WITHDRAWN

A COMMON GOOD

A COMMON GOOD

*The Friendship of Robert F. Kennedy
and Kenneth P. O'Donnell*

HELEN
O'DONNELL

WILLIAM MORROW AND COMPANY, INC.
New York

Library of Congress Cataloging-in-Publication Data has been applied for.

ISBN 0-688-14861-1

Printed in the United States of America

First Edition

1 2 3 4 5 6 7 8 9 10

BOOK DESIGN BY FRITZ METSCH

www.williammorrow.com

This book is dedicated to Michael L. Kennedy,
who had the faith in me when others did not believe,
whose friendship made A Common Good *possible.*

You are loved and missed.

AUTHOR'S NOTE

Much of the material in this book has been gathered from the private tapes of my father, Kenneth P. O'Donnell. A grateful thank-you and acknowledgment to my brothers, Kevin and Kenny, for making them available.

ACKNOWLEDGMENTS

I wish to thank the following people who made this book possible.

First, I would like to thank Ethel Kennedy for her help, support, and understanding. Her early support of this book gave me the strength to take on those who doubted. Knowing she was always there pulling for me, in my corner, made it possible, as well as the various other members of the Kennedy family, who each in a different way contributed to the endeavor.

Special thanks should go to the numerous friends of Robert F. Kennedy and my parents. Their willingness to open up and respond, to bare their souls and their love for these two men, made the words in this book come alive. As I spent time with each one of them, I was reminded of how lucky Bobby and my dad were to be surrounded by such wonderful, faithful, and loving friends.

The efforts of the John F. Kennedy Library staff, Will Johnson, Megan Desnoyers, Stephen Plotkin, Donna Smerlas, and Allan Goodrich, as well as so many others at that library, were indispensable.

At William Morrow, Paul Fedorko for being the kind of person my dad would have loved. I am only sorry they never got to meet. My editor, Claire Wachtel; Kim Lewis, for her faith and patience; and Jessica Baumgardner, for keeping me sane and organized.

Special thanks to my many friends who contributed in a variety of ways, especially Suzanne Farmer; Kelly Paisley; Kathleen, Mark, Gary, Chuck, and Christine Daly; Paul and Gail Kirk; and so many others.

"The boys"—Nick Rodis, Paul Lazzaro, Wally Flynn, Sam Adams, Chief Bender, Chet Pierce, Dave Mazzone, Jerry Bruno, Jimmy Kenary, John Trainor, George Sullivan, John Reilly, John Nolan, John Siegenthaler, Jack Miller, Ed Guthman, William Orrick, Louis Oberdorfer, Sander Vanocur, Barrett Prettyman, Joe Dolan, John Douglas, Paul Schrade, and John Caufield. Thanks to them for sharing their laughter and memories of these two extraordinary men. Michael and I were honored that they trusted us enough to share their memories.

Finally, I owe a debt of gratitude to Robert F. Kennedy, Jr., and Christopher Lawford, who stepped in when Michael died and saw me through the difficult last months of this book. Without their faith and support of me and this book, *A Common Good* would not have been completed.

In closing, I would like to thank my parents, and my aunts Justine and Clareann, for teaching me that toughness and grace under pressure are the keys to survival, for giving me the faith to believe in myself against all odds, and for, as my father would say, "having the courage to see the game through to the end." No matter what the odds.

CONTENTS

INTRODUCTION:
A DAUGHTER'S STORY

This book began as the completion of a conversation I had with my father throughout my childhood. I grew up with Robert Kennedy. He was part of my waking life. I can remember him as clearly as I can remember my father—and yet I don't know that I ever met him. He was assassinated when I was six years old. In life and death he was a part of our household, as a man, a refuge, a set of lasting aspirations, and a figure of tragedy. The events of my life and, of course, the life and times of my father, Kenneth O'Donnell, are completely intertwined with Robert Kennedy, or "Bobby," as my father always called him. I bristle when people say to me, "You know, he preferred to be called Bob—he disliked being called Bobby." I don't know what the rest of the world called him. I do know that my father was his friend beginning from their days at Harvard College, loved him all his life, treasured his friendship, was challenged by his life and devastated by his death, and always called him Bobby. That is what I will call him in these pages.

The last conversation I had with my father was about Robert Kennedy. At the time of his death in 1977, my father was deeply disturbed that people were going to forget what Bobby had lived for and what he had ultimately given his life for. My dad was worried that his work—and their work together—was in vain, and that Americans didn't understand who Robert Kennedy really was. I am not even sure my father completely understood him. I know he did not always agree with him; from football games to Vietnam, they disagreed, argued, and remained friends. But what my father did know in his heart and his gut about Bobby Kennedy was that he had the talent, the brains, and ultimately the courage to change this country. He really believed, as did Bobby Kennedy, that the system can work to help those most in need. He wanted to ensure that America would not neglect Bobby's life work and his own. At the end of his life, my father knew well what the passage of time could mean for their story in the hands of unscrupulous journalists and uncaring historians if neither he nor Bobby was alive to keep vigil on the truth.

He often said, "We mustn't live on might-have-beens." Sadly, he didn't follow his own advice. He became trapped by the deaths of John and Bobby Kennedy in a realm of lost possibilities. My father never recovered from Bobby's death. Two years later his own beloved brother Warren was shot while attempting to stop a robbery in progress on the way home from work, and he later died from complications from his wounds. This may have been the final blow to my father's will to live. After those two tragedies, he never cared about politics again, and he never gave his heart over to another politician again. "When tragedy struck," my father's confidant and protégé Paul G. Kirk, Jr., would explain to me, "your dad not only lost his best friend. His professional life lost its compass and its direction."

My father tried hard; he wanted to move forward but he seemed frozen by tragedy. My mother's growing alcoholic illness and his own skyrocketing dependence on alcohol were contributing factors. After my mother's death, my stepmother would try valiantly to help him, to get him on track, but it was too late; the fight in the man was gone. Though it was alcoholism that would be the technical cause of both my mother's and father's deaths, in reality they died long before their last breath was released.

My father was a public man. As a member of the inner circle of both John and Robert Kennedy for his entire adult life, he moved in the realms of power and helped shape the agenda for a newly reinvigorated nation. Because he was also an intensely private man, a man who shared his deepest feelings and thoughts with only a few others and whose public presence, in the set of his jaw and the coldness in his eyes, radiated a warning to any and all who might presume to pry into his inner world, it is with a certain sense of trepidation that I presume to tell part of his story, which is an integral part of Jack and Bobby's story as well. But I believe there is so much in his life from which we might all learn, and, in the end, that outweighed my reservations.

While I grew up surrounded by Robert Kennedy, indeed all the Kennedys, I also grew up very much my father's daughter. I was his favorite; he was my friend, my confidant, and my pal. As a child, I enjoyed being the center of my father and mother's attention. My aunt remembers one evening when several couples had joined my parents for dinner. As a six- or seven-year-old sitting next to my dad as the adults were talking politics, I tried to speak. My mother and father immediately ordered all conversation to cease. "Be quiet," my father commanded. "Helen has something to say." I doubt whatever I had to say was earth shattering, but the story illustrates how I grew up with the assurance that I had a right to a place in the world, and that whatever came my way, I could handle it: After all, I was Kenny O'Donnell's daughter.

We spent a lot of time together. Those who knew Kenneth O'Donnell as President John F. Kennedy's taciturn doorkeeper, intimidating people with a simple stare, would be startled by his gentleness and his delight in his children. Our routines included walks around Jamaica Pond with my cocker spaniel, Biscuit, and my dad's longtime friend Junior Carr. I rarely spoke on these walks, but I would get to listen to the two men talk and reminisce about past glories during their campaign days and Kenny's time in the White House. Some nights my dad would come by my brother Mark's and my room about 3:00 A.M., and we would sneak downstairs without my mother knowing, to join him for Charlie Chan and Sherlock Holmes movies, complete with bowls of chocolate and vanilla ice cream, laden with chocolate sauce and tons of Cool Whip. We would sit in the dark, watch the movie, and try to guess the killer. Whoever guessed wrong had to get everyone else more ice cream.

Funny, but my brother and I don't remember my father ever guessing wrong.

My father taught me how to play tennis, which was quite an effort for him, since from the time I was a child his hands had been crippled with Depuytren's contracture. He had to force a tennis racket into his hand with my help. Unlike my brothers and sisters, I was not gifted athletically, but my dad was tremendously patient. The first time I got the ball over the net, he was clearly proud of me. "You can do anything you set your mind to," he told me. "You will always have to work harder than the next guy, but you are tough and you will succeed." I could never have imagined on that sunny afternoon how often I would need to rely on that counsel.

During many of the times my father and I spent together, we had a third companion—the spirit of Robert Kennedy. Some afternoons my father and I would go to tea at Boston's distinguished Copley Plaza Hotel. I would have my tea and cookies, he would order a stiff drink, and then we would chat. After I had finished the story of my day, he would eventually begin to tell stories about Bobby. One such story that I remember vividly was about the time that Bobby and Ethel and my father and mother had gathered at Cronin's, a local Irish pub on Beacon Hill. Bobby and my mother soon became involved in conversation, leaving my father and Ethel to trade barbs with one another. My father dearly loved to tease Ethel because she inevitably gave as good as she got. At one point, however, my father may have gone too far, because without warning, Ethel reached over and poured the contents of her mug of beer on my father's head. Ethel had little time to enjoy her victory before my father upended his mug of beer over her head. Bobby and my mother continued their conversation as if nothing at all unusual was happening around them.

The Kennedy brothers were integral to our lives at home on Lochstead Avenue in the Jamaica Plain section of Boston. The living room was my father's bastion. It had once run the whole side of the house, alongside a meandering porch that during the summer became an outdoor playroom for kids. Someone had put in a shelf wall that cut the room in two. The second room became a den, where we would watch television and where my mother would escape the world to hide in the past, where she seemed to find some comfort. The living room itself had a large open doorway, a dreadful orange couch, a fireplace that faced you as you walked in, and an old radio and record player, circa 1939. It looked like something out of a movie set from *The Thin Man*. When my dad wasn't home, it was on this classic old phonograph that my brothers and sister played the Four Tops and the Temptations, and where a few years later I rocked out to Steven Tyler and Aerosmith. Sometimes my father and I would listen to Aerosmith together, playing our air guitars. My father insisted that Tyler was not speaking the English language; at age thirteen, I, of course, knew all the words to the band's songs and informed my father quite confidently that I was going to marry Steven Tyler and that he had better learn to like the music. I'm sure my father was skeptical of the marriage part, but he did understand enough to buy me my first guitar and my first microphone.

Sitting over the fireplace, watching the sometimes strange antics, music, dancing, and general disarray in our household, was a stunning charcoal sketch of John Kennedy. John Kennedy was God in our house. As a child, I did not understand he was a real person. Only as a teenager was I able to view him as someone who had dealt with shyness and awkwardness, someone who had to struggle to fit in. But Bobby was different. My parents never kept a photo of Bobby in the house. My dad said he simply couldn't bear it.

I always felt like Bobby was my friend. My dad used to put on his Irish music, which my mother hated; she used to hide herself in the den with the television volume up full blast in order to block out the music. (Once she resorted to stealing his Irish records from the living room and baking them in the oven. He just bought another set.) I would sit on the orange couch with Biscuit and listen to my father talk about Bobby. The stories were always amazing to me. Bobby Kennedy was a man who didn't wake up perfect every day, and he overcame all kinds of early difficulties in life to contribute so much. Did his example mean that maybe I could do the same? Who was this man who had such a tremendous impact on my father and hung over this house like a ghost?

My dad always said, "Bobby Kennedy's life is a lesson in the art of the possible." That phrase always intrigued me. I have come to learn over the years that Bobby wasn't a giant killer but just a man. Having written this book, I finally understand that my father was talking about perseverance, guts, and working for the common good, no matter the difficulties, the inconvenience, the criticisms, or the danger.

My mother had a much more personal understanding of who Bobby Kennedy was. Some afternoons I would sneak out of school early and go home just to sit with her. She never got me in trouble for that and never told my dad, although I always believed that he knew. (One day, as I was eating breakfast and he got up to leave, he turned to me and said, "Now don't get caught.") My mother savored those afternoons; my presence lifted the burden of her loneliness. She had struggled against alcoholism and addiction to tranquilizers, and during much of my childhood her demons were winning. My father knew she was sick, but it hurt him too much to face her problems; and he seemed powerless to help her.

As she and I sat together on those afternoons, my mother's conversation always turned to Bobby and Kenny and their days at Harvard. She was only nineteen when she married my dad in 1947. He was a returned war hero and a star on the Harvard football team. She was a Sullivan from Worcester. Her father, Bart Sullivan, had come over on the boat from Ireland. He was a small, wiry man who struggled with bouts of anger, depression, and the Irish cancer, alcohol. Her mother was a short, heavyset woman named Hilda, but we called her Darby. What I remember most about Darby was her milk-white, beautiful skin inherited from her parents who were Swedish. I still recall that she always spoke with a distinctive lilting accent.

My mother's parents were relatively young when she and her brother were born, and my mother's childhood and later years were marked with troubles. After her parents fought, this young girl, with auburn hair, stunning blue eyes, and an athletic, small frame she had inherited from her dad, would drive around Worcester to various bars that her father might have disappeared into, sometimes for days at a time. She married my dad because she was smitten, because he was an O'Donnell from Worcester, and because marriage offered refuge from the madness at home. It was not easy for my mother to be thrust into the vigorous, confident world of postwar Harvard. My father, busy with school, football, and friends, did not ever really make the transition from college boy to traditional young husband.

At Harvard in the late 1940s, one of the few people who seemed to understand her frustration was the young Bobby Kennedy. As she and I sat together in the kitchen on my truant afternoons, my mother told me how he would come visit them at their small apartment in Cambridge, one of many prefab apartment buildings thrown up to house the married GIs returning from the war. (The walls were so thin that, as one member of the Harvard football team later told me, my father once put his fist through the kitchen wall while demonstrating his boxing prowess to his friends.) Bobby would come over there, have a beer, and sit and talk with my mother. Mostly, he just listened.

What they talked about was not as important to my mother as the very fact of the conversations. Passing the time with the wife of his best friend was probably not a significant event to Bobby, but it meant the world to a woman who had little money, a baby, twins on the way, and a husband who was rarely home. Bobby Kennedy cared and he listened. It was a simple gesture that later in life she would treasure and hold on to, especially as she felt her grasp on life slipping away. It was not the attorney general or the presidential candidate that my mother loved; it was the man who demonstrated such simple human concern. In a move that would become a pattern of his life, Robert Kennedy, a man of wealth and incipient fame, had immediately understood, cared, and taken action. That was the Bobby Kennedy my mother told me about.

A Common Good is a daughter's fulfillment of her father's dying request. It is a daughter's attempt to explore her father's life and his profound friendship with a man who continues to have a tremendous impact on how the nation shapes its aspirations.

If I grew up feeling that I knew Bobby Kennedy, in writing this book I have learned far more about a complex, courageous, and considerate man. This book is a memoir of sorts, the story of two men and their friendship, whose influence I felt in my own life. For those readers who are not able to guess, I should state that this is not an unbiased tale. When I began this project, I was besieged by journalists, family friends, and others telling me, be wary, don't write a hagiography; you must be critical to be correct. I am not a historian and I do not pretend to be. The story written by a daughter about her father and his best friend could not but have its biases. I also do not believe one has to be "critical to be correct." Like many people, I am tired of revisionist histories and long for a good book about two good men and a challenging time for our nation.

I began this project with immense respect for the Kennedys. Through the process of researching and writing this book, my respect has grown into great admiration, not only for the Kennedys of my father's generation but for those who are my contemporaries. Having written a book about my own father, I am now painfully aware of just how deeply Joe, Michael, and all the other children understood the sense of paternal loss that I feel, which still continues to make a difference in their lives.

I have also come to realize the special debt I owe to Jacqueline Kennedy Onassis. My father admired her and loved her. He first met her when he was becoming more and more involved in Jack Kennedy's political campaigns and, at the time, he paid little attention to her. My father was not a man who was, at that time, terribly sensitive. Just as he wasn't attuned to my mother's difficulties with political life, he was less than sympathetic to Jackie's position. Eventually, and especially after they had won the White House, he really began to value her contribution. He also realized how tough she was. As my father himself observed, the word "tough" is not one that people naturally associated with Jackie. But time and events would prove Jackie one of the strongest people among the Kennedys and their circle.

During the White House years, Jackie's social events at first drove my father crazy. He saw them as a frivolous intrusion into the president's valuable time. Eventually, as White House social secretary Tish Baldrige explained to me, "Kenny began to understand." As Tish recalled it, "Kenny would come to me and say, 'Look, you have got to talk to Jackie. You can't take up the president's time with this junk, it's foolishness.' Finally, after Kenny came to several events, he would stand against the wall with his arms folded and simply watch. Now and again, Jackie would look over at him, and he would get the tiniest smile at the corner of his lips. We knew then he understood, he saw the value. They were like the king and queen of this country at these events. The public loved it, and Kenny understood Jackie really knew politics — she just practiced it differently than he did!"

Later, after tragedy, it was to Jackie that my father would turn in time of incalculable pain. They could share their losses with few others. My mother, for one, knew of the bond her husband and Jack's widow possessed between them. Once she said to me, "I wasn't there. He can talk to her about things that he could never bring himself to tell me." I never knew exactly what she meant, but as I get older, her meanings — and her sympathy — become clearer. Jackie saw all the horrors Kenny O'Donnell did and somehow was able to endure. She understood and even shared his pain, yet she was able to move forward; I think he admired and envied her that ability. While I was growing up, my father always urged me to conduct myself in the manner that Jackie did. I know he was referring not only to the White House years but to that dreadful day in November and its aftermath, when she was able to hold them all together.

My father died six months after my mother's death in the same year. It was horrible. It was as if my world had ceased to exist. I was fifteen years old. Both my parents were dead, and all that I knew and loved was behind me now. My future looked bleak, unsure, and frightening. At the funeral, I mostly remember being jostled by photographers trying to get a better shot of Jackie and the Kennedy family in the midst of the service. I left the church to the heart-ripping sounds of "O'Donnell Abu," my father's favorite song, and I rushed to the limousine, to hide from all the people, all the sad faces and the funeral-goers with their halfhearted reassurances that it would be all right, when they all knew that none of us had any idea if we would ever be all right again. I jumped into the limo, closed the door, and began to cry. Suddenly, the door opened and the light from outside flooded in. I saw cameras flashing and then, suddenly, Jackie was sitting there next to me. She put her arm around me, hugged me, kissed my cheek, and in that soft voice my father called "pleasant to the ear," told me it would be all right. Softly, but with a firmness of tone that told you she meant business, she said to me, "If you ever need anything I will always be there. Even when you don't see me, I will always be there for you. All you need to do is call. Your father was a wonderful man. Bobby was his hero and my hero. Don't be sad. They are together again, and it is up to us all to carry on. They would expect nothing less. As hard as it is, remember that they loved you and they loved us all and they are always, always with us."

She kissed me again and then she was gone, flashbulbs popping. I was left with her warmth, love, and reassurance. At a time when I thought nobody understood the pain and certainly nobody could give the pain life, she was able to do both. From then on, I knew I would be all right. Although my father was gone, I understood that I would never be completely alone. In that one brief moment, I understood the bond my father had with Jackie. And from her I learned that pain can teach us wisdom.

Finally, this book has helped me to realize my full debt to Edward Kennedy. Without Ted Kennedy's love, support, and faith in me over the years, I might not have been here to write this book at all. He was always there whenever I needed him, and sometimes when I didn't even know I was in trouble. Only a very special person could be so strong and so present. As his former aide and close friend Dave Burke pointed out, "Ted combines the best in both Bob and Jack—the political sagacity of Jack and the unbridled compassion for a cause that was Bobby's hallmark." My life is certainly a personal testament to that special blend of wisdom and compassion that is Ted Kennedy.

As Bobby Kennedy and Kenny O'Donnell both would tell you, their story at its heart is not a tale of sorrow but a narrative of hope. For all the tragedy and foreshortened fates, this book is not an account of death but a testament of overcoming. It is a story of a friendship between two men working to accomplish a common good for future generations. *A Common Good* is a daughter's fulfillment of a promise made to her father who did not live to write it himself. It is their story for those who truly knew Bobby and Kenny and for those they never had the chance to meet.

TRIBUTE TO KEN O'DONNELL

Page 16, The Sunday Post—*January 15, 1978*
WITH POETIC LICENSE
Martha Vrakas Poetry Editor

They spoke of the Irish Mafia
And the ones who got ahead,
"Kenny didn't make it"
Is what the article said.

Return with me to Camelot
The country's shining hour,
Jack gave the quiet Irishman
A uniquely "different" power.

Kenny was the man to see
They came to him one by one,
I doubt that he played favorites
He did what had to be done.

Through the years he did his job
In his quiet sort of way.
Then came the visit to Dallas
On that bright November day.

Those bullets claimed our President
The country was torn apart.
Yet, no one seemed to notice
The bullet that pierced Kenny's
*   heart.*

Kenny was lost and lonely
Now Bobby needed him too,
Kenny picked up the pieces
And did what he had to do.

Bobby was busy campaigning
For him success was in store,
But in the city of angels
A shot rang out once more.

Once more Kenny felt the pain
Of loss, and in his grief,
The sparkle left his Irish eyes
Like the dropping of a leaf.

Kenny made it all the way
"In the noblest race of all"
He may have stumbled once or twice
But, never did he fall.

The years passed by for Kenny
His "scars" just wouldn't mend,
On a September day his voice was
*   stilled*
His pain was at an end.

May you rest in peace and smile
*   once more,*
"May the wind be at your back"
May you spend part of your heaven
With two friends, Bobby and Jack.

—ANONYMOUS

THE PLAYING FIELDS
OF HARVARD

The best thing that ever happened to Harvard was World War II.

—PROFESSOR GEORGE GOETHALS

On a September day in 1946, in the locker room at Harvard's Dilllon Field House, a war hero named Kenneth O'Donnell came face-to-face with a young man he had never seen before. He was struck immediately by the man's intense blue eyes and his tousled mop of hair. "I'm Bob Kennedy," the young man said. Kenny thrust his hand out and was surprised by the strength of his grip. He could not imagine how that introduction would change his life or that he was beginning a friendship that would span time and transcend death.

Kenny O'Donnell, son of football coaching legend Cleo O'Donnell, had returned from Europe a genuine war hero. His father had been furious when, in the days following Pearl Harbor, Kenny had taken early enlistment in the air force at age seventeen. Even though Kenny was eager to get in the fight and ready to get out of the family house, his father strongly objected to Kenny's signing up under the legal age and doing so without even so much as a "by-your-leave" from his father beforehand. Even before he enlisted, he hadn't planned to go to Harvard, where his older brother, named Cleo for their father, had captained the school football team before leaving to fight in the Pacific. "Clee," or "Sonny," had always been the star, his father's favorite, and the two brothers were fierce rivals. Clee, Kenny knew, had it tougher in some respects, bearing as he did his father's name and the accompanying burden of having to live up to his father's achievements. Kenny was the second son, the third child, and "his mother's favorite," as his younger sister Justine would recall years later. "But nobody knew exactly why," Justine said, smiling. "After all, we were much nicer than he was."

Philip Kenneth O'Donnell was born on March 4, 1924, to Cleophus Albert O'Donnell and Alice Mae Guerin O'Donnell. His father, Kenny said, was "the most literate man I ever knew," with a passion for football, history, government, and politics, all of which he instilled in his second son. Kenny's father was a man of ambitions and determination. He had left the family home in Houlton, Maine, at age nine, taking his younger brother with him. Cleo was unable to stand his father's new wife or his father's drinking. Cleo headed for Massachusetts and ended up in Everett, living with his father's two sisters. Following the route of many of Boston's ambitious Irish, including, some four years later, a young man named Joseph Patrick Kennedy, Cleo attended Boston Latin School. After taking off a few years to work and earn some money, he went on to Holy Cross College in Worcester. At Holy Cross, Cleo quickly distinguished himself as both a scholar and an athlete. Cleo played on the Holy Cross football team nicknamed the "Elevens" and was, in the words of one sportswriter of the time, "one of the greatest ends to ever play the purple." (Purple was the school color of Holy Cross.) Fiercely competitive by nature, Cleo often played his best games against Harvard and Yale, never suspecting that years later he would watch all three of his sons, Cleo, Kenneth, and Warren, play for Harvard. After his marriage on September 16, 1916, to Alice Mae Guerin, a beautiful young woman blessed with milk-white skin, black hair, and green eyes who came from a socially prominent family in Worcester, Cleo would begin a career that would make him one of the nation's most successful coaches, taking him from Everett High School to Purdue, St. Anselm's, and Holy Cross.

Cleo and Alice would have five children in all, a rambunctious brood that would keep Alice busy and Cleo often on the edge as he tried to maintain the discipline and order he felt befitted his children. Their first child was a red-haired beauty named Phyllis; their second, his father's namesake, Cleo Jr., otherwise known as Sonny; and Kenny was third in line. Besides these three, the young couple would go on to have another daughter, Alice Justine, and last, a son named Warren.

Justine remembered family life as something of a mixed blessing. On the one hand, their father was a very good provider, even through the Depression. "Somehow," Justine recalled, "there was always food on the table, even in the direst of times." She also recalled that the household was very strictly regulated. For instance, the children had to be seated at the dinner table, dressed in nice dresses for the girls and shirts and ties for the boys, by the time their father pulled into the driveway, which he did at the same time each and every day. Before they sat down, the children would all jostle one another to make sure that they would not be the ones who sat closest to their father during dinner. He made it a regular practice to grill the children over dinner about current events, school subjects, and the like. Those who did not answer correctly or quickly enough earned his strictest disapproval and, for the boys who were unlucky enough to be seated within reach of their father, even a smart slap. Alice, when Cleo was not present, ran a much more relaxed kind of household. Where Cleo was strict and stern, Alice was his opposite, fun loving and indulgent in the occasional vice of smoking.

Justine recalled that the boys, especially Kenny, were her assigned protectors on their way to and from school. She wasn't all that thrilled with their guardianship, because "they always seemed to be in fights of one kind or another." At a time when being Irish in Worcester made them the objects of taunts and insults, the O'Donnell boys soon learned that they had to be as good with their fists as they were with their mouths. "And the boys could really be rebellious when their father was away from home. As soon as it got dark outside, up would go the windows and off they'd go to run the streets of Worcester, no matter what my mother would say to the contrary," Justine remembered.

Sent to fight overseas, nineteen-year-old Kenny exhibited a confidence in the face of prospective danger that was a combination of the fearlessness of youth and an early sign of the coolheadedness that would mark his years in the political arena. Though he was not much of a letter writer, he wrote home regularly to his mother, missives that were clearly designed to allay his mother's fears. It wasn't until many years later that anyone was to know the true extent of the dangers and how near he came to getting killed. Kenneth did not cheat death once, but twice.

He served in the Army Air Force, based in Britain, and was part of the famous Eighth Division that played such a decisive role in the war effort. A first lieutenant, he flew more than thirty bombing missions; as a bombardier often in the lead plane, he would be the first to let the lethal cargo go over Germany. One time, on an early mission, as his plane was flying directly over a target, he simply froze. He couldn't remember which way to turn the lever controlling the bomb. He was forced to guess. Fortunately, he guessed right and the bomb descended to its target. It would not be the last time that he was scared, but it would be the only time that he froze under fire.

Kenny quickly developed friendships with several of the pilots he flew with, and he became lifelong friends with one of them, Ken Kavanaugh, or Kav as he was called, who was himself a football star who had played for Louisiana State in a legendary game against Holy Cross College in 1940. Kav would later play for the Chicago Bears and then the New York Giants; one of his teammates was the "Gentle Giant," Roosevelt Grier, whose life would, years later, intersect with Kenny O'Donnell's own, in the midst of tragedy.

During the final push that would end the war, it was with Kav at the helm that Kenny received a citation from no less a person than the famed British field marshal Montgomery, after he and Kav dropped a steel "calling card" in the middle of a bridge to the German retreat. As Kav remembers it, the United States Army was hesitant to give O'Donnell a citation, citing the crew's failure to take out the entire bridge. Monty had no such hesitation; the bombs had damaged the bridge beyond repair, and he made sure O'Donnell got the citation. What Kav recalled the most about the incident was how little O'Donnell cared about getting the recognition. "He simply shrugged his shoulders and said, 'No big deal, as long as I get outa here in one piece—that's all I care about.' When he did receive the citation from Monty, he just stuck it in his sack and never mentioned it again. Stuff like that really didn't seem to matter to him too much. It was really kind of refreshing."

Kav came out of the war without a scratch, but Kenny was not so

lucky. At Christmas 1944, during the Battle of the Bulge, when the
German field marshal Albert Kesselring was certain that he had the
Allies cornered and could turn the tide of the war, the AAF was called
upon to thwart the determined German drive. Kenny's B-17 was on a
bombing mission when the plane was hit and began a plunge into the
Rhineland. Six members of the crew were able to parachute out, but
Kenny, who had been wounded by gunfire, was forced to go down with
the plane. With two other members of the crew, he rode the plane right
into its crash landing, which luckily turned out to be on Belgian soil.
The plane had been turning to return to Britain when it was hit, which
was good, but it had crashed right between German and Allied lines.
Climbing out of the wreckage into no-man's-land, Ken could see the
Germans approaching and knew he had to run for his life. Remembering his father's football advice on how to run, and with his mind firmly
set on a mental picture of his mother, he dashed for the Allied lines.
Despite a severe wound to his leg—shrapnel that would never be totally
removed—Kenny made it. He collapsed bleeding into the arms of an
American soldier on a reconnaissance mission.

The Americans sent him directly to an army hospital in Belgium,
where he was to stay for the next six months while his leg healed. At
the end of the six months he was able to return to Britain and to his
beloved B-17. On one of his first runs back, his plane was shot down
again, but this time he was a little luckier. He was able to parachute to
safety and run quickly to the American lines.

In one of his last trips over Germany, as the plane was traveling at
some 26,000 feet, with oxygen masks the only way to breathe, Kenny
was forced to climb down into the bay and manhandle a bomb that had
become stuck in the bay instead of dropping on its target. He knew he
had no choice; if they couldn't force the bomb out, the plane would
blow to pieces. In order to free the bomb, Kenny was forced to jump
up and down and dislodge it. He opened the bay door, but the bomb
stayed stuck. He had no choice but to crawl into the bomb rack to kick
the deadly device loose. As he gave the bomb a final kick and dislodged
it, suddenly black spots appeared before his eyes and he felt light-
headed. The oxygen hose had parted from his mask.

Keeping his head, Kenny inched his way back to his place and managed to reconnect the hose to the mask. Life-giving air pumped its way back into his lungs, and slowly he felt the sickening fear in his stomach loosen its grip. He looked up and gave the crew a thumbs-up. They had all watched terrified, unable to help.

Having flown this fifteenth mission with his regular crew, Kenny was stunned to receive orders switching him to another crew for what would be his sixteenth mission. He and his regular crew joked about the bomb incident and made plans to go out for a beer upon everyone's safe return from the next foray. The men waved goodbye to each other, climbed into their planes, and took off. Kenny would never see his regular crew again. They were shot down over Germany. There were no survivors. He was not fated to be on that plane, but the sadness of losing his whole crew brought home to him the real horror of war. He understood all too well what it meant to send young men to fight and to die. Some twenty years later, in 1962, that fear would manifest itself in his complete and total opposition to the growing American presence in Vietnam.

Kenny O'Donnell would win the Distinguished Service Cross with four Oak Leaf Clusters, the Air Medal, the Purple Heart, and no fewer than six citations, including the one from Montgomery. He never wore any of his medals and never told anyone of his heroics. Cleo and Alice never even knew that their son was wounded or was in a hospital. Ken made sure that they were never informed; his positive, ostentatiously unworried letters continued to arrive home in Worcester. It was only after the local press began to write about the new 1948 Harvard football captain from Worcester as a genuine war hero that his family finally understood the extent of his valor. Despite all these honors, journalist Fletcher Knebel said that the war gave Kenny "a distaste for glory grabbers, the fakers and the phonies."

A young lieutenant in the navy, who was nearly killed when the Japanese sank his boat, who survived a broken back and malaria and would never fully recover his health, shared O'Donnell's reticence. John F. Kennedy also understood Kenny's sense of loss. Among the men who didn't come back from the war would be Jack Kennedy's older brother, Lt. Joseph P. Kennedy, Jr., killed on one of his last flying missions over

Europe. That death would devastate his father and force Jack Kennedy into a political role he would never have envisioned otherwise. It was this shared experience in hell and understanding of the evil that war really is that would bond Jack Kennedy and Kenny O'Donnell later in life, helping them understand, along with Robert Kennedy, what was really at stake during the Cuban Missile Crisis and in Vietnam.

With his black eyes, chiseled features, and the coal black hair still cut into the crew cut he would maintain until President John Kennedy asked him to grow it out because he "looked too young to be in the White House," Kenny O'Donnell was a powerful presence on the post-war campus of Harvard, both at the Varsity Club where he lived and on the football field. A tremendously gifted athlete, Kenny quickly won a spot on the Harvard football team. With so many soldiers not yet returned from the war, the 1945 season would consist of mostly informal, non-league games. However, 1946 was a different matter; it would be Harvard's first regular season since the war. Although his start on the team began with a tense and uncomfortable meeting with Coach Dick Harlow, whose coaching technique Kenny did not find appealing, he was not deterred. He and his brother had both survived the war and were relaxing into the promise of the postwar world that lay open before them.

The years 1945 and 1946 brought tremendous changes for Harvard and for young men like O'Donnell. "The War had changed the University as much as it had the country," says historian Richard Norton Smith in his book *The Harvard Century*. Like most of America, Harvard had been reluctant to get involved in a foreign war; up until the last minute, the university elite had hoped that the British alone would somehow take care of Hitler. Under the leadership of President James Bryant Conant, Harvard was slowly brought around along with the rest of the nation and, by the time of the attack on Pearl Harbor, may have been more prepared for the war than many realized. A close adviser to President Roosevelt and a scientist by training, Conant was influential in the war effort, first by supporting the British with such programs as the Lend-Lease Act and later by working on the atomic bomb.

Conant had left much of the running of the university to his provost, the only one in Harvard's history. Paul Buck, a promising historian of American reconstruction, was, according to Smith, "a loyal second in command for a full decade. Short and balding, he reminded Cambridge observers of Sancho Panza to Conant's Don Quixote." Buck perhaps more than Conant realized that with the war's end and the advent of the GI Bill the Harvard they had known was gone. The traditional Harvard elitism that had up to this point characterized the university would be relegated to dusty books and fading pictures on the walls of the Varsity Club.

"You must be trained to win the Victory," Buck told the incoming freshman class of 1946, which included Kenny and Cleo O'Donnell, Bobby Kennedy, and their friend and fellow football player Nick Rodis. "You must be prepared to live in a postwar period, and both of these tremendous tasks must be achieved in a relatively short period of time. There can be no wastage, no misspent effort, no luxuries. We have work to do and we must do it well and quickly. More than our own destinies are involved." Kenny O'Donnell, having been shot down over Belgium with the shrapnel still in his leg to show for it, and Bobby Kennedy, with a brother killed, another severely wounded, and a sister whose promising life would soon be cut short by a plane crash, couldn't have understood or agreed more that time was short and there was much to be accomplished. They, like their friends, were more than ready and eager to take advantage of the opportunity that was presented to them by postwar Harvard.

The changes the veterans brought to Harvard were immediate and complete. In the words of Richard Norton Smith, "Returning veterans brought to the classroom a seriousness and maturity that were the joy of their instructors." Most of all, the GI Bill had literally changed the face of Harvard more than James Bryant Conant could ever have imagined. "Nationwide, some 2.3 million veterans studied in Universities and Colleges, at least one third of whom could never have taken advantage of such schooling without incentives that the bill contained." In the decade from 1939 to 1949, the number of people in the United States receiving college degrees nearly doubled. The effect was to "convert what had been a privilege of the few into the right of all. The new waves of students forced educators at Harvard and elsewhere to revamp their standard curricula, to emphasize science and technology, to dispense with old entrance requirements, and to experiment with fresh approaches to those whom Robert Hutchins [the enfant terrible and president of the University of Chicago] publicly disdained as 'educational hoboes.' "

Kenny O'Donnell would have disdained the term "educational hobo," and it certainly did not apply to Bobby Kennedy, son of the wealthy former ambassador to Great Britain and Harvard graduate Joseph P. Kennedy, Sr. However, the influx of this new breed of student at Harvard was an adjustment that the still-traditional college would find difficult to make. The war had made possible the influx of such first-generation, ethnic "educational hoboes" as the tough Irish Catholic O'Donnell brothers; Nick Rodis, a Greek American from Nashua, New Hampshire; Chester Pierce, the first black man to play football at Harvard; the Irish Americans Wally Flynn, the son of a policeman from Arlington, Massachusetts, and Jimmy Kenary from Worcester; and Paul Lazzaro, from a poor Boston Italian-American family. Before the war, the school had been a Yankee bastion, its blood more blue than red. While Protestant students, such as Jack Kennedy's confidant Torbert MacDonald, still strolled the campus in great numbers, they were nearly a minority after the war. When Johnny came marching home, he brought a multiethnic army with him. Coming from all races and classes, they would make the transition from being the ultimate outsiders to becoming insiders, the generation that would in ten or twenty years be running the country. Harvard and schools like it would prepare them to follow the lead of a young Robert Kennedy, who had with his family wealth at one time represented all that was beyond their reach, and yet whose father, an Irish Catholic of no great wealth, had blazed the way a generation before.

The changes the war brought to Harvard made possible that meeting between Kenny and Bobby in the Dillon Field House that cool fall September afternoon in 1946. Although he had to admit to himself that his new acquaintance hardly looked the type to make the varsity squad, Kenny knew from his strong firm handshake and sharp blue eyes that there were more intriguing depths to this young man than were immediately visible. Introductions aside, the two athletes, both naturally shy and reserved, made their way toward the lush practice fields with their teammates for an afternoon of practice with Coach Harlow. Quickly, the pair found out they had a mutual dislike for the coach. Bobby's was based on Harlow's treatment of his older brother Joe; Kenny's antipathy arose from a combination of his father's views and what he perceived as Harlow's heavy-handedness as a coach. As the two continued talking, they realized they shared an interest in politics as well as football. Then the discussion turned lively. Kenny O'Donnell's first indication that this was no ordinary young man would come about on the football practice field. But that was only the beginning. In the meantime, it would take Kenny some six months to realize just who this very unordinary young man was. By the end of 1946, Bobby and Kenny would be inseparable friends.

Nobody could ever accuse Robert Francis Kennedy of being ordinary. The tenacity and toughness he would show on the football field at Harvard, and later in the spacious committee room in the Senate Office Building, the attorney general's office, and the presidential campaign in 1968 were bred in Bobby Kennedy from the time he was a small child. The seventh child born into what would be a formidable brood of Rose Fitzgerald and Joseph Kennedy's nine children, Bobby would learn early that just to survive in such a clan took guts and endurance. The challenges he faced growing up in the Kennedy clan would prepare him well for his experience at Harvard.

Rose and Joe had met as children at various points, becoming reacquainted as young adults during summer vacations at Old Orchard Beach, Maine, where so many Irish retreated from Boston's summer heat. "During the few days we were together," Rose would recount later, "we became friends, then affectionate friends, and later began to think of ourselves as sweethearts." Young Joe went on to attend Boston Latin School and eventually Harvard. Like Cleo O'Donnell, who also attended Latin School and then Holy Cross, education would further propel Joseph Kennedy up the ladder of success. Harvard at that time was an absolute bastion of the Yankees. Even as the Irish established a place for themselves in Boston's economy and took political power in the city, it would be a long time before very many would be able to penetrate the venerable walls of Harvard College. Joe Kennedy was not deterred. His father, P. J. Kennedy, understood only too well that he personally had achieved as much as he could in the Irish political and business arena; if his son was to proceed further than he, young Joe would have to go directly into the lion's den.

Joe did well at Harvard but never was completely accepted. The experience made him even more determined to win the key that would open the doors of the American establishment to him. It would take a lifetime of trying, and only the election of his son as president would open those doors once and for all. Even after 1960, the Kennedys were aware of the risk they were taking to break down the barrier barring Irish Catholic America from national political power. When asked if he'd broken that barrier, Jack Kennedy, then president, would answer, "No, I have not broken it. I have only been given the opportunity to break it. If I am not a successful president, the barrier will be back higher than ever."

Joseph Kennedy was, as Rose would recall of her late husband, "tall, thin, wiry, freckled, and had blue eyes and red hair . . . sandy blond with a lot of red highlights in it. His face was open and expressive, yet with youthful dignity, conveying qualities of self-respect, and self-discipline. He neither drank nor smoked . . . he was a serious young man, but he had a quick wit and responsive sense of humor." He was, Rose declared, "the boy I fell in love with, the man I married, the father of my children, and the architect of our lives."

Rose and Joe were married in October 1914 in the private chapel of Boston's Cardinal O'Connell, who officiated. Joe had by this time saved his father's bank, Columbia Trust, the local bank that catered to the Irish, from being bought out. Having access to their own financial institution was crucial, for even with the election of Patrick Collins as the first Irish mayor of Boston, the Brahmins could still maintain control of the city purse strings and therefore still retain power for themselves. Joe beat back a takeover attempt by the Brahmins and in the process became, at age twenty-five, the youngest bank president in the country.

As his family grew with the births of Joseph Jr., John, Rosemary, and Kathleen, the family moved from their Beales Street home to Brookline; it was here that Eunice and Patricia were born, followed by Robert Francis Kennedy on November 20, 1925. Joe was then often in New York City working as a "lone wolf" investor on Wall Street. Eventually he moved his growing family to New York. While he handled the business, Rose was the major influence on their children's early years. Eunice would later remark to her mother that, in fact, Rose was "in charge of us and raised and trained us while we were children. And then when we began turning into young people, Dad took charge the rest of the way." Rose agreed with her daughter's assessment.

Bobby, as the first son after the births of four girls, was especially eager to gain his father's attention and approval. "Bobby was the seventh child," Rose would say, "which is supposed to be lucky. On the other hand, by then even the most enthusiastic parents may feel less excitement about 'another baby.' We were all happy he was a boy baby, after four girls. It was wonderful for the girls. And for us . . . By the time Teddy arrived in 1932, Bobby was already more than seven years old. So there he was, with two older brothers and one very much younger brother, none of whom were much use to him as boyhood pals, playmates." As a result, Bobby was often left to his own resources. This may have lent somewhat to his tendency to keep to himself and his difficulty in making friends; it probably added in no small way to his sense of independence. Moreover, as Rose recognized, "he had to listen for many years to kudos about his two brilliant, older brothers, so when his turn came, he had to work extra hard to make his record equal theirs. I don't think I worried much about the situation," she said about Bobby, "but I remember my mother did. 'He's stuck by himself in a bunch of girls,' she would say; he'll be a sissy.' But of course this didn't happen. Bobby never did become tall, but he became strong, muscular, fast and a fine athlete, in fact, a rather famous varsity football player, an end at Harvard."

Rose was firmly convinced that Bobby's success against such odds was in fact "the result of raw willpower. When he was grown up and in politics, reporters wrote about his toughness, and said he was ruthless. I think this is mistaken. He was determined, dedicated, loving, and compassionate. He was a thoughtful and considerate person. He always had the capacity, and the desire, to make difficult decisions. Those who loved him saw this in him, and understood. As I did, as we all did."

"Bobby may have been quiet and caught among all those children," says Pat Kennedy Lawford, "but his basic shyness to the outside world gave way to fun, humor, and wit whenever he was with his family."

Bobby would constantly view life as a series of challenges to be overcome. He constantly felt the need to prove himself, first to his father, then his older brothers. Rose was sometimes overprotective and overly cautious with Bobby. Joe, who was often away during his childhood, according to Arthur Schlesinger, could be on occasion impatient and rough with Bobby. Schlesinger felt that problems with his father created in Bobby a sense of inadequacy, which inspired him to work twice as hard to prove himself and ultimately win his father's approval and love. He had a difficult time of it. "I was always dropping things, getting hurt or bumping into things," Bobby said years later. Pat Lawford recalls an incident when Bobby was young that set the tone for much of his childhood experience. "There was a large living room, and that's where Bobby was when the call came for supper. We had been brought up to be prompt, very prompt—one had to be on time! Dad was extremely punctual, so Bobby was in the living room, and between it and the dining room there was a passageway under a sort of grand staircase, and in that was a big heavy sheet of glass. I suppose it slid back into a groove in the wall, to join rooms, but it was closed then. When the call came, Bobby took off and ran right into it and smashed it! The pieces cut his head and he fell down and there was blood all over the place, a horrendous scene. It turned out to be not nearly as serious as it looked, with no effects on Bobby after he had some stitches taken." Said Rose of the incident, "We certainly wanted him to be prompt. But not that prompt."

Joseph Kennedy went on to work for President Roosevelt, whom he had met when they were both involved in the war effort in 1917. As the family grew and Joe's career took new turns, for Bobby this meant repeated moves to new homes, new schools, and new schoolmates; making new friends would be hard for him, but he was loyal to those he made. When the family moved to England, when Joe became ambassador, Bobby found the adjustment another challenge to be overcome. He developed a come-from-behind attitude and a devotion to the underdog that he retained all of his life. "Growing up," recalls Ambassador Jean Kennedy Smith, Bobby "seemed to have innumerable problems. He was the smallest of the boys (although he was five foot nine), immersed between four older sisters and myself. Everything seemed to come harder for him—school, sports." Struggle, toughness, and persistence were Bobby's answers to having to come from so far behind.

As was the custom with families of the Kennedy financial means, by age fourteen Bobby was sent away to school, to St. Paul's in Concord, New Hampshire. It was September 1939; Joe and Rose were in England, and war was looming. Joe had picked St. Paul's thinking that he wanted Bobby to have the same sort of secular education that had benefited him. But St. Paul's turned out to be the wrong choice. While Joe struggled with the war he had so desperately hoped to avoid, Rose was horrified to learn from Bobby's letters that the Protestant Bible was read throughout school. "It was for that reason that I withdrew Bobby," she said later, sending him to Portsmouth Priory, a Benedictine school near Newport, Rhode Island. The school's morning and evening prayers, with Mass three times a week and High Mass on Sunday, served to confirm Bobby's already strong religious beliefs. Rose Kennedy remarked that Bobby "was probably the most religious of all of my sons."

Luella Hennessey, the Kennedy nurse who worked with the family for twenty-five years, declared, "Bobby was people-minded. . . . Bobby's deep love for people made me think that one day he would enter a seminary and follow a religious life. But it was not so; he was a lay apostle." For instance, at Brompton Oratory, which the Kennedys attended while living in London, Bobby, during spiritual counseling sessions, noticed that the priests had to supply their own fuel for the fireplace in their offices. When one of his priest friends was short of funds, he was also short of fuel. Upset, Bobby spoke to his father about it, and Ambassador Kennedy arranged for a year's supply of firewood to be sent in for the priests.

Bobby stayed at Portsmouth until 1942, when his father shifted him to Milton Academy, to give him another venue for the secular education his father admired, to keep him from becoming too indoctrinated in the religious life, and to give him an academic boost. The shift to Milton did not particularly improve Bobby's grades, but it did broaden his world, even though the transition was not easy. For a shy Irish Catholic boy who had already attended six schools in ten years and was now plunged into what a prep school friend described with precision as "a consummate WASP school," Milton was an ordeal. He continued to have difficulty with schoolwork and problems fitting in with the rest of the students. He did succeed in making two lifelong friends: David Hackett and Sam Adams, who would follow him to Harvard. "My first real insight into Bobby's character came from football," Adams says. "Bobby ran every practice play and tackled and blocked dummies as if he were in a hard-fought game. To another sixteen-year-old kid like myself, this gung-ho attitude seemed a little weird." As his sister Jean recalls, at Milton Bobby was "constantly struggling to make the football team against boys who were taller and stronger. Nothing came easy for him. Perhaps that gave him sympathy later in life for those who were less fortunate. He, in some peculiar way, understood their soul."

Bobby's letters home from Milton and later from Harvard confirm his fascination with and love of the sport and underscored his determination to succeed. It was a quality that Adams would find himself emulating when he himself faced difficulties later with Coach Harlow at Harvard and was forced to turn to his pal Bobby for support.

Dear Mother & Dad,

Back once more at school and by the looks of things the first few days, it's going to be pretty tough. I am taking English, French, Math, History (instead of Chemistry) and a war course in geography. Football has started and it looks like a good team from what I can tell. There are 4 boys going out for blocking back, and we have a scrimmage tomorrow. I am alternating first string now, but I hit my shoulder during blocking practice so I'm not sure whether I'll be able to scrimmage or not. My shoulder is getting better though and I give it heat all the time and the doctor has seen it. We scrimmage South Boston a week from Thursday so I don't know how many of us will be left after that. We open with Thayer the 9th of Oct., Gov. Dummer High School, St. Marks, Groton, Milton High School and Nobles make up the rest of the schedule with Groton the worst.

If Fury seems pretty lonely at the Cape which I imagine he does I am quite sure I can get permission for him to stay with me here at school, but I'll phone you later about that.

I saw in the paper where you all went to the race track. It must have been quite gay.

Well that's about all the news. I'll keep you posted on all new events. By the way Dave Hackett and I tried out for Glee Club and we sang a duet which went over very big with the singing master. Dave is one of the few people who rivals the Kennedys in his singing so you can imagine how good we were. We have not yet heard, though, if we got in.

much love,
Bobby

Dear Mother & Dad,

We had a football game here yesterday against Thayer Academy and won 19–0. I didn't even play so I guess they don't think much of my football abilities. Portsmouth played Thayer last year and I started the game so it's quite a drop. The team played well and it ought to have a good season.

The work is quite hard, but I'm having extra help in math so that's coming along better. How are Joe & Jack getting along? Jean said that Jack had been promoted [in the Navy]. I hadn't heard anything about it!

Well, that's about all the news from here. It's been great weather as I imagine it has been on the cape. School is fine and I will write again soon.

Love,
Bobby

There was a chapel on campus, but it was nondenominational, so Bobby with his pals Sam and Dave in tow would trek across the river to go to the Catholic church in Dorchester. "It was a good half mile to the nearest church, but Bobby rarely missed a Sunday or a holy day," recalls Adams, who, like so many Yankees of his time, regarded Bobby's religion of chants, incense, beads, and medals with some degree of scorn. "I think," says Hackett, "what we learned about Bobby Kennedy's life throughout his experience at Milton was that he was the real thing. There was no phoniness here, this guy was real, he knew who he was and what he was about. It was unusual for such a young kid."

But it would be the game of football that would begin to forge Kenny O'Donnell, Bobby Kennedy, and their melting pot of friends—fresh from war and new to Harvard—into the "band of brothers" who, later, under the leadership and guidance of Bobby Kennedy would make an impact far beyond the playing field.

"The GI Bill allowed even the poorest boys to seek an education in our best universities, and Harvard was overflowing with the finest collection of athletes to be found anywhere," Kenneth O'Donnell recalled. At Harvard Nick Rodis was teased unmercifully by Kenny, Cleo, and Bobby Kennedy. They called him "the Greek," since his ethnicity made him a singular character at the college. "In 1946 there were no Greeks at Harvard! I will tell you one thing," Rodis says of his admission to Harvard, "I kept waiting for them to tell me it was a mistake." Like so many other young men of his era, Nick went right from preparatory school into the war. Stunned by the postwar opportunity of attending Columbia or Harvard, he was recruited to play football for the Crimson.

Another of the band, Wally Flynn, recalled how after graduating from Arlington High School in 1942 he had decided to go to Dartmouth, feeling that he had a better chance at success there than at Harvard and was more likely to meet a crowd with which he would be comfortable, but the war would intervene before Wally could enroll at Dartmouth. After the war, a member of the football squad at Harvard saw the young man play at Arlington and went after him, convincing him that if Wally chose Harvard his parents could simply hop on a trolley and come over to watch the games. "The last piece of the puzzle," Flynn remembers, "was where to live. Again, I couldn't afford to live on campus, so Coach Lamar made it possible for me to join the guys at the Varsity Club." With his choice made, Flynn arrived at Harvard, settled into the Varsity Club, and headed over to Dillon Field House for practice. As would also be true for Bobby and Nick, the first person he was destined to meet in 1946 was Kenny O'Donnell. Flynn was struck by how slight a figure Kenny appeared to be. "He couldn't be that tough," Flynn remembers thinking. Kenny greeted Flynn with a firm handshake and immediately began to pick on him. Wally "knew right away that I had made the right choice and we were gonna have some fun over the years."

Kenny then took it upon himself to introduce Wally to his friend Bobby Kennedy, who, because he was a member of the Naval V-5 Officer's Training Program stationed at Harvard, was still in his sailor's uniform. Bobby had played on the 1945 squad, and because of his naval duties he had already been at Harvard a year when Wally met him. So even though Wally was older, Bobby had been around the school longer and certainly knew more people. Flynn was struck, as Kenny had been, by Bobby's youthful appearance. "He was really nice and just incredibly low-key," Flynn remembers. "It took me months to realize that he was Ambassador Kennedy's son. I had no idea and he never mentioned it. I do know that Bob Kennedy won three Harvard letters because he played in '45, '46, and '47 . . . pretty impressive stuff. He earned that just like the rest of us."

Soon, Kenny, Cleo, Wally, Nick, and Bobby began to form the core of a gang of friends that would endure over their lifetimes. What was really remarkable about these rough-and-ready guys—all from backgrounds with little money and invested with incredible experiences in the war—was not only how well Bobby Kennedy fit in with them but how quickly the group accepted Bobby as their leader. Bobby seemed to thrive not on being recognized as exceptional, but on the easy acceptance he won among the athletes. For the first time in his educational experience, he was accepted simply as Bobby Kennedy and not as Ambassador Kennedy's son.

As the football season progressed, the group that would form the core of the "Kennedy Debate Club" began to both join the team and find lodgings at the Varsity Club. One member was Jimmy Kenary, an affable young Irishman with sparkling blue eyes and wavy red hair. One of Kenny and Cleo O'Donnell's old-time pals from Worcester, though much younger, Kenary was recruited by the O'Donnell brothers to join them at Harvard. "There was no real mystery to my decision to go to Harvard," Kenary says. "I went in large measure because Kenny was there and he was sort of my hero." Ultimately Kenny and Bobby would become mentors for the young man as he made his way through college. "I remember one of the best things about those guys was that you knew they kept their eye on you, and you knew they made clear that you didn't have to do the kinds of things that you get pressured to do as a young man at college," Kenary says. "Both of them were very protective, and Cleo too." Kenary liked Bobby immediately and felt sympathy for him. "I remember Kenny telling me that his dad was the former ambassador to Britain. I was so naive that for the longest time I really felt bad for Bob because I thought that his dad was out of work, and I remember thinking how tough it had to be for him with his father not having a job. I mentioned this once to Cleo, and he just burst out laughing and told me who his father was. Well, I was just stunned. I never, ever would have guessed that Bobby Kennedy came from money, not ever."

Chet Pierce's being black made no more difference to the group than Robert Kennedy's wealth. Walking to class one day, he was surprised to see Bobby Kennedy drive by in a car, waving and honking. Cars were terribly scarce in post–World War II America. As Bobby drove off, Pierce turned to one of his roommates, Howard Foster, himself a person of some wealth, and said, "My God, Howard, I wonder where Bobby borrowed that car?" Foster stared at his friend in amazement. "You goddamn fool. He is Ambassador Kennedy's son — he is a Kennedy, for

Christ's sake. He could buy himself ten cars if he wanted to!" Pierce was "shocked, really," he now recalls with a laugh. "I had no idea who he was. I mean, I had known him by then for a long, long time. I first met him in '44 and I never imagined or had any idea that he had grown up any differently than I did.

"What is funny," Pierce continues, "is that when I met Kenny O'Donnell—it would have been the spring of '46 for practice—I remember I was really impressed with him. Kenny was a genuine war hero. He had been written up in newspapers and was the son of the great coach Cleo O'Donnell, and when he arrived on campus he was sort of a celebrity. Cleo didn't arrive on campus until the fall of '46, but by then, you know, everyone knew who Kenny was and he was a real celebrity. He and Bobby became fast friends, but even though we all knew who Kenny was, many people didn't realize at all who Bobby was." Kenny understood and respected Bobby's wish to keep his family background quiet.

"I can't remember exactly when I first met Bobby or when Kenny first talked about him," says Justine O'Donnell, Kenny's younger sister, who was then home in Worcester. "It was, I think, a quick introduction, but all of a sudden he was like part of the family, you know, part of the group. Kenny and Bobby hit it off right away because of their mutual interest in politics. Bobby became the sort of brother that Kenny never had growing up. Kenny and Clee were close, but Cleo was older and they were so competitive. . . . Kenny admired the fact that Bobby Kennedy, coming from such a wealthy family, spent time with the real people. That was what made him special and different than you would expect. Kenny really liked that about him."

The return of so many young veterans eager to attend school and start families had led to a critical housing shortage for most colleges, and Harvard was no exception. Despite the addition of cheap, hastily constructed buildings in Cambridge, the returning vets had problems finding places to live. For the football team, Harvard's easiest and most obvious choice was to provide quarters at the Harvard Varsity Club. Kenny and Bobby would center their lives on the Varsity Club at college and crystallize their friendship there. The two-story brick building, which now houses the Harvard Medical Center, was dormitory, hangout, and with the arrival of Bobby Kennedy, a sort of political debate club. "By the end of the season," said Kenny, "Robert Kennedy was a member of the Varsity Club, admired and respected. By then his deepest friendships had been formed with a group at the Varsity Club, which became known at the 'Great Kennedy Debating Society,' with debates covering generally, football, politics, and girls! Occasionally," Kenny chuckled, "the order was reversed."

The Harvard Varsity Club was just the sort of collegiate space to be expected at Harvard, its walls paneled in rich dark woods and featuring photos of past athletes and shelves with the trophies they had won. The game room contained a pool table alongside the large windows and a Ping-Pong table. Bobby didn't live at the Varsity Club like the other players, however; he could afford housing on the campus and chose instead to live at Lowell House. Often on Friday nights after the famous Harvard Torchlight parades, Kenny, Bobby, Cleo, and the others would end up back at the Varsity Club playing a game of pool and drinking a few beers.

The Varsity Club also had something else that made it a natural attraction for both the players and for young George Sullivan, a local youth who was paid a dollar a day to be a ball boy. "They had something many of us had never seen before, and that was a television," Sullivan says. "Most homes didn't have one then because they were new and it was right after the war and money and goods were really scarce, but because it was Harvard and it was for the football team they made sure that the Varsity Club had one." Sullivan remembers his father's delight when he told him about his after-school job. "Specifically, he told me to keep an eye out for the O'Donnell brothers, Kenny and Cleo, the sons of the famous football coach." George's dad reminded his son how significant it was that both O'Donnell boys chose Harvard over Holy Cross. "My dad also told me to watch out for Ambassador Kennedy's son, that one of his younger sons was supposed to be part of the team that year."

One cold Friday night, following the Torchlight Parade, Bobby spied young George and his pal Teddy Ratigan, inviting them to come to the club to watch television. As Bobby walked away he gave the boy a playful cuff behind the ear. "We didn't know if he was serious or not," Sullivan says. "We climbed up on the ledge of the windows and knocked on the glass and yelled, 'Hey, guys!' Nick, Bobby, and Kenny were in there playing pool and they signaled for us to come in there, and we did—it was great!" Kenny and Bobby would become George Sullivan's surrogate older brothers. Every Friday night for the next two to three years he would go over to the club, watch television, and run errands for his heroes.

There may have been a slight ulterior motive to the kindness of Bobby, Kenny, and the other guys. The Varsity Club had a pay phone that was literally in a front closet as you entered. Because most undergraduates couldn't afford private phones, George Sullivan would stand by the phone ready to track down Kenny and Bobby when Friday plans were made for the weekend. Sometimes Jack Kennedy, who would be elected to Congress in November 1946, phoned to track down his brother. George would run wildly through the house seeking Bobby out. "We would always find him," Sullivan says now. "It was great fun for kids."

Bobby's letters home at the time reflected not only his wide interests but also his slowly increasing interest in a young, lively brunette named Ethel Skakel, from Groton, Connecticut. She was a friend of Bobby's sister Jean, and although Bobby had originally been interested in her sister Pat, Ethel slowly won him over.

Dear Mother & Dad,

. . . Am swimming for Winthrop House tonight for the finals between the houses & if we win I hear we go down to Yale to swim against their best house for the Championship. I almost die from exhaustion every time I swim 50 yrds but it will be pretty good fun if we win & I've been practicing my stroke in my room all day which I'm sure will bring results in the pool this evening.

Jean, Ethel & another friend of hers are coming up this weekend. I'm taking Ethel out & will probably end up at the H-Y basketball game this weekend. Dave Hackett & Charlotte Crocker are announcing their engagement this Saturday which makes things very interesting. It's taking place in Groton so I'm taking Jean & Ethel up to it. . . .

Can hardly wait to get down again which will be in less than three weeks.

Love,
Bobby

Football practice, not swimming, was Bobby's real passion. Kenny and Bobby would regularly try to meet before practice began in order to give Bob extra time to work on his game. Kenny, having grown up with a father like Cleo who believed that football forged character, just as Joe Kennedy believed education and athletic prowess made the man, quickly found they had much in common in their attitude toward the game.

Their late-night practices were as much about friendship as football. They became the scourge of equipment coach Jim Farrell because they regularly swiped footballs, which sent young George Sullivan scurrying to make sure the footballs were returned. Sullivan used to stay and watch his heroes play, often sitting on the hard wooden benches on the side. One night, with the New England wind howling, George waited with teeth chattering, wishing that they would grow tired. He suddenly realized that both Bobby and Kenny had stopped throwing the ball; he thought with relief that maybe they were finished and he could get home and get warm. Bobby walked toward him and, placing his hand on the boy's shoulder, reached for his old coat that had been thrown carelessly on the other bench. He draped the coat around the young boy's shoulders. "Thanks for waiting, pal," he told Sullivan. With that he went back to Kenny on the field and they resumed play. George forgot about the cold wind.

"They would be out there," George Sullivan says, "under the street lights on the practice field, and play after practice that day. The rest of the guys would either be in the showers or already showered up and gone, but Bobby and Kenny would always have me hold them out a ball and they would stay out and practice. . . . Sometimes they would have someone else with them kicking and they would both receive, but mostly it was just the two of them. Nobody wanted to stay out that long. You know, Kenny would be throwing the ball and Bobby would catch for a while and then they would switch up."

The two men would work late on the practice field the whole three years they were at Harvard together. Even after Kenny married Helen Sullivan from Worcester in 1947, the football practice ritual remained. Kenny and Bobby would be out there in the night practicing while the supper Helen had prepared cooled considerably waiting for Kenny's return home. Regularly, she would don a short winter coat and walk slowly down Bank Street to the practice field, trying in vain to get Kenny to come home to supper. It was a foreshadowing of how she would spend much of her life.

2

THE HARVARD IRREGULARS

All but a few started with only their hands and hope.

— WILLIAM SHANNON

Even at Harvard the ivy walls could not entirely blot out the horror of war. Nick Rodis and Kav Kavanaugh remembered that Kenny's life was interrupted briefly and terribly when columnist Drew Pearson wrote an article about Captain Jimmy Doolittle and a young bombardier on his plane, Philip Kenneth O'Donnell, who accompanied him on an infamous flight that dropped a bomb on a German hospital, killing all the inhabitants.

Kenny was devastated by the article. He insisted to friends and family that the young fliers used only coordinates in their bomb drops; if they did hit a hospital it was because they were given those coordinates by their base. The article made a big splash on campus. His teammates and fellow students supported him, well aware of the moral quandaries soldiers found themselves in. Kenny turned to Bobby for help. What should he do? Should he respond? Bobby Kennedy suggested that O'Donnell talk to his father and ask him how to handle it. Bobby arranged for them all to meet when Joseph Kennedy, Sr., was next in town. Joe listened patiently to his son's friend's problem and had terse advice for him, which Kenny took to heart for this situation and for the rest of his career. Ambassador Kennedy said, "Don't ever talk to the press about it, or anything, if you can avoid it. If you are wrong, they will nail you for jaywalking for the rest of your life." Convinced that the ambassador was right and that he couldn't spend his life worrying about what others might say about him, Kenny moved on. "The episode did serve," said Jimmy Kenary, "to make Kenny more famous than ever on the campus, although I am not sure he liked all the attention." As time went on, Kenny would turn to a supportive Joe Kennedy for guidance on many things, including what he should do for a career.

In the 1940s, Harvard University and its football team were much more a congenial part of the Cambridge neighborhood than they are today. For all of Massachusetts around and above the Charles River, Harvard's was the local sports team, and college football games were where most people would spend their Saturday afternoons—after Friday evening's Torchlight Parade.

The parade itself was a Harvard tradition and quite a spectacle. The Harvard band would march around Harvard Square and play fight songs as the students, faculty, and people from the neighborhood gathered around singing, many of them bearing real torches, complete with wicks, as the band paraded into the Indoor Athletic Building, built in the thirties on Holyoke Street, where the football team would wait behind the closed doors. As the starting players—Kenny, Bobby, Cleo, Nick, and the others—heard the emcee announce their names, each one would come charging out from behind the door, go up to the microphone, and say something stirring for the crowd. Nick Rodis remembers he would come running out and declare something like, " 'We're gonna beat Princeton!' and the crowd would go wild and start screaming and singing! It was great fun, because the whole campus and neighborhood got into it." Last of all, the emcee would call out the name of the captain. One year, the name called out was Captain Vinny Moravic; another year it was Captain Cleo O'Donnell. And one year it was Captain Ken O'Donnell. After the captain spoke, the emcee would announce the rest of the team, and as many as forty players would charge through the doors and out into the streets.

"The band would play, everyone would sing, and then with Kenny, Nick, Cleo, and Bobby in the lead, we would march over to Cronin's and have a few beers. Then from there we would go to the Varsity

Club," Rodis recalls. "It's amazing that we didn't burn down half of Harvard with all those torches. There were dorms right across the street and there would be students at the windows with torches and other kids with their bedsheets hanging out, having painted signs on them for the team. The Indoor Athletic Building was surrounded by these big beautiful trees that cover so much of Harvard, and there would literally be people hanging from all these trees—kids, students, neighborhood people, and faculty. It was all really part of the Harvard experience, but it was different for us—because, until the war changed things, this was something none of us could ever have done, and because of surviving the war, events like this were so much more special."

Life at the Varsity Club quickly became dominated by the "big three," as they were called: Kenny, young Clee, and Bobby. Dr. Ralph Bender, another member of the team, captures the spirit of Kenny and Bobby and the way it dominated the team's life. Graduating from Peabody High School, he had chosen Harvard and quickly ended up as part of the team. He was, he recalls now, "one of the babies. I hadn't been in the service myself. Bobby and Kenny were sort of the established leaders by the time I got there. I remember my first impression of Kenny was during the freshman football scrimmage with the varsity. I saw this little bitty guy over there playing wing back and I was playing defensive end and I figured, hell, this is going to be easy—this guy is so small. So I went in there and I swatted at him and I missed. Next thing I knew, he had his hand on my belt and he was holding me and wouldn't let go! I just couldn't shake him. It was unbelievable. He was like that—no matter what he wanted to do or which way he wanted to do it, he would do it. Once Kenny set his mind on something, whether it was football or politics, you couldn't shake him. He was just determined to always win. After I met and got to know Bobby, I realized why they got on so well. They both had the same approach to life. No matter the circumstances, they weren't afraid of anything and they would take it on. Both of them were always like that. It could be sort of intimidating sometimes."

When they were not in class or on the practice field, often the teammates ended up in the game room of the Varsity Club, playing pool, drinking beer, and debating politics. Says Bender, "We just listened. Kenny and Bobby used to debate all the time. They just loved it. Kenny had a comment about everything, and Bobby was often the only one who challenged him. Kenny would start talking, and then Bobby would jump right in and take him on. I remember sitting around and listening to these old men argue about the future of our country. To me, they were old men, because they had been through so much more than me. It was quite an education."

"Bobby and Kenny would come in together," recalls Wally Flynn, "and we might be studying or reading or maybe even watching the TV. Immediately, and I mean immediately, one of them would start discussing the postwar political situation and start a debate." Pretty soon the debate would erupt into argument. "I think it was the street fighter in Kenny that attracted Bobby," reflects Sam Adams. "He was in so many ways such a sheltered kid, and Kenny was anything but. It was a good balance." Kenny and Bobby would make sure that everyone got involved in the debate. All the participants could be provoked into opinions because, as Nick Rodis says, "we had all been through the war, so we all had pretty strong views on what should happen" in a nation flush with success, regearing its society for postwar growth and about to face a new, cold war. Kenny and Bobby had both grown up with fathers who deliberately stirred political debate among their families, and thus they were in their element in these arguments and were often much more adept than their friends. "Kenny and Bobby would have these conversations and discussions and we got to sit in on them, but really they were in a different league than any of us or anyone else at the school," remembers Jimmy Kenary. "The way they grew up with their fathers' influence I think really shaped who they were and, in a funny way, why they became so close."

"They would argue about anything, but most especially about politics," adds Jimmy Noonan, another veteran who entered Harvard in 1946. "I remember the first time I met Kenny and Bobby. Kenny walked right up to me and said, 'My God, there is somebody here smaller than me!' The debate about who was taller or weighed more went on for years, and I don't think we ever solved the question. I do remember the club arguments. You could just sit there and listen to them and learn so much. It was great."

Nick Rodis recalls a favorite trick of Bobby and Kenny's. "They would come in and get something going and the next thing we knew it would develop into a full-scale argument and we would all be involved. It would get really heated sometimes, and it would make you think about the tough things. Well, suddenly we would look up and realize that Kenny and Bobby were gone! They would literally start these arguments, debate with us for a while, and get up quietly, grab a football they had snagged from poor little George Sullivan, and go out and toss around the ball for several hours. After they had left we would all stop and look at each other. Finally somebody would ask, 'You don't think they did that on purpose, do you?' Then we would all laugh and go try to find them."

Kenny was notorious for wanting to be right at all costs. "Kenny was known to lie," laughs Jimmy Kenary, "and it used to make Bobby, Cleo, and the rest of us crazy. He would state something like it was a fact and because of the way he said it, most people never challenged him." Jimmy remembers Kenny declaring with an air of finality that 80 percent of all big league baseball players were from the South. "Everyone kind of looked at him and then looked at each other, and finally I said, 'You don't know that!' He said, 'Yes I do! Name one!'" Jimmy thought a moment and then threw out the name Tommy Hendricks. "Athens, Georgia!" Kenny said with absolute confidence. Furious, Kenary said, "Kenny, hell, you don't know that! You are just making that up!" Kenny smiled at Kenary and said knowingly, "I do know it. Go look it up!" Bobby sat looking quizzically at both of them, but said nothing. Several days later Jimmy returned to the Varsity Club triumphantly; he had looked it up, and Tommy Hendricks was from Massillon, Ohio. "That was the only time I ever got Kenny, but every time he would open his mouth to state a fact about some sports figure, I would grab that book and hold it up just to remind him. Bobby used to laugh. He thought it was great that we had finally caught Kenny. It was rare to be able to catch him at anything."

*   *   *

With his leadership skills, football prowess, and his reputation as a war hero, Kenny quickly became the dominant figure on the campus. For Kenny's older brother Cleo, life at postwar Harvard required more of an adjustment. Returning to the campus in 1946, he was elected team captain again and developed a friendship with Bobby over the course of his time there, but it was never the fast friendship that Bobby and Kenny had. Clee was older than Bobby by two years, and, although he enjoyed the debates and discussion to a degree, he did not share Bobby and Kenny's passion for politics. Recalls one veteran and Harvard graduate, "I think Clee's interests were a little different. He was older and different than Kenny was, and I think he didn't want to be seen always hanging with his younger brother and his friend."

The difference between the two O'Donnell brothers was considerable. Both lived at the Varsity Club, but having spent their youth tangling with each other at home on Worcester's Pleasant Street, they relished the chance to live in different rooms and with different roommates. "Clee and Kenny would argue," Noonan says, "but it was not usually about politics. It would be usually Kenny trying to drive Cleo crazy deliberately." Cleo was fastidious about his clothes, his personal grooming, his room, and the way he conducted himself. Clee had taken on much of his father's habits and comportment. And, like his father, he had also developed into a bit of an intellectual snob. For his younger brother, the opportunity to compete with Cleo was simply too much to resist. When his brother was elected football captain in 1946, Kenny made sure that everyone knew it was his influence that had won Cleo the honor. Jimmy Noonan also says the morning routine at the Varsity Club became dominated by the O'Donnell brothers. "Clee would come down, and he would be just going to class, but he would be dressed to the nines, every hair in place and impeccable. You would not find a speck of dirt on him, not even on his shoes. Kenny would walk up to him and give him the critical once-over and then say, 'God, Clee, you gonna wear that shirt?' Clee would immediately say, 'Why not? What's wrong with it?' Kenny would look at all of us, roll his eyes, and shake his head and say, 'Oh, never mind. Nobody will notice.' We would all shake our heads in agreement with Kenny. Appalled, Clee would rush upstairs and come down again with a different shirt on. Kenny would say, 'Much better,' and we would all agree. This might happen three times in a row on any given day." When Cleo left for class, Kenny would go upstairs and take his discarded shirt out of the laundry and wear it. Kenny said to his buddies that it made a great deal of sense to just wear Cleo's shirts, even though the two were different sizes. After all, it saved money and then he didn't have to wash them; because after he'd worn them he would simply toss them back into Cleo's pile. "Kenny was like that. He was a real wise guy. The original wise guy," muses one friend from that time.

Unlike his brother, Kenny was without question someone who just made do when it came to clothing and personal appearance. One time, when one of Kenny's shoes developed a hole in its sole, Bobby Kennedy was appalled to find out that instead of buying a new pair Kenny had put folded magazine pages in the loafers and worn them anyway. Bobby, who understood but never said out loud that Kenny didn't have the money to buy new shoes, promptly loaned his friend the cash for a new pair. "He never had any money," says Nick Rodis. To combat the constant shortfall, Kenny decided to draft the thrifty Rodis to be the treasurer for the group. "If they didn't pay back a loan, they couldn't get any more money," Rodis recalls. "I kept a record of who borrowed what. Even Bobby borrowed money from the till; he lived just like the rest of us, from hand to mouth. I am sure that he didn't have to, that his dad probably would have helped him, but he didn't ask. I think he enjoyed the fact that he didn't have any money either, so that we were all equals. He really didn't have a lot of time or interest in the fancy people on campus. He was just one of the guys. He was always the first one who wanted to help and be with you when the chips were down. As far as all of us are concerned, he never changed."

While life at the Varsity Club was punctuated by football and political debates, occasionally class work was part of the equation. Schoolwork was something that Kenny didn't enjoy. From his days as a star on the high school team at Classical High School in Worcester, he had little time or patience for classwork. For Bobby Kennedy, classwork remained the struggle it had been at Milton. Sam Adams, Bobby's friend at Milton, joined the team and the gang at the Varsity Club in 1947. "School was difficult for both of us. Bob had to work very hard for everything. He had a slight learning disability, dyslexia, really. I had it too, and he and I used to joke about it all the time. But both of us overcame it. Bob's was worse than mine. His handwriting was awful. Mine was too. But the teachers were always commenting on his small, cramped handwriting." Bobby's other pal from Milton, Dave Hackett, who would go from Milton to McGill in Canada, agrees that studies were hard for Bobby. "I think he was an average student," says Hackett. "He got average grades; I think he was obviously very intelligent." Bobby may not have been gifted academically, but he would succeed by sheer willpower and bravado.

"These guys," Nick Rodis adds, "Bobby, Kenny, and Cleo, would never study. They would have an exam in the morning in, say, government. I would be going to every class, studying, taking notes, and these guys didn't go to class and didn't take notes. They never went to class; then they would breeze into the exam and pass. I couldn't believe how calm they were about it. They had such confidence in themselves."

For Kenny the idea of winging exams was less difficult than might be expected. He rarely took notes, and his legendary memory would become increasingly useful over the years, during his political ascendancy with John F. Kennedy. He almost never studied, preferring instead to scan the material briefly shortly before an exam and then take the test— almost without exception passing, much to the frustration of his friends. "Both Kenny and Bobby were avid readers," Jimmy Noonan says. Kenny's interest in the world had been motivated by his war experience; Bobby's engagement with current events arose from having grown up in a family that was able to travel a great deal. Both men were intellectually influenced by their fathers' engagement with political ideas.

Football was the center of life itself for Kenny O'Donnell and Bobby Kennedy at Harvard. Not a natural player like Kenny or his brother, Bobby probably worked harder than anyone else to earn and keep his spot on that team. According to Nick Rodis, Dick Harlow, the football coach, "told me one day, 'Bobby is the toughest boy pound for pound that I have ever coached since Bobby Green [Harvard Captain Robert C. Green, '38]!' "

Harlow took the game very seriously. Before the war, he had been considered crusty, difficult, and very firm in his views about how football should be played and how his team members should conduct themselves. Like many of his players, he had left Harvard to fight in the war and returned a changed man. If people thought him ornery and a bit eccentric before the war, many felt now that Harlow was almost impossible.

Kenny and Harlow disliked each other immediately. Kenny would, in the words of Sam Adams, "become very active in dumping Harlow." Not only was Harlow generally difficult, but Kenny, Bobby, and many of the players felt he capriciously singled people out for a hard time. Sam recalls vividly how, after having transferred with some public fanfare from Tufts University, he felt excited about playing football for Harvard. Harlow decided that Sam needed to be put in his place. Harlow, Adams says, made it "as difficult as possible. He developed really unreasonable prejudices toward certain players. He hated anyone who came in with any publicity or held any status on the campus, so his idea was to tear people down and mold them to his idea of the game. He would grind you down to a different size until you fit his mold."

Kenny believed that Harlow would make snap judgments and not allow certain players to play. He took the risk of insisting to Harlow that certain people be allowed in the game. "Somebody would screw up and then Harlow would just sit them out," Sam remembers. "Kenny's view was 'In the end it's just a football game!' " Bobby in particular was very good with Sam. "I would get so frustrated with Harlow," Sam says. "I had never had these kinds of problems with a coach before. Bobby was great. He was very encouraging because I was going bananas and I really was ready to quit the team. Bobby would say, 'Hang in there, Sam — the coach is just riding you, just keep your cool.' He was very good that way. If you were having a tough time, he was the first guy there; Kenny too."

Bobby went through his own difficulties with the coach, just as his brothers before him had. Harlow had coached both Joe and Jack Kennedy. The ambassador was particularly furious at the way Harlow treated Joe Jr. In the fall of 1937, during Joe Jr.'s last year of school, during Harvard's traditional final game of the season with Yale, Ambassador Kennedy sat in the stands waiting for his son to play. The only way to get a letter at Harvard was to play in the Yale game. You could miss every other game of the season, but if you played in the Yale game even for one play, you got your letter. As George Sullivan heard the story years later, the clock was ticking away the afternoon and Joe Jr., a sub, still hadn't gotten in the game. The score was close, and for whatever reasons, Harlow never put young Joe in the game, not even for one play. He would leave Harvard without the letter. Sullivan says he heard that "the ambassador tore down to that field and collared Harlow right on the gridiron at Harvard stadium and read him the riot act right in front of everyone! Fans were running by, people were yelling, and the players were walking by, including Joe Jr., and there was the ambassador blasting Harlow in public. I guess it was really an awful scene."

Harlow seemed determined not to let Bobby Kennedy forget the incident or escape payment for his father's actions. According to Sam Adams, the coach would look for every chance to embarrass Bobby in front of his teammates. "I think it was sort of his way of getting back at the Kennedys, and Bobby really resented it. He felt he had earned his right to play on the team through hard work and grit, and he resented Harlow insinuating that he was only there because of his father." "Bobby took some needling," says Nick Rodis, "but it just served to make him more determined."

Harlow would situate himself on the wooden platform he had built on the side of the field, where he could stand over the players and bark out orders or comments. Sam recalls one time hearing the coach yell at him, "You have all the alacrity of a water buffalo, Adams!" Kenny told him to just ignore it. What Bobby dealt with was perhaps much worse. According to Sam, "Harlow would stand on that platform and we would be in a scrimmage and something would happen—maybe the play would go well, maybe Bobby missed a tackle. Nothing huge—it was practice, standard stuff. Well, Harlow would suddenly start to yell, 'Mr. Bobby Kennedy, don't you know how to—' And then he would suddenly turn as if he were talking to someone on the ground, and he would say, 'Oh, excuse me, Mr. Ambassador, I didn't see you—isn't your son a wonderful player? Good job, Mr. Kennedy!' It was awful. Bobby hated it."

The coach's treatment made Bobby simply redouble his efforts. "He would," said Sam, "make a face and grit his teeth and just get back in the huddle. He never complained or said a word. He just worked even harder. I think that made Harlow even madder that he didn't get to Bobby. Bobby just kept his cool." Kenny, whose natural ability far outstripped his friend's, admired Bobby's courage and tenacity, says Nick Rodis. "It was kind of a mutual admiration society. Bobby admired Kenny's ability and Kenny admired Bobby's flat-out courage." As he had been all his life, on the football field Bobby was the runt, and he took to his role with relish.

In addition to picking on certain players, Harlow would often put in other players in key slots in which the team had no confidence. Other, better players might fall out of favor, and the coach would not play them again. Another classic incident with Harlow involved the Harvard kicker Bucky Harrison. When his attempt at a field goal was blocked, "it wasn't his fault," says a teammate, "but Harlow was furious and announced to the team in a voice loud enough for all the players including Bucky to hear, 'That boy will never kick another field goal for me!'"

The coach had little tolerance for the players' own antic delight in the game. "One time Cleo, Bobby, and Kenny all crashed into each other during the middle of the Dartmouth game," remembers Wally Flynn. "It was part of the play and it was a hard tackle and they all kind of crashed heads. Afterward they got up and began talking to each other in a kind of jibberish. It was hilarious, but the referee didn't realize they were kidding. He called a brief time-out and went over to see if the guys were okay. Well, they were in a circle sort of talking in jibberish and bowing to each other. The whole team just broke up over it! The poor referee thought that they really might have hit their heads too hard. He didn't realize they were just being wise guys." Needless to say, Coach

Harlow, who was never much amused, especially with Kenny, found even less to laugh about that day.

Kenny found it harder and harder to tolerate the coach's behavior with his players. By 1947 the situation had become impossible. "Kenny was really the reason that Harlow was gotten rid of and Arthur L. Valpey was brought on to coach in Kenny's last year." With his war hero status, a father revered on the gridiron, and a brother who had been team captain, only Kenny had the influence to get rid of Harlow. "Kenny really risked his future by taking on Harlow," says Sam Adams, "but neither he nor Bobby could stand around and allow people to be treated that way. And really they were the only ones in a position to do something about it. They wouldn't make a huge deal about it, but they would put a stop to it, no question." For Kenny, a natural risktaker anyway, fair was fair, and Harlow was not being fair to his players.

Harvard football and the national issue of race would soon collide on the playing field. Only the fourth black man ever to attend Harvard, Chester Pierce would make history as the first to play racially integrated football south of the Mason-Dixon Line. He was not one who would have sought out the role. A quiet, unassuming man, Pierce would go on to be a doctor, psychiatrist, and Harvard professor.

The first time Pierce ran out on the field during a Harvard game at the serene and history-laden stone stadium, he was met by a shout of "Hey, my God, look—it's a nigger!" The crowd was not yelling it in anger, Pierce explains, but in absolute astonishment. He had challenges off the field as well. There were establishments that at first refused to serve Pierce because he was black. The crisis of racial integration that Robert Kennedy would address as attorney general and senator would not begin to boil until the next decade, but Pierce addressed the problem personally and directly, taking some of his teammates with him to various places that refused him service and confronting the management directly. There never was any major direct confrontation, but the point was made. The team always backed him up. For Bobby, Kenny, Cleo, Nick, and the others, it did not matter that Chet Pierce was black and they saw no reason that it should matter to anyone else.

In October 1947, Harvard University was scheduled to play football against the University of Virginia in Charlottesville, the school where Bobby Kennedy would later become president of the Legal Forum and get his law degree. When the game was scheduled the year before, Harvard's athletic director, Bill Bingham, had informed the University of Virginia that Harvard had a black player, whom they intended to bring with them. In what would become an interesting foreshadowing of an incident that Bobby Kennedy would deal with just a few years later, the university first indicated they had no problem with the presence of the black player. But a few weeks before the game, University of Virginia officials called Bingham and told him not to "bring that black boy" with them. Bingham was furious; he informed the officials that Harvard had every intention of bringing Pierce and intended for him to play. "It was all or none," Wally Flynn recalls. "Either he was playing or we were not going."

The Virginia players themselves had taken a vote, and they had agreed unanimously that Harvard should bring Pierce and that he should play. But University of Virginia officials, wary of breaking the segregation barriers, were worried about how the crowd would react to seeing a black player on their field being treated as an equal.

"Bill was a tough guy, and he didn't back down on a principle or shy away from controversy," says Flynn. Pierce, Kenny, Cleo, and the rest of the team made the trip. Bobby Kennedy was left back in Cambridge, having broken his leg earlier in the season. Pierce played the game with the quiet grace of a young man certain of himself and comfortable with breaking the barriers he needed to. Kenny started the game at quarterback at Scott Field at the University of Virginia, which has a normal capacity for 22,500, but on this day held some 25,000 spectators. Back in Cambridge, Bobby holed up at the Varsity Club, listening to the game on the radio. Harvard, suffering the loss of several injured players, including one Bob Kennedy, would go down to defeat, but history had been made. "It was something that just wasn't done in those days," says Pierce of his appearance as the first black man to play on a southern gridiron. Only four years later it would be Bobby Kennedy who would force the very same university to break its long-standing segregation laws for yet another black man and another precedent-setting event.

The kind of loyalty that buoyed Chester Pierce would extend from team member to team member, from the football field to the poolroom in the Varsity Club to a candlelit St. Patrick's Cathedral in 1968.

At Harvard, Kenny was the quarterback and Bobby was the receiver. Over the years, at the Senate rackets committee, in political campaigns, and in the White House, the relationship would change: Bobby would become the quarterback and Kenny the receiver. But while at Harvard, football was where Kenny held command. His interception record as quarterback would become part of Harvard football history and still stands unbroken to this day. "It was no accident that Kenny broke all the interception records," says Wally Flynn, who often played defensive halfback. "Of course, his father Cleo's influence and advice had a lot to do with it. But Kenny figured out that something like seventy-eight percent of all passes are overthrown. The way his mind worked, he could figure out those kinds of things." Such savvy would later in life be one of the reasons he was inducted into the Hall of Fame at Harvard. Sam Adams remembers Bobby pointing out how Kenny had a mind for calculation, "so with football he can judge where a ball is going to end up by the wind condition and speed of the player involved in the play." Bobby understood that Kenny's technique was to watch the arm of the quarterback move forward, time the ball in his mind, and then time it against the possible receiver, and most often he could anticipate and be where the ball was being thrown. In what would become a clear Kennedy trait, whether with football or government policy, Bobby would identify someone he could learn from and then do all he could to gain as much information as that person had to offer. For Kenny, caught up with politics and savvy enough to know that Bobby's older brother, Congressman John Kennedy, had serious ambitions, it seemed an even exchange of knowledge and acumen. Such an understanding helped to develop a solid bond of friendship between them and the beginnings of a powerful partnership.

In the opening game of the 1947 season, against Western Maryland, Bobby caught his first touchdown for Harvard. Harvard scored an impressive fifty-two points, and Western Maryland went completely scoreless throughout the game. Bobby Kennedy scored the second touchdown on a quick six-yard pass from Kenny. It was a fake buck play and perfectly timed, "right out of their nightly practice sessions," according to George Sullivan.

The football season for Bobby that senior year in 1947 would be short-lived, however. During a particularly rough practice session, Bobby attempted to tackle somebody twice his size and crashed full force into the equipment cart. Nick Rodis remembers that Bobby was really badly hurt—"at least we found out afterwards that he was." Ignoring the sudden surge of pain in his leg, he jumped right up and got back into the game, recalls Flynn. "I remember asking him if he was okay, because he sure hit that thing hard, but he said he was fine and he finished out the practice."

Bobby said nothing to his friends, although he did ask Kenny if his leg looked crooked. Kenny replied, "Yeah, but no more than usual." In excruciating pain, he completed practice and showed up the next day for practice and played. By the third day, midway through the practice, Bobby collapsed on the field during a play. Flynn found out later that Kenny had known right away that Bobby was hurt more severely than he said. As he said to one pal, "I told Bobby not to worry—since his other leg was cockeyed, now they both matched. Bobby didn't think it was that funny." A true son of his ironfisted father, Cleo, Kenny thought nothing of the incident and wasn't even middling impressed that Bobby had continued to play. Pain was just pain, and you never complained or showed that it bothered you. Bobby of course had grown up with the same credo of toughness; and as his father would have it, he just bounced back up and played until his broken leg gave way underneath him. But not even a Kennedy could overcome a broken leg.

Sullivan is quick to point out that "Bobby was not a fool. He was tough as nails, but he knew enough to know a broken leg wasn't going to get better without treatment, so he couldn't have realized that it was broken. But he could get up and put pressure on it, so he thought it was okay. Granted, I think most people couldn't have played under those conditions, but God—both Kenny and Bobby played with broken legs."

The football season traditionally ended with the Harvard-Yale game, held that year at the New Haven bowl before close to eighty thousand fans. One of the fans was the star of the baseball team, a fellow New Englander and future president, George Bush. Bobby played the game with his leg in a full cast. Despite the pain, he caught a pass for a touchdown. It was only the second of the two touchdowns Bobby scored while at Harvard. It earned him his third Harvard letter. He was the only one of the three Kennedy brothers to earn three letters. "Although," Flynn points out with a smile, "his leg was still cockeyed even after the cast."

In an ironic twist of fate, Kenny was to break his leg the next year. Bobby had gone on to the University of Virginia Law School, but the two were still close, keeping in touch with constant letters. During a game with Princeton, Kenny brushed off the injury, a hairline fracture, and was fitted with a full leg cast. He demanded to play, especially in the last game of the season and his collegiate football career—the game with Yale. He wanted his letter. Although he had already won three of them, his brother Cleo had won four and Kenny had to compete. The new coach, Valpey, agreed to let him play. Valpey expected, as did the rest of the team, that Kenny would just lie low during the game and not get into too much trouble. That was not his style. Like Bobby, injury or no, he had to be where the action was.

The old Harvard stadium could not hold a crowd the size of the Yale Bowl, but it could contain fifty-four thousand fans, and during the big games the college brought out wooden benches for extra seating. With his father, Cleo, in the stands, Kenny wanted to put on a show. He scored the winning touchdown with his leg in a full cast. Running for a few feet, feeling his leg give way, he dove over the goal line, and Harvard won the game. It was a story that Kenny loved to tell, and the incident captured much of his spirit.

The Harvard that Kenny and Bobby knew for their two full years together changed even as they were leaving the university. By 1948 a backlash had begun to grow against the Varsity Club. "There was a feeling that the Varsity Club had become too exclusive and that the team was not mixing with the general student population, which of course we weren't," says Nick Rodis. The team had established its own world, with friendships that for Bobby Kennedy and his circle would last until his death in 1968 and beyond. Bobby and Kenny had formed a bond that would change both of their lives. Sustaining their relationship would be their firm and mutual belief that action was the key to change. Neither one had been raised by his father to stand still. Each had had great expectations placed on him from childhood. Growing up in the shadow of older brothers made it all the more important to prove that they were worthy of their fathers' admiration and the gifts that had been given to them.

In 1948, Kenny and Bobby engaged in a mock presidential debate at Harvard's cavernous Memorial Hall. Each took a different side, one representing Truman and the other Dewey. For the first time in such a public setting, they went after each other's representative positions as tenaciously as they always went after each other in their own political discussions within the walls of the Varsity Club. Neither gave any quarter, nor expected any to be given. When the dust settled, the issues dividing the two had been given an airing that left no questions where either Truman or Dewey stood in the upcoming elections, and no one who did not know them well would have believed that the two representative speakers were in fact not political rivals but actually the best of friends. Just four years after that debate, the two of them would run Jack Kennedy's Senate campaign and beat Eisenhower's favored candidate, Henry Cabot Lodge. Four years after that, in 1956, they would narrowly miss winning Jack the nomination for the vice presidency but, in so doing, prove to themselves that they could win it all. Four years later, they would again team up to run Jack Kennedy's campaign for the White House and win. Without question, time was to prove what the boys at the Harvard Varsity Club knew all along—that, as Jimmy Kenary said, "Kenny and Bobby were really in a league of their own."

3

BEGINNING THE MARCH: THE 1946 CAMPAIGN

Give me the toughest part of the district.

— BOBBY KENNEDY

"Hi! I'm Jack Kennedy!"

Startled, Pasquale "Pat" Fuccillo turned to face an extraordinary-looking young man, thin, with pale skin, blue eyes, and a mop of reddish-brown hair. Then he recognized the face. This was Ambassador Kennedy's boy, the war hero. What was he doing here? It was early in 1946, and Pat and a group of young men were standing at an East Boston streetcar stop, waiting for the trolley to Revere Beach. Freshly returned from his service in the war, Pat had never met a politician before, let alone a Kennedy. The Fuccillo family lived in a second-floor walk-up in East Boston. Like most Bostonians, they were familiar with the Kennedys, especially the ambassador, who had founded Columbia Trust Savings Bank and gone on to even better things, and they followed the story of the Kennedy clan, from the transatlantic adventures of the beautiful Kathleen to the tragic death of Joe Kennedy, Jr. A sports fan, Pat had also heard of Cleo O'Donnell, Sr., the football legend, and his Hall of Fame coaching exploits at Everett, Holy Cross, and most recently at St. Anselm's. Everett, where Cleo had started his career and gained notoriety, is a neighbor of East Boston. Pat had also heard that two of Cleo's boys were attending Harvard. He hoped to get over to the stadium to see them play at some point.

What struck Pat the most was how extraordinary it was for a politician to hit the pavement in search of votes. Young Jack Kennedy told the gathered group that he was running for Congress and he wanted their help. In rapid fire, he asked them about themselves, where they lived, and what they thought of life after the war. Pat was impressed with the strength of his handshake; the candidate certainly didn't look that strong. The group of young men watched the young war hero work his way down the sidewalk, regularly stopping people along the route to ask them about themselves and seek their vote. As he and his friends boarded their streetcar for Revere Beach, he decided that if he had Jack Kennedy's millions, he'd be off living a life of leisure and enjoying himself, not searching out handshakes from returned vets and little old ladies. As the streetcar lurched to a halt at the next stop, Pat turned to one of his friends and said, "You know, that guy's got something. I don't know anything about the race, but he has guts and I'm going to vote for him!" Jack Kennedy won at least one vote that day.

A few days after his meeting with Jack, Pat's younger sister Matilda received a phone call from one of Jack Kennedy's sisters inviting her to a tea with Rose Kennedy and other members of the Kennedy family on Sunday at a well-known Boston hotel. Matilda was thrilled. A tea — nobody did teas, and it was a chance to dress up and meet Rose Kennedy! Honey Fitz, otherwise known as former Boston mayor John Fitzgerald, was a legend, his daughter a celebrity. Matilda went and was delighted; she had met "all the beautiful people," she told her family, "and they were so ordinary and very nice." Pat was pleased that his sister enjoyed herself, but he was also amazed she'd gotten the invitation at all, because he didn't even remember giving his name to Jack Kennedy, let alone his phone number. But clearly he had, his sister said; Jack had mentioned to her how nice it was to meet her brother. Jack Kennedy had now won two votes from East Boston. His sister was so impressed that she would go on to actively support and eventually work for the Kennedys for some thirty years.

Although his brother was running for Congress at the time and Bobby Kennedy was involved in the campaign, he continued to keep a low-key presence at Harvard. While he might argue politics with Kenny O'Donnell at the Varsity Club, he would not bring the Kennedy congressional campaign onto the football field or into the poolroom on Friday nights. But the campaign itself would not only be a new act in the Kennedy family drama. Jack Kennedy's race for Congress would mark the beginning of a new life for twenty-year-old Bobby as well. From 1946 until the end of his life, he would remain in the public arena.

In 1946, said Kenny O'Donnell later, Bobby began to meet other kinds of people—people who didn't give a damn who he was or who he was related to. Kenny knew that very early in his adulthood Bobby had made the choice to forgo the easy social life he could have led among the Harvard and Boston elite. Instead, he had chosen to associate himself with the rough-and-tumble veterans who made up the Harvard football team. Similarly, Bobby would enter the rough-and-tumble of politics instead of sitting back and staying out of the action.

At Bobby's insistence, Kenny went with him to the Bellevue Hotel, where Jack was living, for a brief meeting with the candidate and older brother. It was a year when the votes of the veterans were to be the big factor. None of Kennedy's opponents had a war record worth talking about, and Jack's well-known display of courage in the South Pacific gave him an aura of glamour that overshadowed his political inexperience and the charges that he was a carpetbagger whose wealthy father was trying to buy him a seat in Congress. As they headed over that spring day from campus, Kenny made clear to Bobby that he was only accompanying him out of friendship. "I'm much more interested in meeting your war-hero brother than I am in meeting your brother who is running for Congress."

"Fine" was Bobby's reply.

They arrived at the Bellevue. Bobby made introductions. Kenny liked what he saw, but was still suspicious of how serious the young man really was about making a difference in Congress. Kenny, having grown up with a father for whom the three courses at dinner were football, politics, and history, didn't think at the time that the reserved, polished, and remarkably thin Jack Kennedy had much of a future in politics. He did like that he was a veteran, and he liked his firm handshake, which surprised him, considering Jack's gaunt appearance.

Kenny would stay clear of the 1946 Kennedy congressional campaign, keeping apprised of it mainly through listening to Bobby's adventures as a lieutenant in his brother's army of Kennedys. Kenny himself had football to play, courses to pass, and a woman from Worcester, Helen Sullivan, to court. It would be 1948 and in Paul Dever's Massachusetts gubernatorial campaign where Kenny would really test the political waters as an operative. By then, Jack's work helping to draft and hone the Veterans' Housing Bill and other issues would convince a skeptical O'Donnell that Kennedy was not only serious but intended to make his mark and change the political landscape. By 1952, Kenny would jump at the chance Bobby gave him to become really involved in the Kennedy political machinery.

For the time being, on the late spring afternoon in 1946 as he accompanied Bobby to the Bellevue Hotel, he was content only to meet Jack Kennedy the war hero, his friend's brother; he was content only to wait and see. Kenny made clear that if Bobby wanted his help, he would do it as a favor to his best friend, and that was all. Jack Kennedy, candidate for Congress, still had to prove himself as a serious candidate to this veteran.

Billy Sutton, or Whiffle, as he was known in the Charlestown neighborhood where he grew up, walked slowly up School Street in Boston. The year was 1946 and he was anxious. Still wearing his brown army uniform, he carried his final mustering-out pay from the army in his left breast pocket. He was glad to be out of the service and glad to be home, but now he was unsure of what to do. He could go back to his old job at Consolidated Gas, but it didn't hold any real interest for him. Still, it was a paycheck, and with the waves of returning vets, jobs were scarce.

"Whiffle. Billy." Billy turned to see Joe Kane on the other side of the street. Billy crossed the street; he liked Joe Kane and knew that he always had something to say. Joe was Ambassador Joseph Kennedy's cousin and always had the political beat of the city close at hand.

"Have you ever heard of Jack Kennedy?"

Billy thought for a moment. Sure, he knew the Kennedys. The Kennedys of New York, Cape Cod, and Palm Beach—they had money, nothing but money. But Jack? "No," Billy replied. "Never heard of him."

"Well, I want you to meet him. He's running for Congress and I want you to help him."

Since he had nothing better to do at the moment, Billy followed Joe Kane up the slightly sloping street. As they walked past the City Hall building, Sutton remembered something else about the Kennedys: Rose Fitzgerald Kennedy was Honey Fitz's daughter and a real beauty. Now there was a real lady, Billy thought. She knew Boston, she knew politics. The Fitzgeralds and the Suttons had all grown up in East Boston. His father and sisters were born on Charter Street and Rose was born a few streets over. East Boston was a small, Irish enclave; everyone knew one another.

As he walked into the Bellevue's dark lobby with its overstuffed chairs and people milling about for lunch, it took a moment for Billy's eyes to adjust to the dark. He followed Joe directly to a young man standing in the middle of the room. He was thin, almost gaunt, and he reminded Billy of Charles Lindbergh.

"Billy, this is Jack Kennedy."

"Hi!" The young man grasped his hand. "I could really use your help. I'm running for Congress and I need someone who knows the district. Can you do it?"

Sutton found something about this guy appealing. He was different. Maybe it was his youth; maybe it was that he was a veteran. Maybe working for him would be better than a job at Consolidated Gas. "Sure," Billy heard himself saying.

"Call Paul Murphy," Joe Kane told him, referring to a New York aide to the ambassador. "Give him your social security number and he'll put you on the payroll." Billy Sutton did as he was directed. Still in his army uniform, he began his first full day of work for Jack Kennedy.

John F. Kennedy formally established his own residence in Massachusetts in the fall of 1945. He set up housekeeping at the Bellevue Hotel, not far from where his grandfather Honey Fitz lived. As much as the Kennedys were associated with Boston, in truth, Jack Kennedy had never really lived in Boston with the exception of the time that he attended Harvard and lived at Cambridge. Ambassador Kennedy had managed to secure a position doing an economic survey for then governor Maurice Tobin. The job had two key benefits for both the ambassador and his son. It allowed Joe Kennedy an excuse to meet with and win over as many of the political movers and shakers in Massachusetts as possible, which was no small feat. It had been quite some time since the ambassador had paid any real attention to Massachusetts, and as he well knew from his own family background, the Irish have very long memories and can be an unforgiving group. The second benefit was that the survey allowed Jack and his father time at the end of each day to meet at the ambassador's normal hotel, the Ritz-Carlton, to talk and to plan political strategy. Both father and son would survey the territory, and Jack, new to politics, would get his feet wet.

For Jack, the first and perhaps most difficult part of his entry into the political arena was convincing his father that he should run for Congress and not for the lieutenant governorship of Massachusetts. The ambassador thought Jack should make the statewide race in large measure because he was deeply concerned that Jack would not be able to win a bruising congressional battle for the seat recently held by Boston mayor James Curley. Part of Joseph Kennedy's concern stemmed from his own father's brutal experience in politics. Despite Patrick Kennedy's having served only one term before being defeated and turned out by the very voters he spent a lifetime helping, a combination of events made the congressional race for Jack the inevitable choice: Joe Kane wrote the ambassador a frank memo saying, despite his father Patrick's bad experience in electoral politics, it was clear that Jack should run for Congress. In addition, the ambassador himself had a private poll taken that convinced him that Jack's running for Congress was the best option. The decision made, it was now up to Jack to make the announcement and set himself apart from his father and his father's generation.

It was a delicate balance to achieve. Jack realized that his political future lay in his ability to distinguish himself from the prewar isolationism his father had championed and from the old-time politics represented by his beloved grandfather Honey Fitz. When he announced his

candidacy on Monday, April 22, 1946, Kennedy immediately made it
clear that his political outlook was his own. He quickly identified himself with the returning veterans and with the risky internationalist era
that he felt was the inevitable result of World War II:

> The people of the United States and the world stand at the cross-
> roads. What we do now will shape the history of civilization for
> many years to come. We have a weary world trying to bind the
> wounds of a fierce struggle. That is dire enough. What is infinitely
> far worse is that we have a world which has unleashed the terrible
> powers of atomic energy. We have a world capable of destroying
> itself. The days which lie ahead are most difficult ones. Above all,
> day and night, with every ounce of ingenuity and industry we pos-
> sess, we must work for peace. We must not have another war. It is
> no answer to the problem to say that we shall not go to war again,
> no matter what the cost, and leave it at that. If another Hitler were
> to appear on the world scene, if totalitarianism were to threaten
> once again to engulf the world, then we would face the same sit-
> uation which we faced so recently and the only course would be
> war. We must see to it that such a situation is never allowed to be
> created again. To accomplish that task calls for abilities of a high
> order. It calls for intelligence, for firmness in speech and for ac-
> tion. . . .

With these words, the twenty-eight-year-old John Kennedy was speaking to Kenny O'Donnell, Bobby Kennedy, Nick Rodis, and all the other
veterans in Boston and beyond who saw themselves at a personal and
generational turning point. "The country was really at a crossroads," says
Bill Connors, a veteran who would later become head of the Veterans
Administration in Boston, "and Jack Kennedy sort of represented the
future." It was the first but not the last time that John F. Kennedy would
put himself forward as both leader and emblem of a new generation.

The campaign and the candidate quickly attracted the interest of a
great many young people who had never been involved in politics before. Peter Cloherty, one of Kennedy's campaign secretaries, says, "It

was a rather unique campaign inasmuch as there were a great many young people who I don't think had ever been interested in politics before." Whether it was the temper of the times, the glamour of the candidate, or the Kennedy money, the result was a new type of political campaign, one that would help to set the terms for how America conducted politics in future years.

The campaign would continue to be a battle between Jack Kennedy's understanding of the electorate and that of the Irish politicians with their cigars and smoke-filled rooms. The pols believed that political decisions about candidates were best made by a chosen few, while Jack Kennedy espoused a greater participation by the general public in such matters. The battle would continue through much of the campaign and would not come to a head until the 1952 Senate race, where under the leadership of his brother Bobby and with the support of Kenny O'Donnell, Dave Powers, and Larry O'Brien, Jack Kennedy would ensure that his new brand of politics would replace the old. First, though Jack knew he had to win, and to do that this first time he knew he needed not only his father's and Joe Kane's help but their network. Once he had won the seat, he could really begin to build his own future and his own network.

Despite the help of his father's influence, his grandfather's friends, and his family's money, Jack's first political race started out as an uphill fight. The race to fill Curley's seat turned into "a wild free-for-all," says historian Doris Kearns Goodwin, with Mike Neville, the mayor of Cambridge, the clear favorite, despite Jack's grandfather Honey Fitz himself having represented the district in Congress at the turn of the century.

Jack had picked up the help of two local political hands who were as much responsible for his winning the election in 1946 as Ambassador Kennedy and Joe Kane. The first, Bill Sutton, had urged both Joe Kane and the candidate to meet one very important young man in Charlestown. Bill had known Dave Powers since the two were boys and played hockey together; he was there when Dave caught a hockey puck in the eye that nearly blinded him. Bill had worked for Dave selling newspapers in the Charlestown Navy Yard, "and so right there," Sutton pointed out with some urgency, "was ten thousand people!" In Sutton's mind, the personable and charming Powers seemed to know just about every-body.

On the evening of January 21, 1946, Jack Kennedy climbed the three flights of stairs to the top floor of a three-decker house at 88 Ferrin Street in Charlestown. The knock at the door startled Dave, who was in the kitchen with his widowed older sister and her eight children. Three-decker families always gathered in the kitchen, especially during the New England winters, to be close to the warmth of the stove. Like his pal Bill Sutton, Dave was a returned veteran. He had just recently been discharged from the Army Air Force, after having served his time as a sergeant in China.

As he opened the front door of the cold-water flat, Dave could not really see the face of the caller. "I could barely make out this tall and thin, handsome young man in the front hall, hidden in the half-lit dark-ness by the dim light of a twenty-watt bulb." Startled, Powers invited the young man into his sister's home. After some discussion, Dave told the young man what he was seeking, but at Jack's urging, he did agree to attend a Gold Star Mothers meeting two days later at American Le-gion Hall where Kennedy would be speaking.

The meeting changed his life. As he listened to Kennedy talk and watched the emotional responses of all the mothers who had lost chil-dren in the war, Dave learned what Pat Fuccillo and Bill Sutton already knew, that there was something different about this returned war hero, son of Ambassador Joe Kennedy. "I had been to a lot of political talks before," Powers said of his first experience listening to Kennedy speak, "but I never saw a reaction like that one." Powers said he thought to himself as the candidate finished speaking, "I don't know what this guy's got. He's no great orator and he doesn't say much, but they certainly go crazy over him." Completing his speech, Jack struggled through the throng of Gold Star Mothers, all of whom were reminded of their own lost Bill or Bob. He responded uncertainly to their grasps and ready smiles. This was new territory to him, and he was determined to over-come his shyness and reserve.

Shaking hands, making small talk, Jack fought his way through the crowd, and he and Powers finally found themselves in the fresh air outside. "How do you think I did?" asked Jack, staring hard at Powers's face for the slightest sign of sycophancy.

"How do I think you did?" thundered Dave in his rich Boston twang. "You were terrific!"

Relieved, Jack let out a sigh and then said seriously, "So, then you'll be with me?"

"I am already with you! I've already started working for you!"

Jack had forged what Dave would later come to call a "magical link" between himself and the people in that room. As Dave headed back to his sister's house, he knew this young vet was a different kind of politician. He would remain associated with Jack Kennedy in a variety of roles until November 22, 1963.

Because Jack Kennedy was a veteran and a war hero, young men like Sutton and Powers were drawn to him. Like him, they were freshly returned from the war, and Jack represented to them a new kind of politician. Despite his wealth, he seemed to have a certain understanding of their fears and concerns. Just as they had trusted each other in wartime, they could trust each other now as well. "Being a veteran," says Bill Sutton of that time, "was why I was able to work with and gain the respect of these really incredible men, Jack Kennedy, Bobby Kennedy, and Kenny O'Donnell. We all had a bond. The bond, of course, was the war. It really did make all the difference."

Bobby was nine years younger than Jack, and although they had always been close, the death of Joseph Kennedy, Jr., propelled the brothers together in a way that might never have occurred otherwise. Jack had always been protective of his younger sibling. When Bobby had enlisted in the army, Jack's intercession with his father as much as his father's own intervention prevented Bobby from seeing real action. When Bobby began to work on Jack's campaign, the relationship between the two brothers would change once again. They had to figure out who they were and how they fit together now that Joe was gone.

"When Bobby first came into the campaign headquarters, he was very polite, nice, and what I would call very shy," says Sutton. "He wanted to help out in the campaign. What struck me was the first thing he said to me: 'Give me the toughest part of the district. I'll take it.' Then I

realized that underneath this kid was really tough. Bobby wanted East
Cambridge because he knew that was Neville's area and it was going to
be a really tough race," Sutton remembers. Just as he had done with
football at Milton and Harvard and with the debates at the Varsity
Club, Bobby was naturally drawn to the toughest front in the battle.
Rather than being intimidated, he saw it as a natural opportunity to
prove himself.

"We were trying to get this man elected to the congressional seat and
he really was an interloper and people knew it," says Sutton. The Kennedys of New York, Hyannisport, and Palm Beach had traveled far from
the North End where Joe Kennedy's and Rose Fitzgerald's parents had
grown up decades before. The real key to his success, Jack knew, was
his mother. She was an excellent campaigner, who knew the district
better than her son did. Moreover, she was a competitor who understood
instinctively how politics worked and how to win. She put in her all
and brought along not only Bobby but her daughters Patricia and Eunice. It was through Rose that Jack overcame the charge of carpetbag-
ging. During the heat of the campaign, as his mother's popularity
continued to grow, Jack would often joke that if he had ever had to run
against Rose, he most certainly would have lost. "Our best weapon,"
says Billy Sutton, "was Mrs. Rose Kennedy. There was a lady who should
have been in office."

One of the most formidable of the nine other candidates competing
for the seat, Mike Neville, mayor of Cambridge, was not intimidated by
Ambassador Joe Kennedy's son. Neville was a tough campaigner and
judged that the young Kennedy brothers weren't really going to like the
rough-and-tumble of politics. Neville believed that he knew Boston and
Cambridge and that he had paid his political dues; people knew who
he was and where he was from. The Kennedys had long been gone from
Boston and had to make an effort to ensure that people were reminded
of the very real Kennedy roots among the Boston Irish regardless of their
later accumulated wealth. Jack had to find a way to introduce himself
to people anew, making himself appealing without sacrificing the things
about him that made him different and more attractive than the other
candidates.

The campaign was conducted mostly door-to-door and over the radio; very few people owned televisions. Jack Kennedy proved himself to be a tremendous campaigner, but it was much tougher for him than for Bobby and the Kennedy women. He was far sicker than anyone realized at the time. Plagued with a damaged back from the war as well as various illnesses, he spent much of the campaign feeling ill. "What I remember most," says Sutton, "is that I knew he was in pain almost all the time and he would have to stand for hours and walk up and down these stairs and these streets. He never, ever complained and he acted as if he was the healthiest person in the world. I think it was the Kennedy credo of toughness."

The daily routine often began about 5:30 or 6:00 A.M. "We would go have breakfast," continues Sutton, "and then Jack would go speak at the United Way and then at some high school. He would go to maybe City Hall for some meeting and then just stop and talk to people on the street. It was a really long, long day. And always at the end of the day— and sometimes it would be very late at night—he would ask, 'Is there one more place we should go? Have we done everything we can do today?' " Both Sutton and Powers learned that the Kennedys not only were tough but worked hard and expected everyone around them to do the same.

Dave Powers first met Bobby Kennedy in Jack's Bellevue Hotel room, where most of the key players gathered in that first campaign and where the important decisions were made. "Jack introduced Bobby to me in the living room, and then Jack excused himself. He had to get dressed for a political event we were attending that evening. Bobby turned to me and said very quietly and sort of in a shy way, 'How is my brother going to do in Charlestown?' I explained to Bobby that the people of Charlestown really admired his brother. They admire courage in Charlestown. It is a working town and they admire courage along the docks and shipyards of Charlestown, so I told him I thought his brother would do all right there. Bob looked over at me with that mixture of shyness and youth and said, 'My brother has more courage than anyone I have ever met.' "

As they stood in the tiny living room waiting for Jack to finish dressing,

Dave was struck by the twenty-year-old's sincerity. "Bobby was so certain and so admiring of his older brother that I realized for the first time that there was a special bond here between the brothers."

Bobby had volunteered to campaign in East Cambridge, a Neville stronghold. The man who would take over the seat in 1953, future Speaker of the House Thomas "Tip" O'Neill, and all the political pros in Cambridge were supporting Neville. Bobby took over Precincts 4 and 5, in Ward 1. "Bobby was only twenty and was too young to vote, but he went door-to-door, literally door-to-door in East Cambridge, and met every single person who lived there," Billy Sutton relates. "People just fell in love with him. He was so young, handsome, and sincere, so quiet and well spoken, that people really loved him."

"Unfortunately, people didn't fall in love with him enough to carry the precincts, but enough to seriously cut into Neville's plurality. Bobby showed he knew what he was doing," Powers says. "The week after the primary, Jack invited me to the family home at Hyannisport and asked me to bring all the figures from the election results. As Jack studied the results, Bobby was there. He quietly asked only one question, 'How did we do in Precincts Four and Five in Ward One?'" Jack looked up, smiled, and read him the results:

> Precinct 4—Neville 315   Kennedy 169
> Precinct 5—Neville 259   Kennedy 169

"Bobby just smiled and said, 'It proves I campaigned equally hard in both precincts. Next time I will campaign harder!' Jack laughed." The total vote in Cambridge was Neville 7,606 and Kennedy 6,472—not a bad first effort against the heavily favored hometown mayor. Kennedy won the primary, and since the district was so heavily Democratic, the general election campaign promised little or no opposition.

Kenny O'Donnell's views on Jack Kennedy and politics in 1946 reflected those of many returning veterans. Although they returned with a fistful of medals, they were frustrated by the public's reaction in the United States to the end of the war. The country Kenny and his comrades returned to was still suffering the effects of the war and eager to put it behind them. They did not share the returning veterans' fear of the future or their sense that the United States must become an active and ready world partner, or that the real foreign threat now lay with the Soviet Union.

It was a frustration that Kenny shared with Jack Kennedy, Bobby Kennedy, Bill Sutton, Dave Powers, Nick Rodis, and other returning veterans. It would be this underlying political frustration and unease that Jack Kennedy would capitalize on as he began to build a bridge from the Bellevue Hotel to the White House. He understood the mood of the country and the world war veterans more than Kenny realized when they first met that spring afternoon in 1946. It was that political instinct and that "magical link" with the voters that Jack would turn to his own advantage. It would change the destinies of both his younger brother and his friend Kenny O'Donnell.

With the primary victory assured, Bobby returned to his full-time life on the Harvard campus and his developing friendship with Ken O'Donnell.

4

"GOD'S PLAN . . . OF
ASSETS AND BLESSINGS"

*There is no greater need than to educate men and women to point
their careers toward public service as the finest and
most rewarding type of life.*

—BOBBY KENNEDY

"His death," wrote Jack Kennedy of his brother Joe, "seemed to cut into the natural order of things." In May 1948, the natural order of their lives would be interrupted yet again.

It was while Bobby was traveling in Europe after receiving his A.B. from Harvard in March of '48 that the Kennedy family received the second body blow from fate. Kathleen "Kick" Kennedy Hartington, the second daughter of Rose and Joe Kennedy, was killed in a plane crash in Europe. After the death of his brother Joe in the war just four years before, Bobby was again reminded that fortune did not guarantee anyone a future. He would always be hesitant thereafter about plans beyond his control. By now it had become a Kennedy family credo to retain a positive attitude and look past disaster. While some critics of the family have seen such determination as a negative characteristic, for Bobby and his siblings a fierce forward-mindedness became a way of life that could rescue them from depression and recrimination. Rose, her own bearing buoyed by religious faith, would remind her son that "a healthy attitude can change a burden into a blessing, a trial into a triumph."

Kathleen's death, and Joe's before it, were tastes of tragedy that helped make Bobby particularly understanding of those to whom fortune had been unkind. This characteristic would mark him throughout his life — leading those who knew Bobby to find it difficult to understand the often-mentioned charge that he was "ruthless." "I think that when he came upon people's deep problems later on," says his friend Dave Hackett, "it was a natural thing for him to have compassion and some understanding for them. I think what he never had any understanding or compassion for was arrogance, or wealth that was not used properly by the privileged; he had very little compassion for that!"

Kenny's new wife Helen Sullivan experienced Bobby's compassion very early in their friendship. Bobby intuitively understood that she was having a difficult time making the transition into married life. He took the time to provide her with the ability to laugh at herself and her troubles. Helen Sullivan was a pretty, slim, auburn-haired girl with stunning blue eyes. A natural athlete with a quick mind and disciplined body, she had met Kenny in the summer of 1947 while he was working at Morgan Construction in Worcester. They had been introduced by Kenny's younger sister, Justine. Kenny would regularly make the trip back home to Worcester on weekends. Often, he and pal Jimmy Kenary would catch a ride with Kenny's father, Cleo, who would make various stops along the way selling carpeting out of the backseat of his car since losing his job at Holy Cross after two losing seasons in a legendary career of victories. During those trips, Jimmy Kenary remembers being struck by the sadness of this older, elegantly dressed man, a legend in coaching, having to go door-to-door to sell carpeting to make ends meet. Jimmy also remembers how painful it was for Kenny to see his father in this state.

Kenny had dated various girls both in Worcester and back in Cambridge, but he didn't seem to be serious about anyone in particular. "I never got the impression," says Nick Rodis, "that there was anyone special. I mean, I always thought he enjoyed being with us more than anyone else."

The introduction took place at a drugstore in Worcester's Tatnick Square, where Kenny, Cleo Jr., and many others gathered. Justine and Helen attended Salters Secretarial School together. "Helen always had a million guys chasing her," Justine remembers. "She kept asking to meet my brother Kenny, who was such a hero because of the war and his playing at Harvard. I tried to put her off as long as possible. I liked her, but I just knew they would meet and fall in love." Justine's fears that this meeting would change the relationship between her and Helen from school friends to sisters-in-law were well founded. Kenny and Helen did fall in love, and during the summer of 1947, the relationship became even stronger. Jimmy Kenary remembers how at the close of the workday at their summer job with Morgan Construction he and Kenny would follow the railroad tracks from outside of Worcester to Tatnick Square and the drugstore where Helen would be waiting.

With his older brother Cleo still in Cambridge—in fact rooming that summer with Bobby Kennedy—Kenny was forced to wear his own clothes, not his brother's, which inevitably led to problems. Jimmy was always struck by Kenny's careless appearance, especially when he was meeting a beautiful girl like Helen, whom all the boys were chasing. Kenny let his white shirt hang and the tail come out of the back of his slacks. He still wore his military khakis, kept in place by a tired-looking belt, his broken pants zipper replaced by a safety pin. His personal self-confidence was such, Kenary remembers, that his clothing simply didn't matter. If it bothered Helen, she never mentioned that she took any particular notice. Jimmy knew Kenny liked Helen, but not once did Kenny ever give Kenary any indication that he felt something special for this woman. Kenny's decision to marry Helen caught more than just Kenary by surprise. By the end of that summer, the couple was married in Worcester in a simple ceremony.

Planning his return to Harvard that fall, Kenny kept his marriage a secret because of his rocky relationship with Coach Harlow. A player who married could lose his place on the team and would forfeit his lodging in the Varsity Club, which in postwar Cambridge, with housing at a premium, was not a prospect taken lightly. He returned to the Varsity Club room he had shared with pal Nick Rodis, who was startled to come back from class to find Kenny packing his things. Astonished and worried that he had done something to upset Kenny, Nick pleaded with him to know what he had done wrong. "Did I offend you?" he asked. "I haven't even seen you all summer! What's wrong? Why are you leaving? At least give me a chance to address the problem!"

Kenny finally looked up from his packing and said with mock seriousness in his voice, "Geez, Nick, you didn't do anything wrong, but
the problem is that when a guy gets married, the girl expects you to
move in and live with her! By the way, can I borrow thirty-five dollars
for the apartment we are renting on Bank Street?"

Stunned and a bit relieved, Nick gave Kenny the loan, but not before
demanding to know the whole story. Quickly, Nick learned that not
only had Kenny gotten married but they were expecting their first child
shortly. "Here was this guy that didn't have two nickels to rub together
and yet he had gotten married," Nick remembers. "I couldn't believe
it. That was Kenny. He hadn't said a word. He just went and did what
he thought was best. He wasn't worried."

Mr. and Mrs. Kenneth P. O'Donnell moved to the shabbily built
housing that Harvard provided for married students. Soon Helen had a
child, a boy named after his father. Kenny Sr. was not often home. He
did not easily adapt to the bonds of married life. In a foretaste of his
habits for years to come, he would spend his days on campus or at the
Varsity Club and his evenings with Bobby practicing and throwing footballs or talking politics at Cronin's. Later in life, politics more than
football would occupy them. Helen was ill prepared and perhaps ill
suited for a way of living where she was so much on her own. She
immediately had to deal with the realities of married life, including a
brand-new baby, and to do so without any help or support from her
parents. Instead she relied heavily on Alice and Cleo to help, often
spending every single weekend at the O'Donnell home in Worcester
while Kenny was away campaigning with Bobby and Jack.

Ethel Skakel, Bobby's new girlfriend, developed a friendship with
Helen through Bobby, which helped Helen make the adjustment to her
new married life in Cambridge. Ethel was sympathetic and understanding of Helen's situation and encouraged Bobby to reach out to her.
Over the next several years as Helen and Kenny struggled financially,
coping with one and soon after three children on a small income, Ethel
would often help without being asked. She would arrange for the young
couple to stay at her future brother-in-law Jack's apartment at 122 Bowdoin Street; years later, she would have them to stay at Jack and Jackie

Bouvier Kennedy's home at Hyannisport for a long overdue vacation. Helen was always forthright and direct in her relationship with Ethel. She never felt the need to cater to or fawn over Ethel and Bobby. "It was mostly that they were comfortable with each other," recalls one friend. Over the years, as their men encountered challenge and tragedy, they would come to rely on each other more and more.

In July 1948, when Helen O'Donnell wrote to Bobby in Berlin to sympathize with the loss of his sister, his response would suggest the growth of his faith and the persistence of the Kennedy optimism.

12 July

Dear Helen,

It was so very thoughtful of you & kind of you to write me that letter. It was appreciated more than I can ever tell you. I think as you said it is most difficult at times to understand what gods plan is in the world. I should think it would be particularly difficult for my Mother & Father & people like them. I believe though that if one can't find the answers in god one certainly can stop feeling sorry for oneself by considering the many assets & blessings that one has received.

Bobby's rigorous optimism and absence of self-pity indicated how he, the rest of the Kennedys, and Kenny O'Donnell, as well, would handle misfortune in the future. The inner toughness instilled in them by their fathers—together with the gentleness of spirit that they could share only with their close friends—would always get them through the difficult times by not allowing them to sink into self-pity or despair.

Bobby had heard about the arrival of Helen and Kenny's first son, Kenneth P. O'Donnell, Jr., in May 1948. Possessed of his father's black, "Indian" eyes and athletic build, the little boy would soon be nicknamed "the monster" by the Harvard gang for both his size and rather rambunctious behavior.

. . . Was very excited to hear about the arrival of the heir. All I can
say is that the best thing to do now is to literally feed him a football
so he can get off in the right direction. What a life he will have
ahead of him!

Even as Bobby celebrated the birth of Kenny and Helen's firstborn, he
could not resist taking a jab at one of his former teammates:

Nick [Rodis] certainly sounds as if he's gone downhill since I left
him. He was such a good little boy & I can't help thinking it was
Kenny who corrupted him as he did me also. In a few private little
chats I used to have with brother Cleo he also put the blame on
Kenny for being the way he was. I think this is a little overdoing it
but one must admit there are some grounds for suspicion.

Love
Bobby

Hope you all have a good summer.

Robert Kennedy had returned from his European tour by August 1948
and began law school at the University of Virginia on September 14 of
that year. He became president of the Student Legal Forum and rapidly
revived what had been a moribund student organization. As it had been
at Harvard, schoolwork remained difficult for him, but he attacked it
the way he had at Milton and Harvard, and the way he had played
football under Coach Harlow—with tenacity and a lot of very hard work.

Gerald Tremblay was also a law student at UVA and remembers Robert Kennedy's arrival vividly. "He showed up in a rather old convertible,
a Chrysler that his father had given to him. Bobby was dressed in an
old pair of khakis, and he really looked very loose. He looked like a
young guy in his first year of college, more than a young guy coming
down to law school." Tremblay and Kennedy enrolled in the same
section at school and studied together, developing an enduring friendship that would eventually include Tremblay in Kenny and Helen
O'Donnell's lives.

Bobby and his friend George Terrien, with whom he had traveled to

Europe, rented a tiny tenant house for a while on Route 250 West in Charlottesville. The tiny house was about thirty or forty feet from a railroad track; every time a train went by, the entire structure shook. The place had a small living room, a tiny kitchen, and no central heat. George and Bobby survived the cold winter by the use of space heaters and a lot of sweaters. "Bobby always had a dog," Tremblay recalls. "At that time he had a great big young German police dog that often thought nothing of going for your leg. Bobby didn't seem to notice.

"Bobby was different than the rest of us and didn't fit in with the rest of his schoolmates," Tremblay continues. "He was courting Ethel Skakel and would often fly out on weekends to Florida, Connecticut, or Massachusetts to meet up with Ethel, Kenny, and Helen, whom I had not yet met." Because of this schedule, Bobby kept largely to himself. When at school he focused on classes, sports, and the Student Legal Forum. "Often he played golf. He would play five or six holes at a time and then shove off," according to Tremblay. "He didn't have the patience for the whole game, but I remember he would always have at least one dog with him, sometimes two or three, and he would bring them on the golf course, which drove everyone crazy. His equipment was terrible. You would figure that with all his money, Bob Kennedy would be the kind of kid who had perfect equipment. He enjoyed the game, but I think he played to be friendly with me because I didn't play tennis. He wasn't arrogant; he just sort of marched to his own drummer and seemed unaware that bringing your dogs on the golf course and cutting in front of people because they were too slow was just not the way to operate. He had a lot of advantages by being able to do anything he wanted, and he didn't let anything deter him."

Tremblay remembers his study habits with some awe. "He was kind of a crash artist at studying. He would go along and take good notes, and he didn't miss too many classes, except sometimes when he was going away for the weekend he probably would cut his Friday and Monday classes and not come back until Tuesday. In spite of that, Bobby did just about as well as the average person in the class. He received average grades. There were some subjects that just bored him to death. For instance," Tremblay recalls, "there was the legal bibliography class that was taught by Miss Frances Farmer. She and Bobby became fast friends later, but this was his first year and she gave him a zero." Tremblay got the distinct impression that Bobby not only found the course boring but didn't feel that he would ever be in a position to do research work. Tremblay puts part of that blame for those feelings on the way Bobby was raised. "I think it's the way he was brought up. He saw how his father operated, and some of it had to rub off on him. He saw how his brothers operated, and I guess he figured if he ever practiced law that he wasn't going to be spending much time looking up law precedents in some law library, that somebody would be doing this for him, so it didn't interest him.

"I felt that throughout law school he sort of focused in on things that he thought were going to be useful to him in the future," Tremblay continues. "The things that he felt were not going to be useful he didn't give much attention to." Bobby seemed very early on to have a real sense of how to use information and his own time effectively. As his career continued, it would be those administrative and management skills honed to efficiency that would be demonstrated again and again.

"He was very impatient and he didn't like small talk, although in later years he mellowed a great deal," Tremblay says of his classmate. If it wasn't politics, public affairs, or football, Bobby could be particularly short. "He was so intense that it created a barrier between him and even his closest friends." Tremblay would grow to see what Bobby's other friends, like Sam Adams, had realized: It took time to get to know Bobby Kennedy and be admitted to his confidence.

For Kenny and Bobby there was no barrier; their bond had solidified over practices at Dillon Field House. Although separated by geography, Bobby remained connected through phone calls and letters not just with Kenny but with Nick Rodis and Wally Flynn. Most of his letters to Kenny, addressed to "Jimmy," "Benny," or "P.K.," which were nicknames whose particular meaning remained secret between the two of them, recounted the progress of the Harvard football team as he followed the games from Virginia. Bobby continued to be passionate about football, often writing for tickets to various games. The letters were also an excuse to give the occasional jab to Kenny's ego.

Dear Jimmy,

Thanks a bunch for the tickets. You're a peach. Looked for you all after the game for I thought we maybe could have a few beers together, but the situation was reminiscent of Howie Horton's wedding, for I just kept chasing myself around the block getting nowhere! Believe if you fellows had the downhill blocking you had against Columbia the results might have been different & also when the refs missed the call down in the 3rd period when both sides were penalized, it might have made the difference. Also if you had me! [Here Bobby drew a caricature of himself.]

I'm counting that there's going to be a war so it will be up to the Dartmouth game. If you can it would be great if you have a few extra tickets to the Dartmouth game . . . in the next section where they put all the former athletes. I don't mind & a student of the game such as I am it takes to see what's going on from every possible angle.

. . . Please don't think that this isn't being motivated by sheer friendship & that I just write when I want tickets, not me! Your old pal, remember . . .

Muscles

The letters exhibit the Kennedy wit that would become familiar to the public more than a decade later.

As they all got married—Nick to Eve, Kenny to Helen, and eventually Bobby to Ethel—the group simply expanded to include the wives. Saturday football would be a constant in their lives, long after they had all left school and were all ensconced at the White House.

Dear P.K.,

Here is your favorite correspondent once again letting you know how his large, well formed muscular body is doing while at the same time asking for 4 tickets to the Army game. I realize what an immense request this is but you remember me your old buddy, your pal, your friend, buddy, all that sort of thing, the kid that knocked down that big tackle in the BU game & made it easy for you to go 8 yds, old RK. Well anyway we had the same classes together, & you used to copy from me. Well we went to the same school. Anyway if you can get the tickets & it doesn't matter where & it really doesn't matter, it would be appreciated. If you can get them would you send them to Ethel's at Lake Avenue Greenwich Conn. with the two you were going to get for me.

Your friend Harvey if you can believe it was carried out of our [UVA] stadium on the shoulders of a cheering, hysterical mob. He looked like he hated it. He was Captain & played well, though they didn't run near his side more than 4 times the whole day. They had a fairly good time, but I thought lousy backs though wonderful passes, but then all passes look good against Va.

Ethel was wondering if Helen & Eve were coming down to the game on Saturday if you & Nick & the gang would come to Greenwich over Saturday night that is if you have to be back in Cambridge. If you would like to you can let me know after the game anyway.

give my love to Helen & the monster & good luck to you all Saturday.

[Here Bobby inserted another caricature of himself.]

Love Bobby

p.s. Nice game last Sat.

During his term as president of the Student Legal Forum Bobby would become involved in a dispute reminiscent of the Harvard/University of Virginia controversy of 1947, when Virginia tried to force Harvard not to bring the black player Chester Pierce to play football at their stadium. Bobby, back in Cambridge with a broken leg at that time, was as outraged as the rest of the team by the university's ultimately unsuccessful attempt to keep its hometown games segregated.

Barrett Prettyman was a first-year law student at the university when Bobby was a president of the forum. "Bobby was not only interested in running the Legal Forum," he remembers, "but in his usual fashion he was interested in improving the organization and choosing who would run it the next year. He somehow got it into his head that I would be a good person to run it, because I had Washington, D.C., ties, as he did, and he realized that meant that we could bring new and different speakers to challenge the students. Because of his contacts through the Kennedy name the Legal Forum presented speakers like Supreme Court Justice William O. Douglas, columnist Arthur Krock, Senator Joe Mc-Carthy, Congressman John F. Kennedy, and Dr. Ralph Bunche, the internationally known Nobel Peace Prize winner and Harvard professor of government. Bobby even had his father come to speak to the students.

"Bunche refused to speak unless the audience was desegregated, be-cause as a black man he refused to ever address segregated audiences," Prettyman recalls. "The university wasn't willing to make an exception. Bobby was determined to set things right."

Gerald Tremblay also saw Bobby's convictions in action. "He believed that just because someone was black he shouldn't be a second-rate cit-izen. Certainly, this segregation bit didn't go over with him! He'd always had a feeling for disadvantaged people—people who were deprived of their rights, or people who were not able to achieve what they could possibly achieve because they were Negro or they were Polish or they were labor union or out of labor union . . . I think he felt he was brought up with so many privileges, and he'd had such an easy life himself, that he had to really do something for the people.

"Bobby was really furious about the university's hesitation on the Bunche lecture. I think he simply couldn't believe that they were un-willing to provide him with a desegregated audience," says Tremblay. On March 7, 1951, Bobby wrote a letter in his capacity as president of the Legal Forum demanding that the university rescind their segregation policies and allow the audience to be integrated for this event. The letter read in part:

At the outset permit us to say that at no time did we consider the invitation one calculated to embarrass the University of Virginia. Quite the contrary it is our belief that this is calculated to rebound to the great credit of the University. It is hardly necessary to recall that through his activities with the United Nations Dr. Bunche is internationally known and respected, that he is a Nobel peace prize winner and that he has accepted a position as Professor of Government at Harvard University. The invitation to him was one of a series of invitations and acceptances which have included a former Ambassador to the Court of St. James and a Supreme Court Justice.

The letter goes on for some four typed pages to outline the arguments for allowing Dr. Bunche to speak to an integrated audience. Kennedy points out to university president Colgate W. Darden:

> ... There [does not seem to be] any problem calculated to embarrass the University, unless the University should decide that it is necessary to create the issue itself by invoking an education segregation policy which, as we shall attempt to point out later, is, in this instance, legally indefensible, morally wrong and fraught with consequences calculated to do great harm to the University. There is no question that Dr. Bunche will be compelled to cancel his engagement if an educational segregation policy is invoked.

The letter is an interesting combination of legal argument and underlying moral statement of the kind that would come to characterize Robert Kennedy's work on Capitol Hill and later as attorney general.

Bobby won a victory. The University of Virginia agreed to suspend its segregation policy, but only for the lecture of Dr. Bunche. After the lecture the university returned to its previous position, reinstating the segregation policy. It was a small win, an accomplishment that would be one of the many small stands made on behalf of racial equality during the first half of the 1950s. The Bunche incident also indicates how Robert Kennedy was slowly beginning to expand his view of the world. He may not have completely understood all the issues of racial justice at the time — few white Americans did — but he was carried through by his evident sense of moral outrage at the way Dr. Bunche had been treated by the university. To Robert Kennedy, the issue was one of simple justice and common sense. Again and again in his lifetime, Robert Kennedy would be caught between his belief in the senselessness of racial bigotry and his awareness of how rooted it was in American society.

*   *   *

In 1951, as he was finishing law school, Bobby became one of the last of his close friends to marry. His relationship with Ethel Skakel had grown increasingly serious, so that by 1949 even the gang from Harvard had begun to realize that Bobby was serious about this woman. "Cleo and I were with Bobby one day, driving Ethel back to school after one weekend football game where he had come up from UVA," Wally Flynn remembers. "We were in the front seat and they were in the back of the car, a convertible. We were talking about the game and chatting away and all of a sudden it got very quiet. I turned around to see why Bobby hadn't answered me, and then I saw the two of them kissing. You know, Bobby was a real Boy Scout, so I knew this had to be really serious. I told Clee, don't turn around—just keep your eyes on the road. We did, but you know we kind of gave each other a side look. We knew then that Bobby was really in love."

Ethel Skakel and Robert Kennedy were married on June 17, 1950. The wedding was held in the Greenwich, Connecticut, Skakel family home. Among the ushers were Kenny and Cleo O'Donnell, Nick Rodis, Jimmy Noonan, and many other members of the "Kennedy debating society" from the Varsity Club. In an interview with George Plimpton, Kenny O'Donnell remembered his best friend's wedding with relish. "Most of us football players were ushers at the wedding. They were so big they couldn't get down the aisle side by side. They wouldn't buy their morning suits, because they cost too much." He and Helen were living on seventy-five dollars a month. He told Bobby, "To hell with it, we were going back to Boston, we don't want to go to the wedding. Bobby ended up paying for them. The in-laws, the Skakel family, were horrified by his friends—not so much the father, who loved the fellows and joined right in with the fun, but the mother. She couldn't understand how Bobby had got these characters around him who all weighed 250 pounds, were Greeks and Italians, and were such cutups.

"We had a party the evening before the wedding at the Harvard Club in New York," Kenny recalled. "John Kennedy was there and he agreed that he had never seen such an outrageous, irreverent group of characters in his life." "It got really rough," agrees Nick Rodis. "Everyone got very, very drunk and pretty obnoxious. I didn't drink, even then, but in looking back it's kind of embarrassing. Of course Kenny was the instigator of a lot of the trouble, as he usually was both in college and afterwards." The Harvard Club was not amused and promptly sent the Kennedy family a bill for the damage the group had caused. Bobby took it all in stride, shrugging off his friends' shenanigans and probably quietly enjoying the discomfort it provided to more proper elements.

After the wedding the couple settled in Charlottesville. Bobby, who had grown up alone much of the time because of the time he spent away from home at school, found married life sustaining. Ethel was more forthrightly engaged with people than her husband, balancing his inner shyness and bringing him out more. He also conveyed to her a sense of calm that she had not known before. Bobby received from her the kind of love and acceptance he needed, which would revitalize him in times of trouble and difficulty. He trusted her judgment, appreciated her wit, enjoyed her as a mother, and loved her fiercely. "It was a perfect match," says a college friend of Ethel's. "I knew that Ethel was it," Nick Rodis says now. "They were just perfect together and perfectly happy. We teased him a lot, but we were all very happy for them. He made the best choice."

As he settled into married life in Virginia, Bobby urged his Cambridge friends to visit him whenever possible. His and Ethel's open-door policy became famous among their family and friends. Wally Flynn remembers one visit in particular. "Bobby was really swamped with schoolwork. He was trying to be entertaining, but I think he had a paper due the next day, so he was in one room studying. Ethel was not feeling well; she was pregnant with their first child and really having a tough time. I told Bobby not to worry—I would just take care of myself. Thinking I would make a nice dinner for them and surprise them, I went into the kitchen. It was an unbelievable mess. There were dishes stacked in the sink, no food in the fridge, and just frozen steaks in the freezer. So I defrosted the steaks, went shopping, cleaned the kitchen, and made a nice sit-down dinner with wine and everything. Bobby and Ethel came in and they were just stunned. They looked at me like I was from outer space. Finally Bobby said, 'Geez, Wally, where did you learn to do all this kind of stuff?' He was really surprised. 'My mother!' I said. 'God, Bobby, you two really need to hire help.' I think they did shortly after that."

If the Ralph Bunche incident forecast an issue Bobby would face a decade later, Senator McCarthy's visit to the university would portend more about the fate of America's most rambunctious anti-Communist in the next several years. As Barrett Prettyman remembers the events, "Joe McCarthy knew Bobby and his family pretty well and so he agreed to come down and speak. This was right during the beginning of the 'Red scare' period and shortly after he had announced that he had a list of two hundred something Communists in the State Department. He came down and gave his talk to an unusually large crowd and then afterward, as was tradition, Bobby and Ethel hosted a coffee at their house near the university. It was really a revealing event and I will never forget it."

After the lecture, a group of students, their wives, and some professors gathered for drinks and sandwiches in Bobby's small but pleasant living room. McCarthy arrived, helped himself to a drink, and then sat down on the couch, surrounded mostly by the law students' wives. Most of the men sat on the floor. "The crowd was amiable at first," Prettyman says, "and then slowly, as McCarthy continued to drink, he got more outrageous and the students began to really challenge him. I remember a couple of times he would reach down and pat the knee of the woman sitting next to him. She was quite embarrassed by it. McCarthy responded less and less coherently. He began to make one outrageous charge after another. I don't want to overdramatize this," Prettyman continues, "but it was almost like a preview of what was in store for him in the next couple of years" as he would grow less and less credible in his accusations against supposed Communist sympathizers.

Bobby wandered in and out. With his nervous energy he seemed unable to sit long and listen to McCarthy, but Prettyman noticed that on several occasions he stood in the doorway listening to McCarthy's ramblings with real intent. "I got the impression that he viewed

Alice Guerin O'Donnell,
Kenny's mother.
*Courtesy of
O'Donnell family.*

Cleo O'Donnell, Kenny's father.
Courtesy of O'Donnell family.

Kenny's high school class. Kenny is in the top row, at right. *Courtesy of John F. Kennedy Library and Museum.*

From Worcester Telegram; *courtesy of O'Donnell family.*

THE O'DONNELLS GATHER ROUND THE BOARD—A tasty scene before the Thanksgiving kick-off in Worcester as Cleo A. O'Donnell and his family prepare to celebrate. Cleo, Jr., Harvard football captain-elect, has first chance at a drumstick. The O'Donnells, (left to right) Kenneth P., 18 years; Justine A., 16 years; Cleo, Sr., Cleo, Jr., Mrs. O'Donnell, Phyllis M. 20 years; and, Warren F., 12 years.

TOP LEFT: Helen Sullivan's high school graduation photo, 1947. *Courtesy of O'Donnell family.*

TOP RIGHT: Kenny's high school graduation photo, 1942. *Courtesy of O'Donnell family.*

Kenny *(top row, third from left)* and his crew after flying the last of his thirty missions over Germany. He was awarded the Distinguished Flying Cross. *Courtesy of O'Donnell family.*

Kenny with Arthur Valpey at Harvard. *Courtesy of Harvard University.*

BOTTOM LEFT: Bobby Kennedy's Harvard football picture. *Courtesy of Samuel Adams.*

BOTTOM RIGHT: Kenny on the playing fields of Harvard. George Sullivan, the eleven-year-old "team mascot," took this photo. *Courtesy of O'Donnell family.*

In front of the Harvard Faculty Club, 1947. Kenny is second from left in the middle row. *Courtesy of John F. Kennedy Library and Museum.*

On the steps of the Varsity Club, 1947. *Left to right:* John Fiorentino, Jim Noonan, Walt McCurdy, and Bobby Kennedy. *Courtesy of John F. Kennedy Library and Museum.*

1947 HARVARD VARSITY FOOTBALL SQUAD

Left to right, front row: Feinberg, Warren, Moffie, Freedman, Lazzaro, J. Noonan. Second row: Kennedy, Drennan, Pierce, Kenary, Gannon, Captain Moravec, Rodis, Houston, Coulson, D. Stone, O'Donnell. Third row: End Coach Jacunski, Line Coach Kopp, Backfield Coach Margarita, Foster, Markham, W. Flynn, Hill, Bradlee, Roche, Head Coach Harlow, Trainer Cox, Manager Judkins. Fourth row: Sullivan, Hickey, Drvaric, Harrison, Guidera, Shafer, Goodrich, Miklos, Bahn, Stensrud, L. Flynn, O'Connell, Nolan. Back row: Fiorentino, Peabody, Howe, Gorczynski, Middendorf, Mazzone, Reed, Leavitt, Davis, A. Stone, Glynn.

A young Bobby Kennedy and future bride Ethel Skakel, circa 1949. *Courtesy of John F. Kennedy Library and Museum.*

Ethel and Bobby with their bridesmaids, June 17, 1950. Eunice Shriver is in the lower left corner; Pat Lawford is next to her. *Courtesy of John F. Kennedy Library and Museum.*

Ethel and Bobby with their wedding ushers, June 17, 1950. Cleo O'Donnell, Kenny O'Donnell, and Nick Rudis are third, fourth, and fifth from right. Jack and Ted Kennedy flank the bride and groom. *Courtesy of John F. Kennedy Library and Museum.*

McCarthy as a friend of his family and sort of felt sorry for him as the evening continued.

"In the end, as McCarthy got more and more drunk and made less and less sense, all the students, their wives, and the professors wandered off and left him there alone sitting on the couch. He was very, very drunk by the end of it, just sitting there alone on the couch and still talking like he had an audience. At the time I thought it was a very dramatic moment, without realizing that this was exactly how Joe Mc-Carthy would end up—alone and drunk, making charges about invisible evils to an invisible audience."

While Bobby progressed through law school and got married, Kenny graduated from Harvard in 1949 and enrolled in Boston College Law School. He had never enjoyed classwork and relished it even less now. For Kenny, law school lacked the camaraderie he had had at Harvard. As he attended law classes, he worked in a paper plant to earn money to support his family. Even with his work and veteran's stipend, money was tight. Helen's parents had little income because of the toll alcoholism had taken on Helen's father. It rendered him unable to work even though he still had a child at home to support. What little income they did have came from her mother's cleaning rich people's homes. Kenny knew well that his father did not have extra money and would never have asked. Fortunately, it was not long before Bobby and the tug of his brother's political ambitions would rescue Kenny from the paper company and the drudgery of school. But now, just as he had when he had worn through the soles of his shoes years before, Kenny felt comfortable turning to Bobby for help. Bobby complied, with a combination of humor and a little solid advice.

Dear Kenny,

Please don't spend all of this money for drinks for that would be very disgusting. Why don't you start a bank account. That's what I do & you'd be surprised how much easier it makes everything. You just write your name on a check & they give you money—

If you change your mind about the game at Miami, you & Helen are both welcome for Christmas. I should think you would go down for it would undoubtedly be bully fun & besides let's face it after this year you've shot your bolt unless you put on five pounds & play pro ball with the Greek.

Must hustle & hit the books. If the Kennedy's are going to be honored by your & Mother's [Helen's] presence please let Ethel & I know. Say hello to all my friends for me!

Not just football games but weddings also helped cement the Harvard gang after graduation. Often the men all served as ushers at one an-other's weddings. After the wedding reception for Jimmy Noonan, Kenny, Bobby, Nick, Jimmy, their wives, and various others retired to the posh Ritz-Carlton Hotel bar, across from the public garden in Boston, where Bobby and Ethel had a room. They were all seated around one of the small tables in the dark, immaculately tailored bar, arguing football and politics. Next to them was a group of young Boston blue bloods, who were growing increasingly irritated at the noise and the political direction of the conversation of the Harvard gang. Finally, one fellow came over to the group of five or so to join in the debate. The young Brahmin, whom Kenny continued to call Coolidge Wofford Wadsworth, the fifth, despite the young man's protest that that was cer-tainly not his name, got into a hot discussion of politics. "Well, the discussion got hotter and hotter," recalls Jimmy Kenary, "to the point where this guy said something to Kenny, Kenny said something nasty back, which made Bobby laugh, and then suddenly Kenny leaned for-ward, black eyes flashing, almost nose-to-nose with the guy, and said, 'You are full of shit. You know that? And you and your kind are finished!' Horrified, the young fellow pulled back, almost falling into the cushion of the chair, and said with a raised voice that sounded almost female to the gathered vets, 'I am not! And you, sir, are uncouth, mean and have no class.' 'Really?' Kenny asked, and like lightning, he knocked the poor fellow out cold, causing him to fall over backwards, chair and all!"

Kenny calmly sat down and ordered another beer. Bobby leaped from his seat, looked at Kenny for a moment, tried to stifle a grin, and instead shook his head and then bolted for the door, leaving Kenny and the rest to deal with a very annoyed hotel manager. "About ten minutes later they shut us off and we had to get the heck out of there before the fellow woke up. But Bobby was gone! There were times, I guess, that Bobby decided discretion was the better part of valor." "Strangely enough," remarked another one of their pals, "it was that side of Kenny that I think Bobby just loved. Clearly, Bobby was keenly aware of who he was and knew he had to exhibit a sense of responsibility for such shenanigans. But he didn't mind being part of the fun." As for Kenny, he merely finished his beer, stepped over the supine fellow as his friends urged him to hurry up and leave before the guy woke up and called the cops. As they all headed out the door, Kenny insisted they track down Bobby in his room to let him know what he had missed.

In the summer of 1951 Robert Kennedy got a law degree, a new job, and a new baby, the first Kennedy grandchild. Kathleen Hartington Kennedy, named after his late sister, was born on July 4, 1951. Following Kathleen's birth, still unsure of his next career step, Bobby was sent by the *Boston Post* to cover the Japanese Peace Treaty Conference in San Francisco, where fifty nations were gathering to conclude a peace treaty with Japan, formally ending the war that had concluded nearly six years before. Returning from the trip, Bobby took a job at the Internal Security Division of the Justice Department. Ethel found a house for the young couple at 3214 S Street in Georgetown. Bobby soon moved to the department's Criminal Division, where his first major case involved charges of corruption against two former members of the Truman administration.

Meanwhile, in Massachusetts, Congressman Jack Kennedy was planning an upstart Senate campaign against the well-established incumbent, Henry Cabot Lodge. Although Bobby was not yet directly involved in the campaign, he sought out Kenny O'Donnell to join in the effort. For Kenny, struggling with law school, work, and family, it was the kind of call he had been waiting for. He did not hesitate; he took time off from his law program and never returned to it. Rose Kennedy would comment that for Bobby, calling in his longtime friend made sense. "Bobby brought in a number of his friends, notably the talented, tough-minded, loyal and tireless Kenneth O'Donnell, who, with Larry O'Brien, spent the next decade working in close rapport with Jack and Bobby in politics and government," she would write in her memoirs. Still, as Rose pointed out, "Bobby and Ethel had barely settled in Washington, and he had no intention of taking part in the campaign. Nevertheless, when problems developed and he was needed, and was asked . . . he put aside his personal concerns and willingly came in as campaign manager."

5

THE 1952 SENATE
CAMPAIGN

Unless you come, I don't think it's going to get done.

— KENNY O'DONNELL TO BOBBY KENNEDY

"If Bobby and Kenny were your friend, they were your friend forever," declares Nick Rodis, "and whatever they got involved in, we all got involved in. Whatever one of them was doing they would both do, because they were friends and supported each other no matter how often they argued or disagreed. It began with Harvard, then the fifty-two campaign, and beyond. One time Kenny said to me, 'You know, Nick, this guy Bobby Kennedy really feels for the underdog. He isn't saying what people want to hear. From the time we met at Dillon Field House, this guy was real, no bullshit. He understands, he cares, he'll fight for you no matter the cost, he feels it coming right from within his gut. He is the definition of a friend.' To them helping people was a way of life; it was like breathing with them. Kenny and Bobby did so many things for so many people," Nick recalls. "They didn't do them because they were looking for favors or had plans for the White House or whatever. They did them because these guys felt that they were gifted and they were in a position to help people. Their teamwork from Harvard, they took it right into the White House. They decided, I am convinced, when they became friends on the football fields at Harvard that this was going to be their lifestyle: helping people. And in the end that is what they did."

*　　　*　　　*

In 1951, those people who knew that Jack was headed to the White House were scarce indeed. Very few political observers had originally thought much of Jack when he ran for Congress in 1946. They wrote off his victory to his father's money, and thinking him very young and not too serious, they paid little attention to him during his first two terms in the House. Jack Kennedy did spend much of his first term getting his sea legs under him. As he became more and more comfortable with political life, he began to slip away from his father's sphere of influence and make notable contributions to public policy that were genuinely his own. More than most national legislators, including many of his generation, Jack was quick to realize that the returning tide of veterans and their families represented a change in the political landscape. He felt that he could best represent those new voters and communicate their ambitions and frustrations. The change, Jack sensed, was occurring under the surface of political discourse and, in Massachusetts, was not immediately noticeable to the typical, Boston Irish politicians who had supported his grandfathers, Honey Fitz and P. J. Kennedy, and who were often closely allied with his father. For Jack, the question was when and how he could seek to lead this newly redefined citizenry.

Early in his House career, Jack made two political stands that made him a symbol of promise for people like Kenny O'Donnell, who would later describe him as "a symbol of hope for the returned veterans, who were home from the service feeling left out of the establishment and ignored by the older politicians who were trying to keep things the way they were before the war had started." Jack's first act of independence from the Democratic political establishment was his refusal to sign a petition asking for a presidential pardon for rightfully convicted Boston mayor James M. Curley, who was then doing time at the federal penitentiary at Danbury, Connecticut. Jack's decision was especially bold because it was Curley's decision to step aside, in a deal made with Jack's father, Joseph Kennedy, which had opened up the congressional seat Jack now held. By taking this stand, he not only violated one of the axioms of the status quo politicians that "to get along, one had to go along"; he also went against his father's wishes in a very public manner.

His second act of independence was his attack on the American Legion for its opposition to low-cost public housing. With so many veterans living doubled up with their parents and moving into substandard housing, basements, and garages, Kennedy was incensed that the leadership of the American Legion would take such a stand. Congressman Kennedy declared from the House floor that "the leadership of the American Legion has not had a constructive thought for the benefit of this country since 1918!" The harshness of the attack sent his fellow representatives ducking for cover, but it was applauded by Kenny O'Donnell, Nick Rodis, and many other veterans still struggling to get on their feet.

By 1951 Jack wanted out of the House. He found the pace frustrating and slow, and he disliked being one of 435 members, and one whose low seniority made it difficult to have a dramatic impact on public affairs. Although his seat was safe, Jack began running for higher office in earnest in 1948, hoping and waiting for the right opportunity. The question was simply one of timing. It was, in the words of historian James MacGregor Burns, "surely a remarkable thing—a thirty-two-year-old congressman, still hardly more than a freshman, launching an intensive statewide campaign at a time when he did not know the office he was seeking, the year he would seek it, or the man he would run against!"

"I first heard about Jack running from Bobby," Kenny O'Donnell recounted years later for George Plimpton. "He had graduated from Virginia Law School and gone to work at the Justice Department for a fellow named Jim McInery, who is now dead. Bobby was up in New York working on investigations—it was his first real assignment. He called me. He knew I really liked politics. He told me his brother John was going to run for governor or senator—he didn't know which, since it depended on what the then governor did. He asked me if I would go to work for his brother. That was December 1951." Kenny was intrigued. As Sam Adams remembered it, Kenny was just waiting for the right opportunity to enter the political fray.

Henry Cabot Lodge, Jr., whose Senate seat was not up until 1952, was the son of the gentlemanly Boston blue blood who had single-handedly defeated President Woodrow Wilson's League of Nations' proposal in the Senate in 1919. Lodge was a formidable political figure and toppling him was going to be tough. Yet 1952 was a particularly vulnerable year for him. Lodge had spent a great deal of his time focusing on General Dwight D. Eisenhower's incipient campaign for the presidency. In Kenny's judgment, he "had pretty much ignored his home state." Kennedy was poised to take advantage of his vulnerability when word reached him through the grapevine that then Governor Paul Dever was considering running against Lodge. Kennedy was then forced to wait until Dever, a Democrat, made his decision. Even if Jack survived a primary fight against Dever, it would weaken him considerably in a general election fight with Lodge.

When Dever finally decided to run for another term as governor, Kennedy made the decision to go against Lodge. Soon Kenny, Dave Powers, and many other World War II veterans had signed on to the campaign. Kennedy appealed to them because he was a new generation of politician. For Kenny and the other veterans freshly returned from the war, still in their twenties, but already feeling the weights and worries of old men, the time had come for one of their own to take command. Having survived the war a hero, John F. Kennedy now represented the potential of the ethnically diverse group of young men that the war had brought together at Harvard in 1946. For them, Jack Kennedy's election to a Senate seat, especially against a WASP establishment figure like Henry Cabot Lodge, would announce the ascendancy of a fresh brigade of leaders who would soon take command from an older generation responsible for the depression, the war, and a nation averse to challenges and eager to turn in on itself.

However, for Joseph Kennedy, Sr., and the Boston Irish politicians ensconced in their local power, Jack Kennedy's candidacy was something else altogether—a natural next step for an Irish Catholic family of ambition. Massachusetts pols expected that supporting Jack would yield them as much patronage as they had received in the era of Honey Fitz or Curley. As the Senate campaign started to come together, they were most concerned about what Joe Kennedy thought and wanted, paying far less attention to the needs of the candidate or the upstarts around him. Kane Simoneon, a local product of the political machine, remembers: "When I met Jack Kennedy, I thought he was a charming, handsome, and really nice fellow. But we weren't concerned about how nice he was or if he was handsome. We wanted to know if he could win, because in politics in Boston it wasn't whether you like a guy or didn't like him. It was whether or not he could win. We thought with the support of the father, the kid could win. It was strictly a political decision, like a football game. We weren't concerned about the issues or new generations or anything. After all, you could have the nicest fellow in the world running, but if he can't win, he can't take care of you, your family, or your friends. So what good is he?"

Rose Kennedy understood immediately that this race was going to bring a showdown between generations. "My father, with his love and pride for Jack and thinking of him as torchbearer of the Fitzgerald name and fame and achievements, would have thought of Jack as an incarnation of himself and would have tried to mold him to his own pattern," she wrote. "And, frankly that would have been a disaster. They loved each other dearly, but seldom were two people less alike."

The inevitable clash of cultures and generations began to occur almost immediately after Kenny came on board in December 1951. With his quick mind and natural sense of organization, he began quickly to pull together the threads of the campaign, which meant reaching out to new people. "The campaign began as an absolute catastrophic disaster," Kenny remembered in conversations with Sander Vanocur. "His father had come up and associated himself with the elder statesmen who knew nothing about politics of that day and age. He had not been in Massachusetts for twenty years, but he had such a strong personality that nobody could—nobody dared—fight back. I was too young and I didn't know anything about politics." The only time the campaign received any direction was when John Kennedy came up from Washington and overruled his father. As much as Joe enjoyed Kenny and knew that Bobby valued him, in the ambassador's mind he knew nothing of politics and had no experience, and therefore his advice was not to be taken seriously. Through the winter the campaign lurched along, but it was clearly headed into a stall, with Kenny and the father locked in a battle over who was in charge and what the message of John Kennedy's candidacy should be. There seemed to be little doubt that the campaign would inevitably fail. As strong and as self-confident as Kenny might have been, this was his first campaign; he had come in strictly as a friend of Bobby's; and he did not have the credentials or the will to challenge Joe Kennedy over the direction of his son's campaign.

It was clear to Kenny that, aside from Jack Kennedy himself, there was only one other person who could manage both the patriarch and the campaign — Bobby Kennedy. It became evident when Kenny had his first major run-in with John Kennedy directly. "The congressman and I had a big fight one day, and I told him that the campaign could only be handled by somebody who could talk up to his father; nobody had the courage to, and I certainly didn't have the qualifications, and it just wasn't going to work unless Bobby came up. If Bobby hadn't come up to take over that campaign and if he hadn't been Jack Kennedy's right-hand man from that point on, without question, Jack Kennedy would have lost." Kenny saw that Bobby was the logical choice. Unlike Kenny, he had the political experience, having worked in the 1946 campaign, and Kenny concluded that, based on that experience, Bobby had friends in Massachusetts, knew the state, was familiar with his brother's organization, and most of all, was the only one who could stand up to his father.

At first, Bobby tried to avoid the summons, but Kenny persisted with Bobby directly and with the candidate. "I called Bobby and got him in New York, and he was very angry," Kenny would remember. "He was right in the middle of an investigations case; he loved what he was doing. He said to me, 'I don't know anything about Massachusetts politics; I don't know any of the players, and I'll screw it up and . . . I just don't want to come.' So I said, 'Unless you come, I don't think it's going to get done.' "

The friends hung up the phone, both angry and hurt. Kenny didn't know what to expect and Bobby needed time to think. About a week later, Bobby called Kenny on the phone. "I'm coming up," he told him. "I've thought it over, and I suppose I'll have to do it."

"Bobby Kennedy, twenty-six years old and knowing nothing about Massachusetts politics, and not particularly caring much about politics, had given up his job in the Justice Department to manage his brother's campaign for the Senate." "He was the most unhappy fellow that you ever saw in your life. "But after he got to Massachusetts, he put it together. It was difficult because nobody felt his brother was going to win; the politicians were hanging around because they figured that Joe Kennedy was going to spread a lot of money around and that would be helpful to everybody; that was their only interest in John Kennedy. It was a rough campaign and Bobby put the whole thing together."

Bobby officially took over as campaign manager on June 2, 1952. "I still remember his first day at the campaign headquarters," Kennedy confidant Dave Powers recalled. "The headquarters was at 44 Kilby Street in Boston. Bobby was wearing what were called 'suntans' at the time—they were what you might think of as loafers. He had a blue shirt with sleeves rolled up to his elbows and open at the neck. He was really a well-tanned, muscular, and ruggedly handsome young fellow. He arrived at the headquarters every day at eight-thirty A.M. and was always the first to open up the place. He left at midnight every day for the next five months. Bobby, simply put, worked longer and harder than anyone. He opened and closed the office and would be the one who locked up after the last Kennedy reception and rally and when the last volunteer had left."

Bobby saw immediately that the organization had been stuck in neutral, just as Kenny and Powers had been saying since December. As Bobby moved to take charge, he began putting into place the pieces of what would become known as the vaunted "Kennedy machine." The first question he asked Dave Powers showed his seriousness: "Dave, how many cities in Massachusetts?"

"When I told him three hundred fifty-one communities, of which thirty-nine were cities and three hundred twelve were towns," Powers said, "he said to me, 'Fine. I want a map of the state about six feet by six feet and I want it now.'" Powers, who amused Jack Kennedy endlessly with his enormous knowledge of statistics, from baseball scores to the number of votes in a particular town, was surprised that Bobby wasn't impressed by his immediate knowledge of the state. Shrugging it off then, Dave would come to learn that Bobby expected that you would know your job or you wouldn't be there. Dave found the map and watched as Bob tacked it up in his tiny office. "The map became our Bible, really. We could keep track of rallies, teas, and receptions. We all campaigned five days a week until Labor Day; after Labor Day, Bobby moved the schedule for us up to seven days a week for the last two months. We were exhausted, but Bobby had been working seven days a week since June, so Ken and I couldn't really complain." Bobby's organizational and leadership skill allowed Jack to concentrate more fully on the campaign itself and on attracting voters, without having to be tied up in the details of running the organization. Kenny wasn't surprised at Bobby's talent; he'd seen him perform this way at Harvard. If Bobby would rather have been back at the Justice Department, he gave little indication of that as he drove himself uncomplainingly along with everyone else as hard as possible.

At the start of the signature drive to get Kennedy on the primary nomination ballot, Jack announced Dave Powers had mailed nomination papers to everyone on their lists from previous campaigns. Bobby wanted the campaign staff to add to the list any new names that might lean toward a Kennedy candidacy — especially those voters who were not Irish Catholic. For Bobby, it was important for the long term to show that Jack could appeal to voters beyond his ethnic base in order to truly be free of the established Irish pols. Bobby would not win this battle within the campaign organization, and it would take the presidential primary battleground of 1960 West Virginia before he could really make his point. "We had received some hundred thousand signatures with more coming in every single day and still Bobby wanted more. He wanted to be over the top," said Powers. On July 28, 1952, Jack Kennedy filed 262,324 names on his nomination papers. "It was at that time a state record," Powers pointed out, "and it was Bobby who wanted to make the point that Jack *could* win and that Lodge *was* vulnerable."

Bobby quickly rid the campaign headquarters of the so-called elder statesmen. "All they want to do is talk and advise," he complained to Dave Powers and Kenny. "They just want to talk, give advice, and pose for pictures." According to Kenny, "Seeing them sitting around reminiscing at the Kennedy headquarters on Kilby Street in Boston, he was likely to ask them to address envelopes." Bobby and Kenny wanted to build an independent political organization that represented the young former soldiers and their families. Just as Jack and Kenny did, Bobby understood—instinctively and from his experience with his veteran friends at Harvard—that the political future for Jack Kennedy lay in the hands of the young soldiers returned from the war. To make Jack a plausible candidate to this new breed of voter, Bobby needed to move out the old, Irish political guard that had been so successful in Boston and from which his grandfather Honey Fitz and his own father had benefited so much.

Increasingly, Joe Kennedy was forced to step into the background as Bobby took control of the campaign apparatus. He was pleased with Bobby's performance and was increasingly paying attention to his seventh child. Still, he was often surprised when Bobby insisted on making the campaign decisions and running an independent operation, to the amusement and relief of his brother Jack.

It was a daunting task and one not designed to make a lot of friends for the young man. "When Bobby arrived," Kenny said, "he understood a couple of things right away. He realized he didn't know all about politics; he listened when he should have listened; he was tough enough to handle his father; and he was tough enough to handle the organization. The politicians up there didn't like him because he didn't do what they told him to do; he built an independent organization because we all agreed that was the only way to do it. Whatever we suggested, he always stood up for us, even when we were wrong and made mistakes; and he could stand up to his father, and he could stand up to the powers; we didn't have that capacity until he came, we didn't have any real muscle. He supplied it, which began the controversy about his ruthlessness."

It was in this his first real campaign that the complaints about Bobby's supposed ruthlessness began to emerge. He drove himself and the campaign volunteers as hard as possible. Kenny said that "if he couldn't find someone to do a particular task, he simply did it himself." He was not concerned with the political niceties of Massachusetts politics. Jack was the one who had to worry about his public image; it was Bobby's job, in his view, to be the persistent commander who made victory possible. It didn't bother Bobby. He knew who he was and he knew what his job was; it was that sense of himself—developed in no small part from growing up in a large, competitive family headed by a driving father—that would allow him to take on the tough tasks without regard to the personal cost to him.

While Kenny traveled constantly with Jack, responsible for scheduling, advance work, and special events for the candidate, Bobby recruited into the headquarters young people who would not ever have naturally been tapped by the Boston Irish political machine. For both volunteers and paid staff he put into place simple rules that maximized the work effort and minimized sitting around the headquarters and just visiting. Nobody at headquarters was allowed to have coffee and sandwiches—a traditional staple of the standard campaign. Instead, Bobby instituted a rule whereby staffers and volunteers who came in faithfully would receive "supper slips" good for a free dinner at Hylighs, a small diner around the corner. "It was a wonderful idea," recalls volunteer Pat Twohig. "We would all get these supper slips and we could go over to Hylighs in shifts. We would have dinner and coffee and visit. Then everyone would go back to the campaign recharged. It was a very smart move, because it built up a great reservoir of loyalty and support for Bobby Kennedy and he was able to develop a cadre of volunteers who felt not only committed to Bob Kennedy but committed to the cause, which was getting Jack Kennedy elected to Congress.

"He was tough," continues Twohig. "If you didn't work or you were just there to talk, he wouldn't tolerate it. Bobby brooked no foolishness. This was very serious business to him; it was an uphill fight and Bobby knew it. Anyone who was very serious about the whole thing and about Jack Kennedy's future really loved Bobby. Those who didn't, didn't— because they weren't there to work and Bobby wouldn't tolerate it."

Understanding just how tough the fight was going to be and having lost time early, Bobby knew that one key to victory was to reach out to the young people. He set up College Students for Kennedy and urged all the young people involved in the campaign to bring a friend to headquarters to help out in any way they were needed on any given day. "We wanted to keep them all busy, because for so many people this was their first campaign and Bobby knew how important it was to keep them on board," Twohig says. "He designed what you might call make-work, writing thank-you notes and the like, just to keep people busy. Bobby inspired people to work; they would stay there until literally eleven at night doing this work! That was just how Bobby made you feel, like everything you did was crucial." The volunteers would stay loyal to the Kennedys for decades to come. They could be called up in 1960 to head to Wisconsin in the cold and West Virginia in the crunch, to New York in 1964 and to California in 1968.

Bobby's decision to build an independent campaign organization was one that Kenny, Dave Powers, and newcomer Larry O'Brien agreed was vital for success. Bringing O'Brien on board was a significant contribution to that effort. O'Brien was from Springfield, Massachusetts, knew the western part of the state, and had more political experience than anyone in the campaign, except maybe Joe Kennedy himself. "Larry was Foster Furculo's close friend and executive assistant in Washington for three years and they had a falling-out," Kenny recalled. The affable O'Brien would become extremely close with Kenny O'Donnell and Dave Powers, and his sharp mind would make him a central contributor to the 1960 presidential campaign that Bobby would also run, with the help of Kenny O'Donnell. Now with O'Donnell and Powers already on board and the addition of O'Brien, the beginnings of the so-called Irish Mafia were well under way.

O'Brien and Kenny began by naming Kennedy secretaries in each city and town to set up local organizations. One of the first secretaries that Kenny chose had a very Irish and family connection for him: Dick Maguire, whom he had met at Harvard, and who was to develop a close friendship with Kenny and a tense and turbulent relationship with Bobby. Maguire was a raconteur and a rogue, all qualities that Kenny loved because from his early childhood he himself always pushed the boundaries and rules whenever he could. Bobby would eventually come to feel that Maguire's antics would go beyond the amusing to the potentially politically embarrassing for the Kennedy campaigns—a trend he felt Maguire would continue after he had assumed the post of DNC chairman, where his personal secretary was none other than Kenny's youngest sister, Justine.

Among the other prospective Kennedy secretaries Maguire suggested was a partner in his law firm, W. Arthur Garrity, who is today a federal district court judge in Boston. Garrity and Kenny were both from Worcester; Garrity's father knew Kenny's father when Cleo Sr. coached at Holy Cross. Arthur Garrity was chosen by Kenny to be the Kennedy secretary for Wellesley. With his scholarly precision, he possessed exactly the kind of organizational skill that Kenny required.

Garrity's attention to detail aided the campaign in other areas. "I worked with Kenny and Larry O'Brien on designing Jack Kennedy's schedule. The schedule was designed so that every little thing was accounted for; it was quite grueling really," he remembers. "The first time I ever met Bobby Kennedy was at a meeting on Broad Street. There were only eight or ten people in the room, but what I remember most vividly was how terribly shy he was. It was not what I expected before I met him. He sat during the meeting in a chair, leaning against the wall, lifting the front legs of the chair off the floor and sometimes rocking slightly back and forth. He rarely made eye contact with us. And yet even at that early time he had this direct, intense fashion of his. It was a strange combination of shyness, directness, and intensity. I really believe in some manner that is where the 'ruthless' charge sort of incorrectly began and it was inaccurate from the beginning. It was his style as much as anything that led people to misunderstand him and his motives. He was tough and direct and yet you had a sense of a certain gentleness underneath."

The establishment of local Kennedy secretaries in each town was a masterstroke for the campaign. Previously all campaigns had been run from one main headquarters located in Boston, and all the campaigns for Democratic officeholders were coordinated from there. Bobby's decision to set up a completely separate and independent campaign caused a great deal of tension and certainly did not win any friends for him, but proved to be a key factor in Jack's success. It also was a precedent-setting move. From that point forward all candidates ran their own operations independent of the formal party structures within the state.

Governor Dever, busy running for reelection, was happy to be separated from what he saw as John Kennedy's fool's errand of a campaign
against Senator Lodge. "Dever and his associates were eager to avoid
being involved in Kennedy's campaign against Lodge. They thought that
Lodge would be the winner and they regarded Kennedy's followers as
inept and inexperienced, likely to be a hindrance to their fight to retain
Dever in the governorship. Yet as the campaign proceeded under the
direction of Bobby, the Kennedy campaign began to gain momentum
and the Dever campaign began to falter. Dever's staff suddenly changed
their minds about running a joint campaign, using Ambassador Kennedy as a go-between with Bobby and Jack to get the Kennedy organization to agree to work with Dever. Jack, Bobby, and Kenny discussed
it and decided to go it alone. The decision was not well received by the
Dever organization, who blamed it squarely on Bobby Kennedy. Kenny
remembered that "Bobby went to Dever and told him flatly that there
would be no joint Kennedy-Dever headquarters outside of Boston.
Dever was furious with Bobby, and so was the ambassador, but Bobby
stuck to his guns and his decision stood firm." Fortunately, due to Joe
Kennedy's influence, there was, according to Kenny, "no open warfare
between Dever and the Kennedy brothers, but the governor sent out
word that he would deal with our organization only through the candidate's father." Dever was quoted as saying in part, "Keep that young
kid out of here," referring to Bobby Kennedy.

As Kenny O'Donnell recalled for George Plimpton, "Late one night
we were at the Kilby Street headquarters. Everyone had gone for the
evening and Bobby was allowing us to have our first beer, and Dave
remarked that Bobby was not too popular with the Democratic pols in
Boston. 'I don't care if anybody around here likes me, as long as they
like Jack,' Bobby said. Bobby's insistence on keeping the Kennedy state
organization over his father's objections was the thing that gave Jack an
image of his own, different from the rest of the losing Democratic ticket
in that Eisenhower year."

The magnetism of the Kennedy family itself was a major campaign
resource — starting, of course, with the candidate himself and with his
brother Bobby. The Kennedy machine was built on personal loyalty to

Jack and Bobby Kennedy. "The Kennedys were rich and famous," Pat Twohig says. "We were just regular people, and to have Jack and Bobby treat you the way they did—it sounds foolish now, but at that time it was simply unheard of for politicians to be so nice and spend time with, well, regular people. We would have all these volunteers in the campaign headquarters and they would often work until late at night, because Jack Kennedy always would come by towards the very end of the evening. He was always 'running late,' Bobby would say. I realized later that Bobby planned it that way, because that way most of the people would stay hoping to get time to visit with the candidate. Jack was really good about that. He would come in with Bobby and he would greet every person individually. He knew and remembered everyone's name and something about them. It was amazing. I think to be honest," says Twohig, "a lot of the young girls were really hoping lightning would strike!"

Mary Jo Gargan, Rose Kennedy's niece, remembers that "Kenny and Bobby would go out at night and make speeches. Eunice, Pat, and Jean would be out making talks and showing sound films of a terrific interview Jack had given on the TV program *Meet the Press*. All of us were doing something ten to fifteen hours a day. Everybody contributed." Throughout Massachusetts, even today, thousands of citizens possess a thank-you note from Eunice Kennedy Shriver or Jack Kennedy or recall a special meeting with Jack, Bobby, or Ted Kennedy. During the 1952 effort, every Kennedy would write down the name and address of a prospective supporter and send the list back to the headquarters, where Bobby would have the volunteers add the name to the database. That person would immediately get a letter or a card automatically signed by Jack Kennedy. "It made a tremendous impression on people," Twohig says. "In those days old-style Irish politicians didn't bother with such details—chasing after voters and making them feel part of the organization."

The family rallied to sponsor thirty-three of the so-called Kennedy teas. In all, they hosted some seventy thousand guests, all of them women. Very early on, Robert Kennedy understood the power and the strength of women voters. The tea tactic, as historian Doris Kearns

Goodwin points out, was "a masterstroke, for it brought the entire Kennedy family in direct contact with tens of thousands of women who looked upon them as royalty and saw their own dreams and success mirrored in the Kennedys' achievement." The Kennedy teas and receptions were tremendously successful, much more so than Jack, Bobby, Kenny, or Dave might have imagined, but they required an immense amount of family effort to accomplish. "Eunice Kennedy especially was very giving of her time in those things," Pat Twohig recalls. "It had to get tedious, but she never complained. She was so bright and so talented; she had a mind like a steel trap and would remember anyone she had already met and, like her brother, remember the smallest detail that may not have been important but made that person feel so special." The teas became major social events. "We wore black dresses and white gloves and always wanted to look perfect. It was always fun to be included in those events."

The Worcester tea and reception was held on May 18. It was important to Kenny to get a good turnout in his hometown, so he pressed his reluctant family into action. Given her lifelong sentiment that proper people just did not unduly call attention to themselves, especially in public, Alice Guerin O'Donnell normally did not attend such events, but at the urging of her son both she and daughter Justine showed up. Justine agreed to work as an usher. Wearing the regulation black dress, pearls, and white gloves, Justine was just seating somebody down near the front of the reception when she began to hear everyone whisper that Rose Kennedy had arrived. Looking up toward the front door, Justine almost doubled over in laughter. It was not Rose Kennedy who had arrived but Alice O'Donnell. Her jet-black hair styled in the latest fashion, she was wearing a suit and her only mink jacket, decades old. At a distance, in the fading afternoon light and with her regal bearing, she might have passed for Rose. Justine couldn't believe her mother would do such a thing. Certainly Cleo would not have been amused. As she was escorted to the front row, Alice stole a look over at her youngest daughter and gave her a "don't tell" smile. Justine laughed. "Only for Kenneth would she pull something like this. My God, she almost never left the house for public events of any kind at that point, but she went to this because Kenneth was her favorite." (The whole mistaken identity prank was completely in keeping with Alice's character. Later, after Jack had been sworn in as president, when the newspapers called her to ask if she had enjoyed the Inaugural Ball, she told them what a wonderful time she had had, how delightful the president and Jackie were to her. She then went on to describe in the greatest detail the dress she had worn to the events. When her interview made the papers, Kenny thought it was hysterical, because his mother didn't go to Washington at all! She had stayed in Worcester! Justine was horrified, but Kenny thought it was great—who was to question his mother's story after all? When told later by Kenny about Alice's prank, the president and Jackie thought it was really very funny and loved it.)

The Worcester tea and reception drew some five thousand women, some of whom certainly didn't mind that John F. Kennedy was still an eligible bachelor. The teas were so enormously successful that they would lead pundits to declare that John Kennedy had "floated into the Senate on an ocean of tea," a description that over time Jack would find increasingly tiresome, although he never for a moment doubted the teas' enormous value. He and Bobby would use them again in 1960 when the stakes would be even greater.

Kenny O'Donnell spent most of the campaign traveling the state with the candidate. Jack had grown comfortable with Kenny. They had the war in common and a certain sense of reserve in public settings. Because of the amount of time they were spending together, Jack slowly began to trust his brother's friend; and Kenny also came to know the tremendous amount of pain Jack was enduring during this period—pain perhaps aggravated by the intense schedule of statewide drives they'd done from 1948 leading up to the 1952 race. Kenny recalled that Jack "traveled with crutches, which he concealed in his car when he arrived at the hall where the audience was waiting. Dave would notice him gritting his teeth when he walked with a determined effort from the car to the door where the chairman or the committee members were waiting to greet him, but then when he came into the room where the crowd was gathered, he was erect and smiling, looking as fit and healthy as the light heavyweight champion of the world. Then after he finished his speech, answered questions from the floor, and shook hands with every-body, we would help him into the car and he would lean back on the seat and close his eyes in pain." Dave Powers said that "when he would go back to the hotel, out would come the crutches from the floor of the backseat and he would use them to get upstairs, where I would fill the bathtub with hot water, and he would soak himself in the tub for an hour." Jack spent most of his life in pain, Bobby said once, but this was a particularly bad time. At the Worcester tea and reception he had been on crutches, something he always tried to avoid in public. However, the pain had become so intense it was simply impossible to walk without them.

As the campaign concluded, the relationship between Kenny and the Kennedy brothers was rapidly rising to a new level, tested as it was by their alliance on the senatorial race. They all recognized how good they were for each other. Jack, Bobby, and Kenny realized, said Sam Adams, "that they all made a hell of a team, and I think that was one of the most important elements that came out of that campaign, for it would prove crucial in 1960."

Election Day dawned dubiously for the Democratic presidential can-didate, Adlai Stevenson; the latest polls foretold an Eisenhower land-slide. Eisenhower had made one final stop on his presidential campaign: He came to Boston and spoke on behalf of Henry Cabot Lodge, under siege by the Kennedys. Both Lodge and Eisenhower were hoping that a huge Republican national victory would sweep Jack Kennedy and his cadre of volunteers away, once and for all. In his speech Eisenhower urged voters to return Lodge to the Senate, saying that the Republican was "a man of courage and conviction, a vigorous opponent of the men-ace of godless Communism."

Would the voters of Massachusetts decide that Jack Kennedy couldn't defend them from "godless Communism"? According to Pat Twohig, "We could feel victory in the wings as our headquarters began to fill up with smiling faces waiting for our final count." Yet the race was breath-lessly close throughout the night. Twohig remembers Kenny and Bobby standing on tables with Jean Kennedy Smith's husband, Steve, who also was a Kennedy political operative. "They were just so happy and so young. I can just picture them—Bobby with his tan, his blue eyes, hair askew and shirt sleeves rolled up, shirttail hanging out; Kenny standing next to him with those black, intense eyes and crew cut. They sort of gave each other a kind of football players' hug; it was great. Bobby was so tired, he had worn himself almost thin, he had dark circles under his eyes, but nevertheless he stood up there and all night long kept reading off the precinct results from each area. Each time he read something in our favor an enormous cheer would go up from the crowd." At 7:34 A.M. when Bobby read aloud Lodge's concession telegram that assured a Kennedy victory, the crowd burst into applause and shouts. The uncertainties and the difficult start had been overcome and the triumph won.

Jack, who had really only gotten to know his younger brother well in recent years, realized perhaps for the first time what so many of Bobby's friends had known all along: Bobby Kennedy was an amazing organizer, a natural leader, and a taskmaster who kept his eyes firmly on his goals. "Until then," said Jack's longtime friend Lem Billings in George Plimpton's *American Journey*, "I don't think Jack had been aware that Bobby had this tremendous organizing ability. But during the campaign Bobby had proved himself again and again, forging a partnership that would last until the two of them died."

Not only had Bobby proven himself to his brother, his parents, and so many others, but he and Kenny had realized that together they made a formidable team. They were comfortable with each other in a way that required minimum communication and ensured maximum success. Thanks to their partnership in the campaign, the bond they had forged at Harvard had become essential and unbreakable.

6

OF JOSEPH McCARTHY
AND "A CORD OF WOOD"

It is absolutely impossible to slaughter a man in this position with-
out making him a martyr and a hero, even though the day before
his rising he may have only been a minor poet.

—LETTER TO THE *DAILY NEWS*, LONDON
MAY 10, 1916

"We went down to the Cape to celebrate victory, those of us who had
been most involved, and we sat in the ambassador's living room and
talked. Out on the lawn we played football," Kenny recalled. John Kennedy had left for Washington. For the moment he would set aside Massachusetts politics to pursue his courtship of a young Washington
reporter, Jacqueline Bouvier. By the end of the 1952 campaign, Bobby,
Kenny, Larry O'Brien, and Jack were exhausted. Bobby alone had lost
some ten pounds. Now with their families they retreated to Hyannisport
to relax, talk politics, and ponder their futures.

Helen O'Donnell was equally in need of a break. She had given birth
to twins in November of 1950, a boy, Kevin Michael, and a girl, Kathleen Helen. Their births had made Boston's local paper. *The Record
American* ran a photograph of Helen, slim and beautiful, holding her
two children in her arms, under the heading TWINS FOR EX-CRIMSON
GRIDDER. Kenny, the "younger brother of Cleo, Jr., who captained the
'46 eleven, is son of Cleo O'Donnell, legendary ex–Holy Cross Coach,"
the caption read. Helen hoped that after the campaign Kenny would
focus on getting his law school degree. She had difficulty adjusting to
his prolonged absences due to his political work; she hoped they weren't
necessarily going to be a way of life. She thought politics was fun and

enjoyable, but it still wasn't a profession. Money was still tight; the campaign salary was very little to get by on, and with three young children she was in no position to contribute financially.

Ethel had given birth to her second child, a son, on September 22, 1952, right in the middle of the campaign. Ed Wagner, the campaign publicity director, wrote a press release announcing the birth of the first male Kennedy grandchild.

> Robert Kennedy, who is managing the campaign of his brother, Congressman John F. Kennedy, candidate for the United States Senate, was presented with a baby son by Mrs. Kennedy in St. Elizabeth's Hospital in Brighton, yesterday. The baby has been named Joseph Patrick Kennedy, II, after his grandfather, Joseph P. Kennedy, former Ambassador to England. The Kennedys have a daughter. Both mother and son are reported to be doing well. The new arrival is the Ambassador's first grandson.

Bobby, Kenny, and the rest of the Kennedy team had won a significant victory. The Democratic party in Massachusetts hadn't elected one of its own to the United States Senate since the 1920s. They had built an impressive organization that they could and would employ again. But Kenny would remember how, as they gathered in the ambassador's living room on one windswept November evening, they were not allowed to rest on their laurels. "We thought the world was our apple that night, and we were sitting there, and Mr. Kennedy was listening to us congratulate ourselves and with some frustration and annoyance in his voice he said to Bobby, 'What are you going to do now? Are you going to sit on your tail end and do nothing for the rest of your life? You'd better go out and get a job!'" Joseph Kennedy was not a man who would encourage his children to sit back and rest on their laurels.

For Bobby the question was where in government he wanted to go next. He knew he wanted to return to Washington, possibly back to the Justice Department. While Bobby would take his father's harsh admonition to heart as he tried to decide what to do, he had a million-dollar trust fund to cushion his decision. Kenny, on the other hand, had to make a choice quickly. He had no money—when the campaign ended so did his paycheck—and while he had a war hero's record and a Harvard degree, he had been struggling to complete his law degree in the evenings at Boston College. Helen, Kenny, and their three young children had rented an apartment in a two-story home on Temple Avenue in the small suburban seaside town of Winthrop. It was pleasantly situated close to the ocean and, more important, affordable.

The Kennedys were not unaware of this situation. John Kennedy offered Kenny a job in his Washington office, which he turned down flat. The senator-elect was puzzled but accepting. Kenny wasn't ready to go to work for John Kennedy, not just yet. He had a strong sense that there was a definite line between being a Kennedy friend and being a Kennedy staffer, and it was one he didn't want to cross and risk losing the friendship he had with either Bobby or Jack. Bobby Kennedy had another idea. "Go see my father in New York," he told Kenny as they worked to close down the headquarters. "He might have some ideas for you."

Kenny returned briefly to his paper company job, but in early December he took the train to New York and went to Ambassador Kennedy's apartment in the Waldorf-Astoria, seeking advice and help, just as he had done some six years before when he was troubled by publicity around the wartime Doolittle incident. He brought with him a worn brown paper sack. As he entered the ornate lobby of the Waldorf, Kenny spied the men's room as he walked along toward the elevators, and went in. There Kenny opened his paper bag. Inside, carefully folded by Helen, were his tie and his one white shirt. Kenny ducked into a stall and quickly changed. As he exited he stuffed his old, dirty shirt into the paper sack, rolled down the top of the bag, and unable to find a safe storage place, carried it under his arm as he took the short elevator ride up to Ambassador Kennedy's suite.

As he arrived at the ambassador's suite, he stepped off the elevator directly into a hallway where he was immediately greeted by the ambassador's butler. The butler looked the jacketless young man up and down, pausing to notice the crease marks on the recently unfolded white shirt, and then on to Kenny's slightly wrinkled trousers. "May I help you, sir?" he asked as his eyes came to rest on the paper sack tucked under Kenny's right arm. "Yeah," Kenny replied defensively, sensing the butler's disdain. "I'm here to see Ambassador Kennedy. Bobby Kennedy sent me and the ambassador's expecting me." The butler stood in silence for a moment: Bobby Kennedy indeed! The butler told Kenny to wait and headed in to see Joe Kennedy, closing the door on the vestibule firmly and leaving Kenny steaming out by the elevator. Kenny toyed with the idea of getting back on the elevator. He hadn't wanted to come seek the ambassador's help or advice. Bobby had urged it, and when Kenny refused, Bobby joined forces with Helen to push him into it. He turned to press the button for the elevator when the door opened and the butler returned, looking deflated. "Mr. O'Donnell, the ambassador said for you to come right in. He apologized for the delay." Kenny glared at the butler for a moment. Then, taking the paper sack out from under his arm, Kenny unrolled the top, reached inside and pulled out the slightly soiled shirt he had worn on the train to New York. He handed it to the butler, who, stunned, reluctantly took the shirt with two fingers. "Here, James," Kenny intoned in his best Cary Grant imitation, "take this, would you? I'll find my own way." Rolling the bag into a ball, he tossed it at a side table, where it landed amid pieces of decorative china. Kenny headed in to find the ambassador.

After greeting Mr. Kennedy, who, in quick succession took a few phone calls, Kenny sat and listened while Joe listed an entire series of jobs that Kenny shouldn't take and career decisions he shouldn't make. Kenny grew increasingly frustrated. At last, he interrupted the ambassador midsentence. "Look, Mr. Ambassador, you have told me what I shouldn't do, what I can't do. I came here because Bobby told me to come, you asked to see me, and now you are wasting my time! What the hell do you want?"

Stunned, the ambassador stopped for a moment, staring at the young man, his steel blue eyes meeting Kenny's black stare. Finally Joe burst out laughing. He slapped the young man on the leg. "You've got guts, kid—I like that. You aren't afraid of anyone. That's why Bobby likes you! You two are good for each other! Don't ever back down when you know you are right." With that, the ambassador offered Ken a beer, and while he had a soft drink, the two got down to the business: Jack and Bobby's future, and how Kenny could best help them win their goals.

Joseph Kennedy's plan involved great risks. It had several parts. The ambassador would arrange for Kenny to get a job with a liquor wholesale warehouse through some of Joe's contacts. The money was fair and the job would provide flexibility for what was to be Kenny's real task—as a political operative. Next, according to the ambassador, Kenny was to try to convince his friend Bobby to stay in Massachusetts and run for at-torney general in 1954. By doing so, the newly formed and very suc-cessful Kennedy campaign organization would be primed for Jack's 1958 reelection. Kenny agreed to sign on with the new job, since it would lead him further into the political arena, which is where he wanted to be. He went back to Massachusetts, wearing his one good white shirt, ready to argue Bobby into going into electoral politics. Kenny believed that Joseph Kennedy's plan made sense. "Larry O'Brien and I were both distressed when we realized that our excellent Kennedy organization, with its enthusiastic workers in every Massachusetts city and town, would probably never be put to any good use again until the senator ran for reelection in 1958." The organization would be at least as loyal to Bobby as it was to Jack if Bobby chose to run for attorney general or governor. "I also frowned on the thought of Bobby Kennedy leaving Massachu-setts, where he had built up considerable popularity as Jack's campaign manager, and tried to talk him into running for governor or for attorney general in 1954."

Kenny could not persuade Bobby to make the leap into electoral politics. "Bobby was not particularly interested in the idea," said Kenny flatly. "Although he was a great political campaign organizer, he did not care much for politics. In fact, I don't think that Bobby ever acquired a taste for politics and political campaigning until he became involved in the presidential primaries as a candidate himself in 1968, just before his death. So Bobby turned a deaf ear on my pleas."

His bag packed, Bobby headed home to Washington, to Ethel, Kath-leen, and the new baby. He returned to his job at Justice but soon accepted another job that would mark a major turning point in his career. Though he held his next position only six months, the post would offer him some fierce political lessons, propel him in a direction he might not have previously contemplated, haunt his later career, give his enemies recourse to attack him, and seal his lasting public image as the "ruthless" Bobby Kennedy.

In January 1953, Bobby Kennedy went to work for Senator Joseph McCarthy's Government Operations Subcommittee as assistant counsel and deputy staff director. His decision to work for McCarthy was controversial among his family and friends. Theodore Sorensen, who joined John Kennedy's staff when he became senator in 1953, says Jack told him directly that—despite his family's friendliness with McCarthy—he, Jack, opposed the Wisconsin senator and did not want Bobby joining the committee's staff. "John Kennedy told me that he hoped Bob would not take the job with McCarthy. His reasons were political, not ideological." Jack was realistic enough to see that McCarthy would ultimately destroy himself. By the time of Dwight Eisenhower's inauguration that winter, McCarthy had become an increasingly polarizing figure as he sought to root out supposed Communists from government. Sorensen feels that Bobby went into the job without yet knowing all the policy ramifications involved and without the breadth of experience and insight he would later develop. "The simplest views of militant patriotism, anti-Communism, and internal security which were part of his upbringing had, in 1953, not yet been balanced by the deep devotion to constitutional rights and civil liberties that he would ultimately hold."

Kenny put it even more directly to George Plimpton and friends: Bobby "didn't know Joe McCarthy from a cord of wood; he went to work for a fellow named Francis 'Flip' Flanagan, who had been in the Justice Department with him and who was then counsel for the committee. He worked there until the confrontation on the Army/McCarthy hearings, when he resigned and joined the minority staff as legal counsel." Kenny was adamantly opposed to Bobby's decision, not just because he wanted his friend to stay in Massachusetts and run for attorney general or governor, but because he felt that tying his sailboat to McCarthy's battleship could ultimately hurt him when he did decide to run for office. If Bobby had been clear with Kenny that he wasn't entering electoral politics, Kenny wasn't entirely taking him at his word. The controversy over Bobby's decision to join McCarthy's committee would be the strongest test of their friendship so far and led to debates that would have made the Kennedy debating club at the Varsity Club look like country club chitchat in comparison.

McCarthy was not unknown to the Kennedys. Bobby's sisters knew and liked McCarthy; he had at one time briefly dated Jean Kennedy. Bobby's brother-in-law Sargent Shriver was a personal friend of the Wisconsin senator. John Kennedy, wrote Ted Sorensen, "as a member of the House Labor Committee, had made headlines in the conservative Boston Irish press by stiffly cross-examining suspected Communists in the union movement; and no one in that family had the background to understand the motivations of anyone who was blinded by either the despair of the Depression or the hopes of the postwar period into collaborating with the Communists."

It was, however, Joseph Kennedy, Sr., who had the closest ties to McCarthy — ideological, political, financial, and even in terms of ethnic attitude. Kenny at the time thought it understandable that the ambassador would admire McCarthy. "I think it was natural that Joe Kennedy, who had been so assaulted by the press himself — and who had the kind of personality that would react — would think Joe McCarthy was being unduly put upon and come to his assistance." The senior Kennedy did make financial contributions to McCarthy's campaigns; as a businessman, he often gave money to candidates on both sides of the political fence, depending on who best served his business interests at the time. Joe also shared much of McCarthy's professed suspicion of Communism. And finally, McCarthy was a fellow Irishman. As historian Arthur Schlesinger points out, there was something about McCarthy, "perhaps this instinctive insolence toward the establishment, that may have reminded Joseph Kennedy agreeably of his own youth."

Joseph McCarthy would come to embody the Irish "chip on the shoulder" mentality — a defensive mentality with which he would go through life looking for offenses to his ethnicity, imagined or real, at every opportunity — an attitude that might explain, first, Joseph Kennedy, Sr.'s support of him and then, later, why young Bobby Kennedy did not immediately see the danger that lurked just underneath McCarthy's devotion to publicity. The fifth of seven children, McCarthy was three-quarters Irish and one-quarter German. His early political career was marked with a mix of outlandish grandstanding, exaggeration, and an almost demonic push for power that found its focus by 1950 in the nation's growing fear of Communism. The country was eager to return to the relative safety and isolation it had felt before World War II — an urge that frustrated veterans like Kenny O'Donnell. Instead, the nation contended with the fear that its government was rife with traitors and that it would forever have to become embroiled in foreign conflicts. The Korean War would provide fuel to fire McCarthy's charges, as the public's growing fear of the evils of Communism — a fear shared by young Bobby Kennedy — began to grow furiously.

By 1950, having battled his way to the Senate, Joseph McCarthy seized on the issue of Communism as a way to pull himself out of political obscurity. Always prone to exaggeration and storytelling, McCarthy was now in his element, center stage, flinging charges with abandon and with little concern for the truth or the consequences of his actions. McCarthy himself was reckless in his charges but somehow whimsical too. As he plunged forward, destroying lives and careers along the way, McCarthy could at the same time suggest that none of his rantings should be taken too seriously. As author William Shannon points out in *The American Irish*, "He never believed in any principles or body of political convictions, least of all in the movement that was given his name, 'McCarthyism.' Even when he appeared most dangerous and aggressive, one always had the lurking sense that he might on a whim drop the whole thing and skip to Mexico."

The conservative era made many Americans at first sympathetic to McCarthy — especially the Irish, who continued to struggle for political power and independence at the national level. Many Irish, long discriminated against and often culturally isolated, felt that the Catholic Church had a special mission to save the world from Communism. Although very few Catholics might have been able to state it directly, some came to believe if the Church said that Communism is a threat, then it must be so, and since Joe McCarthy was an Irish Catholic, then he must be right. "It follows, furthermore," points out William Shannon, describing this attitude, "that only Catholics can fully grasp the sinister nature of communism, an avowedly anti-religious movement. Communism," it followed, "was the work of Satan in politics; one should not compromise with Satan in politics any more than one should compromise with sin in one's private life." Father Coughlin, the right-wing radio priest of the 1930s, had spoken much the same rhetoric, linking the irresponsible rich with the atheists and Communists of Russia. That combination of fear of Communism, a protectiveness of the anti-Communist mission of the Catholic Church, and the contempt for the Wall Street establishment made McCarthy a potent figure for many Irish Americans seeking to communicate their resentment and fear. While Joseph and Bobby Kennedy may not have embraced any of these attitudes, they operated in an environment where such notions were prevalent.

McCarthy's first opportunity to manipulate the issue came when Millard Tydings, a Maryland Democrat, was asked to head up the Senate subcommittee that was to look into the issue of the Communist threat in America. Tydings, scion of a wealthy Maryland family, was a friend of Joseph Kennedy. Majority leader Scott Lucas must have surely believed that Tydings could control the committee, contain the press, and most of all control Joe McCarthy. Tydings failed and would ultimately lose his bid for reelection when he was tarred with being "soft on Communism." (Tydings's son Joseph would serve in the Senate with Bobby Kennedy, only to lose his seat when anti–gun control lobbyists opposed his efforts to regulate handguns after Bobby's assassination.) In Joe McCarthy, the Senate had a dragon by the tail. Before he was done he would have the very veterans of the Senate in all their power and prestige cowering under the barrage of countless, usually baseless charges flung at everyone, from the State Department to the newspapers to Hollywood. His charges, says Shannon, would in the end "destroy a Secretary of State, helped drive one national administration from office, and wrung with humiliating concessions from the next administration." McCarthy, with the formidable help of his associates Roy Cohn and David Schine, would "ravage the diplomatic service and other branches of government, breaking careers, unmaking hard-fought reputations and generally immobilizing policy."

Into this volatile situation, with McCarthy now chairing his own Government Operations Subcommittee, Joseph Kennedy pushed his son Robert. Sometime in the fall of 1952, he had called McCarthy and asked him to appoint Bobby as the chief counsel to his Government Operations Subcommittee. It was in some ways an awkward request for both McCarthy and Kennedy—the ambassador disliked calling in political markers unless he was absolutely sure of their benefit, and McCarthy, who did not like having such an appointment look like political payback, had already decided to appoint a twenty-five-year-old lawyer for the spot. His choice was a New York attorney already well known for his anti-Communist zeal: Roy Cohn. Cohn shared McCarthy's appetite for publicity, his air of menace, and his disregard for pursuing the truth behind the charges he made. Robert Kennedy was picked as assistant counsel, working with a young assistant named LaVerne Duffey. Together they began to investigate the trade carried on with Communist China by America's allies.

Despite having known McCarthy through family connections and having seen him in action in his own living room in Charlottesville, Bobby seemed wholly unprepared for the depth of McCarthy's reckless willingness to destroy the careers of all those around him. The entire experience, all six months of it, would shock Bobby's sense of propriety and honor and provide him with a costly education.

"I used to tell Bobby what I thought of Joe McCarthy on the telephone, and at the other end there'd be silence," Kenny O'Donnell remembered. "After a while he'd say, 'He isn't that bad, but I agree, you know.' Bobby had the greatest capacity for the underdog. He thought that there were unfair aspects to the criticism of the senator. If he had a weakness, that was his weakness—whenever somebody was in real trouble or being unfairly treated, he was for him, whether the issue involved him or not."

LaVerne Duffey remembered that he joined the committee in the spring of 1953 as a part-time clerk. "My best memory of that day," says Duffey, "is my introduction to a young man named Bob Kennedy who asked me to help him with some research involving trade of Western nations with Red China. That was his first major investigation, and I soon learned the characteristics that were to mark all the cases that followed—hard work and long hours!" The committee offices were housed in a small room in the Senate Office Building. "I remember wondering on that first day if Bob's attire was standard for Senate staff members," Duffey recalls. "His sleeves were rolled up past the elbows, his collar was open, and his tie was pulled loose. Most remarkable, however, were his sweat socks. During the first year I knew him, he invariably wore those sweat socks until somebody—perhaps it was Ethel—convinced him that they weren't appropriate accessories for business suits!"

His work was far more methodical and research-oriented than that of McCarthy and his sidekick Roy Cohn. His investigations were conducted properly, with facts checked and carefully presented; he did not fling charges first and then grope for evidence to support them. Quickly he uncovered a case where two ships had been flying the British flag while carrying supplies up the Chinese coast to the Communists then newly in power, just at the time the United States was fighting in Korea. Kennedy was largely responsible for marshaling the facts, which he then presented at public hearings and preparing the subcommittee's report, which was filed with the Senate on July 1, 1953. In his private, closed papers at the John F. Kennedy Library in Boston, Robert Kennedy himself pointed out at the time of the release of the report that "Senator McCarthy announced the action of the shipowners out of New York and there was immediate furor raised by the critics of Senator McCarthy stating that he was entering into foreign policy, which was the prerogative of the Executive Branch of government. The criticism is just not justified." Kennedy went out of his way to point out that as uncomfortable as many people may be with McCarthy's tactics, he had every right, and that the congressional committee itself had every right, to look into this issue. Bobby continued, saying that, in fact, "America's policy at that time was against vessels going into China and that had been clearly understood for a number of years so we are not making up any new policies as far as the United States is concerned!"

Arthur Krock, in his column in *The New York Times* on Sunday, July 19, 1953, referred to Robert Kennedy's work and subsequent report as "an example of Congressional Investigation at its highest level with documentation given for each statement represented as a fact and with conclusions and opinions expressed dispassionately, despite the provocations of what it disclosed. F. D. Flanagan and Robert F. Kennedy, the Subcommittee Counsel and authors of the report which sums up the information which they acquired by arduous effort and far exceeds what the Executive Department had when they began their search, share largely in the credit for this production."

The results of the work of Kennedy, LaVerne Duffey, and Jim Flanagan meant that some 327 vessels pledged to refrain from trade with Communist China. "This single effort," pointed out Bobby in a rough draft of the final report, "greatly reduced the number of allied vessels which were engaged in this trade." McCarthy was by his side when the cases and the results were announced in the hearing room. But even though McCarthy appreciated the publicity, he was less interested in foreign policy than he was in digging out native-born American spies lurking in the government.

Bobby not only saw the lunacy and paranoia increasingly evident in McCarthy but was bothered by the haphazard, dangerous, and sloppy investigative work of Roy Cohn. The differences in style would inevitably lead to a headlong clash. Bobby did not take part in any of McCarthy and Cohn's investigations into subversives in the State Department, the Voice of America, and various other governments and organizations. He never was involved in any of their Communist witchhunts. In the words of Arthur Schlesinger, Bobby found that Roy Cohn often catered to "McCarthy's hit-and-run inquisitorial instincts . . . personal dislike was compounded by genuine concern." The situation grew worse with the arrival of G. David Schine; hired by Cohn as "chief consultant," he had previously attracted attention by writing a pamphlet called "Definition of Communism," copies of which had been placed in hotels owned by Schine's father. After he and Cohn had, in the words of Arthur Schlesinger, "terrorized" the Voice of America, the two left for a "magical mystery tour of Europe and terrorized American Embassy employees by plucking offending books off the shelves of offending embassies."

For Bobby, the Communist menace was real enough, but the methods used by McCarthy and Cohn were making him increasingly uneasy. His regular conversations with Kenny compounded his concern. Their discussions were often punctuated with either long silences or heated disagreements. Kenny continued to urge Bobby to leave his job. Bobby said little, but he listened a great deal. McCarthy was a friend of his father's, of his entire family; wanting to remain loyal, he found it difficult at first to make the break with McCarthy. But as he watched Cohn prod McCarthy further into anti-Communist mania, Bobby knew he would have to leave.

Even during breaks from the committee hearings during congressional recesses, the issues McCarthy raised would not go away. One weekend, Bobby and Ethel joined up with the rest of the Harvard gang to go to the Harvard/Yale football game, this year being played in Connecticut. After the game ended, Kenny, Helen, Nick Rodis and his new wife, Eve, Sam Adams and his wife, and Jimmy Kenary joined Bobby and Ethel at the Kennedy apartment in New York for dinner. "Inevitably," recalls Nick Rodis, "Kenny and Bobby got into one of their great Kennedy debates over McCarthy. It got pretty heated. Everyone got pretty uncomfortable. Bobby was defending McCarthy and Kenny was really going after him. I remember Kenny was saying, 'He can't prove one thing; he made all these charges and it's a bunch of shit! You know it's a bunch of shit—get outta there. What the hell is wrong with you?' Bobby came right back at him, trying to explain that McCarthy had a lot of problems but he was a good guy and, you know, we gotta get the economy going again . . . and the debate went on like that. It got really rough and they were pretty tough with each other."

Sam Adams remembers it similarly. "Here they were, Kenny and Bobby, and they were best friends, but there was this disagreement and they were really going at it. It didn't affect their friendship, but it was a very, very strong debate. Here the rest of us were just sitting around watching and listening to them debate. Both had their facts and they were well prepared. It sort of developed out of nowhere; we didn't know this had been a long running conversation between the two of them. But Bobby by the end of the argument was clearly coming around to Kenny's viewpoint with regard to McCarthy."

Arthur Schlesinger says that by the end of Bobby's time with the committee, "Kennedy considered it all madness." Bobby went to McCarthy and told him the committee was being poorly run and he wanted out. Later, in an interview with Arthur Schlesinger, he said he had told McCarthy "that the way they were proceeding I thought it was headed for disaster . . . I told him I thought he was out of his mind and was going to destroy himself. Cohn and Schine took him up the mountain and showed him all those wonderful things. He destroyed himself for that—for publicity. He had to get his name in the paper. . . . He was on a toboggan. It was so exciting and exhilarating as he went downhill that it didn't matter to him if he hit a tree at the bottom." McCarthy wanted Bobby to stay.

Bobby's letter of resignation was dated July 29, 1953. The letter was a graceful but clear exit from the chaos of the McCarthy committee. It read in part:

> Please accept my resignation as Assistant Counsel and Deputy Staff Director of the Senate Permanent Subcommittee on Investigations, effective as of the close of business July 31, 1953.
>
> With the filing in the Senate of the Subcommittee report on Trade with the Soviet Bloc, the task to which I have devoted my time since coming with the Subcommittee has been completed. I am submitting my resignation at this time as it is my intention to enter private practice of law at an early date.

McCarthy's acceptance letter was equally gracious, but it is clear that he understood that Bob was not pleased with his methods and work chasing Communists.

So ended his brief sojourn into the world of McCarthyism. McCarthy himself would inevitably crash and burn only months later, when his televised inquest into the army would redound on him. He would be censured by the Senate and, his feverish power broken, die ignored, drunken, and disgraced.

Later, when his tenure with the Wisconsin senator would come back to badger him, Bobby would refuse to minimize his association with McCarthy or deny his responsibility for his part in the committee's efforts. He had learned valuable lessons in how not to run an investigation, which would aid him as he took over as chief counsel at the McClellan Committee and still later when he was attorney general. He had also learned that he did not have to be perfect—that he could make decisions that were mistakes, face up to them, and still go on in public life. That capacity for character growth would prove him a rare public figure.

His father understood the difficulty Bobby went through. When Robert Lovett, the former secretary of defense, inquired of the ambassador about how Bobby was holding up, Joe Kennedy responded, "Put your mind to rest about that. Bobby is just as tough as a boot heel."

"I felt," Bobby Kennedy said of his work with the committee at that time, "that there was valuable work to be done." After a pause, he quietly added, "I was wrong."

While Bobby struggled with McCarthy, Kenny went through his own trials, beginning in February 1953 with the death of his father, Cleo. The older man had a speech to give one afternoon and had spent the morning putting the finishing touches on his notes. Still in demand as an inspirational speaker to young people, Cleo enjoyed the chance to extol the value of education and declaim about how football forged character. He never was paid for these appearances. That morning he was not feeling quite himself and asked first Justine and then his son Warren to accompany him to his speech. Both had other things scheduled and declined. He then asked his daughter Phyllis, but she had several young children to care for. Cleo left and went off to give his speech. "I wish," recalls Justine, "that one of us had gone, but we were all so busy with our own things; it was inconvenient. I just wish that we had taken the time." Cleo arrived at his destination, and after a lengthy introduction, rose and strode with confidence to the speaker's platform.

He had just begun speaking and was working up to his best line when he suddenly stopped talking, dropped his notes with one hand, and grabbed his chest with the other. Cleo A. O'Donnell, who had left home at the age of nine and worked his way up through college football to become a coaching legend, was dead before he had hit the ground. "It was exactly the way he would have wanted to go," Justine says now. "Well, maybe not exactly. He probably would have preferred to be on a football field."

From the disciplined dinners he commanded to the daily discussion on football and politics he would lead, the family's life had revolved around Cleo. That was the way Cleo had wanted it. From the time he was a child he had envisioned what he pictured a family should be; when he had a family of his own, he created that picture with an intensity and ferocity that made living without him hard to imagine for his family. As difficult as Cleo's life had been for so many years, he had always managed to make it seem as though the world were under his control. It had seemed to his children that he would go on forever. With all two sons now graduates of Harvard, Cleo felt they would transcend the struggles that had consumed him and so many Irishmen of his generation.

For Kenny and his brothers especially, Cleo was a challenging and demanding man, but he was also the force behind their forward progress.

With Cleo gone, Kenny was even less sure of his own direction. Politics was his love, but he didn't want to work as a staffer for Jack Kennedy. The timing still just wasn't right. He continued to work at the liquor sales job arranged for him by the ambassador while struggling with Boston College Law School at night and keeping active along with his cohort Larry O'Brien, holding the Kennedy campaign organization together through constant communication with the secretaries around the state.

He began to harbor his own political ambitions. He quietly returned to Worcester, renting a small office in a building downtown. Jimmy Kenary, who had returned to Worcester after Harvard, believed that Kenny "wanted to keep in touch with everyone and keep the Kennedy machinery in place." In reality, Kenny quietly nursed the hope that he might be able to build enough of a base in Worcester to run for the

United States Congress himself—not as John Kennedy's lieutenant, but as his own man. He spoke only to a few friends about his plan.

Using the Kennedy campaign machinery as a cover, Kenny decided quickly that he had the base and the connections to make a serious run at the office. He lacked only one crucial thing: money. But with three young children of his own, law school at night, and a limited income, he pragmatically realized he would have to defer his ambition and bow to financial realities. Kenny was no Kennedy in financial terms; he would have to hitch a ride with Jack Kennedy or with Bobby. Ultimately, Kenny quietly closed this office and returned to Boston. He continued to harbor the urge to represent the public himself. He would try twice later, coming very close in 1966. Perhaps he did not know what was best for him. "He was a great behind-the-scenes guy. He was a master at it," Kenary says. Perhaps even if Kenny had had the option of public office he still would have been most comfortable and most effective as a behind-the-scenes political technician.

Kenny often saw the other members of the team who were still around Boston, and occasionally they would rendezvous as they had in New York for the Yale/Harvard game. Occasionally he and Helen would meet up with Ethel and Bobby at Hyannisport for a long weekend. Helen was busy with three young children and was somewhat happier with Kenny in law school, out of politics, and home more often. She quietly began to hope that the long absences of the 1952 campaign were over for good.

Bobby had left the Government Operations Subcommittee and joined the Hoover Commission to work for his father. He still was not interested in running for public office as Kenny still urged: They would right now be gearing up a campaign for the governorship or for attorney general if only Bobby had given the word. But he was not happy working for his father, nor was he particularly engaged with the work of the commission. Although he admired the former president, Bobby was quick to point out that he most appreciated Hoover's early career before he was president and before he started his commission. "He had lots of frustrations," recalls Kennedy pal Lem Billings. "He wasn't happy at all. He had decided to dedicate himself to the government, and he hadn't found his niche and didn't know where he was going to find it. This made him at the time an unhappy, angry young man." Yet despite his own personal frustrations at the time, others were beginning to recognize more and more the work of the younger Kennedy brother. In 1954 he was chosen for one of the Ten Outstanding Young Men Awards given by the Junior Chamber of Commerce. He was also president of the Joseph P. Kennedy, Jr., Foundation, which during the previous seven years had contributed in excess of six million dollars for assistance to homeless and mentally retarded children. While other people might have been more than satisfied with accomplishing so much at such a young age, Bobby knew that he was not reaching his potential and it was not good enough.

Relief came in the form of a phone call from Senator John McClellan of Arkansas. In 1953, the Senate Investigative Subcommittee had become divided over McCarthy's tactics. The three Democratic members of the committee, Senators Henry "Scoop" Jackson, John McClellan, and Stuart Symington, had, according to historian Arthur Schlesinger, "walked out when the Republican Majority gave McCarthy control over the hiring and firing of Committee Staff." By January 1954, the Democrats had forced McCarthy to relinquish control over the hiring and firing of committee staff. They worked out a settlement with McCarthy and immediately called Robert Kennedy, asking him to come onboard as Democratic minority counsel. Bobby accepted instantly. This time, Bobby would be sure that the investigations were run the right way, not McCarthy's way. The post would also put Bobby in direct conflict with Roy Cohn. It would mark the start of a new period in Bobby's life, as he came into his own as an independent and powerful Washington player. The new minority counsel was barely twenty-seven years old.

The call from John McClellan had brought Bobby back into the action and into immediate conflict with his nemesis Roy Cohn and Senator Joseph McCarthy. In an advisory memo, written in his capacity as minority counsel, to committee member and Missouri senator Stuart Symington, which responded to the threats to call Symington before the committee and examine his positions on Communism, Bobby is blunt in his criticism of both McCarthy and Cohn.

Looking over the Committee Record, McCarthy seems to be using the tactic of repeating over and over again about your testifying. The theory is one that has been used by Hitler and again by Stalin that if you repeat something often enough people are going to believe it. Of course, Democracy and our way of life is based on the theory that the people have greater intelligence and will ultimately recognize the truth no matter what tactics are used by those who peddle lies and falsehoods.

The long arguments and continual political debate with Kenny and his other friends had clearly begun to hit home. Bobby now was providing Symington and the committee's Democratic minority a strategy they could use to counter McCarthy's ever-expanding excessiveness.

. . . Any witness called before a Congressional committee can demand successfully that the Senator or Congressman sitting on that committee be called as a witness and cross-examined . . . certainly a long step towards completely destroying the power and prestige of committees in Congress. That is what Senator McCarthy wants to do. If Senator McCarthy has any charges against you then let him make them on the floor of the Senate. . . . Senator McCarthy talks as if this is a plot by you [the Democrats] to destroy the Republican Party and present Administration. It certainly seems somebody in this committee room is bent on doing that. . . .

"These," concluded Bobby Kennedy, "are some thoughts that you might throw in during the Hearings if there is any trouble."

McCarthy and Cohn were continuing to splatter the government with groundless, hysterical charges with little regard to the facts or the consequences. Now McCarthy was going after the United States Army, choosing Fort Monmouth, New Jersey, as his point of attack. McCarthy was convinced that there were spies and Communists among the ranks of the soldiers and civilian employees in the Signal Corps installation located there. Even as McCarthy scoured the barracks for Communists,

Roy Cohn fought furiously to get special privileges for his confidant David Schine, who had recently been drafted into the army. Unable to obtain the privileges that he sought and upset at the disregard with which he believed the army treated Schine, Roy Cohn made the mistake of urging McCarthy onward.

The constant clamor of charges and countercharges, according to Arthur Schlesinger, "produced a general cry for investigation" of the army overall. On April 22, 1954, the army/McCarthy hearings officially began. Under the white hot lights of the television camera and with an audience upward of twenty million, Robert Kennedy and Roy Cohn were soon at each other's throats. Kenny, who was kept apprised of the situation by phone with Bobby, sensed Bobby was growing ever more resentful of the tactics used by McCarthy and Cohn. "When they got to the army hearings, I used to talk to him twice a week," Kenny said. "He was really upset. Bobby was incensed at the way they were treating witnesses; he was incensed at the Cohn-Schine investigations, and he thought they had lost all sense of direction; and he wanted out without any question."

Kenny was still in Boston maintaining the Kennedy organization while working at the liquor wholesalers job that the ambassador had arranged for him after their meeting at the Waldorf. Kenny recalled Bobby making clear his feelings during the height of the army/McCarthy hearings that involved both Fort Monmouth, and, in particular, Captain Irving Peress, whom McCarthy and Cohn suspected of getting his original appointment, subsequent change of orders, and promotion due to his participation in a Communist plot within Fort Monmouth. Now that the public could see McCarthy in action on television, they could witness his tactics firsthand. The increasingly overzealous machinations of Cohn and McCarthy were beginning to wear thin on citizens weary of the Korean War and tired of Communism and conflict.

The hearing escalated as the army retaliated against McCarthy by charging that Roy Cohn had tried to get special privileges for Private Schine. Kenny knew how infuriated Bobby was. "There was not much doubt where Bobby stood," Kenny would say later. "He and Cohn almost came to blows one day before the nationwide television audience watching the proceedings."

During the hearings themselves, Bobby sat behind the Democratic senators and wrote pertinent questions for them to ask. Senator Jackson was interrogating McCarthy about a supposed anti-Communist plan proposed by Schine. Cohn took exception to the questions, convinced they were directed personally at him, Schine, and McCarthy. When the hearing recessed, "Cohn had taken out a file marked 'Jackson's record,'" said Arthur Schlesinger. As one reporter had it, "Carrying it like a weapon, he headed for the Committee table," where he found Bobby. "I want you to tell Jackson," Cohn said furiously, "that we are going to get to him on Monday."

Bobby Kennedy later told reporters that Cohn was going to accuse Jackson of having "written something favorably inclined towards Communists." "His blue eyes snapping," according to the New York *Daily News*, Bobby said, "You can't get away with it, Cohn."

Bobby later said, "I told him he had a nerve threatening me. I told him he had been threatening all the Democrats and threatening the army and not to try it on me!" Bobby felt the threats were directed at him because he knew that Cohn recognized Jackson's questions as coming from Bobby, who he believed had a personal hatred for the McCarthy side. Cohn replied to Kennedy with equal venom, saying, "I'll make any warning to you that I want—anytime, anywhere!" And then he added, "Do you want to fight right here?" Not waiting for Bobby's response, Cohn began to swing at Kennedy.

It was at that point, Bobby later confided to Kenny when they talked by phone after the incident, that he lost complete control. Bobby advanced toward Cohn, but several newspapermen succeeded in separating the two men. The *Daily News* headlined the incident as COHN, KENNEDY NEAR BLOWS IN "HATE" CLASH. Unhappy that he had allowed Cohn to get to him, Bobby retreated with LaVerne Duffey to the Senate cloakroom to find his brother. Jack, always cool, calmed his brother.

Kenny would say later that Bobby was unhappy with himself for losing control; but at the time he teased Bobby by saying that, considering

McCarthy's and Cohn's behavior, he was surprised it hadn't happened sooner.

The army/McCarthy hearings were the Wisconsin senator's Waterloo, leading to his censure on December 2, 1954. His downfall was a difficult experience for both Kennedy brothers. For Jack, concluded Kenny, "the fact remained that his brother Bobby had been closely associated with McCarthy and Cohn a year earlier." "How could I demand that Joe McCarthy be censured for things he did when my own brother was on his staff?" Jack asked Kenny and Dave Powers. He had been strongly against Bobby's joining McCarthy's staff. As it turned out, Jack missed the censure vote for McCarthy, having entered the hospital in New York for back surgery. His absence would come back to haunt him as political pundits tried to ascribe all sorts of motives to the timing of the surgery.

For Bobby, McCarthy's demise was both expected and sad. He had grown deeply opposed to the senator and condemned his methods and his association with Cohn, yet he saw McCarthy as a tragic figure responsible for his own downfall. Bobby also resented how so many of those who had stood behind McCarthy urging him on during the height of his power now walked away, anxious not to be besmirched themselves in the wake of McCarthy's downfall. But Bobby possessed what his grandmother Rose had called an "exacting sense of responsibility": After the senator had died, drunken and disgraced in 1957, it was that sense of responsibility that moved Bobby to go to Wisconsin for McCarthy's funeral.

In the fall of 1954, the Harvard/Yale game was held in New Haven, and Bobby invited his Harvard friends to a postgame party his father and mother were hosting at the ambassador's Waldorf-Astoria apartment. The ambassador had also invited his own friends, including politicians, financiers, and movie stars. As Jimmy, Kenny, Nick, and their wives, fresh from the game and disheveled from all the cheering and good-natured rabble-rousing with their friends, piled out of the car in front of the Waldorf, they were greeted with baleful stares by the doorman in front of the posh hotel. As they entered the lobby, Kenny began immediately to get that uneasy feeling that he had had the last time he was here. This place still wasn't his style. Stepping off the elevator and into the front hall of the Kennedy apartment, the gang was immediately greeted by Kenny's old nemesis, the Kennedy butler. Recognizing Kenny, he seemed to decide that discretion was the better part of valor and immediately ushered the group into the main living room where Bobby and Ethel were already surrounded by Joseph Kennedy's glamorous guests. Their entrance brought immediate stares from the crowd. Many looked horrified. In their mismatched jackets, sweaters, and casual pants, Jimmy, Kenny, Nick, and their wives looked decidedly un–Park Avenue. Everyone in the gang looked to Kenny for direction. Kenny surveyed the bemused expressions of this high-toned crowd. Then, turning toward the remainder of the group, Kenny barked, "Let's go to the bar."

It was there, with everyone enjoying a beer, that Bobby and Ethel found them. Both seemed relieved to see their friends. Bobby began talking to Jimmy "Squash Head" Kenary about his stint in the marines, which had always fascinated Bobby. He fired dozens of questions at him about the corps, about Worcester and how he grew up. His work in Washington had refined his curiosity and further developed his habit of exhaustively firing questions at everyone he knew or met.

The ambassador spied the group from the other side of the room and strode over to the bar to order a soft drink. As had become their custom, he and Kenny went on to discuss politics and strategy for much of the afternoon, until Rose finally shooed her husband back to his other guests. She also tried to get Bobby to mingle, but he stuck with Jimmy Kenary. Squash Head was both flattered and amazed by the attention. "Here was this kid with all this money and stuff, and all these famous people, and both he and his father would rather have spent the whole afternoon with us." As the crowd thinned, the group decided to go out to dinner. Bobby and Ethel joined them.

Kenny was not surprised by Bobby's and Joe's behavior. "Why the hell would Bobby want to talk to those fakers?" he asked Squash Head. "That's not who he is." As the group made their way out, Squash Head thought to himself, it takes an afternoon like this to kind of remember who Bobby Kennedy really was. Even after several years among the most powerful and prominent people in Washington, he was just himself no matter the consequences. No wonder he and Kenny got along, Kenary remembers thinking as the elevator descended. In his own way, Kenny was just as centered and comfortable with himself among the prominent people and just as impatient with the fakers as Bobby was.

The midterm elections of 1954 had changed the power dynamics of Congress, which after two years of Eisenhower-induced Republican control was back in the hands of the Democrats. John McClellan replaced McCarthy as chairman of the Investigations Subcommittee and quickly moved to appoint Bobby as chief counsel. The committee would continue the investigations into Communist influence in the American government, as Arthur Schlesinger reflected, "no doubt because the Democrats didn't want to seem less zealous in saving the Republic than their Republican predecessors." However, Bobby was determined that this time the investigations would be done properly. He would finally be in a position to conduct the kind of investigations he felt were long overdue, and he would be able to come into his own. He began by cleaning the mess that the now disgraced McCarthy left behind. In Bobby's view, "the mess" stemmed from the shoddy investigative methods used by Cohn and McCarthy. Those methods had lodged all sorts of false charges against people who should never have been brought into the investigation in the first place. He started by informing the press that the committee would return to its original mandate, "looking into waste, fraud and corruption in government." Then Bobby went on to complete the investigations begun by McCarthy, but used a much more "skeptical approach to witnesses," says Schlesinger. In fact, he turned more to scholars and educators familiar with Communism and away from the more "voluble and imaginative witnesses" preferred by McCarthy and Cohn.

In March 1955 the committee began investigations into allegations of Communist infiltration surrounding the questionable promotion of Captain Irving Peress by the army. In setting out his goals for these investigations, Bobby was quite blunt about what he thought the Peress hearings should accomplish. In a memo to Senator McClellan, he wrote:

During the Army–McCarthy hearings the question of those responsible for the mismanagement of the Peress matter arose. Secretary Stevens said that the Inspector General was making a report and as soon as it was complete he would furnish it to the Subcommittee. . . . Many of these questions are still unanswered. It would seem only fair to all concerned that this Subcommittee strive to obtain some of those answers. I would suggest therefore, that this Subcommittee continue its investigation, hold hearings, and learn once and for all the facts behind the Peress matter. If there is a rotten situation in the Army it should be exposed; if there is not, the bogeyman should be put to rest.

Bobby's report on Peress was submitted in July 1955. The committee found nothing to substantiate McCarthy and Cohn's charges that "the original appointment of Peress, his subsequent change of orders, and his promotion had been, in fact, inspired by subversive interests." The committee report did go on to "criticize the Army for forty-eight errors of more minor importance." They concluded that Captain Peress's "subsequent promotion and honorable discharge resulted from individual errors in judgment, lack of proper coordination, ineffective administrative procedures, inconsistent applications of existing regulations, and excessive delays, not from treason."

With these conclusions Bobby had put more than the army's "bogeyman" to rest; through exhaustive and thorough investigative work, he resolved his own concerns about "sloppy investigations and hysterical charges" by performing what Kenny called "proper and appropriate investigations."

As the McCarthy-era hysteria waned, Robert Kennedy told the Louisville *Courier Journal* that "the Committee itself would gradually return to its old functions — looking into waste, fraud, corruption and mismanagement in government." These investigations included inefficiencies in the Department of Agriculture with regard to the grain storage elevators in Pakistan. Kennedy also looked into wiretapping in Washington, which brought him into conflict with the FBI and J. Edgar Hoover, with whom he would come to have a strange relationship in years to come.

Gone was the white-hot press coverage brought by McCarthy's constant charges—except in the case of the investigation of Harold Talbott, Eisenhower's secretary of the air force. The investigation—prompted by the reporting by Charles Bartlett, a reporter who was friendly with John Kennedy—would lead to a memorable cross-examination involving thirty-year-old Robert Kennedy and the congenial sixty-seven-year-old Talbott. Bobby, says Bartlett, "did fight. He just wouldn't let go. In 1955, I got a lead that Harold Talbott, then secretary of the air force, had been running a management-personnel concern in New York. I talked to Bobby about doing a sort of joint investigation. . . . He used the committee's facilities, and I used what I could, and we pulled together the fact that Talbott had continued to operate this management-advisory firm even though he was secretary of the air force; he was, in fact, doing some soliciting for this firm from his official position. Bobby was persistent in that. He just bird-dogged him. We finally got to a hearing which was highly dramatic because there was not a senator who supported what we were doing, because they were all very fond of Mr. Talbott. But Bobby kept pressing. It was only Bobby's persistence that made a success of the hearings, which finally broke in such a way that the president had to request Mr. Talbott's resignation."

The entire affair, says Schlesinger, "led to Talbott's resignation, Bartlett won a Pulitzer Prize, and Kennedy confirmed his reputation as a relentless prosecutor." Bartlett concluded, "I got a Pulitzer Prize out of it, but Bobby's slice of the Pulitzer Prize was just tremendous."

One of the staff consultants Bobby most relied on was accountant Carmine Bellino. He had an ability to spot any kind of scam hidden in any set of financial papers, and soon even Teamsters Union leader Jimmy Hoffa would have to bow to Bellino's genius with figures. Bellino and Bobby began a useful friendship that later would include Kenny and extend into the White House. But in 1954 Bellino performed another service for Bob Kennedy; he convinced his sister-in-law Angela M. Novello to come to work for the committee.

Angie, as everyone knew, wanted to work in government. When Bellino first approached her about working for the committee, she demurred. She had heard about Bob Kennedy—especially that he worked very hard, and so did all of his staff. Carmine insisted: "Look, you must, we need you." Angie finally agreed to go up to room 201 of the Senate Building and take the secretarial test, which she passed easily. She was placed in the steno pool and took dictation from all the agents who were doing the investigations. By the end of 1955 the committee's purview extended into the activities of labor unions, and Bobby found he would need a new secretary. Carmine urged Bob to talk to Angie.

Angie was busy working at her desk when she suddenly realized that Bob Kennedy was standing in front of her. "Oh, hello," she said, immediately suspicious.

"Maggie is leaving and I want you to be my secretary," said Bobby with a tone that was more of an order than a question.

"Oh. Well," replied Angie, "I will have to think about that."

Bobby looked at her for a brief moment. "You have to think about it? It is either yes or no, and it can't be no."

Startled, Angie stared at him. She was not one to be pushed around. "Well, then the answer is no."

Bobby's blue eyes glinted with the slightest hint of amusement. "Well, you are hired anyway." With that, he turned to leave.

Not wanting him to get in the last word, Angie called after him, "Now wait, if in two or three months you don't like it, you can fire me, or if I don't like you, I can quit."

"Fine," said Bobby, shrugging.

Angie recalled almost thirty years later to Michael Kennedy, "We never discussed it again. I was too busy and so was he." Their relationship, begun with the edge of such playfully caustic communication, lasted throughout the rest of Bobby's life, ending, suddenly, in June 1968. Over the years, Angie would move from her beginnings in the committee's secretarial pool to become Bobby's constant and ever-vigilant sentinel at the gate of his office and professional life. She sums up the often whirlwind working relationship between the two of them in her characteristically direct and to-the-point manner: "It was just wonderfully busy and hectic. He had a wonderful sense of humor, which is why we got along so well. I wouldn't have missed a moment of it."

7

TRIAL RUN: 1956 AND THE RUN FOR THE VICE PRESIDENCY

In a moment of triumphant defeat, his campaign
for the Presidency was born.

—JAMES MACGREGOR BURNS

John F. Kennedy never meant to run for vice president, and Bobby Kennedy and Kenny O'Donnell never meant to help him. But in the confusion of the 1956 Democratic convention, the first-term senator from Massachusetts suddenly found himself a national figure, when he very nearly became Adlai Stevenson's running mate in his second campaign against Dwight Eisenhower for the White House. The prospect of victory for the nomination was followed quickly by a hair breadth defeat. But as Kenny, Bobby, and Jack himself would soon recognize, the loss was itself a victory.

During the first four years of his term in the Senate, John F. Kennedy had garnered a reputation as an up-and-coming, post–New Deal Democrat. He had also married Jacqueline Bouvier, and the two of them were already becoming a glamorous public couple on the Washington scene. He and Kenny were already planning Jack's 1958 reelection campaign, which they intended to win by a large margin, in their continuing and slowly escalating effort to make Jack a national figure. Kenny was now working for a public relations firm but spent most of his time running the Kennedy state organization.

In August of 1956, Bobby, Kenny, and Jack gathered in Chicago for the convention where Democrats would select a slate that would have the daunting task of trying to defeat a popular incumbent president. Along with introducing the thirty-nine-year-old senator to a national television audience, the Kennedy team aimed to use the convention to solidify their own base in Massachusetts. Thanks to his chief lieutenants, Larry O'Brien and Kenny O'Donnell, Jack had recently won an impressive victory over the Massachusetts political organization. They had battled to replace William "Onions" Burke as chairman of the convention delegation. Burke had come to resent the young senator and was a consistent source of problems for Jack. Initially Jack had wanted to replace him with another young Irishman, Dick Donahue, who later would go to work in the White House with Charles U. Daly, another Kennedy lieutenant from Chicago. But according to Kenny, "It was clear that Dick simply couldn't be elected because he was too young and inexperienced and not part of the political crowd. So the decision was made to go for Pat Lynch." Lynch, the small, bald mayor of Somerville, who favored wide-brimmed hats and velvet-collared coats, was exactly the kind of Irishman that Jack and Bobby had worked hard to distance from their organization. When Kenny first brought Lynch to meet Jack at his Bowdoin Street apartment, Jack was shocked. Calling Kenny into the bathroom of the tiny two-bedroom apartment, he asked, "You didn't make a commitment to this guy, did you?" "Not yet," replied Kenny with some amusement. "Well, don't," responded Kennedy. Kennedy pressed Kenny to promote Dick Donahue, who was the young Henry Fonda type that Jack thought would exemplify his future-oriented attitudes. But as Kenny, ever savvy in his analysis of a political situation, knew from experience, Jack had to settle for Lynch.

When Bobby asked Kenny to come to Chicago, no one knew that Jack had any interest in the number two spot. "Bobby and I never discussed it with any seriousness," Kenny said later. The only hint that Jack could get the number two spot was a column in the Chicago *Sun-Times* mentioning Kennedy as a possible dark horse candidate whose youth and region could benefit Adlai Stevenson's presidential bid. Arriving in Chicago, they went to the penthouse apartment kept by Peter Lawford, the actor, who had married Jack's sister Pat in 1954. Kenny was disappointed when Bobby announced he didn't want to stay in such opulent surroundings and decided that the two of them would share a room at the Ambassador East Hotel.

Kennedy's recorded narration of the opening-night documentary on the party's history gave wings to the talk about his taking a place on the national ticket. After the film was shown, he appeared on the platform before the crowd and received an extended standing ovation. "Suddenly there seemed to be this feeling that Jack Kennedy was the man to be vice president," Kenny recalled. "The delegates would say, 'Where is he? Can I meet him? Isn't he attractive? Can I get an autograph — he's so good-looking.' Suddenly it seemed to me he was a force at the convention." Kennedy's youth and vigor appealed to the convention, which was one of the first to be televised nationwide; with his easy grin and assured good looks, he came across quite well to the viewers at home.

After Stevenson easily won renomination against New York governor Averell Harriman and Tennessee senator Estes Kefauver, his decision to let the convention select his running mate threw the gathering into a frenzy. Stevenson's lieutenants, according to Kenny, were worried that if they didn't choose Jack Kennedy as their vice presidential nominee, they would lose support and credibility with Catholic and ethnic voters. They decided to throw the convention open. "The logic of the party bosses was, throw the convention open, let it be decided on the floor, and we will defeat Kennedy on the floor," Kenny said. "After all, if Kennedy is anything like his old man, he will not get into a fight he can't win. He will recognize he can't win a floor fight and he will stay clear."

Jack made his decision quickly. Turning to Bobby, he said, "Call Dad and tell him I'm going for it!" Bobby found Kenny and the two retreated to Jack's room, where Bobby called the ambassador, who was vacationing with Rose on the French Riviera. They had all discussed the possibility beforehand, with Joe Sr. making it clear he opposed the idea of Jack's being on the ticket. Stevenson, he thought, would lose; voters didn't connect with him as a candidate and were generally satisfied with Eisenhower. But because Jack would be the first Catholic on a national ticket since Al Smith had lost badly in 1928, he could be blamed for the loss. Thus, being Stevenson's running mate would do his national prospects no good at all. The logic, at the time, had seemed sound to the Kennedy team. But now that the opportunity had actually arisen, the competitive Kennedy spirit could not resist the challenge. "Bobby placed the phone call to the ambassador's home on the French Riviera, by no means an enviable assignment," said Kenny. "Jack had disappeared. When the calls came through, the ambassador's blue language flashed all over the room. The connection was broken before he was finished. Bobby, relieved, quickly hung up the telephone and made no effort to get his father back on the line. 'Whew,' said Bobby, letting out a sigh of relief that it was over. 'Is he mad!' "

Rose, sitting in the room with the ambassador, was reluctant to call his language "blue"; she preferred the word "emphatic." "He felt sure," Rose wrote later, "that Jack was being very shortsighted and he did say so, quite vigorously."

"I listened to his father's conversation with Bobby," Kenny remembered. "I was in the room. You got a real sense of the difference. Bobby's father was not parochial. He was more worldly than we were. He was not caught up in the moment and could see the big picture that we were simply not able to see. We were not sophisticated enough, too parochial and too young, frankly."

Immediately Jack sent Bobby and Kenny into action to woo as many delegates as possible to the Kennedy cause. From the start they were short of time, lacking in organization, and unfamiliar with many of the major players who controlled delegate votes. "Bobby and I ran around like a couple of nuts and tried to make believe we were busy," Kenny said later. The question was, of course, whom could they talk to? Like Jack Kennedy himself, both men were less than chummy with the bosses who could influence or supply delegates, so they immediately tried to talk to various congressmen and senators they knew from Washington. That was itself a valuable lesson, for in most cases legislators had little influence over the conventioneers; in fact it was the governors who controlled these things. "It was a joke," Kenny said. "We didn't know two people in the whole place. It was John Kennedy by himself doing the work. Pat Lynch knew more people than any of us. He didn't like Estes

Kefauver, and he [Kefauver] had captured the enthusiasm of the galleries and the delegates" and was now the convention favorite. Many others shared Lynch's antipathy for the often self-righteous Tennessee senator.

At the height of the frenzy, Kenny was standing on the convention floor with Senator Albert Gore, Sr., from Tennessee and watched helplessly as Tennessee signaled to House Speaker Sam Rayburn, the chairman of the convention, that it wanted to switch its votes. It announced it had shifted its votes from favorite son Gore to Kefauver. That was enough to give Kefauver the momentum he needed to put him over the top.

Lack of time, knowledge, and preparation had handicapped the Kennedy team from the beginning. Jack—as Bobby knew and Kenny was fast learning—hated to lose anything. Kenny and Bobby went over to see him immediately. "Bobby sat down across from him and said, 'You know you are the luckiest man in America!' " Kenny remembered. "The whole tenor of Bobby's conversation was to joke, in case Jack was down, which is what the Kennedys always do in moments of crisis and hardship. In moments of crisis that Kennedy wry humor is at its best. Jack seemed upset, mad much more than he was concerned. But he was more angry than anything, because the Kennedys first of all hate to lose. And, secondly, Jack felt that he may have been 'jobbed' out of the election, which was something that he couldn't stomach, to lose in that manner.

"I will say after Bobby and I talked with him for a while, I got the feeling that he didn't feel it was the crisis of his life, that he had done better out of the convention than he expected to and, most importantly, lessons would be learned for the next time. When we left he was doing reasonably well. He was concerned but not upset. Before we left, Bobby outlined everything that had happened from beginning to end . . . so that we could all get a sense of what had gone wrong and what we would learn for the next time through. By the time Bobby was through, he was in agreement with Bobby and me that this had not been the worst thing that ever happened to him. And that Bobby was probably correct—he was the 'luckiest man in America.' "

As soon as the convention ended, Jack took off to the French Riviera to join his irate father. Jackie headed to Newport, where she would lose the baby she had been carrying; Jack would join her there. Later, he would crisscross the country campaigning for the Stevenson-Kefauver ticket, paying his dues with the party faithful, building a reputation, and courting the politicos whom he had needed for the vice-presidential nomination and knew he would need again.

"Bobby and I flew back on the same plane," Kenny said. "We saw Helen, and then Bobby left to go to the Cape. Within a short period of time Bobby called me and asked Helen and me to bring the kids and come down to the Cape. Purely social. Helen and I went down to the Cape and spent a few days with Ethel and Bobby—very nice, relaxing. Sailing, football; talk politics, argue, the usual. It was at this time when we were all together that we received the news that Jackie had lost the baby. She was in Newport. We were trying to locate the senator. Bobby was upset, because he had been concerned. Bobby and I then got in the car, leaving Ethel and Helen, and drove to Newport. Bobby and I stayed with Jackie for two or three days. Jack wasn't back and Bobby wanted us to be with her during this difficult time.

"We stayed at Jackie's house until the funeral of the child. It would have been the first one; it was called only baby girl Kennedy. The child was born and there was a funeral. Bobby handled all the arrangements. When he arrived, we left and went back to Hyannisport and rejoined our wives. We were very worried. Jackie was much sicker than anyone realized publicly; she was very, very sick." Ultimately, Kenny said, "Ethel and Helen talked to their friends, as girls do probably get more information than Bobby and I ever could have. The consensus from the girls and elsewhere was increasingly that Jack Kennedy, well, that Bobby had been right . . . Jack Kennedy was the luckiest man alive to have lost that convention."

Bobby had agreed, at his brother and father's suggestion, to take time off to travel with Stevenson. Just as he had that afternoon in Chicago, Bobby believed that the Democratic ticket would go down in flames, but he wanted to learn how to run a presidential campaign. He learned the opposite. Stopping once with the campaign in Boston that fall, Bobby met Kenny for a drink. "You wouldn't believe it," he told his friend. "This is the most disastrous operation you ever saw!" For Bobby, the Stevenson campaign would basically become a lesson in how not to run for president. He would remember it in 1960. And in the meantime he would be glad that on behalf of his brother he had failed that hectic convention week in Chicago.

In 1956, Kenny O'Donnell was living on hope. After Adlai Stevenson lost and the nation settled back for four more years of a grandfatherly Republican presidency, he was looking ahead. The defeat at the Chicago convention was also a promise. Dave Powers told him what Jack had said that Thanksgiving at Hyannisport: "With only about four hours of work and a handful of supporters, I came within thirty-three and a half votes of winning the vice presidential nomination," he said, smiling. "If I work hard for four years, I ought to be able to pick up all the marbles."

For Kenny, four years was a long way off. He was biding his time, waiting for the call. Unlike some of his friends from Harvard, including Jimmy Kenary and Nick Rodis, he was not out there hustling a career for himself, going step by step up the ladder at some corporate job. He had not finished law school. Though Helen didn't say it, he knew she wished that he would finish his degree and get a regular job.

He had committed himself to politics and the Kennedys, because he had always loved politics and because the Kennedys had the money and needed his brains, savvy, and toughness. Politics — the rough-and-tumble of getting things done — had fascinated him from the time he hung around the corner store arguing politics with his father's friends in Worcester. His arguments with his strong-minded father had toughened him and given him endurance. Politics, his father had told him, was not that different from football. He was right. What had brought them so close in Chicago was the team, the combination they could come up with against the odds.

Next time with the right team, the right organization, and the right timing, Jack was right, Kenny knew — they could win the whole game. They wouldn't go for second prize. They would have formidable obstacles, from Jack Kennedy's youth to his Catholicism, but with Bobby calling the plays they could capture the White House.

After the convention Kenny went to Worcester and had lunch with Jimmy Kenary. Kenary remembers the day very well. "Kenny came in and sat down and said, 'Jimmy, we are running in 1960!' I looked him straight in the face; I was stunned. 'Wait a minute, Kenny, what about the Catholic issue? I mean, you just lost! Are you crazy?' Kenny gave me a cold stare and said, 'Look, losing was the best thing for us!'

"I couldn't believe what I was hearing and I thought all this political stuff was going to his head. Kenny, you have got to be crazy. How can it be good to lose?" Letting out a sigh of frustration at my obvious naiveté, he said, 'Dammit, Squash Head, Jack is the most logical choice for '60. If he came that close at the last minute, even with the Catholic issue, then with some time, organization, and money he can go over the top. It's all very logical, and it's pretty clear really.'

"I was blown away, and of course his analysis turned out to be exactly correct. This was only 1956, so it was hard to imagine the scenario, but he and Bobby could already see how it would play out. To be able to make that kind of prediction and know what was going to happen— that was how he and Bobby planned, from 1956 forward. I really do think it all started with Memorial Hall in 1948. I saw that debate. I think they were thinking about it even then."

"We were back in Hyannisport," Kenny remembered. "The senator and Jackie were there. This was sometime after the baby had died. Helen and I were back visiting Ethel and Bobby for a weekend. Bobby and I went over to see the senator. He was sunning himself on the porch. Some of the girls were there—Jackie, Ethel, and Helen, especially Ethel and Helen chasing various kids, both mine and Bobby's. We all were discussing the situation in general. Jackie went to lie down. We were discussing Jackie's physical condition, which was now improving. The senator then began discussing the political situation. He reviewed the convention and its aftermath. He began to, in fact, muse out loud what his future course was. He explained how he was receiving thousands and thousands of invitations to speak. His mail had tripled. Many of the letters were from people who felt he had been 'jobbed' out of the number two spot. These letters were from all over the country, and they would tell him how great he was and how they would be for him no matter what he ran for. Up until that moment, except upon a rare occasion, he had never received any letters from anywhere else; now he was receiving letters from everywhere. It was such a volume that he had to increase and change his office staff. Bobby participated to some degree. I simply listened. He talked aloud to himself and then to Bobby, but he obviously had his mind made up": He would seek the White House in 1960.

8

※◇※

THE RACKETS COMMITTEE

It seems to me imperative that we reinstill in ourselves the tough-
ness and idealism that guided our nation in the past.

—BOBBY KENNEDY,
THE ENEMY WITHIN

Journalist Clark Mollenhoff summed up Bobby Kennedy's labor racket investigation the following way: "The Teamsters' power was feared in politics. The Teamsters had the money, the muscle, and the audacity to find ways to control city, county, state, and federal political campaigns. No history of American labor can be written that does not include an account of the dramatic nine-year period in which a stern-faced senator from Arkansas and a . . . boyish-appearing . . . young millionaire lawyer from Boston rocked the world of politics and labor."

Bobby Kennedy and his investigation were opposed on all sides, including those sectors of the labor movement vocally opposed to the Teamsters' corruption. Union leaders George Meany and Walter Reuther both objected strongly to Kennedy's investigation. As Kenny recalled, "They felt that government should leave labor unions alone and that it was up to them to clean up their own problems. So there was no individual interest of theirs in this committee, except to be opposed to [the fact] that they were allowing the beasts of management and business, their ancient enemies, to at last have a vehicle to use to impose legislation on them, which under another plan they could not do. So they opposed the committee in general, they opposed the committee intellectually as a body, and mostly they opposed Robert Kennedy."

When Robert Kennedy hurried back to his hotel room at the Palmer House on a cold, snowy evening in December 1956, his arms laden with files and documents, he could not have imagined that he was about to begin the most thorough and exhaustive investigation into the labor movement that had ever been done. "Toward the end of January 1957," Robert Kennedy wrote in his book *The Enemy Within,* "a move developed to create a 'select bipartisan committee' with four Senators from the Labor Committee and four from our Committee [the Permanent Subcommittee on Investigations]. The McClellan Committee was set up and was specifically given jurisdiction to look into matters involving corrupt influences in the labor-management relations. A select committee is set up for a specific period of time; it goes out of existence after it has performed its function, whereas a regular committee continues year after year." The McClellan Committee was specifically set up to address the question of jurisdiction, which both the union and the Republicans were using either delay Robert Kennedy's investigation or simply refuse to answer questions posed by the committee, claiming the original committee lacked jurisdiction. "The select committee was established and went into operation on the thirty-first of January 1957. The original members were McClellan, Ives, Kennedy, McNamara, McCarthy, Ervin, Mundt and Goldwater." The hearings began on February 26, 1957, and continued through March 1960.

Bobby would describe his work to *Miami News* reporter John Keasler as requiring "persistence, untiring spadework and an intelligent approach—then more legislation to take on the findings." Bobby was described as a "boyish-looking but tough-minded gentleman," who could soon have some three-hundred-pound "hood wriggling like flounder on a gig" while testifying in front of the committee.

Bobby was working with greater assurance than he ever had before. The committee's investigations into Teamsters leaders Dave Beck and Jimmy Hoffa would put both Bobby and Kenny in direct conflict with one of the largest unions in the country, lead them into dangerous, even tragic territory, and win them lifelong allies and friends—men such as United Auto Workers president Walter Reuther, at one time a potential target of the committee—who would become crucial in the election of

1960. "Bobby and Kenny's philosophy of life really showed through during the Hoffa hearings," Sam Adams says. "You get kicked around by
life and you gotta keep moving. Bobby used to say it's like a football
game—you got clobbered last weekend, but you gotta come back this
weekend and fight it out again."

Clark Mollenhoff, a reporter for the *Des Moines Register and Tribune*,
was a big man with wide-set eyes who had been investigating evidence
of graft, corruption, and underworld connections among unions since
1953. Bobby would later describe Mollenhoff as "perhaps the nation's
best-informed reporter into the field of labor-management corruption."
Mollenhoff had watched both House and Senate committees threaten
to take on the giant union but inevitably fall victim to the political clout
of the Teamsters and their charismatic leader Jimmy Hoffa. Mollenhoff
liked Bobby Kennedy's fierce style and reputation for determination. But
could he convince Kennedy that his committee had the jurisdiction to
investigate labor corruption and that the fight was worth the effort?
"Those other two congressional investigations were fixed because of political pressure," Mollenhoff insisted to Bobby.

"While the investigation had potential for making the Kennedy name
well known, it also contained great risks. It could just as easily destroy
the political careers of those who meddle with it," Mollenhoff would
write in *Tentacles of Power*, his book about the Teamsters investigation.
"In 1956, I convinced Robert Kennedy of the need for an investigation
of Hoffa, Dave Beck, and other labor officials. Occasionally I taunted
him by questioning his courage to take on such an investigation."

According to Bobby, at the time the select committee was formed in
January 1957, "very few of the Democrats on the Labor Committee were
willing to accept a position on it." Kenny certainly understood the political risks. "At this time the United Auto Workers was totally opposed
to Jimmy Hoffa–type politics and the labor people who had emerged
. . . and were using it for personal gain, like Dave Beck. But their opposition to the government interfering with the conduct of labor unions
was stronger than their dislike or disgust with the Jimmy Hoffa–type
operations."

Bobby's own recollection of how the committee got involved in labor racketeering had less to do with goading by Clark Mollenhoff than with by following one lead that led to another. It disturbed him that Mollen-hoff believed that the Teamsters had the power to fix congressional investigations. Bobby recalled the process in an interview with Wash-ington reporter Kenneth Brodney done on July 2, 1957.

We were the Senate Permanent Subcommittee on Investigations, of which I was Chief Counsel, and Senator McClellan was Chair-man. We had been making an investigation in this matter, held some hearings, and there were those in the Senate that wanted it in the Labor Committee. There was a compromise arrived at and a Senate Select Committee was formed at the end of January, 1957, of which Senator McClellan became Chairman and I became Chief Counsel.

We were investigating procurement, textiles, by the military serv-ices up in New York City. We started back in January of 1955, and there were other investigations included, but we went through 1955 and into 1956. In the course of our Investigation in 1956, we had a man by the name of Kravits . . . and a fellow by the name of Joey Abrams, they had purchased amounts of bonds in fictitious names — about six or seven million worth of bonds, purchased and sold. We were able to determine that they had been making uni-forms in non-union shops in Pennsylvania and New Jersey, that they had been paying for protection, that certain union officials had been running these non-union shops.

The money they were being paid for this protection and for this work with these fictitious bonds — these bonds that were purchased in fictitious names — that some of the individuals [who] were sup-posed to have run these non-union shops were the Dio brothers, Johnny and Tommy Dio. So, we had them down to an executive session about the same time the acid was thrown in [labor reporter] Victor Riesel's eyes, and the District Attorney asked us not to follow up our investigation until they finished their investigation. We waited — and when they finished, the Federal Grand Jury indicted

Dio, [and] we went back in and started anew. From there we branched out. . . . [RFK private papers]

After consulting with McClellan, Bobby decided to at least pursue an inquiry and see where it led. He called Einar Mohn, the assistant to Teamsters official Dave Beck, at the Teamster headquarters—the "marble palace," as it was dubbed, conveniently located kitty-corner from the Senate's own office building—to announce his intentions and to seek their help. Or, as Bobby admitted in his own book about the investigation, "In my naiveté, I called Einar Mohn. . . . At this juncture I had no idea that Dave Beck was corrupt." Bobby recalled Mohn as being "gruff and unresponsive . . . distinctly unfriendly." Mohn made clear that Bob would get no assistance from anyone within the Teamsters Union. He and Carmine Bellino, the extremely efficient tax accountant who would be the key to breaking Beck and Hoffa's schemes, set out for the West Coast to see what the union was up to there; he had already sent investigators to the East and Midwest. Clark Mollenhoff's "Great Investigation" had finally begun.

In early 1957, John Seigenthaler had his hands full leading a seminar at New York's Columbia University on investigative reporting. He had been a reporter for Nashville's *The Tennessean* investigating union corruption and had come to know Sargent Shriver, the husband of Bobby's sister Eunice, who then ran the Kennedy-owned wholesaling company the Merchandise Mart in Chicago and had political ambitions of his own. Seigenthaler wanted to share with Bobby and the Senate investigation the information he had uncovered. Shriver arranged a meeting between Seigenthaler and Bobby Kennedy in New York. Seigenthaler hurried downtown for the meeting and arrived ten minutes early. Entering the office, he immediately encountered Bobby's secretary, Angie Novello, and Bobby Kennedy, who had his overcoat on with its collar turned up and his briefcase in his hand. He glared at Seigenthaler. "You're twenty minutes late," he barked. "Are you southerners always late?" he asked, reminding Seigenthaler why he liked living south of the Mason-Dixon Line.

"I'm not late," John heard himself replying. "I am ten minutes early!"

Kennedy shook his head. "Angie," he asked the woman seated at the table, who seemed a little too serene, Seigenthaler thought, given the tone Kennedy was using with her, "what time was he due here?"

Angie looked at her date book. "Twelve noon, Bob, exactly," she said, looking up with some satisfaction at the stranger.

"Right," Bobby replied.

Seigenthaler felt himself getting annoyed. "Look," he said, reaching into his waistcoat pocket to pull out a small piece of heavy white paper that he held up in front of Bobby. "This note says twelve-thirty and the clock says it is twelve-twenty, so that makes me ten minutes early!" He held it out to Kennedy, who glanced at it and tossed it over at Angie Novello, who discreetly retrieved it.

Bobby shrugged. "Sarge is on central standard time!" Then he laughed, brushing past the stunned reporter. "Talk to Jerry Alderman, the assistant chief counsel, and go over everything you have with him." With that he was gone.

After talking to Alderman, Seigenthaler thought over the incident again as he headed back to Columbia. "What a rich little prick!" he thought to himself. He did not like what he had seen of Bobby Kennedy so far; he doubted he was serious about investigating the labor movement. He didn't think he could work with somebody that arrogant and abrasive and was glad that his association with Kennedy would be limited.

At Bobby's request, Jerry Alderman soon summoned Seigenthaler to Washington, D.C., to deliver a memorandum he had prepared on the Teamsters in Tennessee. Uneasy, he made his way down the maze of marble corridors to room 160 on the first floor of the Old Senate Office Building, where the investigation by the Government Operations Committee had set up shop. His meeting with Alderman was brief; still standing in the cramped reception area, he handed him the memo and asked if there was anything else that they required. "Yeah," said Alderman gruffly, "I'd like some clips that you wrote."

"Fine," Seigenthaler replied. Meeting adjourned, he left to catch the next flight to New York and return to teaching his course at Columbia.

Two weeks later, Alderman summoned him back. When he arrived he was told Alderman was not available, but Mr. O'Donnell would be with him in a moment. "Who the hell is that?" Seigenthaler thought to himself. A few moments later, a young man appeared around the corner. What struck Seigenthaler first were his eyes, which were black and intense, and his army crew cut. He moved with what Seigenthaler thought was great economy of movement, as if he was accomplishing exactly what was necessary and no more. The man stuck out his hand and spoke in a voice softer than John had expected. "Hi. I'm Kenny O'Donnell. Jerry told me you were coming in. Your work is pretty impressive."

Caught off guard by this new staffer's friendly nature, Seigenthaler talked with Kenny amiably for some time about the investigative work he was doing in Tennessee, until Angie Novello interrupted them to inform Kenny he was needed on the phone and told Seigenthaler that Bob would be out in a moment. Just as Bobby entered the room the outer door opened and another young man walked in. Seigenthaler recognized him vaguely as another journalist, someone named Brislin, from Scranton, Pennsylvania, who had also been investigating labor racketeering. Seigenthaler watched as, with no greeting and a wave, Bobby sent Brislin into the inner office behind the closed door. Turning to face Seigenthaler, he said, "I'm tied up right now and don't have time for you. Wait for Jerry Alderman to get back and give him the memo and the clippings. If you need anything else, call me." With that, he left.

John was once again very annoyed, convinced that Bobby Kennedy was not serious about investigating the Teamsters. This investigation would go the way of so many previous ones, with a few useless hearings, a few statements, one or two slightly ruffled feathers, and then disappear.

One spring morning in 1957 at the O'Donnell household in Winthrop, Helen had answered the phone and, amid the clamor of children, said her brief hello to Bobby and then handed the phone to Kenny, who was just headed out the door. Bobby was calling because he needed Kenny's help.

"Thinking of Jack and 1960, I was not anxious to join Bobby on the McClellan Committee; the 1958 [Senate] campaign was going to be an exceptionally tough one because Jack wanted to roll up a tremendous popular vote," Kenny would remember. "I felt this was no time for me to be leaving Massachusetts." Now, as if they were back at the pool table in the Varsity Club, Bobby argued back, telling him, "If this investigation flops, it will hurt Jack in 1958 and in 1960, too." The political pressure was enormous. But Bobby, not Jack, was running this investigation, Kenny countered. "A lot of people think he's the Kennedy who's running the investigation, not me," Bobby claimed. "As far as the public is concerned, one Kennedy is the same as another Kennedy!"

Kenny was still unsure. Things were going well in Massachusetts, and although Kenny was still not officially on staff with Jack Kennedy, he knew the next Senate campaign, if Jack won by the necessary margin, would open the gate for a race to the White House. When Helen learned of the plan over dinner with her husband, she was thrilled at the prospect of moving to Washington; her friend Ethel was already there, and she hated Boston. Bobby was persistent. The investigation had mushroomed and there was much more there than he had first imagined when Clark Mollenhoff and fellow investigative reporter Ed Guthman and others had urged him to get involved.

Bobby was well aware of Kenny's concern for the 1958 campaign, and he had a ready answer. His plan was to have Kenny come down to work on the committee for a year and then return to Boston by June 1958, where he could pick up with Jack's campaign. It was hard to argue with him. The plan made sense. Kenny knew that Bobby was as concerned as he was about Jack's winning big in 1958. And Kenny did have to agree with Bobby that if the investigation blew up in Bobby's face, it was Jack who would feel the repercussions, not Bobby. After all, Jack was the public official. Kenny wanted to wait and talk to Jack, but Bobby insisted Kenny answer now.

Kenny acquiesced. "It was always impossible to say no to Bobby when he wanted you to do something, so I went to Washington as his assistant.

I assumed he had already discussed my departure from Massachusetts with Jack, and that Jack had agreed to it." In the end, Kenny said, as he explained it to Helen, Bobby was right; there was no reason why being away from Massachusetts for a year would hurt anything. He would be back in June, in time for the beginning of the campaign. The Kennedys would have him as their lieutenant in plenty of time, and they'd be in far better shape than they were with their late start in 1952. Helen listened, allowing him to think he was having to convince her. In truth, she needed no convincing.

"I didn't want to go to Washington," Kenny would say later, "but Bobby needed me. He was my friend, and frankly, I wouldn't even have been there if it were not for Bobby. What choice did I have?" Although it would cause some initial conflict with Jack, who would have preferred he stay in Massachusetts, Kenny would manage to be loyal to them both. "I liked them both, I wanted to help them both, but Bobby needed me and he was my friend. He was involved in a dangerous investigation and I could help. That's what you do."

Three weeks had passed since John Seigenthaler had had his third and what he assumed was his last conversation with Bobby Kennedy. One afternoon, he was sitting in the newsroom of the Nashville *Tennessean*, back at work on a new story, when he heard the city editor call out his name. "Yeah," Seigenthaler replied. "Somebody named Kennedy calling you," he was told. When he picked up the phone he heard Bobby Kennedy's I-am-in-charge voice. Surprised, Seigenthaler sat back and, after a minute, stopped typing. For the next forty-five minutes, Bobby asked him such detailed questions that it was evident he had read and remembered everything the reporter had ever written on the subject and understood the case inside out. "I'm sending two investigators to Tennessee tomorrow. Can you meet them and help them?" "Sure, of course I can."

"From that point on," Seigenthaler recalls, "I grew more and more impressed with Bobby Kennedy and I thought the little snot was a great guy, and our relationship warmed tremendously. Who would have guessed?" Years later, in the Justice Department, he would become Bobby's right-hand man.

Bobby told Seigenthaler that his point person on the committee would be Kenny O'Donnell. "Kenny was the most effective, most efficient administrative assistant at the McClellan Committee," Seigenthaler would say later, giving his own version of Kenny's title. "Kenny had thirty-odd investigators to keep track of. I marveled at his ability to keep track of them all; he wrote nothing down. He kept it all in his head." The photographic memory that had allowed him to memorize bomb coordinates, skip classes at Harvard, and remember the name of every Kennedy secretary in Massachusetts was now more useful than ever.

His life in Washington, D.C., would connect him with Bobby and Ethel socially and also with his family. Helen also thrived in these early years in Washington. It took her away from her parents, which she enjoyed more than she cared to admit, and it brought her into a new circle of friends. Living in Winthrop, she had felt alone across the bay from Boston. The O'Donnell children spent a great deal of time with the Kennedys at the family estate, Hickory Hill, which, with a staff to watch over them, meant Helen, Ethel, and their other friends had the time to go shopping and out to lunch. There were dinners at Hickory Hill, the two couples sitting around the pool, and Kenny would challenge Bobby to a sit-up contest or the two men would toss a football around, talking politics. The two political wives grew even closer. Kenny's sister, who also visited, remembered that "when we would arrive, Ethel would immediately grab Helen by the arm and they would disappear into the party, laughing like two schoolgirls."

Angie Novello recalls this of Kenny's arrival at the select committee's cramped offices: "All I remember is, one day he came, everything was organized, and suddenly I could lift my head! I don't know how he did it, how he kept track of everything. That was the beauty; I never had to worry about it after that. I had enough to do keeping track of Bob Kennedy, and that was no easy task sometimes."

"Kenny had total access to Bob," Seigenthaler says. "He had an emotional security that I hadn't seen before and I thought was very impressive. I guess it was because they knew each other for so long. He was unflappable and had a great sense of Irish, self-deprecating humor. He was always laughing or making fun of himself. He and Bob could be very funny together. It was kind of refreshing."

Their humor would temper what was very serious, politically risky work. Bobby, John Seigenthaler, Kenny, and some others were gathered at Bobby's Virginia home, Hickory Hill, one afternoon, preparing for more hearings. The phone rang and Kenny answered it. After a few moments of brief conversation, Kenny rejoined Bobby and the others in Ethel's vast dining room, where he told Bobby that the Associated Press had called to report that the attorney for one alleged underworld figure had described him as, among other things, "a sadistic little monster." Then Kenny added, "I think you ought to sue him. You're not so little!"

Bobby stared at Kenny for a moment, then shook his head. "This is my statement," responded Bobby, deadpan: "I am not so little."

"Bob and Kenny had a good, close relationship," Seigenthaler says. "Different people find genius in different ways. Bob Kennedy recognized Kenny's genius and knew how to use it. Kenny's genius was simply that his mind worked like a computer. In the same way that you punch names into a computer, he logged them in his mind—who they were, where they were, and what their relationships were. He could recall something that Walter Reuther said in a meeting, verbatim! It was just amazing. He never took notes, ever. It was all in his head. He knew the good guys from the bad guys, the white hats from the black hats. He knew who the no-brainers were, who the intellectuals were. And sometimes the no-brainers to him were just as far off the wall as the intellectuals. He had the best-balanced wheel of anybody I had ever seen. The result was that he became crucial to Bob Kennedy and later the president, because he kept them on balance, he had the guts to say what had to be said, and they knew it and appreciated it and they used it."

Back in late 1956, *Seattle Times* reporter Ed Guthman was beginning to think that there was strong evidence linking Teamsters official Dave Beck to union corruption. And there was much more to the Dave Beck story than he had originally thought. "By the autumn of 1956 Clark Mollenhoff and I had been exchanging information about the Teamsters

Union for several years," Guthman remembers. "One afternoon Clark called from Washington, D.C., and said that a Senate committee was going to investigate corruption in the labor movement. 'I've suggested,' said Clark, 'they start with Dave Beck. A young lawyer from the committee is coming out to see you.' 'Who is he?' I asked, skeptical. I had seen committees come and go, especially when it came to investigating Dave Beck and the Teamsters, so I was more than a little wary. 'Bob Kennedy,' said Clark. I said nothing. I knew who Bob Kennedy was — well, I knew he was Senator Kennedy's brother. But that was not why I sat in silence. Clark waited, finally filling that silence. 'He is Senator Kennedy's brother.' 'That's fine, Clark,' I said, 'but can you trust him?'

"Bob arrived in Seattle a few days later under an assumed name," Guthman says. "Openly challenging Dave Beck in Seattle was a tough undertaking and somewhat risky," Guthman says, more than forty years later. "More important was the fact that we had developed informants within the union whose identity had to be protected." Ed wasn't willing to risk the safety of those informants until he was sure that Kennedy was serious. As they sat at dinner that evening, Bob explained in great detail what he was looking for and how he hoped to succeed. He made it clear he needed Guthman's and his informants' help.

Guthman and *Seattle Times* managing editor Russell McGrath would base their decision to trust Bobby Kennedy on two things — "partly our realization that we had gone about as far as we could go in exposing Beck and partly because of the sincerity which Bob imparted."

The key to the Beck case would be the two informants that Guthman was most concerned about — union men who were taking tremendous risks in helping Guthman and now Kennedy. From the start, Guthman wanted Bobby's word that their identities would be protected. Bobby later explained that as far as the public was concerned the informants were "mystery men" whom he didn't want to identify, but without whom "great investigation" work could not have been done.

"Bob kept his word to us completely," Guthman says. "Besides protecting the identity of our informants, we wanted to be sure that the committee would not skim the surface and hold a few highly publicized hearings, but that it would dig deeply for proof of the dishonesty which we believed existed, have the courage to make it public, and then work for remedial legislation. Bob did just that." Twelve years later, it would strike Guthman as surprising that he ever wondered about whether he should trust Bob Kennedy. "Bob's courage and his humor—the jokes, the mistakes, and the good times—come through. Bob could do anything he set his mind on. He left us a bond of friendship and a standard of courage that urges us on."

Since the army/McCarthy hearings, Bobby had come to depend on Carmine Bellino's genius with figures. "An ordinary chief counsel of a congressional committee would be delighted to be able to conduct three or four public hearings a year," Bellino said, but Bobby Kennedy was different. "During the labor-management investigations he held as many as twenty to twenty-five different group hearings in a year. Anyone on Capitol Hill who has knowledge of the workings of congressional committees will tell you that Bob Kennedy was the hardest-working and best chief counsel that ever operated on the Hill." Bellino himself was able to establish that altogether Beck had embezzled over $350,000 from the Teamsters Union," said veteran investigator Walter Sheridan.

His first trip west with Bobby taught Bellino a lot about his chief counsel. "Bob and I once flew from Seattle to Minneapolis, arriving at six on a Sunday morning. We had very little sleep on the plane and we were anxious to get to our room at the Curtis Hotel. Nevertheless, after checking our bags at the hotel, we went first to the nearest Catholic church to attend 7:00 A.M. Mass. The church was not crowded and we sat at a pew about midway. When the priest walked onto the altar, Bob noted he was without an altar boy. Without hesitation, he walked down the aisle toward the altar, jumped over the railing, and served Mass."

Bellino's colleague Walter Sheridan had sparkling eyes and a deceptively cherubic face behind which was a sharp mind and a steel will. When he first met Bobby Kennedy he was employed by the FBI. He had come to room 160 of the Old Senate Office Building for a job interview and waited for some time outside the counsel's inner office, behind the closed door. Finally, the door to the sanctum opened and out came Bobby Kennedy, his sleeves rolled up, tie askew. To Sheridan he seemed thin, gaunt, almost too young for this job. "His eyes were impressive as he sized me up," Sheridan remembered. After a brief handshake and a few pleasantries, Bobby walked out of the office and motioned for Walter to follow. "I never stopped from that moment on, and by the time we reached the top, the interview was over and I was hired. It was to be that way so many, many times over the next eleven years — talking in motion." That was the Bobby Kennedy everyone would come to know. "I think most of my conversations with him were in motion — walking, on elevators, in cars on the way to airports." Often, recalled Sheridan, "it was the best way to catch him, and he somehow seemed more relaxed when he was going someplace."

When you worked for Bobby, you learned your lessons quickly and learned them once, as Sheridan had discovered, along with other new staffers like journalist Pierre Salinger. On his first day on the job, Sheridan recounted, "I was told to go to Chicago to help Pierre Salinger with the investigation of Nathan Shefferman," a potential target of Bobby's inquiry. "One of the girls made a reservation for me on the noon flight. . . . The following morning I was in the file room, going through Shefferman files. Bob came in. He looked startled to see me. 'I thought you were going to Chicago?' " Walter nodded quickly: "Yes, I am going on the noon flight." Bob stared at Walter for a moment and gave him an impatient look, finally saying, "I never go anywhere at noon. It wastes the whole day!" From that point forward, neither Walter nor anyone else who worked for Bob Kennedy went anywhere at noon.

Walter Sheridan and his wife, Nancy, would become close friends of Bobby and Ethel's as well as Kenny and Helen's. Nancy Sheridan and Walter helped Helen find her and Kenny's first home in Washington when the couple headed down to work on the committee in 1958. They chose a small ranch-style home in a cul-de-sac, not far from the Sheridans, one of several homes they would occupy through 1964. For the next several years, the Sheridan and O'Donnell children would easily race in and out of each other's homes. The husbands, working together on the committee, often commuted to the Capitol together, which allowed the wives to have a car to use at home. Helen and Nancy became close friends.

Walter Sheridan would go to work for Bobby Kennedy as an investigator on some of his most important cases, not just when Bobby was chief counsel but for the rest of Bobby's life. When he died he would take "a vast storehouse of information" with him, said Kennedy sister Pat Lawford. Only Kenny O'Donnell might have known more secrets.

George Lodge, assistant secretary of labor, had strong opinions about what Bobby Kennedy was up to. "I had never met him. I had read what he was doing and was convinced that in pursuing evil that a few had committed, he was tarnishing the entire labor movement. I wanted to talk to him about it. So I called up unannounced and unintroduced and asked for an appointment."

Lodge headed up to the Old Senate Office Building. Bobby was seated in a little room off the reception area, a makeshift conference room with a long table. "Bob was sitting there at the end of the table, surrounded by books and papers. He was in his shirt sleeves with two telephones clapped to his ears, barking away at whoever it was, switching over from one phone to the other," Lodge remembers. "I stood in the doorway and shifted as you do, one foot to another, waiting. Finally Bob looked up with those eyes and barked, 'Who the heck are you?' Startled, I replied, 'I am George Lodge.' 'Fine, what do you want?' growled Bobby."

Lodge began quickly, regaining his composure. "Well, I am concerned that your pursuit of these corrupt labor leaders will tarnish the entire American labor movement." Bob stared at Lodge in apparent disbelief for a moment. "Then," Lodge says, "I distinctly recall, he let out a string of expletives, which ended with the line, or amounted to saying, 'Get the hell out of here! I am busy—you are bothering me!' 'Fine,' I said. I was quite put off by his response."

Lodge turned to leave the doorway, which he had never gotten past, when he heard Bobby say, "Hey, wait a minute. What are you doing Sunday?" He turned around, completely caught off guard, and said, "Well, nothing much. Why?"

Bobby smiled the first smile Lodge had seen thus far. "Why don't you come out to Hickory Hill and play touch football?" Then with a mischievous twinkle in his blue eyes he said, "You can captain the losing team!" Never one to not take up a challenge, Lodge immediately accepted.

"Of course," recalls Lodge, "we lost; in fact, we lost quite regularly, until in 1961 I was able to get my revenge!" When John Kennedy replaced Eisenhower in the White House, Lodge was asked to stay on in his post, which he did. He and his wife, Nancy, became regulars out at Hickory Hill for dinner and as guests at Ethel's famous parties. "It was early 1961, I was flying back from Los Angeles and who should I find myself sitting next to but Rafer Johnson. He was the decathlon champion, who had just won a gold medal at the Olympics. We got chatting and so I asked him, 'What are you doing in Washington?' Rafer explained, 'Well, it is one of the president's physical fitness weekends.' A thought flashed into my head: 'What are you doing on Sunday?'"

"Sunday?" asked Johnson. He thought for a moment. "Well, nothing really. Why?"

"Well," Lodge said, barely containing his glee, "how would you like to play some touch football?"

"That would be wonderful," Johnson replied. "Where?"

Lodge grinned. "At Robert Kennedy's house!"

That Friday night Lodge called Bobby at home. "Bobby," he said coyly, "there is this fella in town and I would like to bring him to the game on Sunday. Is that okay?"

"Sure, no problem—you're going to lose anyway!" was Bobby's quick answer.

On Sunday Lodge picked up Johnson at his hotel, and they headed out to Hickory Hill. As they drove up, Bobby was standing on the lawn of Hickory Hill, smiling, in his shorts, with no shirt on, throwing the football up in the air and catching it, looking very cocky. When Lodge pulled into the driveway, Bobby stopped, long enough to see who was in the front seat with him.

"His face," Lodge recalled, "turned to granite. The smile was gone and the football game was forgotten. Anger swept over his face. He ran up to the car, and as we got out he said, "George Lodge, you son of a bitch!"

Lodge simply grinned. "Bobby, let me introduce you to my friend."

"I know who the hell he is!"

Rafer Johnson stood there, watching the friends, completely mystified. "That," said Lodge, "was the only time my team ever won on a Sunday!"

Pierre Salinger was another journalist Bobby had brought under his wing, along with Clark Mollenhoff and Ed Guthman. He too would become an integral member of the Kennedy team. Salinger was writing for *Collier's* magazine about the Teamsters, Dave Beck, and Jimmy Hoffa, when he saw a headline about a new Senate investigation that would change his life. Senator John McClellan was about to convene the Senate Select Committee on Improper Activities in the Labor-Management Field. "It was the precise area in which I was working," Salinger says. The article went on to announce that McClellan had chosen Robert F. Kennedy as his chief counsel.

Salinger had never met Bobby or John Kennedy, but he flew from New York to Washington to meet the young chief counsel. He and Bobby hit it off immediately over a two-hour lunch in the Senate dining room. However, Salinger had originally sought out Bobby in the hope of getting information for his *Collier's* article. "Instead," says Salinger, "I spent most of the two hours answering his questions about Dave Beck and Jimmy Hoffa. It wasn't until the very end I was able to elicit from him the information about when the committee would hold its hearings." The first hearings were scheduled for February, perfect for Pierre's article. Kennedy struck Salinger "as a man who wasted neither time nor words and was determined to pursue the investigation no matter where it led."

When *Collier's* magazine folded shortly before Christmas 1956, Salinger got a call from Bobby Kennedy, who wanted to know what he was going to do with the material the journalist had prepared on Teamsters for his now moot article. Pierre told Bob that the committee was welcome to his records. "A day or two" after, Salinger remembers, "Carmine Bellino, the brilliant chief accountant, and investigator Paul

Tierney" arrived at his office and went through his materials. In February 1957 Bobby finally pulled Salinger all the way into the committee, hiring him as an investigator. On his first day, Salinger got a stern warning from both McClellan and Kennedy not to talk to the press. His first full day on the committee included dinner at the Kennedy home, and the next morning Pierre was on a plane bound for Seattle to join Bellino, who was busy tearing through Dave Beck's finances. Salinger would become an essential member of the Kennedy team.

He and Kenny O'Donnell quickly grew to be close professional associates. Like John Seigenthaler, Salinger would be awed at how much information Kenny could keep orderly in his head. It was remarkable. "Kenny was the traffic cop. He was Bob's executive assistant and he was the guy that kept track of everything, where the investigators were and what they were working on, and kept a central system for Bob on investigations."

They would also become very close personally, as Salinger recounted. "I would say that of all the guys that I associated with during the whole Kennedy years, my association with Ken O'Donnell was the closest. . . . It suffered, it's gone through traumatic periods, because Kenny's a very tough guy and he's not an uncritical guy. We've had our fights, but I think we've emerged from that probably stronger friends than I am with anybody else in the whole crew. . . . I got the impression he was more than anything Robert Kennedy's guy, to tell you the truth." In the end, Salinger adds, "I guess we were all Robert Kennedy's guys."

While Kenny and Bobby were in Washington chasing Dave Beck and Jimmy Hoffa, the Harvard guys were settling into comfortable and successful careers. They kept in touch with Kenny and Bobby and often got together with them when they were in Washington. As the hearings escalated and the real dangers of Jimmy Hoffa and the machinations of the Teamsters were exposed, their friends from school were concerned. They were worried that Kenny and Bobby didn't understand how dangerous Hoffa and his racketeer friends really were. "We were worried that Kenny and Bobby didn't really know who they were screwing with,"

Wally Flynn says. Several friends tried to communicate their warnings; they called Kenny and told him to be careful and even to "back off" a little bit. After all, these guys were mobsters.

Another football friend, Vinnie Morivac, who had captained the team and who Kenny had terrorized on several occasions, now worked in labor relations for Bethlehem Steel, representing management in negotiations with the steelworkers' union. Someone had pulled Vinnie aside and said, "Hey, you know, Hoffa's had people hit before—tell that Kennedy kid to back off or he'll end up in the river." Concerned, Vinnie called on Kenny when he was in Washington and passed along the warning. "He told Kenny because that was something none of us would have said directly to Bobby," says Adams. "They wouldn't have told Bobby, because Bobby would have thought they were being cowards to even raise it with him." Vinnie told Kenny that he believed Bobby should know about the risks. Kenny's response, according to Sam Adams, was classic O'Donnell: "Hey, look, if some jerk threatened me or my family, I can tell you that it wouldn't stop me one bit. In fact, I would be even angrier—redouble my efforts—and I'd make the bastard really sorry!"

Kenny did tell Bobby, who reacted just as his friend had. "After all," says Adams, "you were dealing with these two tough guys who had been in the war, played football and scored winning touchdowns with broken legs, and I will tell you they weren't going to let some creep like Jimmy Hoffa scare them; they were tough, they just didn't scare!"

"Kenny was just as tough as Bob," says Sam Adams. "I mean, that was the basis for a lot of their friendship. A guy like Hoffa, who was in essence screwing his union—that's what really outraged them both. Kenny made it clear that what really outraged him and Bobby was that here was this guy Hoffa who is supposed to be representing the union members and he was sucking them dry and making deals with the companies to give them bargains and deals instead of negotiating properly, giving them sweetheart deals for payoffs." According to Adams, Bob also said that "he and Kenny could think of nothing more despicable than someone who does that—sells out their members."

For Bobby, Dave Beck and Jimmy Hoffa "were just taking it for them-selves and making it worse for the workers." Adams remembers Kenny saying, "It's like a lawyer stealing from the client they have been hired to protect. Beck and Hoffa were put in a position of trust and they turned around and screwed the very people who had trusted them."

"Bob Kennedy was not a foolish man; he understood risk. They both did," says Nick Rodis. However, both Kenny and Bobby made it clear to Sam and the others that they knew how dangerous the work was but felt it was worth it. In a conversation with friends, both men intimated that they believed that somebody had been assigned to "hit" Bobby and take him out of the game. Kenny told Bobby that their lives had been threatened if they didn't back off. Bobby responded that he knew about the threats and that they had to forge ahead anyway. They were willing to pay the consequences. In their position of influence and power, work-ing for the highest regions of the federal government, if they weren't willing to take on people like Beck and Hoffa, then who would be able to? "I mean," Adams says, "they had good judgment, they weren't foolish or reckless, but they felt they could contribute, so they did."

Bobby felt that union members were far more vulnerable than he and that the Senate committee was helpless to provide them real secur-ity against intimidation, assault, and even murder. He believed an "atmosphere of fear" had infected all labor union members in New York; witnesses were growing more and more afraid to testify. The vice president of the Bakers Union had a rock thrown through his window after he testified before the committee. Many were threatened with far worse. Even after the first year of the committee's effort it had become increasingly clear to Bobby that, in his words, "the underworld had become increasingly powerful as a factor in the nation's economy and, second, that this had been accomplished through its active infiltration into so-called legitimate enterprises, businesses and labor unions." Bobby felt that the work of the committee had begun to expose a serious threat.

Victor Riesel wrote a column called "Inside Labor" in which he reg-ularly attacked the Teamsters Union and Jimmy Hoffa. Bobby read Rie-sel's work carefully, following his columns and speeches, as well as potential leads given to him by Riesel. In fact, several times Bobby was the guest columnist in Riesel's place, writing passionately about his frustration with the growing criminal element in the Teamsters Union. Riesel stepped on the toes of many racketeers—among them Jimmy Hoffa and Johnny Dio, who was accused of accosting Riesel on a New York street corner, throwing acid in his eyes, and blinding him for life.

Although Bobby, as Senate counsel, was not able to go after Dio himself, he was able to use the assault against Riesel to go after Jimmy Hoffa and tie Hoffa with Dio and his racketeer friends. As the committee hearings progressed, with Hoffa as a witness, Walter Sheridan said that Bobby began to hone in on the union leader's "relationship to Johnny Dio and efforts by Hoffa to take over Joint Council 16 in New York with the help of Dio and his racketeer friends." As Bobby's questioning grew more and more persistent, Hoffa became more and more difficult to pin down. Sheridan recalled watching from the sidelines as "Hoffa became more and more evasive, claiming over and over again that he could not recall details of his activities with Dio." Bobby was relentless: "You can't remember back—now this is three months ago and you can't remember three months ago whether Johnny Dio was in your room, a man under indictment for throwing acid in Victor Riesel's eyes?" In the kind of response that would become a familiar stance to the public who were watching the hearings, Hoffa was a stone wall: "I cannot remember whether he was or not, as I said . . . I just don't recall." For the remainder of their lives, the battle between Hoffa and Bobby would continue, becoming more and more personal and dangerous.

Johnny Dio, whom Bobby had come to know early in the labor investigations, was not convicted of blinding Riesel. "I'm not optimistic," Bobby remarked after Dio was found not guilty "that things are going to get cleaned up" among the labor unions of New York. When it came to investigating, he said, "I think that you get an atmosphere of cooperation and you do better. I think that the federal government not being able to prosecute Johnny Dio on the acid matter hurt considerably and it's very tough to proceed in the face of that. I don't think these things are ever all cleaned up—it's an atmosphere that leaves it better or worse; now, we're not doing too well. . . . As far as getting information or help from witnesses, the psychological problem is very important. I think it would have been catastrophic if we had started this investigation and ended without at least accomplishing something, or proving something. I think we've done a good deal of that already—I feel a little better about it—but not everything that I wanted to do."

9

"HARDEST OF ALL"—THE 1958 SENATE CAMPAIGN

Change is chance—which, as Pasteur said,
"favors the mind that is prepared."

—BOBBY KENNEDY

In 1958 Jack Kennedy had to "make an impressive show of vote-getting strength in being reelected to the Senate in order to remain in the running as a leading contender for the presidency two years later," Kenny O'Donnell would say. Kennedy had instructed his team to begin planning the 1958 campaign "long in advance, detailing us to work with Pat Lynch, our state committee chairman, in getting fences mended in Massachusetts." This was a race about the White House.

John Trainor, a young Irishman from Worcester, had just taken his bar exam the summer of 1958 and was awaiting the results when he got a call from Francis X. Morrissey, once a "coat holder," or Kennedy hanger-on, for Joseph Kennedy and now an aide-de-camp for Senator Jack Kennedy. Trainor lived a couple of doors down the street from Morrissey and had borrowed the older man's law books when he was studying for the bar exam. Trainor's father had been a friend of Morrissey's from Holy Cross, where he had also known Cleo O'Donnell, Sr. Would Trainor like to spend the summer working for Jack Kennedy? Morrissey asked. Sure, why not? Trainor told him. He didn't know much about Jack Kennedy, but he needed the job while he waited to see if he'd passed the bar.

Trainor went down to the Kennedy campaign headquarters on Tremont Street, right near the Boston Garden. The windows of the headquarters, formerly a high-dollar shoe store, were now filled with life-size photos of young Senator Jack Kennedy, looking sincere and, ideally, presidential. Peering inside, Trainor saw row after row of old ladies seated at card tables with card files in front of them, in one hand holding an index card and in the other a telephone receiver, trying to convince their unseen callers of the importance of Jack's reelection as senator.

As he walked in and looked for a familiar face who might be in charge, he remembered the advice that Frank Morrissey's wife had given him when he'd told her he was accepting a job from her husband. "Now, remember," she had warned, "when you go to work for the Kennedys, you be sure and be friendly with Steve and Jean Smith; they are wonderful people." Jean Smith was Jack Kennedy's sister and Steve her new husband. "But whatever you do, you stay away from that awful Kenneth O'Donnell. He is a friend of Bobby's and he is very mean. You stay away from him!"

When a young woman came up and offered to help him, Trainor introduced himself and asked to see Steve Smith. The girl nodded and went off. She came back shortly and showed him into a room in the back, where four men were seated around a table. Trainor recognized one of them immediately from his father's descriptions and various newspaper photographs: Ambassador Joseph P. Kennedy. But the young man with his back to him rose first, turning to acknowledge him. The man was slim, with black eyes and a small mouth. To Trainor, he looked like someone he might have seen in an Irish pub, plotting revenge against the occupying British. He said little, sizing the young man up. Then he reached out his hand and said, "Hi. Ken O'Donnell. Sit down and tell me what you want."

Trainor felt his stomach clutch. Mrs. Morrissey's words were coming back to him. He grabbed a chair and was promptly introduced to Larry O'Brien, Steve Smith, and the ambassador. Kenny then began to fire questions at him. After a few moments, Kenny realized that Trainor was James A. Trainor's son, his father Cleo's pal. With family connections acknowledged and little time to waste, Trainor could set aside the admonitions he had heard about Kenny O'Donnell and begin his work for John F. Kennedy.

Kenny told Trainor to go get Jacqueline Kennedy's station wagon in Beacon Hill. As he walked out, trying to remember the address, he assumed that this must mean that he was hired. He found the car and then drove it, as Kenny had instructed, to a sign company, where he picked up a three-foot-tall sign that featured a photograph of Jack Kennedy and a sign in big red lettering. The men at the sign company mounted it on the roof, along with two enormous amplifier horns, which were wired to a small record player that sat on the front seat next to the driver. Attached to this was a microphone that Trainor thought was long enough to reach to South Boston from Beacon Hill. After driving the whole contraption back to the Tremont Street headquarters, Trainor learned his job. He was to drive the sound truck, Kenny told him. As he turned to leave, Kenny said, with a cold stare that brought back Mrs. Morrissey's warning, "And remember, that's Jackie's car! Don't screw it up!"

"By 1957, at least in relation to Massachusetts, the senator had come to rely on my judgment and kind of looked to me as his contact in Massachusetts," Kenny would say years later. "The schedule in '58 became much more organized. When we started campaigning we had a problem, which was really beyond belief: I mean, what do you do with that tiger [Jack Kennedy] from eight in the morning until evening? . . . He liked to be busy and wanted to be doing productive things; so you had to balance keeping him active with not overdoing it, with not wearing him out. Eventually we developed a system or a pattern that we followed in Wisconsin and became our standard campaign pattern. We would take him to a plant or something at eight in the morning, then go to a breakfast or something at nine A.M. At ten we would stop in the next town at the town square. We used bands heavily, so there was always a band. He was drawing very large crowds for this type of a campaign, extremely large! He was quite pleased with the way it was going and the utilization of his time. We always had a restful lunch hour in a nice restaurant where he could eat and be away from the politicians if he so chose. Jackie was with us often, not in the mornings all the time, but she would often join us for lunch.

"So we endeavored to really break his day up, so he wasn't overused and so healthwise, for his back, he could actually enjoy himself a bit. ... We would usually get him into the hotel wherever we were staying about five. He would rest and bathe, get up-to-date with what the problems were, making his phone calls, return calls, eat dinner, and then at eight he would go to a reception. We would make sure it never lasted beyond nine-thirty. He would be back home or in his hotel room by ten or ten-thirty at the latest. It was something he was totally unused to. In '52 he had been campaigning and pushing sometimes until two or three in the morning with no break, so this was an entirely new experience for him. So he felt the physical setup of this campaign was much better for him. ... I think because I knew how to utilize his time effectively, we could talk comfortably with each other and there was no nonsense or bullshit. We got along."

At the time John Trainor began to advance his career by driving a Kennedy sound truck, Bobby was still in Washington, absorbed by his work with the McClellan Committee. Although he was not able to become directly involved in the campaign, he did, however, offer his savvy and advice frequently to Jack and Kenny.

The campaign would not be a nail-biter like the race against Henry Cabot Lodge, Jr., in 1952. Twenty-three-year-old Helen Lempart Westbrook, a pretty brunette who was brought into the organization by Jack Kennedy himself from his senatorial office, recalled that "he was certainly a shoo-in, but getting staff members of his up there to keep on top of all of this was the fact that he wanted to get the big vote." Though Jack knew that discretion was the better part of victory, and did not trumpet his planned run for the presidency, his staff knew that he wanted to augment his national presence by winning hugely against Vincent Celeste, the sacrificial lamb the Republicans had put up to run against him.

During Kenny's absence in Washington, Larry O'Brien had worked to keep the Kennedy organization and contacts active and in place. Now, as in 1952, the plan was to get Jack to meet as many voters as possible, primarily through meetings, speaking events, and the famous

Kennedy teas. Trainor's job was to get Jackie's station wagon to Jack's next destination a day before Jack arrived, and then drive around town. Using his microphone and speakers, he would play triumphant music from his record player perched on the seat next to him and then he would announce that the next day Senator Jack Kennedy would be arriving to speak, and what time, and where. As in the 1952 campaign, Ken and Larry O'Brien traveled with the candidate and handled the schedule, which, though not as grueling as before, was nevertheless tough. They tried to avoid large entourages and kept the traveling party to mostly Kenny and Larry, often with Trainor serving as the driver or herald. Jack would spend his time visiting a local war memorial, town hall, or high school gym. Each town had a Kennedy secretary or ward chairman, often a veteran of the 1952 race.

Despite the organization and experience these staffers had, the campaign was not without its glitches and wild moments, some of which Trainor managed to cause. Normally, when they would arrive at a town where the candidate was to campaign, Jack would quickly hop out of the car and begin to walk the nearest sidewalk, shaking hands and introducing himself to prospective voters, just as he had when Pat Fuccillo first met him in 1946 in Boston's East End. As Jack worked the townspeople, Trainor would drive the sound truck along, with various songs playing on his small record player. Kenny was always walking with the candidate, but often quietly in the back, simply watching the candidate as he proceeded along. Several times as the car trundled along, Trainor would hit small bumps in the road, making the entire turntable slide down the slant in the seat. When the needle scratched across the record, Jack would turn and glare.

Once, as Trainor raced Jack and Kenny to a meeting, Jack grew frustrated at what he thought was Trainor's slow driving. He ordered Trainor to pull over, climbed into the driver's seat, and sped at what to Trainor seemed like "eighty miles an hour toward the town of Foxboro." When a car pulled into Jack's way and proceeded too slowly, Jack slammed his hand on the horn and swung into the other lane, quickly passing the slower vehicle and nearly colliding with oncoming traffic. When they arrived in Foxboro, Jack and Kenny leaped out and headed up the small steps to the speaker's rostrum. Trainor climbed out of the car and moved to the driver's side, leaning back and watching his boss begin to address the sparsely assembled crowd.

Suddenly, Trainor felt a tug at his shoulder. "Hey, you!" a voice barked into his ear. He turned to face a police officer. As it turned out, the slow-moving car Jack had passed belonged to this patrolman, who promptly handed Trainor a ticket for speeding. He tried to explain that the car's crazy driver in fact had been the urbane, sophisticated, tanned United States senator currently up on the speaker's platform, but the patrol officer wasn't interested. Although Trainor had been warned about Kenny O'Donnell, he decided that he had more to worry about from Jack Kennedy's wild driving.

Back in Washington, physically and emotionally exhausted, Bobby was wrapping up the McClellan Committee labor investigation. His work had taken a lot out of him. "There was perhaps an aura around him," says his law school pal Gerald Tremblay. "You always felt the guy was not going to blow up, but his energies, when he was working, were so intense that there was hardly ever a relaxed situation. His father made money and made it available to him and his family, and he wanted to devote his time to public things." Now, with the committee work largely concluded, Bobby was writing a book, just as his brother Jack had two years before — the Pulitzer Prize–winning *Profiles in Courage*. Bobby's book about labor union corruption would be called *The Enemy Within*; he saw it as a vital continuation of his investigation into the Teamsters. He would spend long hours writing in longhand on yellow pads of paper for his devoted secretary Angie Novello to decipher. Of the McClellan Committee, Bobby would write, "The investigative work we have done . . . revealed that there is in America today an incredible and hidden web of underworld enterprise. This underworld is not the figment of a detective story writer's imagination. It is a real and present danger to the economy of our nation, powerful, cunning, well-organized and financed. So successfully masked have been these operations that they seldom are exposed to the public eye."

The investigation remained difficult work, and it won Bobby more enemies than supporters. Once, while Kenny was still working for the committee in Washington, Bobby and Ethel hosted a party at Hickory Hill, inviting among others Nancy and Walter Sheridan, and Kenny and Helen O'Donnell. Neighbors and close friends, the couples drove to the party together, Walter and Kenny sharing the front seat, Nancy and Helen in the back. As they drove, Kenny pointed to an article in the newspaper he was reading describing that evening's gala at Bobby Kennedy's house. He quoted the article as saying that several hundred friends were scheduled to attend. Letting the moment of silence settle, Kenny told the others that he really had to point out the article to Bobby, because he was quite sure it was inaccurate. "Inaccurate?" asked Sheridan, puzzled at how such a mundane story could be wrong. "Because," said Kenny, with some satisfaction, "I know for a fact that Bobby Kennedy certainly does not now and never did have several hundred friends." At the party Kenny did go on to mention the article to Bobby, who professed not to be amused.

"We were in Chicopee, Massachusetts," Kenny remembered. "Often when Jackie campaigned with us, we would try to use her especially in racial areas, be they black, Spanish, Portuguese, or especially French, because of her background. Jackie was scheduled to go to a French reception over at a French church in that part of the community. [Jack] said to Larry O'Brien and me, 'I think you had better go with her to make sure everything is all right.' We said we would. He was resting and didn't have an event scheduled, so we didn't need to worry about him at all. We went over with Jackie. As a matter of fact, Larry and I got there ahead of her and we walked into the hall. Nice little three-piece band set up and a nice piano there. Beautiful china coffee cups, teacups and beautifully done cakes, cookies and all sorts of wonderful French pastries, lots of lovely food, tablecloths on all these small tables, flowers. Looked quite lovely. They didn't have any people there, though, but that was okay because we assumed they were going to come later.

"We told Jackie to be a half an hour late, so we figured by then it will be filled about. About fifteen minutes into that half hour, Larry and I are looking around. There are probably four or five people there; they all worked for the reception committee. The half hour passes, Jackie arrives, and so now there are eight of us, including Jackie, Larry, and me. By six-forty it starts to fill up: There are now ten people in the hall, including Jackie, Mr. O'Brien, and myself. By now Larry and I look at each and realize we have a complete disaster on our hands. By now we realize this is a monumental gaffe; for some reason or another nobody was coming.

"The lady who was in charge of the event started to cry, which I don't handle particularly well. We didn't know what to do. At about that moment, Larry sent his secretary Phyllis out to a girls college not far from there and she recruited some young ladies. She raced to this Catholic college down the street and recruited as many people as they could to have the girls come back and make believe they were supposed to be the crowd. So finally these lovely girls in their Catholic uniforms show up and have no idea why they are there, but would love to meet Jackie. None could vote of course. But, so they come and by now the crowd is up to about twenty-five, because I was pulling people off the street — running around asking them if they wanted to meet Jackie.

"Meanwhile Jackie is not saying a word. She is still talking to the same ten people who have been there all the time, watching us out of the corner of her eye and trying to figure exactly what this is. By now O'Brien and I are laughing and being jolly. Every time Jackie catches our eye we smile and wave, laughing, ha, ha, very jolly, everything is fine. Inside of course you are dying. Finally, desperate, we convinced one of the young ladies to play the piano, and O'Brien and I go up to the piano and sing songs. You see, although the piano and the instruments were there, there were no band members either! So this girl plays and O'Brien stands up there singing and laughing. People are looking at us, laughing and smiling; you know they don't know any better.

"Jackie meanwhile is just floating through the crowd, not saying a word. She is watching me intensely the whole time. Finally she walks over to us at the piano and says, 'Excuse me, I hate to interrupt such fun, but could I talk to you a moment?' I almost died. I would have known what to do with the senator, but I didn't know what to do with Jackie. So I excuse myself from the piano and let Mr. O'Brien do a solo. Looking at me with those pools of dark eyes that don't miss a damn thing, she leaned forward with that voice and says, 'Kenny, this event of yours appears to be a bit of a bust, wouldn't you say?' I stared at her. 'Well,' I began, 'this is what you call a monumental bust! I can't explain why, no excuses, but we have to play it off as best we can because the reporters from *Time* are with us.'

"She shook her head and said, 'All right, but let me take it from here, Kenny. If you and Larry have any more tea, you are both going to turn into teacups, and furthermore, I think for all our sakes we can live without any more singing. If you don't mind.'

"I smiled, kind of embarrassed and said okay. With that she glided through the party for at least another hour. She met everyone at least five times. As promised, I didn't sing again, just hummed. Finally about ten minutes before we had to return to the senator, Larry and I began to talk. We could have stood ruining one of his affairs, because he was an old pro, but to ruin one of Jackie's affairs! She hated to campaign to begin with, so I hated to think what she was going to say to him. Mostly I hated to think what he was going to say to me! So as we prepared to leave, she said, 'I don't want to leave right now. I promised Father Bourgeois'—whatever the heck his name was—'that I would drop in and have a cup of tea with him before I left.'

"With that she swept out in her queenly grace and we followed like two errant schoolboys. She swept into the parish house. She had never met the priest in her life. He had not asked her to have tea. She swept into the room, introduced herself, and asked for a cup of tea, like she hadn't just had sixty-two cups in the hall. The old priest was so excited and flattered that when he stood up his knees were shaking and we thought he might fall over. They sat for a half an hour and chatted in French. O'Brien and I stood in the anteroom trying to figure out what was happening and what she was up to. Jackie was her most vivacious self, as they talked about France, her trips there. I gather it was a great conversation.

"As a matter of fact, we were now late to meet the senator, who was going to be furious with us for being late, never mind hearing whatever it was that Jackie was going to tell him about the event. At the proper moment she gets up and says, 'I must leave. I have to join my husband downtown. We have a reception to attend.' She stood up and the priest had tears in his eyes. She swept out the door, into the car, and we drove back. As a result of her visit, the priest gave a sermon at Mass that Sunday, scolding his flock for not attending the reception and all but ordering them to vote for Jack Kennedy, and spent the whole time talking about his lovely French wife, Jackie.

"That evening we get to the hotel and meet the senator, who wasn't too annoyed. We walk in with Jackie and he smiles at us and says, 'How did it go? I figured it must have been a great crowd and success in order to make you late.'

"O'Brien and I exchange glances. Then we look at Jackie who gives us this look. I said, tentatively, 'Fine.'

"The senator turns to Jackie. 'Fine? Was it? Did you like it? The crowd must have been great in order to make you late like this.'

"Jackie smiles in that queenly fashion, gives a look toward me as if to say, you owe me one. She says, in that voice, 'Oh, Jack, it was just lovely, lovely. I had a wonderful conversation with the parish priest and a cup of tea and met all these lovely people. Just wonderful. . . . You know, Jack, it was so lovely, I don't think Kenny or Larry will have to eat another dinner for at least several days, but other than that it was just really, well, fine.' "

Although driving was officially Trainor's job, he spent as much effort staying out of trouble with Kenny and Jack. Perhaps his worst day began in Quincy, where they spent the morning working the streets. Jack had received a cool response from almost everyone he met, and he was furious. The group returned to Eddie's Motel, where they often met to regroup and have lunch. Kenny always booked two rooms, one for Jack to lie down, rest, and sometimes take a hot bath to give his aching back a break, and another room where the rest of them gathered to have a beer, talk, and take care of the business and phone messages that had accumulated during the morning.

They were gathered in one of those rooms enjoying a beer and a steak sandwich when suddenly the phone next to the bedside table rang. It was Jack Kennedy calling from his room. Kenny answered in clipped, almost nonverbal tones, slammed the receiver down, and, swigging his beer, barked to Trainor, "Go down and warm up that sound truck. The candidate wants to go back out onto the streets and see if he can win over a few of those bastards from this morning." Trainor leaped from his chair and they all headed downstairs, leaving behind their half-eaten sandwiches and half-drunk beers. Eddie's Motel sat on a busy stretch of road in Quincy and had a portico that hung over the motel entrance-way. Jackie's sound truck was parked in the driveway and behind it was the candidate's car, a black Cadillac. Trainor leaped into Jackie's station wagon, revved up the engine, and gave the amplifier time to warm up. As he idled in the driveway, out came Jack Kennedy, looking refreshed and determined, followed by Kenny and Jack's driver, Bob Morey, hoping to get ahead of the candidate and get his own car warmed up. Trainor had the window to his car rolled down, so he was clearly able to hear Kenny bark the orders as he hopped into the backseat of the Cadillac. (Jack always rode in the front, next to the driver.)

Trainor heard Kenny yell, "Gas it, Trainor, let's go!" The portico was some twelve feet high and hard to miss. Made nervous by Kenny, Trainor slammed his foot to the gas pedal, causing Jackie's car to lurch forward. Getting a running start, he sped down the driveway. Jack turned around to look at Kenny and smiled his first unforced smile of the day. "Look at that kid go! He's good, Kenny, he's good, a real go-getter. I'm glad you hired him, even if we've had a few problems with him. He'll be fine." Just then Trainor plunged forward in his car, driving straight under the portico, with the Caddy directly behind him. Suddenly the midday quiet was shattered by a sudden BAROOM! Wrenched off by the motel's portico, the amplifiers, the posters, the frame, and the attached microphone came crashing off the top of Jackie's car, landing with a thud on the hood of Jack's car, the whole apparatus tumbling to the ground.

Both cars screeched to a halt. They all sat in stunned silence for a moment. Then Jack turned and gave Kenny the coldest stare he had ever seen. "Let's go," he barked, and they swung around Jackie's car and drove off, leaving Trainor behind with Jackie's injured station wagon and a very angry motel manager. Bobby loved the story. After that, every time Kenny recommended a new hire who he said was really good, Jack would promptly remind him of the incident with John Trainor at Eddie's Motel.

Bobby remained on call to troubleshoot the campaign and form general strategy, even as he began working their national contacts in preparation for a presidential campaign two years down the road. Steve Smith was the campaign manager, depending a great deal on veteran campaign workers from 1952 like Pat Twohig, Polly Fitzgerald, and Helen Keyes. In return for her hard work, Smith arranged for Twohig to join Jackie and some of the other Kennedy sisters and in-laws on a television call-in program; staring into the red light of the camera lens, she tried to look natural as she wrote down the caller's name and passed the slip of paper to Jack, her hand shaking slightly from nervousness. When Jack took the paper he touched her hand lightly and said, "Thank you, Pat." He had sensed her anxiety, and by acknowledging her, had relieved it. As they left the set at the end of the program, she caught Kenny, standing off to the back. He looked at her and smiled slightly.

Thanks to Kenny's intervention, John Trainor still had a job after his encounter with the motel portico. Kenny had pulled him aside, glared at him, and with characteristic directness told Trainor to straighten up. One day later in the campaign he headed off in Jackie's station wagon, which now looked a little worse for wear, to meet Kenny in western Massachusetts. As he left he saw he was wearing the same tan suit he had worn the day he almost took off the top of the candidate's wife's car. It seemed like bad luck. Putting aside his superstitions, he drove off with a load of new records he had bought. Kenny would be impressed. He had told Trainor to go out and get some new music to blare out of the car's amplifiers. Last Saturday as they marched along, with Trainor driving the sound truck and Jack Kennedy walking in front of the car and waving and shaking hands along the side of the road, Trainor had played military marching music. Jack kept turning to look at Trainor, and Trainor had smiled and waved, even though the candidate looked annoyed. Trainor couldn't imagine what the problem was; after all, both Kenny and Jack were veterans.

Kenny, in his familiar campaigning position — unobtrusive in the background, slightly behind and off to the side of the candidate — suddenly headed toward the sound truck, looking grim. Trainor felt his stomach clutch, Mrs. Morrissey's words coming back to him again. Kenny gripped the rim of the window and leaned into Trainor's face as the car crept forward. "Trainor, the candidate would like to know when the fuck we are invading Poland." Trainor began to stammer that it was marching music, band music. The coal black eyes looked unforgiving. "It's fucking German marching music," Kenny barked, "and we won the damn war! Get that stuff off there!" With that he was gone, retreating to his spot along the side of the road — left side, slightly to the back. Trainor grabbed the needle, scratching it across the album as he did so, which caused Jack to turn and glare into the windshield once more. He drove the entire parade route following behind the candidate, silent.

Something almost as bad musically, or maybe worse, happened several days later, when he played the "Colonel Bogey March." Kenny had beckoned him out of the car. "Get rid of that fucking record!"

"Why?" Trainor asked defensively. "Everyone loves it! They're all cheering and clapping."

"It's Foster Furcolo's goddamn campaign song! Get rid of that goddamn song!" Furcolo was the governor of Massachusetts, now running for reelection, and not a Kennedy ally. Furcolo and Kennedy didn't like each other, and the Kennedy men felt that he was involved in making bad press for Kennedy. As Trainor sheepishly retreated to the car, he passed the candidate, who was headed in Kenny's direction. He heard Kennedy say with some annoyance, "Kenny, isn't that the guy who —" Trainor hadn't waited to hear more.

That day, as today, Trainor had worn a tan suit. The day was clear and bright and the campaign spent the morning in Belmont and stopped for lunch nearby, at a homey type of place with a back room that allowed Jack time to talk to his aides privately and visit with various politicians away from the public or press. Every campaign lunch had the same menu—a steak sandwich, a baked potato, and a large slice of apple pie. They made their way to the back room, where they were joined by a local pol whom Jack was trying to win over. Trainor found himself sitting between Jack Kennedy and the cigar-smoking politician, directly across from Kenny. Once he realized where he was, Trainor immediately began to get nervous. He would have gotten up and offered to move, but Jack was talking and the food had arrived. Jack was talking rapid-fire and the pol was being evasive, which left the senator frustrated. Trainor kept moving forward and then backward, trying to stay clear of the line of fire as he worked at his plate of steaming steak and potato, complete with mushrooms and gravy. Trainor was having trouble cutting his steak and staying out of Kennedy's way. Suddenly, Jack raised his voice. "Look, my people are the best—we have top-notch people and a top-notch organization. Right, Kenny?" For emphasis Jack slammed his fist on the table. Startled, Trainor stabbed his knife into his steak and the entire plate shot out from under the fork and landed, a steaming mess, in Trainor's crotch. The room became as silent as death. Paralyzed, the gravy streaming over his tan suit, Trainor looked up into Kenny's black eyes. Amusement crossed Kenny's face. "Trainor? Uncomfortable? Do you want to be excused?"

As Trainor rose gratefully from the table, some of his gravy dripped onto Senator Kennedy's shoes. As he rose from the table, "Sorry, sir" was all he could manage. Kennedy looked at him cryptically. As Trainor retreated from the table, he heard Jack say to Kenny, "Isn't that the same guy who ruined my wife's station wagon? The same guy with the records? The same guy that you hired 'cause your father knew his father and told me was such a go-getter?"

"Yeah, that's right" was all Kenny could muster. He stifled a chuckle as the candidate bent to clean his shoe.

Kennedy sat up and looked at Kenny, for a long moment. "Good choice, Ken, good choice. Where is Bobby, anyway? I'll have to tell him what a help you've been to me! Maybe he needs you back in Washington."

Later as they made their way toward their cars, Kenny pulled Trainor aside. Squeezing his arm lightly, he said with mock seriousness, "Don't expect a raise."

In spite of John Trainor's mishaps, Jack Kennedy would win a triumphant reelection to the Senate. With the path to the White House now open to them, Kenny could only hope that future bumps in the road would be as minimal as these.

10

STARTING THE RACE

*I do not promise you ease. I do not promise you comfort. But I do
promise you these: hardship, weariness, and suffering.
And with them, I promise you victory.*

— GARIBALDI

In 1957, the late Joseph McCarthy's Wisconsin Senate seat was filled by
a very different legislator, William Proxmire, a Democrat. He brought
with him to Washington an astute young man who would become crucial to the political lives of both John and Robert Kennedy. Jerry Bruno
encountered John Kennedy for only the second time on the congressional subway that runs beneath the Capitol; he had first met the Massachusetts senator in 1957 when he had campaigned for Proxmire's
election. As they sat together on the subway, Kennedy remembered
meeting Bruno and asked him to come and see him at his home in
Georgetown. Bruno was surprised and pleased. As they parted company
that day, he thought to himself that the senator had to be planning a
run for the big prize in 1960 and knew that Bruno had maintained
excellent connections with the Proxmire organization in Wisconsin, a
key primary state, where he would have to prove his candidacy by best-
ing a political neighbor, Senator Hubert Humphrey. There could be no
other reason for the invitation. Bruno kept his speculations to himself
and soon was on his way to the federal brick home shared by Jackie and
Jack Kennedy and their daughter, Caroline, on N Street.

As Bruno was ushered into the kitchen of the Kennedy's home, he
received barely an acknowledgment from the senator. He sat there at

the kitchen table feeling a bit awkward and uncomfortable as Kennedy ate his breakfast and furiously read his newspapers, gulping down information as easily as he devoured his bacon and eggs. Bruno was glad when Jackie's maid, Providencia Pareades, offered him coffee; at least he had something to do with his hands while he waited to see just why Jack Kennedy had asked him to come. Caroline ran squealing through the kitchen, calling out to her father as she ran, followed by several dogs in hot pursuit. Still, Jack Kennedy remained engrossed in his papers until he abruptly dropped his paper to the floor and asked Bruno what he knew about Kenosha, Wisconsin. Before he could even frame an answer Jack went on to say, "I'm going to run for president and I want someone to organize Wisconsin and that person is you. When can you start?"

Hiring Bruno was an inspired move, not only because he knew the state well from organizing Proxmire's campaigns but because Proxmire was very close to presidential aspirant Hubert Humphrey, a Minnesotan who would have a natural advantage in neighboring Wisconsin. When the news broke, newspapers across the state read PROXMIRE AIDE JOINS KENNEDY CAMPAIGN STAFF. The next day, Proxmire "publicly denounced" Bruno. As for Jack Kennedy, Bruno recalled that his new boss found the whole incident "very, very funny."

John F. Kennedy's presidential campaign set up shop in the Esso Building at the foot of Capitol Hill. Both Kenny and Bobby had offices there, but they rarely used them. Bobby was often on the road meeting with political leaders, making speeches himself, or building a campaign operation and a strategy in a specific state. Kenny himself was always on the road with the candidate.

For Helen, who had stayed in Washington during the 1958 campaign, it was a difficult and lonely time. By now the three children had grown to four with the arrival of Mark Francis, whose godparents were Bobby and Ethel Kennedy, and Kenny's extended absences had grown more frequent. However, what kept her going was the prospect that Kenny and Bobby would end up in the White House. It was their mutual dream. At times, as she lunched with her friends Ethel, Martha O'Hare, and others, wives also widowed by the campaign, it was hard to believe that the White House was this close.

Just as the Kennedy and O'Donnell families girded for the biggest effort of all, so did the colleagues Bobby and Kenny had recruited into the Kennedy fold over Jack's fourteen years of public life. Dick Maguire, the law partner of Arthur Garrity and another of Kenny's "Irish Mafia" friends, had come on board as treasurer. Justine O'Donnell, Kenny's youngest sister, left Worcester to work as Dick Maguire's secretary and would retain that post after the election when Maguire became head of the Democratic National Committee. She was often the person people went to when they needed to get a message to Kenny and couldn't reach him. Kenny's job was the schedule, as it would be throughout his years at the White House. Ultimately all the advance men reported to Kenny, including Bruno.

Before Bruno left for Wisconsin in June 1959 he stopped in to see Jack Kennedy one more time. "The first thing we want is a headquarters and we want it in Milwaukee. Set it up," he was told. With those simple instructions, Bruno went back to Wisconsin and found what he thought was the ideal location, in a building right across the street from Marquette University, above a drugstore. The rent was reasonable and it was in a high-visibility spot. From the front office windows, you could look directly across at Marquette University Cathedral. Bruno told the owner that he would be back the next day with a final decision, once he'd checked with Steve Smith. When he got hold of Smith he was told that Bobby Kennedy was on his way to Milwaukee and that Bruno should pick him up at the train station. Bruno had yet to meet Bobby, but he was impressed with his efforts against Jimmy Hoffa and now was glad he had already made some progress for the Kennedy cause.

Bruno arrived at the train station early and met the train, introducing himself to a brisk young Robert Kennedy, who despite the June weather was wearing a black overcoat with the collar turned up, its lining frayed and visible at the bottom. Bruno was surprised that a Kennedy, with all his family wealth, would dress this way. As they neared the exit to the station, Bobby strode directly to the newsstand. Putting down his case, he picked up one newspaper after another and rapidly read it through. "He never bought one," Bruno says. "He'd read one, put it back, pick up another, read it and put it back, then another and another." As Bruno stood there counting, Bobby read five newspapers. Then, just as suddenly as Jack had turned to him over his breakfast in Georgetown, Bobby dropped the last paper onto the stand, turned to Bruno, and said, "Well, let's go!" As they climbed into the car, Bobby said, "Tell me about what's happening in Wisconsin."

With all his experience as an advance man, Bruno felt that Bobby shouldn't make him nervous, but he did. "We've got this great headquarters and we're just now starting out organizing by county, and I think it's going pretty good. I am using all of my Proxmire contacts . . ." As he finished, the two pulled up in front of the prospective campaign office. "This is the headquarters," Bruno said with a touch of pride in his voice.

Bobby climbed out of the car, leaving his suitcase behind, and swung the door shut. He stood in front of the building looking up at the second-floor window with the Jack Kennedy posters displayed across them. He lowered his eyes, looking at the drugstore windows and then up again at the second-floor picture window. Slowly he turned around and faced Marquette University Cathedral. It stood huge, dominating the street beneath it, with a massive cross affixed to its facade — its shadow falling almost directly into the second-floor windows across the street.

Bobby's eyes followed between Jack Kennedy's serious countenance and the cross with its image of Jesus crucified. Bruno watched him, his unease growing. Why wasn't he saying anything? Suddenly, Bobby turned facing Bruno, who had not yet left the driver side of the car, looked at him for a moment in silence, and then said with obvious sarcasm, "Do you really think we need the Catholic identity?

"Let's go in," Bobby directed, and the two made their way up the steps to the second-floor headquarters. Walking up the short flight of stairs brought Bobby into the three-room suite where "Kennedy for President" headquarters had been established. They encountered Bobby's Harvard football friend Chuck Roche sitting at the long table, the phone glued to his ear as he made press calls. Roche had been close to both

Bobby and Kenny in their Varsity Club days. Once after he had been told by a professor to rewrite a paper, he let himself be persuaded by Kenny and Bobby to go with them for beer at Cronin's; they told him he could rewrite the paper there. Which is exactly what Roche did — he copied it over, printing it rather than writing cursively this time, and was surprised when the beer- and pizza-stained pages won him a failing grade. A decade and a half later, Roche had responded to a call from Bobby, set aside his career, and gone to work as an unpaid volunteer for the Kennedy presidential campaign.

After greeting Roche, Bobby made his way into the small office that Bruno had made his own. Tossing his briefcase on the floor, he grabbed the phone and began to dial. Bruno walked out into the main room and watched as Bobby talked, his voice rising as his eyes were drawn more and more to the Catholic cathedral directly across the street. His first call had been to Washington, which suggested to Bruno that Bobby was not exactly happy. He overheard Bobby saying that the Wisconsin effort needed help and that Bobby needed the person he was talking to to come out here immediately. Then he came out and announced, "We need to find a new headquarters."

Within two weeks the Kennedy headquarters was relocated to a former store in downtown Milwaukee on Wisconsin Avenue, the main street, with great visibility. Bobby told Bruno that Kenny O'Donnell would be arriving shortly. Bruno had no idea who this Kenny was and what that meant for his efforts in Wisconsin.

John F. Kennedy's Catholicism threatened to cast a shadow over his entire campaign for the presidency. There had never been a Catholic elected president, and the only one who had ever won the nomination, New York governor Alfred E. Smith, had been crushed by Herbert Hoover in 1928. Many blamed his defeat on his religion — just as in 1956 Ambassador Joe Kennedy had feared that Stevenson's loss to Eisenhower could have been blamed on a Catholic running mate, Senator Kennedy of Massachusetts. Would a largely Protestant nation be able to set aside its prejudices enough to elect Jack Kennedy? "Wisconsin," said Kenny, "had a considerable Catholic population, Kennedy's religion was not as bad a problem there as it was later in totally Protestant West Virginia, but it was bad enough." On one occasion in Wisconsin, Kenny recalled, "Jack counted twenty mentions of the word 'Catholic' in one story about the primary contest that ran only fifteen paragraphs in length!" Even Rose Kennedy had been confronted by concerns about her son's Catholicism as she campaigned for him across the country. "I remember hearing variations on the theme," she wrote in her *Times to Remember*. " 'I don't want any Pope running things over here.' I would answer that the Pope lives in Italy but certainly doesn't run things there, even though it's a Catholic country; and that France is mainly Catholic and de Gaulle is a Catholic, but the Pope certainly did not give any orders to de Gaulle; and that Catholics in the United States Congress never voted as a bloc; and therefore the whole 'Catholic' issue was nonsense!"

One of the advance men in Wisconsin, who had survived the Massachusetts Senate campaign of 1958, was John Trainor. Despite his misadventures driving the sound truck that year, Trainor had proved himself worthy and loyal and was happy to be sent to Wisconsin. But Trainor himself was to run headlong into the Catholic issue and the Kennedy brothers' sensitivity over it.

On St. Patrick's Day, March 17, 1960, Jack, Dave Powers, and Kenny, with John Trainor as advance man and Clark Hughes as the driver, had just left an event at the Enjoy Cafe in Cornell, Wisconsin. John Trainor and Kenny were in the backseat, huddled against the severe cold, with Jack up front, in a new car loaned by a local dealer who was a Kennedy supporter. Jack Kennedy loved cars and spent much of the drive peppering the driver with questions about the car. As they raced along, the Kennedy team was followed by a group of reporters and photographers from *Life* magazine, who were doing a story on the candidate. Kenny had planned a lot of events where he thought he could impress the national media. Suddenly Trainor felt Kenny slap his own knee so hard that Trainor felt it too.

"What the fuck is that?" Kenny demanded, his voice rising in anger.

Trainor peered forward to get a better view of what Kenny had noticed, only to meet Jack Kennedy's icy blue eyes. "John, if you . . ." was all Jack managed to say.

In the distance stood what appeared to be a group of penguins blocking the road. As the car raced through the countryside, followed by the
photographers and reporters from *Life*, Trainor finally asked, "What the
hell are a bunch of penguins doing here?"

"you asshole, they aren't penguins," said Jack.

"They are fucking nuns!" barked Kenny. Blocking the entire roadway
were no fewer than 150 nuns, with the Mother Superior at dead center.
Their habits windblown by the bitter cold, they waved their arms and
their Kennedy for President signs, becoming more and more clear as
the cars got closer. As the car slowed to a crawl, Kenny slapped his leg
again. Trainor saw that Jack Kennedy looked pissed, but his gaze was
directed at Kenny. "You son of a bitch," Kenny growled to Trainor,
"you set this whole fucking thing up, didn't you? When I said do anything to get a crowd, I didn't mean get a group of fucking nuns!"
Kenny's black eyes were staring almost straight through Trainor, who
felt his stomach tightening, as if he were back at Eddie's Motel.

"No, no," John protested weakly, "I really had nothing to do with
this!"

"Christ," said Jack Kennedy as the car came to a halt, "the last thing
in the world I need right now with a carload of reporters following me
is either a priest or a group of damn nuns. Shit." Resigned, Jack and
then Kenny climbed out of the car. The candidate's hair was whipped
by the bitter wind, his unbuttoned topcoat blowing sideways as he
walked with hand outstretched and a broad smile behind clenched teeth
to greet the Mother Superior. As he and the Mother Superior got closer,
Jack turned to watch the gleeful group of reporters and photographers
climb out of the car and set up for the shot. Kennedy gave a baleful
glare at Kenny and Trainor, and whispered, "You fucking assholes. What
a team you two make!" Kenny watched Jack shake hands with the
Mother Superior and grimaced, shooting another fierce look at John
Trainor.

The Mother Superior explained that they were from a nearby convent
and had read in the paper that Kennedy was coming through. Kennedy
smiled and nodded, shaking hands with the nuns one by one, the pho-

tographers snapping away. The Mother Superior tried to pin a huge green corsage to Jack's lapel, but he managed to evade her and her flowers until she contented herself by affixing a green ribbon with a snippet of the corsage to his lapel. She was delighted, she told the group, to see a Catholic running for president.

They drove away in silence. Such encounters were exactly the kind of thing the Kennedy team wanted to avoid. In the next town they took a break to eat and get coffee to warm themselves up at a local restaurant, the reporters and photographers still in tow. Just as John Trainor was burying his fork in the warm pie and ice cream, he felt Kenny give him a swift kick under the table. "You son of a bitch. Now look what you have done." Trainor looked up to see that Jack had stopped talking with the reporters and was staring across the table, his face a mix of astonishment and anger. Standing before them was a priest.

"Shit" was all Kennedy was able to manage. The priest was a German and pretty rough looking; he needed a shave, his hair was a mess, and his silk rabat was turned almost sideways and food stained. He smiled and shook Jack's hand, telling the candidate how lucky the nation was going to be to have a Catholic in the White House, and then greeted everyone at the table, including the reporters, who he assumed were part of the campaign staff. Jack turned and shot a look at Kenny, blue eyes snapping. Trainor studied his pie with great intensity. "I just know," he thought to himself, "that somehow this is going to be my fault." Kenny leaned over him so closely that Trainor could feel his breath. "You are to blame for this," he growled, his face more serious than his intentions.

"I know," Trainor answered lamely. The reporters loved it. They were laughing, enjoying Kennedy's discomfort immensely.

Bobby was even less pleased than Jack with the state newspaper headline the next day announcing that Kennedy had been visiting with nuns in Wisconsin, featuring photographs of Irish Catholic John Kennedy greeting an entire gaggle of the religious. The Catholic issue would not go away. Before Kennedy could win the nomination, he would have to face the issue head-on.

*   *   *

Kenny O'Donnell arrived by train a few days later, after the new head-quarters had been established. In contrast to Bobby, before heading to the campaign offices Kenny wanted to go to lunch and have a beer. Bruno was struck by his chiseled features, athletic frame, and firm hand-shake, and how cool and at ease he was as they settled into the dark recesses of the local pub. He seemed almost detached, which, as Bruno would learn, was Kenny O'Donnell's style. It allowed Bruno to open up to him, leaning against the leather back of the booth they were sitting in as he answered Kenny's rapid-fire questions. Before long, Bruno found himself doing most of the talking and feeling comfortable about it. "What about labor? Are you getting support from labor?" Kenny asked at one point, his hand firmly around the beer bottle, legs crossed, with one leg rapidly bouncing up and down as if it almost had a mind of its own, belying his own casual manner. "Tell me how you plan to organize the state."

Bruno, relieved that he wasn't going to have some outsider come in and take over the show, outlined in great detail his plans for Wisconsin. Kenny said almost nothing for the three or four hours the men sat in the bar. At the end of the session Bruno took him over and showed him the headquarters. Then Kenny took his leave and went back to Wash-ington, D.C., leaving no indication of what he was thinking. He told the Wisconsin operative he was going back to talk to Bobby. He would hear from him soon. Bruno had no idea what he thought.

Within three or four days Kenny called. "Jerry," said Kenny, "I'm going to have my people come in from Massachusetts and organize the state. We'll break the state into congressional districts as we did in Mas-sachusetts. I will have one captain for each district; each captain will be one of my guys from Massachusetts." Bruno felt his stomach tighten, but before he could really protest, clutching the phone in his hand, Kenny cut him off, almost anticipating his response. "Your job is to be the liaison. You know the state, nobody knows it better. Your job is to keep all the captains coordinated and on track. Brief them on the state, give them the names you have, and have them set up a headquarters in each district, just like you have set up the main headquarters."

Before he knew it, Bruno heard himself saying, "Yes, sir," and hanging up the phone. Kenny and Bobby hadn't liked Bruno's plan—it was too "old-school" politics for them—but that was just fine. Fairly soon the Kennedy team from Massachusetts began to arrive. They were young, educated, and for the most part World War II veterans, who like Chuck Roche had left their careers and families when Jack, Bobby, and Kenny had asked, heading out to Wisconsin to labor on the presidential campaign of Jack Kennedy, melding into the community and working with established politicians, and independent of them.

Arthur Garrity was one of the Kennedy brotherhood who, having proven himself in 1952 and 1956, found himself shipped out to the bitter cold in Wisconsin as one of Kenny's men from Massachusetts. Garrity had received a call from Kenny only a few days before—his law partner Dick Maguire was one of Kenny's closest friends—asking him to go out to Wisconsin and help the Kennedy campaign get organized. He and Maguire had made the necessary arrangements to ensure their practice was covered at least temporarily; there was of course no salary—he had never asked and Kenny had never offered but simply expected that Garrity and men like him would make the effort. Some of the Kennedy workers didn't need the money; others made financial sacrifices.

"Bobby was a really terribly shy person, even in 1960," Garrity remembers. "I had known him from the '52 campaign and my days as a Kennedy secretary in Wellesley, but I was struck by how, even then, he was still reserved and a shy person," Garrity would recall. Garrity remembers thinking about Jimmy Hoffa that day, "a very terrible and dangerous man, and yet Bobby who remained so quiet and unassuming had actually taken him on."

Nor was Jimmy Hoffa finished with Bobby and Jack Kennedy. Since Bobby had investigated him in 1957 and 1958, he had grown no fonder of the onetime Senate chief counsel, and he would make things as difficult as he could for both Kennedy brothers. During one of his flying visits into the state, Bobby had been scheduled by Bruno for a meeting in Bruno's hometown of Kenosha and then in nearby Racine, where Bobby would speak at a Teamsters meeting. Bruno had been approached by the local Teamsters president, who said the local members were eager to hear from Bobby. Bruno felt confident. He was pleased, given Bobby's record with Hoffa and the Teamsters, that he had been able to arrange the meeting.

When he met up with Bruno in Kenosha, Bobby seemed uneasy. He said little as the two men climbed into Bruno's car and headed through the evening darkness for Racine. Bruno was driving, his hands clutching the wheel, trying to think of something to say to break the uneasy silence. This was only his second meeting with Bobby Kennedy and he still felt uncomfortable. Finally, Bobby himself spoke as the car rushed through the night. Turning to face Bruno, Bobby said softly, "Are you sure this isn't a setup? Jimmy Hoffa would just love to set me up."

So that's what he's worried about, thought Bruno. "No, no," he assured Bobby. "I talked to the local Teamsters president and he said they were going to have a very friendly crowd and they were going to listen to you and hear you out. This is not a pro-Hoffa crowd."

Bobby said nothing in reply. The two men drove in silence the remainder of the way. Bruno sensed that his words had failed to alleviate Bobby's fears. When they arrived in the outskirts of Racine, Bobby spoke up again. "I just can't believe that the Teamsters are going to let me speak. I just can't believe it. Something about this doesn't smell right," he said, emphasizing the last word as he turned to face Bruno again.

"Well, they promised me," Bruno replied, no longer so sure himself. "They said they wanted to hear you out, they wanted to listen to you. They promised me."

Bobby shook his head as he stared out the window. "That may be what they said, but I just can't believe it." They drove along, getting closer and closer to their destination. Bruno felt himself at a loss for words. "How far are we from their headquarters?" Bobby asked suspiciously.

"About three miles," Bruno said. Silence.

Then as they drew closer, Bobby turned to Bruno again. His eyes narrowing, he said, "Look, when we get to the headquarters, drive right by, don't stop there. Drive right by—go slow, though."

"Okay," Bruno said, by now a little put off by the cloak-and-dagger tactics. Maybe Bobby had been in those hearings too long. As they came within a block of the headquarters, Bobby would do something that would momentarily convince him that Bobby Kennedy really had been chasing bad guys too long. He slid down in the seat, crunching down on the floor of the front seat of the car. Startled, Bruno started to brake. "No," ordered Bobby, "keep going. I don't want to be seen."

Completely out of sight, facing the driver and scrunched on the passenger side, Bobby had to rely on Bruno as his eyes. "Slow down," he ordered softly. "Now tell me what you see. How many people are there?" As the car came alongside of the building, Bruno slowed the car to a crawl. He was startled at what he saw. The building was almost dark. "What do you see?" repeated Bobby.

"Well, I don't see anybody really. Well, wait," Bruno said. In the darkness he discerned a car and in the dim light that the building gave out he could make out some figures. They appeared and quickly vanished. "I see maybe three, four people at most," Bruno said, stunned.

"Keep driving," ordered Bobby from the floor. "Don't stop, you hear me? Don't stop. What else you do see?"

As they continued along, Bruno felt his stomach tighten. Something was wrong with this scene, something was very, very wrong. "Nothing," whispered Bruno. "There's nothing but three people there and one car, nothing else! Something is wrong."

"No kidding," Bobby growled. "It's a setup. Let's go!" With that Bruno gunned the accelerator and the car lurched forward and away. Bobby climbed back into the seat, saying little. There was little to say. The local Teamsters president never asked why Bobby didn't show up. Nothing was ever said. Maybe, thought Bruno, Bobby wasn't so paranoid after all.

Working with the Kennedys was challenging. Bobby Kennedy was one thing, but Jack and Kenny combined were supremely intense, as Bruno found out when Kenny, Jack, and Dave Powers arrived on the *Caroline*—Kennedy's campaign plane—for a three-day swing in Wisconsin. As they drove through Kenosha a blizzard began. The wind whipped the snow so hard that they could not see where the road ended and the snowbanks started. As they crawled along, Bruno was reminded of the last time he had been in Kenosha, with Bobby at the suspicious Teamsters meeting. Finally, Jack, sitting in the front seat next to Bruno, asked if Bruno thought the event was still on. "Yes," replied Bruno. He hadn't spoken to his contacts, but it was a good crowd and he knew them well. They would be there. To Wisconsinites, Bruno explained, this was a minor snowstorm.

As the car crept up the hill it began to spin in place. Jack was getting nervous. He had to make it to his speech and then make the train for his next appearance. "For God's sake, let's get this car going!" he barked.

"It's skidding," Bruno said, helplessly pointing out the obvious.

"Shit." With that, Jack Kennedy jumped out of the car, followed by Kenny and Dave Powers. Braving the bitter cold and wind, the three men moved behind the car, and Kennedy with his bad back joined the others in pushing it all the way up the hill. "This is great," Kennedy muttered. "Candidate for president lost in snowdrift in Wisconsin." Jack made it late to the speech, which meant that Dave Powers had to go ahead and single-handedly hold up the train to Milwaukee. Dave did it; Jack Kennedy made his train. Such was the Kennedy machine in operation.

Bobby's strategy, as it had been in the Senate campaigns, was to work the candidate as hard as possible and make him visible everywhere, the idea being that once people had a chance to meet him and hear him out, he could overcome their reservations about his youth or his Catholicism. The strategy involved working the media as well, especially the local press, which Jack used effectively to get out his message and which Bruno coordinated.

In such a tight schedule, the live media events required precise timing. In the heat of the campaign, Bruno watched the *Caroline* land in Milwaukee and taxi up to the gate, as its doors swung open to the waiting ramp. Bruno could tell from where he stood that Jack knew he was late. Running down the steps of the ramp, he yelled to Bruno, "What time is the show?"

"Seven o'clock," Bruno told him, and the two began hurrying through the terminal, followed by Jack's brother Teddy and Kenny O'Donnell bringing up the rear. The men hurried toward Bruno's waiting car, parked in front. "Are we going to make it? How far is the station?" Jack asked, looking nervously over at Bruno as they neared the car.

"Well," Bruno said thoughtfully, "maybe ten or fifteen minutes away if we don't hit traffic."

Jack climbed into the front seat and Kenny and Teddy jumped into the back. Bruno adjusted himself behind the wheel and had just started the engine when he heard Kenny bark, "Let's go!" With that Bruno hit the accelerator and gunned the car out of the airport toward downtown Milwaukee and the television station. Jack Kennedy nervously tapped the dashboard rapidly with his hand as the car drove along. He was in many ways as quiet and intense as Bobby, but in a different way, Bruno remembers thinking at the time.

At a red light, Bruno came to a halt and waited for the minimal traffic to pass. "What the hell are you doing? What are we fucking stopping for?" Kennedy growled, glaring at Bruno.

Startled, Bruno said lamely, "It's a red light."

"Go through!" Kennedy ordered.

Bruno hesitated. "Go through?"

"Go through," Kennedy replied, as if it was the most obvious thing in the world. Bruno obeyed. After nervously driving through the light, two blocks ahead Bruno spotted another red light and prayed it would turn green as they got there. It didn't. Slowing down, he could hear the drumbeat of Jack's fingers on the dashboard and knew he couldn't stop. All of a sudden as they approached the intersection, Kenny yelled from the backseat, directly behind Bruno, "You are all right on the left!"

Startled, Bruno almost leaped from his seat. Then Ted Kennedy barked, "You are all right on the right!"

Bruno pressed on the gas and they raced through the light. At the next intersection, Kenny shouted again, "All right on the left!" "All clear on the right. Go!" said Teddy. Bruno flew through. "Hurry up!" ordered Jack Kennedy, continuing to tap the dashboard. Bruno increased his speed to make it through the next set of lights, when he saw parked at the corner a police cruiser with a police officer clearly visible in the driver's seat. "There's an officer there," Bruno said quietly.

"Ignore him," ordered Kennedy, tapping furiously.

"Ignore him?" asked Bruno stunned.

"Ignore him!"

It seemed like the largest red light Bruno had ever seen. Suddenly, Kenny said, "He's got his back turned, go! Go now! You are clear on the left."

Teddy yelled, "Clear on the right—hurry up before he turns."

With that they raced through the intersection, Bruno's heart pounding hard. "Where the hell is the station?" Jack growled, unfazed by the near run-in with the law. Bruno tried to open his mouth to reply but found he couldn't speak. Suddenly he couldn't even remember where the television station was. "Where the hell is the station?" Kennedy repeated. "Do you know where you are going?" Gripping the wheel tighter, beads of sweat forming on his brow, Bruno still couldn't find the words to reply.

He turned slightly to see Jack Kennedy staring at him, seemingly stunned at his continued silence. "Shit," he heard from the backseat. It was Kenny, and Bruno knew he was in real trouble now. "Where the hell is the fucking station?"

Kenny's tone jolted the words out of Bruno's mouth. "There," he nearly yelled, as if he were finally able to speak of some miraculous occurrence. "Right there," he said again, pointing to the tower that was dead ahead. They pulled into the station parking lot and directly in front of the door, two minutes before the 7 P.M. airtime. Jack threw open the door, leaping out before the car had come to a complete halt. Kenny and Teddy quickly followed. Bruno sat immobile, watching Jack enter the building's glass doors, tapping the knuckles of his hand nervously against the wall as he went, concentrating his energies in preparation for the interview. It was now one minute to airtime. As Bruno watched Kennedy vanish inside, followed quickly by Kenny and Teddy, he suddenly realized he was gripping the steering wheel so tightly that his knuckles were white. He tried to pry his hands loose but couldn't. Sitting still while staring at his hands, Bruno thought, Whew, these guys are unbelievable.

Bruno and Kenny eventually began to develop a friendship as Bruno found himself admiring the talented people Kenny had brought into the state, from the Harvard gang to women like Helen Lempart, from Kennedy's Washington office, and Helen Keyes. Keyes was one of the first women ever to have a powerful and visible role in a national political campaign. The Kennedys wanted deft and dedicated people from all quarters, and that included women too. Her father was their dentist. In February 1960 Bobby called Helen, a schoolteacher in Massachusetts, and told her, "Helen, I want you to come out here as soon as you can and stay until the election is over."

Startled, Keyes started to demur. "Bobby, I teach school. I don't know if I can. Probably you'd have to speak to the superintendent of schools."

Bobby replied quickly, "Oh, fine, I'll do that."

"All right," Helen replied, assuming that would take time.

Bobby was not going to take no for an answer. "Can you come out tomorrow?"

Minutes after she spoke to Bobby, the phone in her home rang again; the superintendent of schools told her that her classes were covered. She could leave in the morning, and she did. That was typical Bobby Kennedy style. As Kenny knew himself, it was tough to say no to him.

Kenny was a very private, closemouthed man. Yet if you demonstrated that you could deliver when needed, even in adversity, as John Trainor had, you quickly gained his trust. Kenny struck Bruno as a very complex man. He rarely exhibited a temper, except when a political situation went badly or was mishandled. He took guff from nobody, including Jack Kennedy. They seemed to have a mutual respect and understanding that was sometimes deeper than people might have realized. Kenny was loyalty itself, which the Kennedys knew how to value.

Since Kenny was always with the candidate, Bruno saw him in private only after Jack had retired for the night. The evening of the red-light-running TV interview, Jack went to bed exhausted. All the others were tired too, but too keyed up to sleep. So Kenny, Bruno, Ben Smith, and a few others went to the hotel bar to try to unwind. It would be here that Bruno would see a rare flash of that O'Donnell temper. As they sat around the bar discussing the campaign, their conversation drew the attention of some locals in the bar. The locals were well on their way to alcoholic oblivion, and they took an instant dislike to the young Kennedy crowd, whom they perceived as outsiders from the East Coast, especially Kenny and Ben. To these midwesterners Jack Kennedy was just a rich man's son. Toward closing time, their comments became more vicious. "Let's go," Bruno whispered to Ben, worried that his colleague might react in anger. Bruno was not concerned about Kenny; Bruno had never seen him lose control. As the drunks' bad-mouthing of Jack Kennedy got downright vicious, Kenny, silent as a cat, leaped across the table, grabbed the biggest guy by the collar, lifted him off his feet, and threw him straight across the room, where he slammed into a wall and slid with a grunt to the floor.

The entire bar became deadly quiet. Kenny said nothing. He returned to his seat and finished his beer. Nobody moved and nobody talked. Everyone just stared at the table of strangers, especially at the black-eyed cat in the middle. Kenny quietly finished his beer, stood up, and said, "Let's get the hell out of here." The group left the bar and nobody said a word. Bruno for one was shocked and awed.

Bobby, Kenny, and Jack often were oblivious to the effect they had on people. Their single-minded intentions—whether to win a football game, run an investigation, or capture the White House—meant that they would push headlong against all obstacles, their eyes on their goal. All their energies were now focused on achieving their greatest goal of all, which could make their campaign at once exhilarating and nerve-racking. Bruno, as a coordinating advance man for the candidate, felt that headlong ambition firsthand. Sometimes, when he could catch his breath, he could even laugh.

It was another bitter cold day in February when the phone at Bruno's desk rang. Jack was flying into Minneapolis for an appearance in Wisconsin, Kenny said: Did Bruno have a guy there who could meet them at the airport and drive them to the event? "Sure," Bruno said. "I've got a great guy for you. His name is Pete DeGal from Cadott, Wisconsin, and he'll be really excited about meeting John Kennedy."

"Great. Set it up," Kenny told him, hanging up the phone before Bruno could reply. When the *Caroline* pulled up to the gate in Minneapolis, Jack and Kenny climbed down the ramp, in a rush as usual, where an awestruck and nervous Pete DeGal was waiting for them. "Nice to meet you," Jack said quickly. "Where's the car? We're late."

"Don't worry," DeGal told them. "Everything is under control. Where are your bags?" he asked as the candidate and Kenny began striding past him. Before they could respond he quickly scooped up all their bags, their coats, and everything else he could grab hold of. Jack and Kenny stopped for a moment. "Let me help," said Kenny, watching the overburdened young man try to balance bags, coats, and car keys. "No, no. Everything is under control. Don't worry. I'll take care of it," DeGal reassured them. As they hurried toward the car, DeGal talked hurriedly about the campaign in Wisconsin and how well he thought the senator was doing. Kennedy's responses were muted. He was gracious but uneasy. His mind was on the next event and he needed to think. As usual, he climbed into the front passenger side of the car. Before hopping into the backseat Kenny turned to face DeGal. "Look, we got to get to Eau Claire. We are running a little behind schedule, so we have to move it."

"Don't worry," DeGal said. "I'll just put this stuff in the trunk and we are off." Kenny watched as Pete struggled to open the trunk and then shoved everything en masse inside. Slamming the trunk closed, DeGal hurriedly slid behind the wheel, still talking about the Wisconsin campaign. Suddenly he stopped talking and froze.

"Let's go, Pete," Kenny said. Staring straight ahead, Pete made no reply. Stunned, Kenny and Jack sat there staring at their driver. "What the fuck is the problem? For Christ's sake, let's go, Pete."

Suddenly DeGal began fumbling through his pockets. "I can't find my car keys! I think I threw them in the trunk with everything else and locked them in!"

"Oh God," Kennedy said.

"Shit," came the oath from the backseat. The two men jumped out of the car and ran toward the taxicab stand, leaving Pete to solve his own problem. From that point forward, every time either Kenny or Bobby would call Bruno to arrange a driver to pick up Jack, they would always end with "Not Pete DeGal from Cadott!"

✻   ✻   ✻

Since the incident with the Teamsters Union, Jerry Bruno had learned to trust Bobby's instincts and came to value the time they spent together when Bobby flew in to oversee the campaign or make an appearance on his brother's behalf. He might not always explain his logic, but there was always a reason behind his actions. One evening, as Bruno sat at his desk finishing up paperwork and seeing off the last of the volunteers, the phone rang unexpectedly. "Yeah, what's up?" Bruno answered nonchalantly.

"I don't know where I am!" replied a clearly frustrated Bobby Kennedy.

Startled, Bruno sat up a little in his chair. He had assumed Bobby was long since back at his hotel with his candidate and the rest of the Kennedy team. "Where are you?" Bruno asked.

"I don't know. That's why I'm calling you," Bobby said, anger growing in his voice.

In the background, Bruno could hear the clear sound of automobiles passing and an occasional car horn. "You are at a phone booth?"

"Yeah," Bobby replied.

"What's the name of the town?"

Momentary silence greeted Bruno's last comment. "If I knew where the heck I was, I wouldn't be lost," Bobby yelled.

"Um, well, describe it, describe the town. Are you alone?"

"Yes, I'm alone," Bobby said. "Describe it? Well, I'm looking out the window of a phone booth and I see one bar, another bar, and on my side of the road a huge cow pasture with a bunch of cows staring at me, wondering who the hell is this jerk in the phone booth at midnight, in the middle of winter, in the middle of Wisconsin! I can't ask someone, because there is nobody up at midnight to ask! Where am I?"

Bruno's mind began to race as he asked Bobby what his schedule was and how he had ended up alone. How could he explain to Kenny and Jack Kennedy that he had managed to misplace Bobby Kennedy, who was found frozen to death in a cow pasture somewhere? Desperate to resolve the situation, Bruno began to press Bobby for more details of the town. "I don't know, I don't know," Bobby shouted through the phone. He was nervous and confused.

When Bruno couldn't find his schedule, Bobby's exhaustion came through. "This is just great," Bruno heard Bobby muttering through the phone. "We are going to blow this whole campaign! This whole thing is too disorganized and we are never going to pull this off! We shouldn't have even gotten into this thing—we are going to blow it! I am not going to be able to pull this thing off and I am going to blow it for Jack! What the hell am I doing trying to judge a prize bull contest anyway!" Bobby yelled into the phone, by now half talking to himself.

"Did you say prize bull contest?" Bruno asked, excited. He might not be able to find the schedule, but he knew exactly where that contest was.

"Yeah," Bobby told him, sounding worn-out.

"Watertown, Wisconsin! That's where you are! Here's how you go from there." Bruno gave him directions, and when he finished, Bobby slammed the phone down unceremoniously in his ear. He was still furious. Bruno later confided in Kenny about the mishap. Kenny told him not to worry; Bobby would get mad, especially when he wasn't in control of a situation, but he never stayed mad unless you really screwed up. Of course as soon as Bruno replaced the phone in the cradle, he found the missing schedule. Kenny decided the whole story was hilarious, and of course it gave him something else to give Bobby a hard time about.

"Kennedy won in Wisconsin with more popular votes than any candidate in the history of the state's primary, carrying six of the ten congressional districts and getting two thirds of the delegates," Kenny would say proudly in an interview six years later. "That seemed good enough to me, but it was not good enough to satisfy the experts, because Kennedy failed to carry the three so-called Protestant districts in the western part of the state, and lost to Humphrey in the Second District, around Madison, which he was supposed to win." And so the religious issue would not go away. With all the effort Jerry Bruno, Kenny O'Donnell, and Bobby had put in, Jack Kennedy had won a hollow victory. It was not enough to beat Humphrey in his own backyard. Now they would have to go to largely Protestant West Virginia and do it all over again. They would have to capture West Virginia and every other primary from there to Los Angeles if he were to win the nomination. Bobby and the exhausted Kennedy team boarded a plane and headed to West Virginia, where the Catholic senator from Massachusetts would make his stand.

※◇※

11

FROM WEST VIRGINIA
TO LOS ANGELES

Those are tasks that need to be done, and done now.

—BOBBY KENNEDY

Kennedy headquarters in West Virginia was located in the Kennawa Hotel, a ramshackle establishment not far from the State House in Charleston. On the mezzanine were the offices of Matt Reese and Bob McDonough, the two local people who were shepherding Jack through the state and introducing him to people. Immediately after the Wisconsin primary, the advance team of John Trainor and Jerry Bruno arrived, with others, leapfrogging from one event to another.

This would be the showdown between Kennedy and Hubert Humphrey. The Kennedy victory in Wisconsin, hollow though the press said it was for Kennedy, had given Hubert little choice but to take Jack on in West Virginia, a largely Protestant, rural, and labor-influenced state that should naturally support Humphrey's candidacy. The primary would prove pivotal for both men.

"All the old troupers," Kenny recalled, "were summoned to duty in West Virginia, along with a few new ones whom we had picked up in Wisconsin, such as Bruno who did our advance work there and stayed on with us as an advance man until we went to Dallas [in November 1963]. Bob McDonough and his able and tough West Virginian right-hand man, big Matt Reese, were understandably perplexed by some of Jack's Ivy League friends and Boston Irish Catholics, who were hardly the type to mingle well with voters in the impoverished coal-mining towns and the firmly anti-Catholic industrial cities."

On a chilly, rainy day in Fairmont, West Virginia, the Kennedy campaign first ran head-on into the anti-Catholic sentiment brewing in the hills and hollows of West Virginia. Trudging through the rain, Jack greeted the voters. Today, he had brought along Sam Huff, the famous football player, and a Kennedy supporter who lived down in one of the hollows. With the Catholic issue looming in front of him and Humphrey doggedly continuing his battle for the nomination, Jack knew he needed all the help he could get. Speaking before a crowd in Fairmont, Jack was constantly interrupted by a heckler. Trainor, standing beside Kenny down below the stage and off to the left, sensed Kenny's growing unease. "He's going to lose his temper," said Kenny to nobody in particular. Finally, a woman in the crowd asked a question about the Pope's influence on Catholics in the White House. It was a question he had heard a thousand times. However, today he had had enough. Jack's eyes grew icy. "I took the same oath, as a naval officer, my brother took it and died for this country, I took it as a congressman, a senator, and I am going to take it again when I am elected president of the United States! Nobody," said Jack—laying heavy emphasis on the last word, his voice rising—"nobody owns me—the Catholic Church doesn't own me, my father doesn't own me, *nobody owns me*. You either vote for me for what I stand for or don't!" Furious, Jack concluded his remarks.

Trainor heard Kenny take a deep breath. Jack said little as he descended; he and Kenny exchanged glances. The event had been filled with television and news media, who made a big play of it the next day. "He had answered the questions over and over again," says John Trainor, "in a million different places and towns, but this was by far his toughest response. His anger was visible." But his anger also got his point across more than his polite responses had. People began to take notice. Sometimes politics worked that way, with the best successes the most unplanned.

While later the West Virginia stories would grow affectionate and rosy in the recounting, at the time, the pain, exhaustion, and grueling uncertainty were all very real. It was hardest on the candidate himself, who despite his health concerns, pushed himself beyond endurance. Bobby worked unceasingly. The campaign had its most risky moment in Elgin, West Virginia, which had always been a stronghold of Adlai Stevenson, who was not running for president this year but had made known his availability as a potential candidate. Trainor had done a lot of advance work in Elgin, and by the time Kenny and Jack arrived, the site of Jack's speech was mobbed. It was a cool, windy evening and the rickety wood campaign platform was bathed in electric lights. As Trainor made a pathway for the candidate, Jack was mobbed by the crowd; people surged forward trying to reach and touch the candidate. Jack was as gracious as thousands of grasping, clinging hands allow you to be. As Trainor got Jack up onto the platform, he turned to leave and realized that his retreat was blocked by well-wishers; he had to stay up on the platform with Jack. He turned and caught Jack's eye and sensed that he should stay. The crowd continued its surge to the edge of the platform. Kenny had to struggle to join the others on the dais, which creaked against the tide of the crowd beside it.

Then, as Jack was introduced and began to speak, a baby appeared, floating across the crowd. The sight was so peculiar that it nearly brought the candidate to a complete halt. People were passing the baby above their heads, the infant bobbing from hand to hand, laughing and giggling. Horrified, Jack urged the crowd to pass the baby forward to him. Somewhere in the back the infant's mother squealed. She so wanted her baby hugged and kissed by the handsome Jack Kennedy.

John Trainor watched Kennedy, surprised and curious. He was not the baby-kissing type. Kennedy moved away from the microphone and knelt so close to the edge of the stage, it looked as if he might fall forward. Trainor felt Kenny move closer up behind him on the platform. As the baby floated toward him, Jack grasped the child firmly, pulling it into his arms and holding the baby tightly; he stood and walked toward Trainor. "Find the damn mother," Jack whispered, "before this poor child gets killed."

Trainor grabbed the baby and started to make his way off the crowded stage. It was just then that he saw what, if possible, was an even stranger sight, unplanned by the campaign and startling to all: Just out of the rim of the crowd was a man riding a magnificent white horse.

Stunned, Jack turned, grabbing Trainor's arm as he cradled the baby. "Look at it! Look at it!" said Kennedy, incredulous. As he moved back to the microphone and began to speak, he kept his eye on the magnificent animal in the background. Concluding his speech, he urged the rider to come forward. Clearly thrilled, rider and animal made their way to the platform. John Kennedy was no fool. He was not going to fight his way out of the crowd when he could ride out on a white horse.

"I remember him sitting on that white horse," said Trainor, "—what a magnificent sight—as they rode through the crowd and to safety."

The Maryland primary would be held a week after West Virginia's. It was a preference primary, meaning that the delegates elected to the national convention were bound to whoever won the preferential primary only for the first ballot. Many candidates and potential candidates chose not to enter the Maryland primary, choosing instead to marshal their resources elsewhere. Joseph Tydings, whose father Millard was the senator Joe McCarthy had smeared as a Communist sympathizer a decade before, explained that Jack and Bobby Kennedy "had other ideas." Political forces in Maryland were committed to Lyndon Johnson and urged Kennedy to stay out of the state. Kennedy came anyway. Joe Tydings, who had a lot of experience working on his father's campaigns, says he told Kennedy that "public perception was that he was going to lose West Virginia, which made Maryland so important." After a heated discussion with Joe Kearnan, an Irish Catholic Boston politician who had been sent in by Kenny and Bobby to organize Maryland and had succeeded only in offending just about everyone, Tydings knew Jack was in trouble. "I was really upset when I was meeting with Kearnan," Tydings recalls. "I told him not only do we have to carry Maryland but we have to carry it big! Kennedy's reputation is going to have to be rehabilitated after he is defeated in West Virginia by Hubert Humphrey." Humphrey had chosen not to enter Maryland, putting all his efforts, win or lose, into West Virginia. Tydings thought that Humphrey's decision would give Kennedy a fighting chance to recover and win the small border state.

Bobby called on young Joseph Tydings to take over the reins in Maryland. Tydings took a leave of absence from his law firm and became executive secretary of the campaign. Not wanting to seem to push Kearnan aside, Tydings decided the title suited him, and in practice it allowed him to run the entire state. Quickly, as was the Kennedy pattern, he set up Kennedy secretaries, region by region. Another benefit of having Tydings involved, Bobby Kennedy realized, was the fact that he was a Mason, one of the group that had long been a bastion of the male Protestant establishment in America. The Masons were largely supporting the candidacy of Texas senator Lyndon Johnson; they liked him in part because he would not allow the Pope to run the White House.

Putting the campaign in Tydings's hands was a stroke of political genius. By the time Jack Kennedy arrived in the state for an entire tour of the Eastern Shore of Maryland, Tydings was able to tell him with some pride, "Senator, do you realize that every county chairman for the Citizens for Kennedy in this part of the state is a Mason?" Kennedy was pleased. "It hasn't been easy convincing them!" said Tydings. Jack knew that he would have to win the support of cautious Protestants one by one, just as Tydings had done it.

On a regular basis, Tydings would make the short trip to the downtown Washington Esso Building, where he would meet with Bobby, Kenny, and Larry O'Brien, outlining the plans and progress in the state. There was little money left over for Maryland, so Kenny made it clear that Tydings would have to "pretty much do it on a shoestring." They agreed with his assessment that Maryland was crucial given the long odds in West Virginia, but resources had to be marshaled in West Virginia. As the four men sat in Kenny's often vacant office, Tydings told them not to worry. "Maryland is Kennedy country really. There is a large Catholic and ethnic base, especially around Baltimore City. With the support of the Masons and Jack's youth, which really appeal to people here, I think we can pull it off." Kenny was encouraged but skeptical. "Just do it," he replied.

Bobby especially pushed Tydings, soon the state's official campaign manager, to make use of his ties with the Masons. Acutely aware that the Catholic issue had not been put to rest in Wisconsin and was proving formidable in West Virginia, Bobby and Kenny met many times with Tydings, mapping out strategy and the best use of Jack Kennedy's time in the state. Jack flew in on the *Caroline* on a Thursday night, four days before the primary in West Virginia and eleven days before the Maryland and New York primaries, to address a huge rally at Washington College in Kent County on the Eastern Shore, kicking off the campaign. He flew out the same night and then came back the following day to campaign from Hagerstown to Frederick and Baltimore County and everywhere in between. When they arrived in Baltimore County after a long day of handshaking and speeches, an exhausted Jack Kennedy, accompanied by Kenny and Dave Powers, climbed into the plane and headed back to West Virginia. Bobby came back from West Virginia and filled in. Tydings had him for half a day. The day started badly. Bobby had used the opportunity working in Maryland to spend time at home across the Potomac with Ethel and his growing brood. He and his driver had gotten a late start that morning, as Bobby wanted to quickly go up to headquarters and check in. Back in Hartford County, in the town square waiting for Bobby, Joe Tydings was a wreck. Kenny had made it clear that he only had Bobby for half the day and already they were behind schedule. Standing at the side of the road, looking hopefully up the highway, Tydings felt himself getting more and more concerned. Finally, he spied Bobby's car coming down the road. Tydings was relieved. He had fought to have Bobby here. "Bobby was the guy to do it," Tydings had said to Kenny. Once Bobby arrived, they hurried into Aberdeen, Havre de Grace, Bel Air, and then to Baltimore County, and then from Baltimore County to Anne Arundel County, down to Baltimore City, and then, after several stops in the area, back in Baltimore City at about 11:30 Friday night. Bobby was spent as he headed back home and from there to West Virginia early the next morning.

Jack Kennedy had joined Bobby earlier that same day and, after spending the night at the Tydings family home at Oakington, gone up the next morning to Havre de Grace, Elkton, Sisel County, Queen

Anne's County, and then down to Easton, the county seat at Talbot, Cambridge, Dorchester, and then to Salisbury. They hit every single courthouse, county seat, restaurant, and town hall they could find; then the group hopped on the *Caroline* and flew to Baltimore. There Jack did another television program and then headed to a speech in Prince Georges County, before boarding the *Caroline* to fly at eleven that evening to Seattle for a tour of the West Coast. It was a typical campaign day for the Kennedys.

The Kennedy team, with John Trainor on lead as advance, was due in the small town of Dunbar, West Virginia, about eight one evening for a rally. Trainor had never been there before; with three states in contention, the advance team was stretched thin. Often Jack Kennedy would go into these events cold. Trainor was driving the candidate there, and they were forty-five minutes behind schedule, which meant the Kennedy organizers in Dunbar were getting panicked. "It seemed we spent the whole campaign making up time," Trainor recalls. Jack had a television appearance to make later, so as the car bearing Kenny, Jack, and John Trainor pulled into the parking lot of the event, he slammed the car into park and rushed into the building to find the people running the event. Spying a small, dark man who seemed in charge, Trainor grabbed him by the arm. Just then Jack and Kenny were walking through the double door leading into the building. "Look," said Trainor, his urgency forcing out his words quickly, "we're running late and we would like to get him off the stage as quick as we can!" The man stared at Trainor, jerking his arm loose, and said very clearly, "I don't understand!" Just then Jack arrived and the man made a beeline for him. As Trainor retreated to stand near the side of the stage, he was puzzled by the fellow's reaction. As the locals ushered Jack toward the stage, Kenny and Trainor hung back. Suddenly, Trainor noticed the same man with the jet-black hair pulling Jack aside and talking to him. "Geez," said Trainor to Kenny, "he looks madder than a wet hen."

Kenny was already gone. Seeing the commotion, he had immediately headed toward the candidate. As Trainor looked up, he noticed that both Jack and Kenny shot him a "now-what-have-you-done" look. The event was in progress; Jack was gracious and gave a strong stump speech; Kenny waited just off the stage. Once the event was concluded and Jack was briefly waylaid shaking hands, Kenny and Trainor made their way toward the car, with Kenny being sure not to let Jack too far out of his sight. "What's wrong?" asked Trainor hesitantly. "What happened? I know I must have done something!"

Kenny turned and looked sternly at him. "That goddamn Boston accent of yours is going to get us all in trouble!" It turned out that when Trainor had rushed in to inform the locals that Jack was "running late and we would like to get him off the stage as quick as you can," the small, dark man, who turned out to be not only a delegate but the mayor of Dunbar and the chairman of the delegation, thought he had said, "We are running late, so I will introduce him." Deeply offended, the man had made it clear to Jack Kennedy that that was not the way things were done in Dunbar and he could no longer count on his vote.

As they climbed back into the car and raced toward the television appearance, Trainor tried to explain and apologize. Fighting exhaustion and focused on the upcoming television appearance, Jack didn't want to worry about Dunbar. "Don't worry about it. It's too late. Bobby will fix it." Bobby did fix it. He made a special trip three days later and apologized in person to the mayor, soothing his ruffled feathers and ensuring his support of Kennedy. Bobby did, however, ask Trainor to speak a little clearer in the future.

John Trainor was once taken to task by Kenny because he rented a convertible for use in the campaign. "Kenny was furious," he remembers. "He just thought it was really arrogant to be driving around West Virginia with such horrendous poverty in a fancy new convertible. He was really mad! He said to me, 'I can't believe you would be so stupid!' " Trainor returned the car to the dealer the next day.

A Kennedy friend, the artist William Walton, recalled that the poverty the Kennedy brothers saw in West Virginia was really a watershed event for both men. "Bobby's early speeches were hardly set speeches. We would arrive at the typical coal mine just as the shifts were changing; and he would just walk up to them in a simple, direct way and say, 'My name is Bob Kennedy. My brother is running for president. I want your help.' And then he would stand with them . . . they, all black with coal dust, and his hands black from shaking hands. . . . His personality came over very well in this intimate face-to-face kind of thing. They dug him. They'd kid him, but he would kid right back." His interest and need to understand the poverty was tremendous, observed Bruno. He seemed intent on understanding how they lived and how difficult it was for them.

Helen Lempart, recruited from Senator Kennedy's Washington office, found herself working for the campaign in Logan, West Virginia, for two weeks making arrangements for opening the Kennedy headquarters. "Logan," Lempart says, "is almost indescribable. It's a town of about six thousand people, and its main industry had been coal mining until the state mechanization of the mines. This was a great experience for me; it was a real enlightenment, because for the first time in my life I realized that there is true poverty here in the United States and that some of these people were living in such misery. . . . It was really the strangest experience because after Wisconsin . . . you ran up against these people who really didn't know and didn't care about anything at all. . . . They were really suspicious about Mr. Kennedy at the time and exactly what his stands were, and the fact that he was Catholic, they didn't appreciate at all."

Helen often got to travel with Jackie, who spent a great deal of time working the stump. Although she was in the early stages of pregnancy, she knew that winning in West Virginia was central to her husband's ambitions. Lempart recalls one day when she was driving with Jackie in the so-called hollows around Logan. Both she and Jackie were struck by the shacks that hardly looked habitable for families, with cars up on blocks and laundry hanging in the wind. Jackie told Lempart to stop at one shack, where a husband and wife sat in rocking chairs on their small wooden porch. Climbing out of the car, she made her way up the muddy pathway to the front porch. Lempart was struck by Jackie's elegant bearing, her nice figure, and her designer suit. Introducing herself, she began to talk with the people about her husband. Lempart, still outside by the car, was astonished when the couple invited Jackie in.

She watched with trepidation as the candidate's wife disappeared behind the screen door. Panicked, she hurried to the door to catch Jackie. Here they were in the middle of nowhere and Jackie has just vanished into someone's house. Lempart did not relish explaining this to Kenny.

As she neared the screen, she came to a halt. Sitting inside on slight wooden chairs were Jackie and the couple, surrounded by their young children. They were sharing coffee. Lempart could hear Jackie's whispery voice coming through the screen. The couple was clearly delighted with their guest. Jackie stayed long enough to finish her coffee and ensure their support for her husband. They had been concerned about Jack's Catholicism. After talking with Jackie, they were concerned no more.

Ron Linton, a onetime labor reporter in Kentucky, had come to Washington on a fellowship for the American Political Science Association and ultimately got the chance to work for Senator Jack Kennedy. He jumped at the opportunity to get in on the ground floor of a political campaign. He was new to the staff, and with the West Virginia primary in full swing he had been one of the few left behind in the Esso Building in Washington.

One day the phone at his desk rang, cutting through the silence. It was one of the operatives in West Virginia, and he was beside himself. Jack was supposed to fly out of one small West Virginia town the next day in a chartered plane, but no one had yet gotten the aircraft. The man began hysterically declaring that Bobby and Kenny were going to kill him if the candidate was stuck there in the morning. "Should I charter a plane? What should I do? I'm just a lawyer from Boston—I don't know how to do this!"

"Geez," Linton thought, "how hard can this be?" Taking a minute to think it over, he told the fellow with all the authority he could muster, "Yeah, absolutely charter a plane." Unfortunately, the next morning there were two chartered planes. Kenny called Bobby, who was back in Washington for the day, wanting to know what idiot had authorized a second plane. Finances were tight; the campaign was spread thin. Linton overheard this exchange and, since he didn't feel secure in the

Kennedy inner circle, told himself that his association with the campaign was going to be a short-lived engagement. When he heard Bobby slam down the phone in his office, he thought, "Better 'fess up."

Tapping on the door frame outside Bob's office, he said softly, "Bob, kinda sorry about the airplane mix-up." Bobby looked up from the stack of papers in front of him.

"What? What mix-up?" Linton had heard stories about how tough Bobby was; he had heard him in action against Hoffa, and now he was waiting for him to blow. Quickly he explained what had happened. Bobby stared right at him, almost through him, it seemed to Linton. He let the silence sit for a moment; then Bobby finally said, "Better two planes than none. You did the right thing—you took a chance and you were right to tell me." With that Bobby returned to his stack of papers. Linton never heard another word about it, but he steadily found himself entrusted with more work.

"You see, the thing that you have to understand about Bob Kennedy and Kenny O'Donnell, and really Jack Kennedy was the same," Linton says. "They all liked people who made decisions—people who took the risk, took the responsibility. Bobby and Kenny would have lost total confidence in me if there had been no planes that morning—if I had told the guy not to charter a plane, or worse, if I had told him I was a new, low-level staffer and that it was not my responsibility to authorize or make a decision like that."

Jerry Bruno agrees. "They might not always be right," he says, "but they liked people who had the guts to make the decisions and take the responsibility. That never bothered them."

The day of the West Virginia primary, Ron Linton got a call from Kennedy's secretary, Evelyn Lincoln, telling him to meet the senator and Mugsy O'Leary, Senator Kennedy's driver, at National Airport and then take him home and stay with him there. Linton liked this idea; he was looking forward to spending some time with Kennedy. When Jack Kennedy slowly came down the ramp of the *Caroline*, he was in a foul mood. As they climbed into the car, Jack muttered, "Well, it's over. We're out of the campaign. We've lost West Virginia. Shit!" he said, banging his hand on the dashboard. Linton's reporter's instincts told him otherwise, and he argued the whole way home to Georgetown, with Kennedy pressing him to explain to him how they could possibly pull out a victory in the state. As they pulled in front of Kennedy's house, Jack waved his hand in the air, wearily closing the argument. "I'm going to take a hot bath, have some dinner, and watch television. Go back to the Esso Building and wait there until I call you to take me back to the airport."

"They told me to stay with you," Linton protested.

Jack looked annoyed. "I can take a bath alone, thanks," he said, ending the discussion with an authoritative slam of the car door as he and Mugsy headed into the house.

Resigned, Linton headed back to the Esso Building, where he sat with a few other staffers. When he picked up the phone he heard Evelyn Lincoln screaming, "I told you to take him to the house and stay with him!"

Ron dropped his feet from the desk and said with some anger, "Look, I brought him to the house and he told me to take off and go to the Esso Building and he would—"

Evelyn cut him off. "When you are told to stay with him, you stay with him. I am going to Kenny." With that she slammed down the phone.

Stunned, Linton began hurriedly dialing Kennedy's house just as the other phone rang. "Why didn't you stay with him?" Kenny's voice was steady and ice-cold. "When you are told to stay with him, you stay with him."

"Yes, sir," said Ron lamely. "No excuse."

With that Kenny hung up. Only later did Linton learn that Jack Kennedy was notorious for getting rid of people or ducking out on them. It was something the Secret Service would learn well. He had gotten rid of Linton, and then, turning on the television, had figured out that he was going to win in West Virginia, and had then rushed to the airport to get on a plane for West Virginia. In the meantime, the campaign had been desperately trying to reach Kennedy on the phone. There had been no answer at the house.

Three days later, Linton was with Jack at a speaking engagement. As the senator descended from the stage, he walked by Linton and said with a laugh, "I hear I got you in a little trouble with Kenny and Bobby the other day."

"Yes, sir, you did," Linton replied with a tight smile.

Kennedy laughed and winked. "Don't worry about it. I'll take care of it."

Later Linton caught up with Kenny. "Next time I'll know."

"Yup," Kenny replied with a grunt.

Remembering the incident, Linton says, "That was the way Kenny and Bobby worked. They weren't really mad. They knew I didn't know, and that Jack knew I was inexperienced. But the point Kenny was trying to make is, you know, when we tell you do something—do it! There is a reason for it. As long as you learned and admitted you screwed up, that's all those guys cared about. They hated people who made excuses."

"West Virginia was different than Wisconsin. In West Virginia we just knew we had won!" said Bruno. At the Kennawa Hotel headquarters Bobby and Kenny had watched the initial returns with trepidation. Jack was still in Washington and would return based on the outcome. As the evening continued, the trend grew. Jack Kennedy had won in West Virginia.

"The spectacular performance in West Virginia wrapped up the nomination for Kennedy," Kenny would say. "It settled the one big question about his candidacy in the minds of the leaders who controlled the delegates in the larger states—whether a Catholic could be elected."

As the concession telegram came in from Hubert Humphrey, Bobby turned to Kenny and said, "God, this must be awful for poor Hubert, ending up this way after working so hard in two states." At the Kennawa Hotel, the party went on, with Pierre Salinger knocking off the only two or three tunes he knew, and by four o'clock in the morning Kenny, Bobby, and Dave Powers had climbed up on a table and were singing any song they could remember. Bruno had never seen Kenny and Bobby so relaxed. It was a view into their friendship—their shorthand conversation, warm embraces, and songs they knew from school through the early campaigns—that he had not seen before. "I guess it was at that moment," Bruno says, "I realized just how damn close those two really were."

West Virginia was the demarcation line. A victory there meant a direct road to Los Angeles. "With that obstacle behind him," Kenny said, "Kennedy could spend the remaining two months before the convention putting together the political bits and pieces that he needed to form a solid bloc of support in Los Angeles." Jack, with Joe Tydings's help, would easily win Maryland and then Oregon, racking up impressive victories as he headed into Los Angeles. Thanks to his own smarts, charisma, and hard work—and thanks to the effort of his brother and his brother's college friend—he would lead the Democrats in 1960.

12

THE 1960 CONVENTION

The spirit of victory was in the air—you could almost feel it!

—KENNY O'DONNELL

"Joe!" barked Jack Kennedy, catching Joe Dolan off guard. It was 1957 and John Kennedy had his eyes firmly on the White House in 1960. "If I run in Colorado, how many delegates would I get?"

"I will personally get you half!" Dolan announced with unearned and presumptuous arrogance.

"Half?" Jack asked. "Is half enough?"

"Sure," said Dolan, hoping that Kennedy didn't catch the bravado in his voice. "Well presumably," continued Joe, "if every state gave you half, you would be nominated because you would get more than half of Massachusetts! Right?"

Kennedy burst out laughing. He liked the arithmetic and audacity of this young lawyer from Colorado. As he headed out the door of his Senate office, he called back, "I'll hold you to that, Joe."

Now, the night before the opening of the 1960 Democratic National Convention in Los Angeles, Joe Dolan had been one of the few given a free ticket to a thousand-dollar-a-ticket party fund-raising event. Dolan had hung out by the door, knowing it would be his only opportunity to get to shake the hand of a man he was convinced would be president soon. As John F. Kennedy entered, he was immediately engulfed by well-wishers trying to shake his hand or get in a word. He quickly spotted Dolan and grabbed him by the arm, pulling him along briefly. "Now remember our deal, Joe," Jack said mischievously, "don't hold back to make yourself look good as a prophet!" With that Kennedy released him and continued working the room. "Whew," thought Dolan, recalling their conversation of 1957, "what a fucking memory! This guy is really something."

Dolan had first gotten involved in government in 1947 and had spent his career shuttling from his practice as a Denver antitrust lawyer to work on various investigations in Washington, which is how he first came to the attention of Jack Kennedy. One day during the winter of 1956, Dolan had seen a letter on his desk bearing a Senate frank from the office of John Kennedy but had decided to ignore it because he was headed out to the Colorado ski slopes. When Dolan didn't reply, Kennedy's assistant Lee White called him; they wanted him to serve as counsel for hearings the senator planned to hold around his bill to amend the Federal Lobbying Act. "Senator Kennedy wants to hold legislative hearings on the lobbying act," White told him. "We've heard that you are a hell of a good lawyer or at the very least a good politician" — White laughed — "because seven out of the ten people we talked to recommended you."

"How long will it be?" inquired Dolan, trying to gauge how well his law partners were going to tolerate yet another Dolan absence. About ninety days, he was told.

"Fine," Dolan said, "let me talk to my partners." His fellow lawyers agreed; such work would be good for the firm. Dolan headed east in his beat-up car. There was something about Jack Kennedy that made you willing to drop everything and just come.

In February 1958, after the hearings were over and Dolan had returned to his law firm, Jack Kennedy came out to Denver to give a foreign policy speech. Kennedy's aide Ted Sorensen had asked Dolan to find a venue for the speech, and he had arranged for the Social Science Foundation at Denver University to host and promote Kennedy's appearance. The day of the speech Dolan got a call telling him that the university had moved the event — from a small hall to an eight-thousand-seat auditorium. They assured him he would have a large crowd. Dolan's experience in politics had taught him never to make such assumptions.

Dolan exploded, exhausted from a long day of litigation. "You can't move it there — that damn place seats eight thousand people! You can't do that. We'll never fill it!"

The caller from the Social Science Foundation was unmoved. Filled with trepidation, Dolan went to pick Kennedy up at the airport. He looked a little wan. After climbing into Dolan's station wagon, Jack said softly, "I need to stop for a drink."

Dolan was startled. Even after working with him in Washington, he didn't even know that Kennedy drank alcohol at all. They stopped at a small place, not far from the airport. Jack ordered a grasshopper. "That's a drink?" laughed Dolan. Kennedy shrugged. It had been a particularly bad flight and the landing had been horrendous, Jack explained. He had gotten bounced around quite a bit. It was only later that Dolan realized that he must have been in incredible pain with his back.

They were running about fifteen minutes late as they drove into the parking lot down below the auditorium. "How many does it seat?" Kennedy asked, bounding out of the car, his energy renewed.

"Damn," Dolan thought. He had been dreading this question since the airport. "Eight thousand."

"Eight thousand!" said Kennedy, turning to stare at Dolan. "Are you crazy?" he asked, his voice rising.

"We've arranged a backdrop to cut off half the space," Dolan said lamely.

As they neared the auditorium, Kennedy started to laugh. "Oh, well, here goes."

As Kennedy, Dolan, and Sorensen walked into the auditorium, Dolan realized he had made a mistake: The auditorium was not large enough. On this bitterly cold February evening, more than eight thousand people had turned out to see Senator John F. Kennedy. The place was packed; people were sitting in the aisles. Dolan and Sorensen exchanged a quick glance. "This guy is going to be president," Dolan said. Sorensen just smiled. As the two men followed Kennedy down the aisle, the crowd went wild. Dolan and Sorensen managed to find the two empty seats reserved for them as they watched Jack Kennedy bound up to the stage. Crowds exhilarated him.

Now after Jack Kennedy had spoken to thousands and thousands more people and had, with his brother Bobby, Kenny O'Donnell, and others, put together a campaign juggernaut, Dolan would witness in Los Angeles the first victory in Jack Kennedy's drive for the presidency, which had germinated more than two years before at events like that cold and crowded night in Denver.

Lyndon Johnson also wanted to be president. He had not run in the primaries, however. His strategy, as Kenny saw it, was to "use the senators and the congressmen. That was his only knowledge of national politics, and it was totally without merit." As Bobby and Kenny had learned the hard way in 1956, it was governors like Mike DiSalle of Ohio who had the real power when it came to influencing the top of the ticket.

As majority leader of the Senate, Lyndon Johnson was used to exerting power among legislators. Bobby Kennedy had had run-ins with him before, especially in the wake of the 1958 congressional elections, where the Democrats had taken electoral advantage of a recession to win even larger majorities in the House and Senate. The following year, Johnson, influenced by labor lobbyists, tried to change the party composition of Bobby's select committee, which had four Democrats and three Republicans, to reflect the larger Democratic margin, bring it into line with the makeup of the other committees, and thus solidify party power. Bobby Kennedy and Senator McClellan were adamantly opposed. Given the type of investigations the select committee was conducting, a bipartisan atmosphere was crucial to its success and credibility.

As it happened, Kenny O'Donnell was sitting in Senator McClellan's office discussing committee business when Johnson called McClellan and informed him that he wanted to change the composition of the select committee to five Democrats and three Republicans. Senator McClellan, who Kenny thought was someone who rather enjoyed "deciding a lot of things for himself, just listened very politely and kept calling him 'Mr. Leader.' He told Johnson, 'Of course I have to go along with what the Leader says. But let me tell you, Mr. Leader, that, number one, I won't serve on a partisan committee investigating anything this sensitive, and number two, you obviously can change the committee any way you want it. Of course, I will have to take it to the floor of the Senate and oppose you, and I intend to put it just the way it is. This is cheap politics,' " he continued, his voice rising. "If you want to work for the labor people, you go to work for the labor people, but I am going to work for the United States Senate!" Finishing with a flourish, he slammed the phone down hard. "Needless to say," Kenny said, chuckling, "the committee never changed."

Lyndon Johnson had made a warm speech nominating Jack Kennedy at the '56 convention—the famous "fighting sailor" speech—but then he had suffered his heart attack, which at least temporarily sidelined him from national consideration. However, by 1959, Kenny recalled, "it became evident that despite everything else he might be a candidate. I think we thought that if there was going to be any opposition it probably was going to be Stuart Symington who would be difficult." But by the primaries in 1960, Bobby and the Kennedy campaign realized they had underestimated Johnson's plans. They realized he was giving financial aid and comfort to Adlai Stevenson, who was not running in the primaries, and Hubert Humphrey, who was. "Humphrey was unelectable and unnominatable at that time, and we knew that," Kenny said. "So therefore he was only in there as a spoiler and was being encouraged by people, which we know to be true, who really had them in there to stop John Kennedy." In West Virginia, Johnson's hand was seen when the state's junior senator, Robert Byrd, attacked John Kennedy harshly. If the majority leader played his cards right, the convention would be deadlocked, and he would be the compromise nominee.

Jack Kennedy had barreled past Johnson's attempts at intimidation and by winning all the contested primaries after West Virginia had accrued almost enough delegates to give him the nomination on the first ballot. "We traveled around the West," Kenny said. "We had won all the primaries and we were sure that we were going to be nominated, but a lot of western states have these conventions at the later dates between the last primary and the convention itself." The pace had re-mained grueling. And at every stop in the western states they ran into the "Leader," Lyndon Johnson, the noncandidate. He kept explaining to all those who would listen that he was a "westerner" not a "south-erner," and he was the right man for the White House. For at that time, as the politically astute Johnson knew, no man from the South could ever hope to become president.

Kenny had a calculated view of Johnson's position in the party and his prospects for the nomination. "Johnson and Speaker Rayburn were certainly much more conservative than we were in a philosophical sense, and so therefore we were not happy with the kind of leadership they were giving. . . . But it was certainly nothing personal. None of us [Jack, Kenny, or Bobby] considered Lyndon Johnson as a formidable contender at that time. He was not well himself, and whether he was ever going to get back on his feet and certainly get back to be a candidate for president was unthinkable to us. And also, I think we [Jack, Bobby, and Kenny] would make as politicians a very cold analysis that at that time a southerner could not be nominated for the presidency under any circumstances, and so therefore we didn't [consider it]."

Johnson was not making a great deal of headway. He was still thinking like a legislator. McClellan, the wily Arkansas Democrat, had taught Bobby and Kenny a cunning and valuable lesson about national politics and power, a lesson Johnson would not grasp until the Los Angeles convention, when it was too late. "They [senators and congressmen] don't have that kind of strength at a convention. . . . I found that out in 1956 with John McClellan, [who] was very friendly to Robert Kennedy. I went to see John McClellan, whom I had never met before in my life, and Robert Kennedy, and I sat with him and he said, 'You know what? With Orval Faubus as governor, I am lucky to be here as a delegate. That was the first time we learned where the muscle was! We learned a great lesson. We realized where the power was in the United States, and it does not lie with the Congress or the senators. Lyndon Johnson and Sam Rayburn were just as convinced that's where the answer was, and I think they got the total shock of their life as they suddenly started to realize that these fellows they were relying on had no political clout at home at all." So the Kennedy team left Johnson to his machinations; they tallied up their delegates, and when they arrived in Los Angeles they were, as Kenny later recalled in typical understatement, "feeling very confident!"

At the fund-raiser Dolan was seated right next to a friend, football legend and Rhodes Scholar Byron White, a lawyer in Denver, a member of the board of the National Science Foundation, and, Dolan thought, one of the most astute political minds around. White had helped create the success of Jack Kennedy's Denver visit in February 1958. His skill would later help Robert Kennedy assemble an impressive team in the attorney general's office until John Kennedy appointed him to the Supreme Court. Unlike Dolan, Byron White was not exactly new to the Kennedy family. He had first met Jack Kennedy when Joe senior was ambassador to the Court of St. James's and White was one of the Rhodes Scholars invited to a reception at the embassy. He and Jack toured Germany together in the summer of 1939, just before the outbreak of war. Later they both ended up in the South Pacific, Jack as a PT boat commander and Byron White as a young operational intelligence officer, assigned to first a PT boat, then a destroyer, and finally an aircraft carrier. White saw Kennedy in combat and admired him: "He was a coolheaded guy under fire, very courageous, an expert sailor and a tough, tough guy." In 1958, when Ted Sorensen was looking for a place in Denver for Kennedy to speak, they called White. Unbeknownst to Dolan, White had deliberately changed the location. "The crowd had gotten so big for Kennedy's speech we had to move it to Municipal Auditorium," White remembers. "It was through Jack Kennedy's speech that my good friend and fellow lawyer Joe Dolan and I became drawn closer into the Kennedy circle."

"We had the votes," said Kenny simply. "We had the votes on the second ballot, the third ballot, or the tenth ballot. Didn't matter—we had the votes!" But the convention would not offer a smooth path to a winning Democratic ticket.

Kenny was in his room at the Biltmore when he heard that Jack had agreed to debate with Lyndon Johnson. Kenny blew up. This was exactly the distraction they didn't need. A debate would give Johnson more visibility and elevate him to the level of the presumptive nominee. He would tell Jack. He called him on the telephone. Jack was in his car. "You know," Kenny began, his anger obvious in his tone, "this is a real error! You don't debate with a fellow when you've got the thing won!"

Silence. Jack didn't like his decisions questioned. He had thought this thing out. He knew he had the nomination in hand, but he still had to win the White House in November. "Look," said Jack, his irritation palpable through the phone wires, "I know Lyndon like no one knows Lyndon, and I can't wait to get there!"

Kenny hung up more than unhappy. What was Jack thinking?

Jack Kennedy had no reservations. He had Johnson and he knew it. "He went in," Kenny would say later, and "that was the end of the Lyndon Johnson debate!" Awesome was the word some used. Kennedy was devastating, a combination of elegance, subtlety, smarts, and wit. "You're the greatest majority leader, and I hope you'll be the same for me," he told Johnson at one point, which made even Johnson's cadre of Texans laugh. If Jack Kennedy had decided then to choose Johnson as his vice presidential running mate, nobody would have guessed it. He didn't even discuss it with Bobby. At least not yet.

With the primaries over, Ron Linton, like the rest of the team, had headed to Los Angeles and the convention. Linton's job was to edit the daily newspaper that Pierre Salinger was publishing at the convention. The paper was a daily update for Kennedy delegates and potential delegates, informing them of the candidate's activities and progress. With part of the Kennedy team, Linton took over an office in an office building about two blocks away from the hotel Salinger was working from, connected by a direct phone line, to put out a four-page paper delivered to the doors of the delegates every single morning. "The paper went out every day," Linton says. "The last day it went out was the day Kennedy accepted the nomination. John Kennedy read the paper every single morning. It was all Bob Kennedy's idea; it became an incredibly effective tool"—and even helped in some unexpected ways. New Jersey governor Robert Meyner had long been a holdout against the Kennedy advance, which had frustrated Bobby. The day the governor arrived at the Los Angeles airport, Salinger and Linton sent four or five straw-hatted "Kennedy Girls" bearing balloons and Kennedy signs, who rushed up to the startled governor, surrounded him, put a Kennedy hat on his head, and smiled and waved at the waiting photographer from their newspaper team. "So the next day we had this great photo of him at the airport surrounded by the 'Kennedy Girls' with their hats and pom-poms, smiling and waving on the front-page news in the Kennedy newspaper," Linton says. Meyner was furious with the Kennedys, blaming Bobby, but once it was evident that Kennedy would be the nominee, politics as usual stepped in.

Early that morning, the solo phone in Linton's cramped office rang. "Come to my room," commanded Bobby Kennedy. Arriving at his Biltmore Hotel suite, Linton quickly saw that Bobby was not in a good mood. He held up a copy of the paper. "What the hell is this guy doing on the front page of my newspaper?" Surprised at the sudden anger, Linton took a step back. However, being a onetime newspaperman, he was not easily flustered. "Wait," he said. "Think about it, Bob," he said, rushing to get the words out before Bobby could explode again. "Think how confused everybody from New Jersey is right now! The governor may or may not ever be able to correct the perception that he is supporting Jack Kennedy—that he is a Kennedy man, even though he hasn't said so publicly. Time is short. Think about it."

Suddenly, Bobby began to laugh. "You know, it is pretty funny, considering he's been playing such games with us! Yeah, you're right—let him deal with it!" Linton smiled, and as he turned to leave, he ran into several people coming to report to Bobby on their state's delegation vote tallies. He stole a parting glance at Bobby. He looked simply beyond exhaustion. Bobby caught his eye and smiled. "Thanks, Ron."

Bobby had asked Byron White, now chairman of Citizens for Kennedy, and Joe Dolan to come out a week early to help prepare for the convention. "Bobby sent us to the hearings on the platform committee. Byron was a delegate and I had a floor pass. We went to those meetings

in room 8215 at the Biltmore, the meetings Bobby ran, giving instructions. He was something. He would stand on a chair or a table and all
these important guys would be gathered around and he would be barking out orders and asking them questions. He was really tough, and they
better have the answers! He didn't care who you were. There he was,
sleeves rolled up, hair all over the place. It was quite a picture to watch
these older guys jump for this young guy. Bobby was very, very direct.
John Kennedy was a charmer, but Bobby was no-nonsense; he couldn't
fake it if he wanted to. I guess the bottom line is that with Bobby you
would eventually learn to love him, but you had to learn. Kenny was
no charmer either. I guess that's why they got along; they were both so
damn direct."

Headed for the convention floor with his pass in hand the night the
different candidates were nominated, Dolan was worried. The Stevenson
people had packed the galleries, and after his nomination speech a noisy
demonstration went on for several minutes. As Dolan made his way
across the floor, he spied the chief of the "Irish Mafia" standing off to
the side, his black hair in a brusque crew cut, eyes narrowed, and arms
folded across his chest, watching the Stevenson demonstration with deep
interest. Was O'Donnell worried? Dolan made his way over to Kenny.
He liked Kenny but was intimidated by him. "Kenny was the politics,
labor, and big-city guy" for the campaign. "They would have all these
meetings, but you knew it wasn't the big time unless Kenny showed
up." Dolan stood quietly by his side for a moment watching and listening to the Stevenson uproar. Finally, hoping to break the awkward silence, Dolan ventured, "A lot of noise, huh?" Kenny said nothing for a
moment, never turning to look at Dolan, never unfolding his arms,
never taking his eyes off the scene occurring in front of them.

Dolan began to feel uncomfortable; maybe he shouldn't have said
anything. Finally, Kenny responded with a characteristic growl: "Last
gasp!" And, indeed, for Stevenson that is just what it was.

The Kennedy operation at the convention was designed to leave nothing
to chance. While many politicians and staffers were on the floor of the

convention, assigned to various delegations and tasks, the real power remained in the hands of Bobby Kennedy, Kenny O'Donnell, and Larry O'Brien. The people on the floor "would receive information and that's it," Kenny said. They would take orders. "And most of them on the floor of the convention would be so-called Kennedy staff. Perhaps outside of myself, O'Brien, and Bobby Kennedy, I don't know anybody that was on the floor of the convention that was really working in sort of a political sense. There were guys like Governor Ribicoff and [future] Speaker [John] McCormack and senators and governors and people like that who would be called Kennedy people, but they were not involved in it." Those working the floor, and in the off-floor "Boiler Room" command post, included political leaders such as Mayor Daley, Bill Green (the mayor of Philadelphia), and others who would get the information that Jack and Bobby wanted them to get and act as the lieutenants for them.

Dave Hackett, Bobby Kennedy's friend from Milton Academy, remembers Bobby's complete control of the convention. Hackett had been living happily in Canada and was even thinking of becoming a Canadian citizen before Bobby summoned him to Los Angeles to run the Boiler Room. "We arrived in Los Angeles two weeks before the convention and set up operations in a locked room in the hotel where we had eight girls and about twelve phones. For some of the biggest people, we'd have two people assigned just to stay with a state delegation and call in day and night any change in the delegate count" of convention-goers supporting Kennedy. "It was a combination of Bob Kennedy, Kenny O'Donnell, and Larry O'Brien," with Bobby like a good football coach, making sure he knew where all his key players were, who looked shaky, and who had to be worked on. Dave was struck by Bobby's single-minded determination, just as he had been back at Milton. "I think he was devoted to just one simple thing, and he wouldn't let anything stand in its way. That was to elect his brother, and that's what he was totally dedicated to doing. This is part of where the 'ruthless' charge began — because he upset a lot of people." At the convention and throughout his political career, Bobby had to make tough and often unpopular decisions. And that, as Kenny recognized, "doesn't always win you a lot of friends; nobody likes to be told no."

After the Wisconsin primary, Bobby had expected Arthur Garrity to move on to West Virginia, which looked like the turning point in the campaign, but Garrity says he "had to return to my law practice. My partners could only allow me so much leeway. Bobby was down on the Cape taking a brief break before really getting into West Virginia. He called and said, 'Arthur, you will of course be with us in West Virginia.' I said, 'I'm sorry, Bobby, I can't. I have to go back to work. I can't have my partners supporting me like this any longer. I'm sorry but the answer will have to be no.'" There was complete dead air. Bobby didn't say a word for a good fifteen seconds. Finally he said, "Well, that's good, that's fine. Lots of luck, we'll be in touch."

"I hung up and thought, boy, I really blew that one," Garrity says. But Kenny and Bobby valued his work enough that before the convention they pressed him into service — this time giving him little chance to say no — by sending him a prepaid airline ticket and putting him up in a small hotel, where he worked on voter registration materials for the fall campaign, so that the delegates could go home with an organized system for signing up prospective Democratic voters. Garrity saw Bobby in action around the delegate count for the Kennedy nomination. He had called a meeting for his suite at the Biltmore; the room was packed.

Garrity watched as the young man, who retained some of the shyness that he had first witnessed in 1952, fired off questions to men, many twice his age. "Bobby was a tough taskmaster," he recalls. "I watched these men stand there and wait to be called on. If you had done your homework you were fine, but if you hadn't, watch out." He stood on a chair in the middle of the room calling the names of area chairmen and asking them, "How's the vote going? How many delegates do you have in your delegation?" The Kennedy man from that delegation would make a report. One man had not done his homework, and Bobby asked him staccato questions: "Why don't you know? When did you last talk to them? What have you done about it? You can't just sit around and wait for them to let you know!" At the next meeting, recalled Garrity, the fellow had all the answers.

Garrity would encounter another Bobby Kennedy quirk during the fall presidential race. When he was finished campaigning or managing the race in a particular town or area, he would just grab his coat and go. If he had brought a suitcase he would just leave and then remember it afterward; somebody else would always have to take care of it. Bobby never asked.

Kenny figured that he had flown some five thousand miles in that damnable rickety old plane, the *Caroline.* "The *Caroline* went about one hundred twenty miles an hour and that's pretty good speed," he would say years later. "You're in the air a long time going between spots. Jack and I would sit and talk, and once in a while we'd discuss the vice presidency. Jack Kennedy never mentioned Lyndon Johnson's name.

"I don't think any of us thought an awful lot about the choice for vice president," Kenny would explain later. "You just try to win and discuss things afterward." On the day that the party would select its presidential nominee, Kenny was on the convention floor amid the chaos of vote counting and cajoling. He heard his name called out and someone shout, "Phone call!" Kenny headed off the floor to the Kennedy trailer, communications central; unlike the amateur hour of the convention in 1956, they were extremely well organized, leaving nothing to chance. Kenny grabbed the phone. It was Pierre Salinger, who had been recruited from the Rackets Committee to be campaign press secretary. "Come up to the room," Salinger told him. "Bobby wants to see you." Kenny put down the phone and felt suspicious. He knew the vice presidential nominee was on the table, and since Bobby had Salinger call them, then something must be wrong. Walking into the suite, he saw Salinger, who "looked glum," Kenny would say later. "Where is he?" Salinger nodded toward the bathroom. Its door was ajar and steam was coming out.

Salinger said, "He just told me to add up all the northern states we think we can carry and add Texas."

Kenny couldn't believe what he was hearing. He couldn't believe his ears. "Texas! You mean Johnson? You must be fucking kidding."

"I wish I was," said Salinger tersely.

"Well," growled Kenny, "I can't go for that myself." Spitting out the last part of the sentence, he turned and walked into the bathroom.

"Bobby was in the usual Kennedy place," Kenny recalled afterward, "in the bathtub." The Kennedy brothers always got lots of work done in bathtubs. According to John Reilly, the aide whom Kenny arranged to travel with Bobby during his years as attorney general, "It wasn't like he sat in the tub and stared at the wall. Usually he would be reading documents, papers, or a book, or have a yellow pad on which he might be writing out things he was working on. You would get back these pages and notes, with the ink blotted and wet where they had gotten soaked from the bathtub. In some ways, I think it gave him a chance to get some work done in peace and quiet, and maybe relax a little anyway."

Kenny and Salinger pushed open the bathroom door. Bobby looked up; he could see the anger on Kenny's face. "Don't tell me it's Johnson!"

"I guess it is," said Bobby wearily. "He's seeing him now."

Kenny shook his head violently. "Bobby, I have always dealt through you, but this is too much! Do you realize this is a fucking disaster? Nixon will love this. Now Nixon can say Kennedy is just another phony politician who will do anything to get elected. I want to talk to your brother myself on this one." Kenny's words were spilling out in anger. "I am not about to stand still on this one. I want to talk to Senator Kennedy myself!"

Bobby was obviously upset. "All right. As soon as I get dressed we'll go up and see him." He dragged himself from the steaming water, tossing the yellow pad and pen aside. Soon they were on their way to Jack Kennedy's suite. Johnson had by then gone back to his own hotel.

"I suppose Jack changed his mind back and forth—as I did—maybe, oh, at least six times," Bobby said later, reflecting on the choice of Johnson. "First we thought it was a good idea, then not. . . ." And so the discussion had proceeded all day until a decision was made and Kenny got his phone call from Salinger.

"Jack Kennedy's suite," at the Biltmore, recalled Kenny, "was filled with a throng of northern Democratic leaders—David Lawrence, Mike DiSalle, John Bailey, and Abe Ribicoff." Also present was Chicago's Dick Daley. All of them had gathered to offer Jack Kennedy congratulations on his choice of Johnson as vice president. Johnson, Kennedy told them, explained he had wanted some time to think it over, although it looked as though he would accept the offer.

Bobby and Kenny stood among the throng, listening to them all take credit for urging the choice of Johnson. Kenny felt himself growing angrier and angrier; he consoled himself by talking to Jack's brother-in-law, Sargent Shriver, who shared Kenny's misgivings. Jack was listening to David Lawrence tell him how, compared to someone like Senator Henry "Scoop" Jackson of Washington, Johnson would provide the strength in the South that Kennedy so desperately needed. Then Jack saw Kenny's expression. Kenny didn't have to say he was furious; his face said it for him. He indicated that Bobby and Kenny should follow him into the bedroom, but it was filled with people. When Jack saw the bathroom light was on, he turned to his brother. "Bobby, I'd better talk to Kenny alone in the bathroom." Bobby nodded. He could see that Kenny was about to explode, an event he had witnessed on various occasions since Harvard, and he didn't need to be on the other end.

Once they had shut the bathroom door behind them, Kenny burst into anger. "This is the worst mistake you have ever made," he said, spitting the words out. "You came out here to this convention like a knight on a white charger, the clean-cut Ivy League college guy who's promising to get rid of the old hack machine politicians. Now in your first move after the nomination, you go against all the people who supported you. Are we going to spend the campaign apologizing for Lyndon Johnson and trying to explain why he voted against everything you ever stood for?" The labor leaders who had backed Jack, and whose help he'd need in November, would feel betrayed by the presence of Johnson on the ticket, since Johnson had not been a major supporter of any labor initiatives in Congress.

Jack Kennedy was stunned by Kenny's attack. Kenny watched as the color drained out of his face and fury rose to replace it. It took Jack a minute to regain that famous Kennedy composure. He didn't like being spoken to this way, and it was only Kenny or Bobby that dared challenge him this forcefully. "Wait a minute," Jack said evenly. "I've offered it to him, but he hasn't accepted it yet and maybe he won't. If he does accept it, let's get one thing clear." Jack Kennedy's blue eyes steadily returned Kenny's black stare. "I'm forty-three years old, and I'm the healthiest candidate ever for president in the United States. You've traveled with me enough to know that. I'm not going to die in office. So the vice presidency doesn't mean anything! I'm thinking of something else, the leadership in the Senate. If we win, it will be by a small margin and I won't be able to live with Lyndon Johnson as the leader of a small majority in the Senate. Did it occur to you that if Lyndon Johnson becomes vice president, I'll have Mike Mansfield as the leader in the Senate?" Mansfield was a huge Kennedy supporter and would back Jack's agenda in Congress with more alacrity and vigor than a Majority Leader Johnson would.

Jack Kennedy waited for Kenny to grasp the meaning behind his words. Johnson was the choice, Kenny realized, and Jack was right about his analysis of congressional power politics. Opening the bathroom door, Kennedy gestured to Bobby to come in and join them. "You get your tail end over and get your labor friends in line. Talk to Walter Reuther and George Meany, get to work on them. You get them and tell them this is the way it has got to be. I don't know whether he will take it or not, but I've offered it to him and I suspect that he will take it." Bobby and Kenny exchanged glances and headed out to find the labor people. This was not going to be pleasant.

Throughout this exchange, Bobby had been standing sentry outside the bathroom, buttonholed by politicians eager to talk to the brother of the nominee. "Robert Kennedy was absolutely neutral in the whole thing," Kenny remembered. "He didn't have a position one way or another, and he was not present at the conversation. Bobby didn't have a strong positive or negative opinion about whether it was Johnson or Jackson on the ticket." When the choice of Johnson began to upset Kenny and threaten the labor constituency, then it became Bobby's problem, because it was Jack's problem.

Kenny came out of the bathroom. "Bobby, we've got this problem," explained Kenny, speaking in the typical Bobby and Kenny shorthand that only the two of them understood. "They"—meaning Walter Reuther and George Meany—"they're not going to listen to me, they're going to listen to you," Kenny told him. "I'm not that big, and you and

I will have to go over and see them. I know them all, but you're the candidate's brother and you've got the muscle. I don't have it."

Bobby understood at once. The two friends headed over to the Statler Hilton where the labor leaders were gathered. Kenny wasn't entirely sure that Bobby understood the depth of anger and betrayal the labor men were going to have over the selection of Johnson. Bobby found out fast. When they entered the suite, the union leaders were shouting and yelling.

Labor was deeply opposed to Johnson because of his conservative, antilabor voting record. Their fear with a Kennedy-Johnson ticket was that they would end up with two conservative Democrats in the White House. After getting assurances from Kenny that it would not be Johnson, labor felt betrayed and lied to. George Meany of the AFL-CIO and Walter Reuther blistered Kenny and Bobby. They were outraged, particularly because they learned about Johnson's selection from television, not from Kennedy's lieutenants Kenny and Bobby, according to Paul Schrade, who was Walter Reuther's aide and was present for the confrontation. "They lamely tried to explain that they had gotten caught in traffic between the hotels," and thus hadn't got the word out. Reuther, said Schrade, was even more angry then, noting that the hotels were only five to six blocks apart; they easily could have walked or better yet, said Reuther acidly, "used a telephone!"

Bobby had been most shaken by the reaction of one of the Kennedys' warmest and strongest allies, Jack Conway, who had approached with a look that convinced both men that he was about to slug Kenny. "I mean they murdered me and it was really rough. Guys, some of them who were great personal friends of mine — I had spent a lot of time socializing with these people and am still personal friends with all of them, families and everything else — they were just so bitter. It was unbelievable." Later, after John Kennedy was dead and Johnson was president, Kenny would sadly chuckle at the sight of these same union leaders telling Johnson what a great guy he was.

After some rough conversations and myriad accusations of betrayal, Kenny and Bobby left the enraged labor leaders and headed back to Jack. They could only hope that Jack was wrong in his belief that Johnson would accept the nomination. "Bobby was ashen. We were all ashen." There was no way that Jack Kennedy or any candidate could survive the embarrassment on national television of having his choice for vice president challenged. With all that time taken up with acrimonious nominating speeches and seconding speeches for the two candidates, Kennedy's opportunity to introduce himself to a national audience would be devastated and Richard Nixon would have a clear path to the White House.

Returning to Jack's suite, the three huddled in the bathroom, and Bobby told Jack the bad news. "At Jack's request," recalled Bobby, "I went down on one occasion" to Johnson's hotel room and told him "he was going to be opposed. How would he like to be chairman of the Democratic National Committee instead?" Johnson, sitting in his suite with his wife, Lady Bird, and Speaker Sam Rayburn, was stunned at Bobby's request. Johnson himself was having second thoughts about accepting the number two spot, but to have the offer taken away was unacceptable. As Bobby told it later, "His eyes filled with tears, and he was very upset, and said that he really wanted to be vice president. And so, he became so committed during the course of the day to being vice president, and Sam Rayburn became so committed, that by the time that afternoon was over, it was decided that he'd be vice president."

As Kenny and Bobby left the Johnson suite, Bobby had sensed the hostility from Rayburn and Johnson. When labor indicated that they were offended by the choice of the Texas senator, Jack had asked Bobby to tell Johnson that it could get ugly. Instead, when Johnson came to Jack's suite, in Bobby and Kenny's presence, livid that Bobby had, in effect, unoffered him the vice presidency, Jack casually told Johnson, "Bobby was out of the loop." Johnson, his eyes still moist, threw an accusatory look at Bobby and told Jack he would indeed take the spot and suffer any fight, if they would have him.

Jack wasn't worried about telling Johnson that Bobby had been unauthorized to say what he said. Bobby would understand. It was his job to be the lightning rod. As on a good football team, everybody had a role to play. Bobby, the dutiful younger brother, did not care if Johnson liked him or not. Jack had asked him to do a job, as he had so many other times, and he did it. Yet his role in the choice of Kennedy's running mate would come back to hound him. Like his decision to work for McCarthy, it would put an early strain on his relationship with Johnson and be misconstrued and misread throughout his career.

In the end, Jack Conway, Walter Reuther's administrative assistant, called Kenny, who was with Bobby and Jack in the candidate's suite. Labor, Kenny reported to them, "would not put up a candidate; they were just angry, but they would not tear up the convention." The shock of choosing Johnson had been a blow that Walter Reuther had not anticipated. After eight years of a Republican White House, Reuther and the other labor leaders had convinced themselves it wasn't worth blowing the election over Lyndon Johnson. Labor would have to fold, Jack would get Johnson, and — Bobby had been right — now the Kennedy campaign could add Texas to the tally of states they could count on at the convention and in November.

Through Kenny and Bobby, working with Walter Reuther, Jack Kennedy obtained a commitment from Johnson in favor of the party's civil rights plank and agreeing to several other key concerns of labor. This satisfied the Michigan delegation, in alliance with labor leaders, which had delayed the entire convention as they debated whether to oppose Johnson on the floor.

Jack's gamble had succeeded, though the battle was not without its scars, the relationship between Johnson and Bobby being the most visible wound. But once they were in power they could try to mend their fences. There would be nothing, Bobby thought, that could really go wrong once they had won the White House.

With the nomination won, Bobby reminded everyone that the fight had just begun. John Kennedy was an underdog in the race against Richard Nixon. Once Jack had triumphed, Bobby ordered the Kennedy staff into the ballroom of the Biltmore Hotel and also commanded the attendance of everyone in the Democratic party operation. He told them what they were expected to do. He also told them they were expected to start right away. This was now Jack Kennedy's Democratic party, and they had better get on board or get out of the way.

13

CINCINNATI AND CHICAGO, 1960

We have every confidence the best-informed citizens in the history
of the United States will return a judgment
in November that will be right.

— BOBBY KENNEDY

One day early in 1958, William Geoghegan sat in his Cincinnati office putting the finishing touches on a nine-page letter to Bobby Kennedy. The letter analyzed in great detail the political situation in Ohio, where Governor Michael DiSalle was making noises about running as a favorite-son candidate for the Democratic presidential nomination in 1960. "I told Bob that I thought it was a mistake and that we could put together a ticket that could win, that DiSalle had no chance of winning the White House, and that the end result of a favorite-son candidacy would be to splinter the delegate vote and eventually the cost would be borne by Jack's candidacy. The only way we can win the White House back is with John Kennedy." Geoghegan addressed his letter to the labor rackets. He wasn't sure what to expect in return. He would have to wait and see. At the end of the letter he included a hello to his friend Kenny O'Donnell.

Bill Geoghegan was yet another Harvard connection of Bobby Kennedy, dating from 1947, when he was a first-year student at Harvard Law School and living in a boarding house by Ridge Tech. Geoghegan's younger sisters Jean and Margie were both students at Manhattanville College in New York and had become friends with Ethel Skakel and Jean Kennedy. When the women came up to visit Boston for a weekend during the summer of 1947, they booked a room at the Copley Plaza

Hotel, where Joe Kennedy often kept a suite. Geoghegan's sisters invited him to join them for lunch at Joe's dining room, where he met Jean Kennedy and Ethel Skakel. "My brother Bobby lives right around the corner from you," Jean told him. "Why don't you go over and introduce yourself? He knows a whole group of guys there."

Geoghegan, who was feeling a bit isolated at the law school, soon made his way over to the Varsity Club, an initially intimidating place, filled as it was with massive football players playing pool and Ping-Pong. Bobby introduced him to Kenny, Nick Rodis, and Paul Lazzaro. As they sat chatting, Geoghegan watched in amazement as a football player named Chuck Glynn crushed the Ping-Pong balls that strayed close to his feet. When Geoghegan mentioned that he was planning to join his roommate on Cape Cod, Bobby said, "My family has a place down there, in Hyannisport. I'm going down there this weekend. Do you want a ride?" Geoghegan quickly accepted and met Bobby back at the club that Friday. Bobby was wearing only swimming trunks in the heat. As they drove down to the Cape in Bobby's convertible, Geoghegan felt overdressed and uncomfortable in his slacks, shirt, and tie, his pale skin burning in the sun. He didn't want to admit it and ask Bobby to put up the top. "He wasn't a real talkative guy," Geoghegan remembers. "We sort of sat there and about every five miles he would or I would say something; the other would answer and then there would be silence for another five miles. It took me a while, but later I realized that he was just kind of shy, a very private guy, and really he did not know how or really like to make small talk. It wasn't who he was."

The two men had kept in touch only intermittently over the last thirteen years. But when Geoghegan, now a lawyer, wrote that letter in 1958, it seemed worth offering the Kennedys what help he could, especially in fund-raising, as they planned the last step in their ascent from Massachusetts to the presidency.

By the late 1950s, Jane Byrne was mourning how her life might have turned out. A Chicago native, Jane Burke had been married in the early 1950s to William Byrne, a pilot in the Marine Corps who also served in the reserves. They had a daughter, Kathy. One weekend in 1959, while her husband was away on routine training exercises, she received a call from the military chaplain. He had terrible news. William had been killed in a training accident. In one awful moment Byrne went from the top of the hill to the bottom of the heap, the plan for her married life in ruins. A woman bred to be a prosperous wife and mother, she was now a single woman on her own with a small child. What made her fate feel worse was the way her husband died — in training, accidentally, not on a battlefield. Having grown up in the World War II era of heroes who died for a clear-cut cause, she had trouble defining herself as a widow of a man who had given his life for no transcendent reason. His fate seemed so unfair, so pedestrian. When other women told her she should be proud, she couldn't believe them or even trust their sincerity.

One day as she drove down Lakeshore Drive to downtown Chicago, she heard a Yankee voice crackle on the car radio: Senator John F. Kennedy, Democrat from Massachusetts. Anyone who dies in the service of the country is a hero, he was saying: Americans should be proud that they were willing to give their life for their country. Every contribution counts, he said, no matter how it was made. Byrne felt almost as if he were talking directly to her; at last someone was addressing her agonized questions and making her feel included. Finally what her friends were telling her made sense as she heard it in the words of a man she knew to be a war veteran himself who had nearly died. For her, John Kennedy could give her situation meaning. He would lead her into political life, a road that would take her nearly two decades later to the mayoralty of Chicago.

Mike DiSalle would in time become a close friend of Kenny O'Donnell's, but in late 1959 as John Kennedy began his run for the White House, the Ohio governor's ruminations about becoming a favorite-son candidate for president were not something that Kenny and the Kennedys were looking upon kindly, as Bill Geoghegan had long since surmised. The Kennedy team arranged to meet secretly with DiSalle in a motel near the Pittsburgh airport. "Steve Smith had reserved two rooms, one under the name Smith and the other under the

name Brown," Kenny recalled in a later interview. Jack Kennedy, accompanied by Kenny and Connecticut Governor John Bailey, arrived
at the motel late. Strong head winds had delayed the *Caroline*'s arrival.
Kenny was stunned to discover that there were no rooms reserved for
anyone by the name Smith and Brown. After much consternation,
O'Donnell and Bailey went out to the parking lot hoping to find Governor DiSalle's car. "John Bailey and I ran around the crowded parking
lot, getting down on our knees to search in the darkness for an Ohio
license plate. The smoothly organized and highly efficient Kennedy machine had collapsed again."

"This is great," Jack growled. "Now you guys have ruined me in
Ohio!" Then the desk clerk mentioned another motel at the other end
of the airport. The Kennedy team went tearing through the airport,
running into DiSalle, who had given up and was just leaving. At last,
DiSalle and Kennedy met and talked.

"DiSalle was evasive in the first meeting," Kenny remembered. Kennedy wanted DiSalle's endorsement, which could open up greater support for him not only in the important battleground of Ohio but
throughout the Midwest. Bill Geoghegan was party to the talks between
the Kennedy brothers and Kenny and DiSalle and his aides. "They told
him, 'Okay, you run as a favorite-son candidate throughout the state,
and all the delegates technically pledged to DiSalle would really be
Kennedy delegates and released on the first ballot for John Kennedy.'"
DiSalle was unwilling to make a final commitment to Jack, but Jack
left the meeting confident he had, as he later told Kenny, "DiSalle
hooked and he would come around."

Bobby and Kenny wanted to be sure. "Bobby went to Ohio with John
Bailey to put more pressure on DiSalle," Kenny said later. "John Bailey,
a veteran politician who does not shock easily, told me later that he was
startled by the going-over that Bobby had given DiSalle. Bobby made it
coldly clear that DiSalle could avoid a showdown fight for party leadership in Ohio, with the Kennedys backing DiSalle's opponent, only by
agreeing to be the first governor of an important state to announce an
endorsement for Jack Kennedy." On New Year's Day 1960, Kenny heard
that Michael DiSalle had capitulated. "A week later, to the great surprise

of everyone in Washington, the newspaper headlines announced that
Governor Michael DiSalle was pledging all of Ohio's delegate votes to
John F. Kennedy."

"That was really the breakthrough," Geoghegan says, "and throughout
the contest DiSalle became one of the strongest Kennedy supporters. It
was hardball politics that Bobby and Kenny were playing, but sometimes
that's just what you had to do, and they knew how to do it. . . . They
knew that it was a key endorsement. I wasn't part of the inner circle, so
I was not part of it, but I do know that as tough as it was, Mike DiSalle
came to love Kenny and the Kennedy brothers."

"That was really where the ruthless thing got going," according to
Bobby's longtime aide Angie Novello. "Bob Kennedy had a job to do.
He was the guy who had to say no to some people and get other people
to say yes when they really wanted to say no. That's a tough position to
be in and it requires an inner toughness to get the job done. Bobby had
that."

After his assistance on the DiSalle endorsement, Geoghegan didn't
hear much from the Kennedy brothers until after Labor Day 1960. He
was vacationing in northern Michigan when he got a call from Byron
White, by then chairman of Citizens for Kennedy, summoning him to
a Cincinnati hotel for breakfast the next morning. Geoghegan went.
Back in late 1959, Bobby had responded to Geoghegan, telling him to
"stand by in Ohio and we will get in touch when we need you." That
was now. White explained to Bill that they needed someone to become
chairman of Citizens for Kennedy in southwestern Ohio. Geoghegan,
who couldn't spare the time from his law practice, spent two days introducing White to eight different potential candidates for the post. At the
end of the second day, as Geoghegan drove White to the airport, he
asked him which person he'd decided upon. White had been polite and
noncommittal during their meetings. The chairman of Citizens for Kennedy let the question hang in the air for a moment as Bill maneuvered
through traffic. "You."

"Me?" said Geoghegan, genuinely shocked.

"Yup."

There was little more discussion. After White made his plane, Bill

Geoghegan headed back to town to become local chairman of Citizens for Kennedy.

A week later Bobby Kennedy was in town to speak at a luncheon that Geoghegan had arranged for him through his political contacts in and around the state. Much to Geoghegan's delight the crowd was about a thousand strong. Bobby had been picked up at the airport and brought directly to the hotel. It had been a rough several days for him; he had been campaigning for his brother in Indiana and it had not gone well. "The schedule was brutal," Geoghegan says. "The Ku Klux Klan was very strong in southern Indiana and I gathered that they had really physically harassed and made things terribly difficult for Bob. I learned later that in fact it had been a pretty hairy situation. Bobby had been pounded there about the religious issue, the Catholic thing, and the Klan had really harassed him and given him a bad time. He was just physically and emotionally drained." In the hotel suite Bobby collapsed into a chair, ashen, and shaking with tremors. Almost as quickly as he had collapsed, he was up again rushing headlong into the bathroom. He had a bad case of the runs, diarrhea — a combination of exhaustion, bad food, no rest, and probably a virus. He told Geoghegan to hold the luncheon without him. "I'll come down and speak," he said, "but I just can't sit through that luncheon."

When Bobby appeared, Geoghegan thought he looked worse than he had when he first arrived. Geoghegan told him that he would make up some excuse, but Bobby was insistent; people had come to hear him speak about his brother, and he wasn't going to let them down. Partway through the speech, Bobby began to grow emotional. His voice began to rise as he talked about the experience in Indiana and the injustice of his brother's being judged by his religion.

Then suddenly Bobby stopped in midsentence, turning as white as the napkins on the luncheon tables, and gripped the lectern, swaying slightly. "He looked as though he were going to faint," Geoghegan remembers. "Tears were coming down his face; then he began wheezing slightly." He looked helplessly at Geoghegan, who hurried to his side and helped him sit down. The room became deathly quiet. A guest grabbed a water glass and thrust it up to Geoghegan. "Bobby couldn't go on. He just kind of fell apart. Later when I realized how sick he really was, I marveled that he had kept pushing himself. He should have been rushed to a hospital, but he wouldn't hear of it. We helped him to his room and that was all he allowed us to do. First, though, he gave me his speech and had me finish it. That was the way he was—for the right cause he would push himself beyond human endurance. It was almost an emotional thing with him. He just could never give up."

The press watching the entire episode played it big in the newspapers the next day, while some Republicans scoffed that Bobby had staged his illness to garner public sympathy. Bobby didn't like the attention at all. "It wasn't his way," Geoghegan says. "He wasn't a phony and he didn't like to show weakness, but he had just pushed himself too hard."

The Cincinnati luncheon was the first time that Geoghegan had met Bobby since their ride to the Cape back in 1947. To him, Bobby was as intensely determined as he had appeared to be some thirteen years before. Though the human cost of such intensity could be high, it was a good way to run a campaign, Geoghegan thought. He would later work for Bobby Kennedy as attorney general and volunteer in his 1968 presidential campaign.

Chicago, like Boston, was an Irish political town. Unlike Boston, Chicago had its political power concentrated in the hands of one man, Richard J. Daley, the master of political life there for upward of two decades. "It wasn't a game to my dad, Kenny, Bobby, or Jack; it was a business that affected people's lives and really mattered," says William Daley, son of the late mayor and secretary of commerce in the Cabinet of Bill Clinton. And in 1960, the business of Mayor Daley was to see that John F. Kennedy swept Chicago and carried Illinois.

Jack Kennedy, Bobby, and Kenny allied themselves with a young Chicago congressman, Dan Rostenkowski, one of Mayor Richard Daley's men. Recently elected to the House, he had worked on legislation with Massachusetts congressman Eddie Boland, where he had caught the eye of the Kennedys and the Irish Mafia. "I got to know Kenny O'Donnell, Bob Kennedy, and Larry O'Brien, and what we discovered is that we had a common ground in politics," Rostenkowski says. "The way things worked in Chicago was pretty much the way things worked in Boston. The year was 1958 and Boston was very political, like Chicago with the Irish. It is a well-known fact that after '56, we all had our eyes set on '60."

While the Kennedy headquarters had been set up in a storefront on North Michigan Avenue, the real campaign decisions were made in city hall. And the real source of the money for the entire Kennedy campaign was located in Chicago: the Merchandise Mart. The twenty-four-story building had been opened by Marshall Field in 1930, boasting ninety-three acres of renewable space. When Joe Kennedy bought it in 1945, he had become the owner of what was then the world's largest commercial building. The Mart became the center of the Kennedy fortune, both politically and financially.

Jane Byrne had gotten a job at the Michigan Avenue headquarters as secretary-treasurer. She wasn't entirely sure what the title meant, but she felt involved and active in a way she hadn't since her husband had died. One of her jobs was to sign for the bank deposits and withdrawals. "I would go home at night and there would be 150,000 dollars in the account, and by the morning the account would be completely overdrawn. It turns out that with limited funds, the Kennedy campaign was using the money, switching it around and moving it to different primary states all across the country that were in need of cash."

The comptroller of the Mart would calm her with a smile and a chuckle. "I know, I know. It will be covered by tonight, don't worry. You realize," he would tease her, "you are actually secretary/treasurer of me, you know!" It became an inside joke between the two and slowly she grew more and more comfortable in her new position.

Quickly three names began to define business at the Michigan Avenue headquarters: Kenny O'Donnell, Bobby Kennedy, and Richard Daley. Conflicts would often arise between the campaign headquarters and the campaign chairman, who was Daley himself. "In any dispute," Byrne says, "they would always call on Kenny O'Donnell to settle anything. He was the man you had to call upon to solve it, especially when it came to the mayor." Sargent Shriver, who worked at the Mart, ran the North Michigan Avenue headquarters. "Sarge really tried to set up kind of an independent operation," Byrne says. "I think he wanted to do more than just have the appearance of independence; I think he really wanted to give the Kennedy operation an opportunity to reach independent voters." In doing so, he made his first critical mistake — hiring Steve Mitchell as executive director of the Speakers Bureau that sent out pro-Kennedy stand-ins to speak in favor of Jack. Mitchell was an independent figure on the Chicago scene who Shriver thought would help bring in the unaffiliated voters and the so-called Lakefront liberals, the affluent population bordering Lake Michigan, who were less dependent on the Daley machine and therefore immune to the orders from city hall to vote this way or that. "He had not taken his loyalty oath — solemn to Buddha and all of this stuff," Byrne says. "Sargent Shriver may have been the campaign manager but nobody in the real political circles paid any attention to him. The real ones who ran Chicago and Illinois for Jack Kennedy were Kenny O'Donnell and Bobby Kennedy, and that was a fact!"

One particularly harried morning Jane Byrne was manning the headquarters phones. "Citizens for Ken —" she answered, before she was cut off by a cold voice on the other end of the line. "Who the hell is Steve Mitchell?"

"Well," Byrne answered tentatively, "he was a candidate for governor here and he is now director of our Speakers Bureau. He's recruiting people to come in and join him, recruiting the independents to give speeches and parties in the suburbs and along the waterfront."

"Do you know who Matt Danaher is?" asked the voice with growing annoyance.

"Yes, sir," Byrne replied. She didn't know Danaher personally, but she had heard that he was very close to the mayor, as the "Buddha," his right-hand man.

"Well, Matt Danaher called me and said Daley is screaming that Mitchell has got to go. So get rid of him. Tell Sarge to get rid of him."

Sensing the caller was about to hang up, Jane asked quickly, "Who may I say —"

"Kenny," said the voice. "Kenny O'Donnell." With that the phone was unceremoniously slammed in her ear. That was Jane Byrne's first introduction to P. Kenneth O'Donnell.

Later that morning when Shriver returned to headquarters, Byrne caught his attention and quickly filled him in on her extraordinary phone conversation. As she spoke, Shriver's face grew more and more clouded with anger. Byrne finished her story by asking, "Who is Kenny O'Donnell?"

This was not the first time that Kenny and Mayor Daley had circumvented Shriver or ordered him to undo some decision he had made. Today, however, Shriver exploded in a rare show of anger. "I am not taking orders from Hitler! Mitchell is a decent man, it's announced, I am not backing down and I am going to the mat for this one! Enough is enough — I won't be pushed around. I'm going to call O'Donnell right now and tell him so!" Shriver turned on his heel and went into his office, slamming the door behind him. Byrne returned to her seat stunned; looking down at the phone, she saw the light for Shriver's private line light up. "I guess he's going to tell that Mr. O'Donnell," said Jane to her coworker Margaret Zulkey, who just chuckled knowingly.

Several minutes had passed when Byrne looked down and noted that the light on the private line had gone out. Just then the door to Shriver's office opened and he walked out. "He looked like he needed a diaper!" Byrne recalls.

"Get me Mitchell" was all Shriver said, his voice barely audible as he turned and walked back to his office.

Just then the phone rang again. Zulkey answered. "Yes, Mr. Danaher," Byrne heard her say. She could hear the other voice shouting through the phone. "This is very serious! You better understand that the 'boss' said that guy goes or that is the end of you guys in Chicago! Got it?"

"Yes, Mr. Danaher," Zulkey replied, hanging up the phone and getting up to tell Shriver.

When the phone rang again Byrne picked it up. "Is it done?" It was that voice. She tensed and sat up straighter. "Look, you people better get this. I want it done, I have to go back and tell them it's done. Whoever the hell Mitchell is, he is not worth losing the support of Mayor Daley. Now you make sure it's done now. I am going to call them back." Jane heard Kenny O'Donnell banging the desk or table in the background as he spoke. Rushing into Shriver's office, she told him

O'Donnell had called again. Shriver was just then hanging up from Mitchell. "It's done," he replied gently, gracious in defeat. As she returned to her desk, she wondered when she would get to meet the man on the other end of the phone who had such peremptory power. She was young and naive, but she knew that these guys didn't play around.

The son of one Chicago mayor and the brother of another, William Daley, secretary of transportation under President Bill Clinton, provides some perspective on the attitudes of the Chicago organization under his father. "You have to look at the times in which they lived, the experiences that formed them," he says. "You have to judge them within the context of their experience and their times: world war, the Cold War, Russia, the Depression. These were the things that formed them. My father was even older than the Kennedy brothers. He was born in 1904. Signs like NO IRISH NEED APPLY were real to them. So to put an Irish Catholic in the White House — for these guys it was pretty amazing stuff. What they overcame and what they achieved! It's amazing!"

John Reilly hadn't expected to be this involved. A Chicagoan, he had first met Bobby in 1957 when Reilly was working for the National Association of Attorneys General, the states' legislative lobbying arm, which was therefore tightly associated with officials in each of the key presidential primary and general election states. Reilly had helped coordinate the information that governors could provide Bobby Kennedy at the McClellan Committee. "We all had an interest in helping get the mob out of the Teamsters Union," says Reilly. Reilly thought Bobby Kennedy was "a good fellow, but hard to read. We got along well and liked each other very much." By late 1959, Bobby had grown convinced that Reilly had excellent political instincts and good judgment — qualities the burgeoning presidential campaign would need. He urged Reilly to leave the Association of Attorneys General and come to work for him on the campaign. Reilly resisted giving him an immediate answer. When Bobby was in town for a speech in Chicago he asked Reilly, "Have you thought about it?"

"Yeah, I have," Reilly said, knowing Bobby wasn't going to like his answer. "I have thought about it and the answer is no." Bobby just stared at Reilly in amazement, saying nothing in reply. "Look," Reilly said, feeling the need to explain himself, "the reality is that I am married with three kids and the pay is less than I make now and I can't afford it and I just can't get up and leave." Bobby kept staring. "Look, Bob," Reilly continued, "I can really do more for you where I am now. I deal with every governor in every single state, their staffs, the legislative bodies—and I can use those contacts to make inroads for Jack and get you names of people within those states to help."

Bobby liked that answer. Smiling ever so slightly, he agreed. "You need to call Kenny O'Donnell."

It was some weeks later when Reilly actually got to meet Kenny O'Donnell. "The first time I met Kenny he was walking in with Kennedy to some event in Chicago. He looked like some guy straight from IRA storm troopers. He just intimidated the hell out of you when you first met him. I had never met anyone who could so intimidate the shit out of you, without ever opening his mouth. Because Bobby had told him I was a good guy, later he invited me for a few drinks. He asked me a ton a questions. I must have passed some kind of damn test, because from that point forward I was always in with Kenny and Bobby. We all became the best of friends. In fact, it was Kenny who arranged for me to travel with Bobby, which was a hell of an experience!" Reilly stayed with the association through the election, spending more time doing jobs for the campaign and taking calls from Kenny and Bobby than he did for the organization. When Jack Kennedy won, Reilly was one of the first to get a call from Bobby. "It's time now. No excuses this time. I will expect you in Washington next week."

"I'll be there," said Reilly. He quit his job that afternoon and went home and told his wife Susan that they were selling their house and moving to Washington to work for Bobby Kennedy and Kenny O'Donnell. "What job did they give you?" Suan inquired.

"Oh," he said, after a moment's hesitation. "I don't know. I never asked."

"My wife," Reilly says now, "thought I was soft as a grape!"

*   *   *

When Kenny O'Donnell first came to the Chicago headquarters, accompanied by the candidate, Jane Byrne was impressed — first to meet
Jack Kennedy, who had so changed her life, and second, to encounter
the man on the other end of the phone. His attitude and his self-
confidence matched his voice. At first she was nervous and uneasy with
him, but he put her at ease quickly. By the time the men had left the
headquarters, she decided he was tough but that he was a committed
professional she needed to know. Kenny and Bobby "were smart enough
to know that this was a new era, this was a tight race, and they were
going to need the independents, the suburbanites — those voters could
make the difference," Byrne says.

Kenny had explained the Daley dynamic to Jack, who was unhappy
with the mayor's petty infighting and turf wars. "It all matters because
it is important to him. You may have to put up with some of this now,
but you have got to win in order to make change." Jack agreed, as did
Bobby, that if working with Daley was required to win the election,
winning the election was what was most important, and they would work
with Daley. "We need to go this route," Bobby said. "I mean, we have
to win, we can work through the problems; the bottom line is we have
got to win in November or none of this means a damn thing."

Advance men under the direction of Jerry Bruno would come in
regularly to Chicago. They were Kenny's boys — Jerry Bruno, Dick Donahue, John Trainor, and others — who, when they arrived in town, first
paid their respects to the mayor. Often they were content with leaving
a note or a memo telling him of their plans and purpose in Chicago
that trip. The mayor liked to know and he liked to know first. Nothing
else in Chicago mattered as much as the opinion and support of Richard
Daley, and everyone in the Kennedy camp had gotten that message.
Almost everyone.

He walked into the headquarters as if it belonged to him. Jane Byrne
had the phone clamped firmly to her ear when a man walked in and
made it clear that she needed to pay attention only to him. His name
was Phil Kaiser, he said; he was "the advance man," he explained with

an expansive wave of his hand. "I'm in town to make all the arrangements for Jack's rally next week." Byrne didn't like the way he said "Jack"
so easily; even his brother-in-law called him "the senator" in public.
Quickly Phil Kaiser was to earn the wrath of the Daley machine. His
style differed sharply from that of the urbane Dick Donahue, who had
been in town only a couple of weeks before. He began by ordering up
sound trucks, having leaflets printed up, and pulling valuable machine
volunteers off the phone banks to distribute news of his upcoming rally.
The headquarters didn't have many volunteers, relying instead upon
Daley's network of some three thousand workers. "This guy is going to
find out the hard way," Byrne told her coworker Margaret Zulkey. Kaiser
left message after message for the mayor. Incensed that his calls went
unheeded, he proceeded to prepare a rally without an ounce of assistance or awareness from mighty Mayor Daley.

Shortly after Kaiser's arrival, Jane Byrne's phone rang. Marion Mullen, the mayor's political secretary, was on the line. Byrne knew she
could be tough and mean. "A flyer landed on our desk this morning
about some kind of arrival of Senator Jack Kennedy at O'Hare Airport?
What the hell is this?" Byrne felt queasy; she had known this was coming. "Look," Mullen said. "His Honor the Mayor doesn't want the arrival
at O'Hare. Nobody checked with him and he has made other arrangements for the Kennedy rally. So cancel it." With that the phone was
once again slammed in Jane Byrne's ear.

It was Thursday. The rally was scheduled for Saturday. Sound trucks
had been booked and paid for, thousands and thousands of flyers dis-
tributed and pasted up, and military bands and honors scheduled for
Kennedy's arrival. What the hell is going to happen now? Byrne wondered as she wrote a note to Shriver.

Quickly, putting his organization into play, Daley went on to announce that Chicago's rally for presidential candidate John F. Kennedy
would be held at Miggs Airport, some thirty miles out of town, smaller
and less convenient than O'Hare. Daley was making a point. This was
his event or the Kennedy event. Marion Mullen called Byrne again.
"You better cancel it. It's going to be at Miggs."

Phil Kaiser was persistent and resistant. "It's too late to cancel," he told Byrne. "He'll capitulate, he will have to come around," he declared, with an air of confidence no one shared.

The phone rang. It was the voice. "Who is responsible?" Kenny O'Donnell asked tersely. Byrne found herself trying to explain the situation without sounding as though she was attacking Kaiser. She didn't get far. "His name. Who is he?"

"Kaiser, Phil Kaiser."

"This has got to be settled, settled today. Matt called, the mayor is furious and this will be solved. Understand?"

Jane didn't bother to answer. He never waited to listen to it anyway.

Hearing the familiar click in her ear, Jane dutifully began writing out the note to Sargent Shriver.

That night, Phil Kaiser returned from O'Hare to his hotel after a successful day planning his rally. Sifting through his messages as he headed to the elevator, the last one stopped him short. "To Home" was all it said. It was from Kenny O'Donnell.

When Kaiser skulked into headquarters the next day to gather his belongings, nobody wanted to make eye contact with him. Standing in the middle of the room, he tried hard to get someone to look up. "I didn't know," he announced plaintively. "I didn't know, I thought . . . what else could I do? He" — meaning Daley — "didn't call me back. . . ." Then he was gone.

"I thought he was going to cry," Byrne remembers. "He came to the headquarters just shell-shocked. I will tell you one thing: It's bad enough to have Daley mad at you, but Daley, Kenny, and Bobby — that is as bad as it can get!"

With Kaiser's banishment complete, Kenny and Bobby still faced a serious problem: They had two rallies scheduled at two different places at the same time for the same man. Kaiser had made the point that Miggs wasn't big enough for Kennedy's Convair to land safely, which was why he had chosen O'Hare. Daley did not appreciate this information. Calling Kenny on the phone, Daley thundered, "I have engineers telling me that Miggs is the safest airport in the country and here is this jerk who doesn't even know where Miggs is telling me it's not safe!" Banging the table so loudly Kenny could hear it over the phone, Daley declared, "It will be at Miggs or nowhere! It will be at Miggs or you can forget Chicago today!" He threw out a personal challenge to Jack Kennedy with thumping directness. "You let the senator decide where. Let him decide."

Jack had avoided resolving the issue; through Kenny he had told Daley he was going to "let the pilot decide which airport was safer." That made no one happy, and the situation remained at a stalemate, with only two days to go before the dueling rallies.

Now it was Joseph Kennedy's turn to call Jane Byrne. "I heard there was a problem in Chicago," the ambassador said, as usual the master of understatement. Kenny had known only the ambassador could solve this one. Chicago was too big to lose, and Joe was the only man who could fix it.

"Nobody is here, sir," Byrne explained, intimidated. She had met Joe already; he had come through the headquarters a couple of times. He was nice and unassuming, quite unlike the hard-nosed entrepreneur she'd read about in the newspapers.

"Tell them I tried to call the mayor and he hasn't returned my call. They've really screwed it up this time. I will do what I can. This stupid thing will be solved tonight. Thank you."

With that, he politely hung up. It was nice, thought Jane replacing the phone in the cradle, to not have the phone slammed in your ear for a change.

Ten minutes later the phone rang again. It was Bobby. Byrne was relieved it was not Kenny.

Jane Byrne had met him for the first time several weeks earlier and decided he had a nuts-and-bolts attitude combined with a certain softness and could sense instinctively when you were over your head. "I remember thinking that he looked like that big award-winning soldier who won all the decorations—Audie Murphy. Bobby had that chiseled, rugged, handsome look. You knew he could handle himself equally well at a black tie affair or in the midst of an Irish brawl." His eyes are what struck her the most. "He had big, blue eyes. They were nice eyes; they didn't look crude or arrogant." Bobby had come to get a firsthand look at the Chicago operation. "He came to the Michigan Avenue head-quarters, because he wanted to talk with people outside the confines of City Hall," Byrne says. "Bobby wanted to know who was doing the real work, where the problems were, who was out beating the bushes—and he knew some of that information he could only get from people when they went outside City Hall." He wanted to reach voters that the Daley machine couldn't pull; Jack had to carry not just Chicago but Illinois. "He wanted to know what size vote the Democratic party had to pull out of the 'collar counties' as he called them, along with the suburban-ites in order to offset the downstate vote, which he knew was not going to be for John Kennedy."

Byrne had watched as Bobby called the election commission directly to find out. "No," he told the man on the other end of the telephone, "I want actual figures and I want them now." Holding the phone in one hand, Bobby signaled that Byrne should stay, gesturing to the lone available seat inside the tiny office. As the man began repeating figures, Bobby began jotting them down on a long piece of white paper. His handwriting looked to Byrne like chicken scrawl. "Get this to Kenny," he told Byrne.

Byrne headed out to track down Mr. O'Donnell—just in time to witness a commotion at the door to headquarters: A disheveled and soiled-looking man was trying to explain that he was looking for Mr. Bobby Kennedy. "May I help you?" Byrne asked, trying hard not to look at his threadbare clothes, stained with indignity. Almost shyly, perhaps intimidated by the setting, the man handed her a piece of paper. It read "Give this man a job," and it was signed by Bobby Kennedy, in the chicken scrawl she had seen only moments before.

Surprised, Byrne asked the man to wait, then turned and went to find Bobby. He was on the phone. Realizing that the man probably hadn't had a decent meal, she fetched him a cup of coffee and a cookie. He said little but seemed to appreciate it. Then she went back and stood quietly in Bobby's doorway. When he looked up from his yellow pad, he managed to motion with his eyes for her to come in and resume her seat. He was talking to Kenny—she heard his name—about Daley's man Matt Danaher. The conversation was mostly unintelligible, consisting of a series of grunts, yups, uhs, okays, and yeses and nos. It sounded like a locker room. Did they even understand each other?

Finally, he hung up and with an easy smile asked Byrne, "What's up?"

"Excuse me, Mr. Kennedy . . ." Not quite sure how to begin, she just handed him the note. "There's a fellow out here, and well, he looks *strange*." That was not the right word to choose, she realized, when she saw a look of disapproval flash briefly across Bobby's face. "He said you recommended him for a position with the campaign?" She heard her voice rise with that last word.

Bobby looked at the note again and his blue eyes focused on her, as if he sensed her discomfort. As Byrne would find out only much later, whenever Bobby was in town he would help serve Mass every morning at Holy Name Church. He had met this man there. Bobby burst out laughing, surprising her. "Look, Jane, I know you think I'm crazy," he said, rising from the chair to seat himself on the edge of the desk, "but"—his voice went soft so that the man outside couldn't hear—"this fellow has had a sad, very sad life, he's in trouble—he had a good job and he lost everything. We can help him and we should help people like that. We ought to, because helping those less fortunate is what my brother's campaign for the presidency is all about. Okay?"

"Yes, Mr. Kennedy," Byrne said, smiling involuntarily as she rose from her chair. "I will personally take care of it."

"Good," he said, turning to pick up the phone and return to his seat. "Jane," he added, before she left the room, "make sure he gets paid. I don't care what he does, but make sure he gets paid. I gave him my word we would help him."

Bobby's fellow communicant from Holy Name was given a paid position on the staff, which was a rare thing. He delivered mail around the office, did messenger runs, made coffee, and performed any other odd job that came up. The fellow did a superb job, got himself cleaned up, and set himself back on his feet. His success had one drawback for the campaign, however: He told all of his friends at Holy Name how helpful Mr. Kennedy had been. Soon the campaign was inundated with down-and-out people looking for Mr. Bobby Kennedy.

Now Bobby was spending his time trying to resolve the crisis over Mayor Daley and Miggs Field. "Where's Matt?" he asked Jane Byrne when he called in from the campaign trail.

"I don't know, Bobby, I haven't seen him."

"Where's Kenny?" he asked, letting out a sigh of exhaustion or frustration.

"I think with the senator."

"Fine. Thank you." With that he hung up.

The phone rang again instantly. It was the voice. Kenny. "This thing is going to be resolved tonight—you tell everyone there that the mayor is going to win."

"Yes, sir," she said.

That Saturday morning Jane Byrne's doorbell rang with a special delivery package. Inside were credentials, in red, white, and blue, with all sorts of ribbons attached, and a telegram inside a special delivery package signed by a Colonel Riley who was the mayor's chief of protocol. She was invited to attend, "at the Request of the Mayor," a rally and reception for Senator John F. Kennedy, next president of the United States, to be held at Miggs Airport.

There was no mention of O'Hare. Byrne laughed out loud. The Kennedys had to give in to Daley after all, she decided. Looking through the envelope she noted that she had been sent three invitations, so she resolved to bring her daughter Kathy and her mother, who had recently organized a tea for Rose Kennedy that had brought in some seven thousand people. She wanted her mother and daughter to meet the man who had changed her life.

At Miggs they were directed to the prerally reception. They walked into it and were stunned. It was men. All men. These were the ward bosses, the people who made the Daley machine work. Jane Byrne had never dealt with them and felt immediately overwhelmed. Soon Colonel Riley appeared, with a flourish, bringing the room to attention just by his entrance. He had a black patch over his eye, and never had Jane seen a man that so relished his role. "The mayor," he said, pausing dramatically, "would be delighted if all of you would join him on the podium, as the senator's plane is about to land. If you will just come this way." The two women and a little girl followed all the big-bellied male ward bosses tramping out to the wooden podium where they would meet Jack Kennedy. She felt absurd.

Coming out onto the podium, she beheld it: the machine in operation. Thousands of women, men, children were standing shoulder to shoulder on the tarmac. All of them bore their Kennedy banners, posters, balloons, drums, and of course posters for His Honor the Mayor — all provided by those machine bosses who had preceded her to the podium. They commanded her instant respect. She had never seen the machine in action. For her, it had only been talk, but now she was seeing the effects of their power firsthand. Years later, she would battle Mayor Richard Daley's son for control of the Chicago machine.

After some delay, three helicopters began their slow descent toward the airfield. They landed in tandem, and soon she saw Senator John F. Kennedy, looking fit and trim, bouncing down the steps. He was followed quickly by Kenny O'Donnell, always in the background, but always visible to those who understood power.

After being introduced by the mayor, Kennedy began to speak. He thanked the mayor and the crowd. Apologizing for the delay, Jack Kennedy explained that the *Caroline* had landed at O'Hare and been greeted by an "unexpected" crowd. As it turned out, that "unexpected" crowd comprised no fewer than a thousand people, more than the Kennedy men had expected, and all of them had gone wild when they saw their candidate. Jane Byrne would read a newspaper account later that called it an "electrifying arrival." The crowd had wanted to see him, touch him, hear him; and then they hadn't wanted to let him go. Squad cars were overturned, people were knocked down, and in the shoving and pushing Jack Kennedy was almost mauled.

Byrne listened, impressed not just by what the man said but by how he had surmounted the conflict between the Kennedy organizers and the Daley machine. He recognized the power of Mayor Daley, but he would not be pushed around. He and his brother would not let down those people waiting at O'Hare or show themselves to be under the thumb of Richard Daley. Later she learned that it was Bobby who had worked out the compromise—that Jack would land first at O'Hare, speak briefly, then fly on to Miggs and the Daley rally. Now when Jack entreated his listeners to "come and walk across this new frontier with me" it felt to her like a truth and not just a slogan.

Later, Kenny told Byrne that there would never have been a separate Kennedy headquarters on North Michigan Avenue if it had not been for the personal intervention of Ambassador Joe Kennedy with Mayor Daley. Daley may have been Chicago's boss but he was also a pragmatic man and a party loyalist. He liked John Kennedy and wanted him to win the White House. He understood Kennedy couldn't win if he seemed like a candidate of the boss. But Daley and Kennedy both understood that there would be no election victory without Illinois. And, there would be no victory in Illinois without the support of Richard M. Daley, mayor of Chicago.

The disciplined machine intended none of the O'Hare frenzy to occur at their Miggs rally. But they were wrong there too. The Kennedy men and the mayor had forgotten the effect Jack Kennedy had on a crowd. As Jane Byrne watched, the machine spun off on its own, the crowd pushing and shoving when he finished speaking, trampling the ropes, struggling to walk with the candidate and touch his hand. They nearly crushed him with their enthusiasm. She monitored their progress as the Kennedy team, led by Kenny, ran interference for John Kennedy, bearing him through the crowd—and into the presidency.

14

TOWARD VICTORY

Coast to coast with the Holy Ghost!

—JACK KENNEDY

"Coast to coast with the Holy Ghost," the first Catholic candidate for president joked as he boarded the *Caroline* for yet another campaign tour. "We're going to win," Sam Rayburn would tell him as he criss-crossed the country. "I never believed it before. I thought we were just going through the motions, but now I know we got it!"

What had convinced the skeptical Rayburn was Jack Kennedy's effect on the crowds, especially in his home state of Texas. Rayburn had turned on the charm in Dallas, warming a reluctant crowd, and Kennedy had stirred them into feverish enthusiasm. "He made a great speech in Dallas," Kenny said. "I will never forget it. He was talking about Democrats and about religion to these rich oil millionaires. He said to them, 'I can remember you when you didn't have a patch on your pants! The Democrats have given you everything you had and now the minute you get rich, you turn on them.' There was silence in the place," Kenny remembered. "He warmed up so much you couldn't believe it as the trip went on. By the time we left we ended up in Texarkana, and we must have had two hundred thousand people in Texarkana!"

By the end of the Texas tour "Mr. Sam" Rayburn even began to warm to the idea of Jack Kennedy making a speech to the Baptist ministers of Houston to confront the religion issue straight on. There had been much debate leading up to the speech about whether it was advisable to face the religion issue head-on. Both Jack and Bobby believed it was the only chance to put the fact of Jack's Catholicism to rest. Rayburn had initially disagreed, saying to Kennedy, "These are not ministers. These are politicians who are going around in robes and saying they're ministers, but they're nothing but politicians. They hate your guts and they're going to tear you to pieces." Kennedy laughed. He was aware of the risks, but believed the risks of not doing the speech were as great as doing it.

Kenny had been at first opposed to his speaking to the Houston ministers, fearing the worst. "I think it would be a mistake," he advised Jack one morning in his hotel room. "If you have to meet the religious issue, Houston is not the place to do it." Kennedy listened, then went into the bathroom to shave. When he came out, he returned Kenny's steady gaze. "Tell them I'm going to do it. This is as good a time as any to get it over with. I've got to face it sooner or later."

"Kennedy's opening speech to the Houston ministers was by far the best speech of the campaign, and probably the best speech he ever delivered in his lifetime—precise, intelligent, forceful, and sharply pointed, without a wasted word," Kenny would declare later, averring forcefully that he was his own man and as president would be independent of all religious influence. Just as under the Constitution a president couldn't tell a religious leader how to behave, so religious leaders could not dictate an agenda to the president. "These are real issues," Kennedy said, "but because I am a Catholic, and no Catholic has ever been elected president, the real issues in this campaign have been obscured. I believe in an America where the separation of the church and the state is absolute—where no Catholic prelate would tell the president (should he be Catholic) how to act and no Protestant minister would tell his parishioners for whom to vote. . . ." He went on from there, Kenny explained, "to state his views on every aspect of the religious issue so clearly and uncompromisingly that he left no important questions for the ministers to put to him during the question-and-answer period that followed. Kennedy's poise and forceful arguments seemed to leave the ministers so overawed and confused, with all the starch taken out of them, that they were in no mood to ask him embarrassing questions anyway. He handled [each question] as quickly and calmly as a major-league shortstop handles an easy grounder and often drew spirited applause from the Texas spectators in the ballroom when he threw back his firm and fast answer."

Kenny and Bobby would both later observe that Kennedy hadn't changed any votes in that room that evening, but as Kennedy himself observed, "I didn't lose any elsewhere!"

"The Speaker and I watched it on TV and he was stunned," Kenny recalls. Jack Kennedy's gamble had been correct. Even the Speaker realized it, telling Jack afterward, "That is the greatest thing I've ever seen in my life."

With the Houston speech, Kennedy was finally able to put the religious issue to rest. Convincing a room full of dubious Baptist men of the cloth that his Catholicism should not be an issue to consider when choosing a president was the key to his election. Kenny would say humorously later that "once again, in deciding to accept the invitation from the Houston ministers, Kennedy had instinctively done the right thing against the advice of all his advisers."

The speech before the Houston ministers, in Kenny's view, "gave Kennedy himself a stimulating psychological boost and an added confidence at a point in the early stages of the campaign, two weeks before the first debate against Nixon when he needed it."

The debates were the key to the Kennedy victory. "There were four of them, not one!" reminds Bill Wilson. "Everyone forgets that." Wilson was the first television producer ever hired as an aide in a presidential campaign—brought in from CBS by the doomed Stevenson team in 1956. The experience taught him a great deal about how television could make and especially unmake a presidential campaign. In 1960, once he won the nomination, Jack Kennedy brought Wilson and his production agency Baskin and Feeley into the Kennedy camp; he and Bobby knew perhaps better than anyone that television would be central to their success. Bill Wilson would produce all Kennedy advertisements and live television appearances during the national campaign. He became the Kennedy campaign's representative to the presidential debates.

Wilson had learned a valuable lesson in working on the Stevenson campaign: to "edit out half the people around the candidate and find out the key guys who have the candidate's ear, who make the tough decisions, who get back to you and get you an answer. In a national campaign with major deadlines, you find those people and you hold on to them." One of those people was Bobby Kennedy. "I met him briefly; he knew what he wanted, and made clear what I was to do, and that was it." Another essential operative was Kenny O'Donnell. "He was tough, direct, concise, but if you asked him a question he would get you an answer. Kenny was one of the few people, besides Bobby, who when he said to you, 'I will get back to you and find out,' actually did." Kenny's effectiveness, Wilson saw, had to do with personality, his own and the candidate's. Kenny had developed a deep connection with a man who had long since grown confident about delegating responsibility to the people he trusted. In turn, Kenny and Bobby had enough confidence in their abilities to be able to hand out responsibility to other powerful and talented people.

"They were not threatened," Wilson says. "In fact I think they welcomed it."

Sam Adams, Bobby's friend from Milton and Harvard, felt he had come to understand the dynamic among those aides closest to the Kennedys, including Kenny O'Donnell. "The Kennedys historically didn't want or need people around them trying to shine in their spotlight. They liked smart, savvy people, but they didn't like people who they knew were trying to use them. Kenny understood that. Kenny was comfortable with being the behind-the-scenes guy. He had all the power he needed, which he derived from his ability to have the ear of Jack and Bobby Kennedy, but he was always himself. He didn't need to be like them; he understood that his value to both Bobby and Jack, why they trusted him so very deeply, was that he never bullshitted them. He always told it like it was; he was always himself and he had no problem telling them when they were full of shit. They needed people like that around them and they liked it."

Wilson perceived that while Bobby was efficient and rigorous in his dealings with people and politics, Jack Kennedy was in many ways much tougher. "Jack Kennedy wasn't looking to hold hands; he was looking for votes, and it was Bob's job to get him those votes."

All three men were fiercely single-minded in their pursuit of a victory in 1960. "Politics," Kenny once said, "is a tough business, especially if you plan to win." These were the first televised debates ever between American presidential candidates. Voters who had grown familiar with Richard Nixon over the eight years of his vice presidency would now have a chance to witness the young Democratic senator from Massachusetts in action. Because the stakes were so high, the preparation for the debates induced immense tension in the Kennedy camp. Jack Kennedy underwent six practice sessions. Bobby delegated to Bill Wilson the negotiations with the Nixon staffer Ted Rodgers over the format and tactics of the debates. Wilson was in essence an advance man for television. The day of the debate he would set up the lighting, the podium, and the sound and work the control room.

Wilson, Bobby, and Kenny met him at the door of the studio in Chicago and took him into a private room they had set aside. As Kenny later recalled, "As everybody knows, the real turning point in the campaign was the first debate with Nixon in Chicago. The contrast on the television screen between Nixon's nervous anxiety and Kennedy's cool composure wiped away the Republican contention that Kennedy was too immature and inexperienced for the presidency and established him as a potential winner." Jack Kennedy with his Palm Beach tan looked healthy and handsome, but both men would still require makeup before going under the harsh studio lights. The day of the debate, neither man wanted to go into the makeup room before the other. Kennedy made it clear to Wilson he wasn't going in there until Nixon had gone into the makeup room; neither man wanted to be perceived by the pool reporter as making the decision to get made up. "You have to realize," Wilson says, "politicians were really thin-skinned about the new medium, about putting on airs on television that would affect the way people perceived them in public. They hadn't yet figured out that this thing called television was going to be a useful tool. I would say Jack Kennedy was way ahead of most politicians of his era when it came to using television as a tool.

"They did their homework; they left nothing to chance. Pierre, Kenny, and Sorensen, everyone would be in the room and they would brief him until the very last moment." Wilson had to shoo them out before doing his final prep with the candidate. Bobby was the last person to leave. Slapping his brother on the back, Bobby said, "Okay, kick 'im in the balls!" The brothers both burst into laughter. "It was a great moment," Wilson says. "Both brothers had wide grins on their faces and it broke the tension and it was what Jack needed at that moment." It was something only Bobby could have dared to say.

Wilson was in the control room during the debate. The Kennedy and Nixon camps had agreed that there would be reaction shots, which meant that each camp could take a picture of the other candidate. Wilson's job was to ask the controller for the reaction shots. He chose moments when Nixon looked most vulnerable—his pale and drawn face, exhausted from the road, just looked worse under the makeup. And Nixon sweated. By comparison, John F. Kennedy always looked not just cool as a cat but presidential. The night of the debate, Kennedy remarked to Kenny, "lightly, but perhaps not too lightly, that he owed it to the country to win the election in order to keep Nixon out of the White House."

Kenny had a context for understanding Jack's success in the debate. "Bobby Kennedy and I both remarked at the time that the first impressive debate with Nixon in Chicago—hardly anybody remembered the other three—seemed to be a rerun of Jack's debate with Henry Cabot Lodge in Waltham, Massachusetts, back in the 1952 senatorial campaign."

Shortly after the Los Angeles convention, Joe Dolan was trying to work his way through the formidable stack of papers that had built up in his law office since the convention when he was interrupted by a phone call from Byron White, who was in New York with the campaign. "I'm staying at the ambassador's apartment up on Park Avenue and Bob wants you to come," White told him. Dolan was relieved to be rescued from his paperwork; he hung up the phone and headed to the airport. Once in New York, and with his luggage misrouted by the airline, Dolan climbed in a cab and headed to the ambassador's apartment. Paying off the cab driver and walking into the lobby, he realized he still held the book he'd taken with him on the flight: *The Enemy Within*, by Robert Kennedy.

White was filling him in on the plans for the national campaign when Bobby strode into the room. Shaking Dolan's hand, he glimpsed his book, now stuffed in the other man's coat pocket. "I see you're reading my book!"

"Yeah," Dolan told him, "but it's a little heavy and when we fly I like to look out the window, so I read it only when I'm on the ground."

Startled, Bobby stared at him and then laughed. "Yeah, I know, that's how everyone reads my book! That's why they told me not to give up my day job." He plopped himself tiredly into a nearby seat. Dolan had already gained a reputation for candor with Bobby and Kenny, which would serve him well later on.

"We're going to Philadelphia. Billy Green had a big meeting and we have got to be there," White told him. The foursome, Kenny, Bobby, Dolan, and White, left Penn Station by train to set up the Kennedy campaign in a city dominated by Mayor Bill Green and rife with Stevenson supporters still smarting over their candidate's defeat at the convention. Dolan would stay on to coordinate campaign manager Jim Clark's Philadelphia effort for Kennedy—no easy task given the fractious party organization. After three days Dolan had run up a two-hundred-dollar hotel bill at one of the nicer hotels. Bobby saw the bill and was furious. About a week later in New York, he called a meeting of all the Kennedy staff people who had been on the road. Climbing onto a chair, holding Dolan's bill in hand, Bobby lectured the team, telling them to cut back on their expenses. The assembled lawyers, politicians, and operatives looked at each other guiltily. Many had all left lucrative careers to work on this campaign, but frugality was also part of this assignment.

"You're going to be restricted now and get only the government allowance of twenty-five dollars per day." Bobby looked around the room, finally making eye contact with Joe Dolan.

"For some reason," Dolan says now, "whenever he would do that, I always took it as a cue to say something." "Plus room," he answered back.

The entire room was quiet; all eyes turned to Dolan. Bobby just stared at him for a long minute. "Oh forget it!" he said with exasperation, climbing off the chair and leaving the room.

Everyone told Dolan he was going to be sent home to Colorado, but he knew otherwise. "The thing about Bobby Kennedy was that he liked people who stood up to him. He didn't like yes-men around him. If you disagreed with him or thought he was being too uptight about something, he would want you to say it. People that were afraid or intimidated by him didn't last long. He couldn't feel comfortable with them."

The room allowance was increased.

"Do you want to do advance?" Kenny asked Ron Linton during the convention. He didn't even look up from his desk.

"Yeah, I could do that," said the former newsman.

"Okay. You're advance. Go see Bruno."

Linton was put into the leapfrog advance-man rotation. Bruno took the formal Labor Day campaign kickoff in Detroit; Linton took Flint, Michigan; and so forth. He and the other advance men reported to Kenny O'Donnell who continued to travel with the candidate, handling all details and logistics. Also working for Kenny was Dick Maguire, head of scheduling; John Nolan, a Washington lawyer, and former Chicagoan John Reilly reported to Maguire. Jerry Bruno, by now the real Kennedy pro, divided the men into teams, and off they went.

Before the first presidential debate, Ron Linton recalls, they constantly worried about corralling crowds for campaign events. "After the debates we never worried again, except occasionally if a trip was badly planned or something—we would always have a crowd." Only occasionally would Linton encounter a major problem, as in late October during a Kennedy train tour through Michigan. It was an exhausting, perhaps unnecessary trip, but long-scheduled commitments had to be honored. Tuskegee, Michigan, a union town, had turned out a predictably strong, pro-Kennedy crowd. But Linton worried over the next stops. He didn't want "old eagle eye," as Kenny had been dubbed, to notice that the crowds were down. At one predebate event he had picked Kenny up at the airport in their rented car and they were headed to the Coliseum in Detroit to check the logistics for a major upcoming rally. As they drove along, Linton asked about John Salter, who had been named chief of staff of the Democratic party, when Senator Henry Jackson had been named national chairman at the end of the convention. The posts had been given purely for political reasons and were just decoration. Jackson and Salter had run afoul of Kenny and Bobby when they thought they actually were running the party. Salter had made the ultimate mistake of taking on Kenny, thereby incurring the wrath of Robert Kennedy. Salter had begun reviewing Kenny's expense accounts and questioned his use of time. He had also begun bad-mouthing Kenny, which several loyal Kennedy men relayed to the team captains.

"I hear rumors, Kenny, that Salter is not going to be involved in the campaign anymore," Linton asked Kenny, "that Bobby wants him gone?"

They drove through a couple of sets of lights before Kenny answered, "Yeah, that's right, he's out."

"Why? I don't understand. He's been with the party—"

Kenny cut him off. "Bullshit. We've been having these meetings with him, and he spends the whole time not doing what we ask and saying that even if we lose, we will build the party. Finally Bobby and I talked and so I told the son of bitch, 'Fuck the build-the-party shit and lose-the-election shit! We are in this to win the election, not build the party! You're out!'"

"Oh" was all Ron said.

That was the end of Salter; like Kaiser in Chicago, he was gone. Bobby and Kenny ran things the way they thought Coach Dick Harlow should have run them at Harvard: You are either on the team, dedicated to the team's success, or you are gone.

On another early campaign trip when the Kennedy motorcade was running late, Linton was having trouble keeping an already thin crowd. Finally, he spied a lone figure walking up the middle of the street, thin, suit coat on, sunglasses on, his short black hair ruffling in the fall wind. Rushing toward Kenny, Ron blurted out hurriedly, "For God's sake, Kenny—where the hell is the candidate with the caravan?"

Kenny stopped dead in the middle of the street and pulled off his sunglasses. "Don't worry about the fucking candidate! He's coming. Where are the goddamn crowds?"

Now, after the debates, Linton's problem was protecting the candidate from the screaming crowds—though Marshall, Michigan, could prove a little different. Finding the local police chief, Linton explained that he represented John Kennedy and he would need the chief's help controlling the crowd. The officer laughed. "This is a community of five thousand people, in the heart of Republican territory—you ain't going to get but fifty people out there, son. You don't need my help."

The officer's words made Linton nervous; he did not relish encountering "old eagle eye" when the train stopped and they were greeted by fifty people. Linton got an idea, one he thought Jerry Bruno would have liked. The next town on the route after Marshall was Elkin—big, Democratic, union—already organized and ready for the train to come. Linton went to the Elkin union headquarters and explained his problem. The Democratic union leaders agreed to his plan. He loaded several buses with supporters from the Elkin crowd and rushed them to Marshall. Now when the train stopped in Marshall, Kennedy and the trailing reporters were greeted by a huge, wildly enthusiastic throng. The local police officer was not amused. Kenny looked impressed.

After the rally ended and the train pulled out, Linton loaded Elkinites up again and beat the train to Elkin by fifteen minutes, hurrying the supporters off the buses and to their designated spots. To be on the safe side, Ron bused the crowd to the next stops as well. Finally he saw Jack and Kenny exchange glances.

Kenny climbed off the train and signaled with his finger for Linton to follow him over to the side. Linton, nervous, knew that he had fooled the press, but he hadn't expected to fool "old eagle eye" and he hadn't.

Kenny took off his sunglasses. His black eyes stared at Linton, who felt his stomach clutch.

"You are one smart son of a bitch," he said. Then he turned and was gone.

The next day's local newspaper headline read KENNEDY PULLS BIG CROWD IN REPUBLICAN RURAL AREAS.

Jerry Bruno saw firsthand the pro-Kennedy frenzy that developed in the wake of the first debate. The evening following his first encounter with Nixon, Kennedy flew into the Cleveland, Ohio, area, followed by about 120 members of the press. Jack Kennedy hurried down the plane steps and climbed into the back of a waiting car so he and Governor Mike DiSalle could talk shop. Kenny climbed in the front; Bruno took the wheel. "Everybody was scrambling," Bruno remembers. "The trip wasn't all that well planned. We had not expected the huge reaction after the debate. The hotels were jammed and there weren't even enough rooms for everyone." Kenny shook his head, throwing a glance at Bruno, who couldn't even move the car forward because the press were surrounding it. As a result Kennedy would be late for his next event. "Beautiful," said Jack from the backseat, observing the chaos. He turned to DiSalle. "I wonder how Hannibal ever crossed the Alps?"

The Ohio governor leaned forward and tapped Jerry Bruno on the shoulder. "Because he didn't have any advance men to screw it up!"

Finally the group made it to the hotel and rooms were found for everyone. The candidate went to bed, and Kenny and the guys went out and had a beer. At seven the next morning, Bruno rose and roused Kenny, who had what Bruno thought was the distinctly unpleasant job of waking the candidate. Kenny was a light sleeper and was half out of bed before Bruno completed the knock on his door. While Kenny headed to Jack's room, Bruno went to get the candidate's breakfast: two eggs, bacon, toast, juice, and coffee.

By the time Bruno returned, Jack was talking rapid-fire about the debate the day before; Kenny was leaning against the wall, listening, sometimes making a terse comment or a grunt or two. He had won; he had Nixon and he knew it. Bruno had never seen Jack so keyed up. Leaving his breakfast untouched and a stack of newspapers unread, Jack paced the room in his undershorts, going over every detail of the debate with Kenny. "I knew I had him!" he announced triumphantly. "I knew I had him. Boy, did I nail him." Jack kept pacing past the untouched breakfast for more than an hour as he replayed the drama of the night before. Bruno kept trying to signal to Kenny that they were running late. Kenny shook his head. "I know, I can't move him, I can't move him!" he whispered. Finally, Jack sat down to his breakfast and grabbed the papers and began going through them. With a fork he prodded his eggs, now cold and hard from sitting untouched on his plate. "What the hell?" Jack asked. "Why the hell do I have to eat cold eggs for Christ's sake! I kicked Nixon's ass and I have to eat cold eggs?"

"Because," Kenny growled, "you goddamn let'm sit there for a god-damn hour, that's why!"

Jack put down his fork, looked up at Kenny, and then the two of them burst into a laughter of relief. "Okay, yeah," Kenny said, in response to Jack's wide grin. "You nailed him last night!"

The Saturday before the general election Bobby Kennedy came back to Ohio for a speech before flying on to Ashland, Kentucky. On this trip Bill Geoghegan met another Kennedy friend, John Reilly, who would in time become very close to Kenny O'Donnell as well. As Geoghegan accompanied them back to the airport, Bobby expressed his appreciation for Geoghegan's hard work but also pointed out how important Ohio was. "He really thought that with all the hard work we had all put in, Jack Kennedy should have won Ohio." Bobby had given Geoghegan his private number at his and Ethel's expansive cottage at the family com-pound at Hyannisport, which served as election night headquarters. "We must have talked five or six times the evening of the election," Geogh-egan remembers. "There were several counties along the Ohio and Ken-tucky border that were bellwether counties. When Kennedy lost those to Nixon, I called Bobby. I told him and he knew automatically what it meant. Kennedy had lost Ohio."

"I am so disappointed," Bobby said.

Geoghegan could hear the chaos in the background, the phones ring-
ing, the voices, the blaring televisions, making it hard to even hear what
Bobby was saying. "Bobby, we are still going to win the election!"
Geoghegan declared, trying to be reassuring.

"Yes, I know," Bobby replied, with resignation. "But we put in so
much time and effort there, it's just awful. I'm really disappointed."

"I understand," was all Geoghegan could say. "I am too." Geoghegan
understood that Bobby wanted to win not only the big prize but all the
hard-fought ones along the way.

Jane Byrne and John Reilly would have the satisfaction of helping John
Kennedy carry Chicago by a large margin, bringing the entire state of
Illinois into the Democratic column and helping Jack garner the electoral votes he needed to win the presidency. Much controversy would
develop over the years about how his margin was obtained, which Reilly
feels is unfair and unwarranted. "The story of Daley stealing the election
for John Kennedy is simply not true. The awful thing is not that anyone
stole the election in Chicago, but that a traditional voting practice has
been used to say that the Kennedys stole the election. The fact is, it was
traditional in Chicago to hold back the reporting of Cook County
votes — the city of Chicago — because downstate Illinois held back votes.
So Daley's procedure was to hold back the reporting of certain precincts,
which was not any big deal. He played the game of political chicken
with downstate; they loaded theirs in and then he loaded in Cook
County's behind that. There has never been any proof that the Kennedys
stole the election. The best proof to the contrary is that Illinois Republicans demanded a recount and Nixon would not do it."

"At three o'clock in the morning on November sixth, 1960, the election
was still hanging at 261 electoral votes," Kenny said later. "It was eight
short of what was needed for victory." As they sat in the dining room of
Bobby and Ethel's Hyannisport house, now converted into campaign
central, Kenny watched Richard Nixon make a short, sad appearance
on national television. He did not concede defeat. Kenny remembered
how often his mother Alice had sent him to the local Worcester drug-

store and how he had stayed arguing about Franklin Roosevelt's policies with the men sipping their coffee at the counter. He remembered how often he, his brother Cleo, Bobby, and the Harvard gang had debated how they could make a difference. He remembered the first campaign in 1952, how everything was falling apart until Bobby appeared. He thought of how hard Jack Kennedy had worked, from 1952 to 1960, at times in serious pain, while taking great political risks. Now everything Jack and Bobby and the rest of the team had struggled for required eight more electoral votes. There was nothing they could do — no more balls to throw or passes to catch, and only a yard from the goal line.

Jack Kennedy got up from the chair, having finished his sandwich and glass of milk. He turned to face the room full of people, "Why should he concede now?" he said, in reply to the grunts and groans from the assembled about Nixon's refusal to acknowledge Kennedy's victory. "If I were him, I wouldn't!"

Then he left with Dave Powers to return to his own cottage across the lawn. Kenny and Helen finally began to take their leave; there was nothing more they could do. Saying good night to Ethel and Bobby, they exchanged hugs. Kenny noticed Bobby seemed worried. "What is worrying you, Bobby? Eight short, we've got it."

Bobby shook his head. He was exhausted, his blue eyes dull and smudged with fatigue like a football player's. "I'm worried about Teddy," Bobby replied. "We've lost every state that he worked in out West. Jack will kid him, and that may hurt his feelings."

Kenny shook his head. "Teddy's tough as nails, don't worry about him." Even at a time of weariness and stress, Bobby would be a brother.

By the next morning, John F. Kennedy was president-elect of the United States. He and Jackie and Caroline took a walk on the serene beach of Hyannisport. Then Jack watched Herb Klein, Nixon's press secretary, read the message of concession. It was over. The Kennedy family posed for a now famous photo, inside the ambassador's living room — the same living room, where after the victory in 1952, Kenny and Bobby had sat around on a similar postelection November day, relishing their victory, only to be startled when Joe Kennedy told them to go out and get jobs. There was none of that today.

"I was standing with Helen on the steps of the armory when we saw John F. Kennedy for the first time after his election as the president of the United States," Kenny would recall, more than five tumultuous years later. "He was already a different man from the Jack Kennedy we had talked with the night before. There was a change in his manner and bearing. He came to us, kissed Helen on her cheek, shook hands with me, and thanked me for the work I had done for him over the past eight years. It was a very emotional moment."

As he and Bobby stood watching President-elect John F. Kennedy and his wife Jacqueline stand before the press corps of the world at the armory, Kenny remembered a fateful introduction at Dillon Field House fifteen years before. The team they had made had won its greatest victory.

15

"THE BOBBY PROBLEM"

You're in politics whether you like it or not.

—KENNY O'DONNELL

Kenny O'Donnell knew what his job would be in the White House. He had been doing it since the campaign had begun: He would be the right-hand guy, the assistant, the scheduler, the decision maker, the guy who said yes and the guy who said no. Kenneth O'Donnell would remain as John Kennedy's appointments secretary, chief political adviser, and—as Bobby sometimes called him—Jack's "general handyman." He came to be nicknamed "the Cobra." For it was Kenny sitting by the door to the Oval Office, watchful and attentive, who would decide who would get in to see the president and who would get told to get out.

"You don't care," Bobby told Kenny jokingly over the phone right after the election. Justine O'Donnell overheard them. "You have a job! I'm the one without a job. What do you care what happens to me?"

"Bobby," Kenny said, trying not to burst out laughing, "for Christ's sake, you're the second most powerful man in the country! You can do anything you damn well want to do! You are the president's brother, his closest confidant—whatever you do you'll be one of the most powerful men in the world!"

"Oh," replied Bobby, sounding surprised. "I guess so. I hadn't really thought about it. I thought maybe I would go teach or do something."

"I don't think so, Bobby," Kenny said, chuckling. "This time you can't change your mind. You're in politics whether you like it or not."

Kenny hung up the phone with a chuckle and joined Helen and his sister Justine in the den of their Washington house. Helen had just finished mixing before-dinner drinks. "What's so funny?" she asked, knowing her husband had just been talking to Bobby.

Kenny shook his head, taking the gin and tonic from her. "That goddamn Bobby! He's upset because I have a job and I know what I am going to do, and he doesn't!" Amused at his best friend's seeming ingenuousness, Kenny walked to the window to watch his kids play in the backyard.

With the election won, Jack Kennedy headed down to Palm Beach for some rest, relaxation, and executive decisions. Kenny, after spending some time at home with Helen and his family recovering after the grueling election schedule, flew down to join him. Kennedy was in the process of selecting his Cabinet. The Kennedy team was undergoing the change of attitude and perspective that comes with assuming power. Kennedy remarked at the time that it was easier to sit outside the White House and criticize than it is to form a government.

Jerry Bruno's hard and dogged advance work had also won him a ticket to Palm Beach. The men were sitting around the pool at the Kennedy estate, enjoying their triumph, lapping in the sun and air, when Kenny suddenly broke the silence. "Jerry," he said, catching Bruno off guard, "You're going to Texas! The president-elect is going to meet the vice president-elect and spend some time down there and I want you and your team to advance it." Bruno was pleased; it was a nice assignment and shouldn't require too much heavy lifting.

Bruno, John Trainor, and Kennedy cousin Joey Gargan arrived at Johnson's ranch and sat down with the vice president-elect to plan out the agenda for Jack's visit. Johnson proudly showed off the cowboy hat that he had bought for the president-elect and wanted Kennedy to wear on his visit—especially in front of the cameras. Bruno knew his boss's style; he explained in no uncertain terms that, in fact, Jack Kennedy would not be wearing a cowboy hat for the cameras. And could they see the room where the president-elect would be staying?

Johnson took umbrage at that. "It's a good goddamn room! What do you mean you gotta look at the room? And, what do you mean you have to have phones put in! I have phones! What the hell does he think, that I am going to be listening in on his phone calls?" Johnson was furious. "For Christ's sake," Johnson bellowed, "doesn't he trust me?" It was the first of many times in the next several years that Lyndon Johnson was to feel at odds with the Kennedys and that there would be strains in what Kenny had dubbed the "Boston to Austin" axis.

When Jack Kennedy arrived, the advance team was lodged in one of the guest houses, some fourteen miles away from the main house, where Jack, Kenny, and Johnson were working on presidential transition matters. At 5:00 A.M. the next morning Bruno was awakened by a strange noise. He rolled over in his bed and found himself face-to-face with an enormous bull, his head protruding through the open window. "Wake up, John! Wake up!" Bruno hollered. "A goddamn bull wants to get in our room!"

Trainor leaped to his feet, brushing the sleep out of his eyes, and stared astonished out the window. The bull briefly surveyed the startled men with a look of what Bruno decided was amusement before it turned and rejoined the rest of its herd. The three men exchanged sleepy looks, when suddenly Trainor, looking past Bruno and out the window, exclaimed, "Holy Christ, there's a car out there!"

The car had pulled just a dozen yards from the window of the guest house. Out of the car strode Lyndon Johnson, wearing his cowboy hat, fancy cowboy boots, leather cowboy jacket, and carrying what looked to Jerry Bruno like a tremendous rifle under his arm.

The car's back door opened and out climbed another occupant of the car, "old eagle eye" Kenny O'Donnell, looking none too happy to be there. He was wearing khakis and a white dress shirt, without a tie, which for Kenny was a rare sartorial departure. Following Kenny out of the car, and looking even less pleased, was John F. Kennedy, the president-elect of the United States.

"Oh shit," mumbled Trainor to Bruno. Kennedy, like Kenny, looked equally ill dressed for the morning's events, wearing penny loafers, sports slacks, a white button-down shirt, and a sports jacket, his hair wild. The men stood blinking in the early morning light. "They looked like they were on Mars," Bruno says.

"They're only like fifty feet from us," Trainor whispered. "I hope they don't spot us, because they don't look happy." The bull had gone around the other side of the guest house. LBJ was talking in his booming voice as he shuffled the unhappy men toward the jeep. They were going out hunting, to bag a deer.

"Kennedy was furious with me," Kenny would recall. "He became even more furious when the guide and the Secret Service men who were with me told him that I had indeed easily knocked off my deer on my first shot." Spending the morning tramping the brush for deer tracks was not Jack Kennedy's sort of activity; his only source of pleasure was going to be watching Kenny be as miserable as he was. "He was mad because I had deprived him of his fun, and because I had shot my deer quicker than he had shot his deer. He did not speak to me for the next two hours."

From the start Jack Kennedy and Lyndon Johnson were men of very different temperaments, even when they were sitting in the same room, wearing their business clothes. But according to Kenny's recollections, Jack tried hard to solicit Johnson's advice about potential members of the administration as well as legislation and executive policy. "The president and Lyndon talked about people that he might know, what his judgment was, and the president did everything in the world, including go down to Lyndon Johnson's ranch, which he detested because it wasn't his cup of tea," to make him feel central to the new administration. Unfortunately, given their distinct characters and the institutional limits of the office of the vice presidency, Jack Kennedy would never really be able to make Johnson feel completely at ease in his new position. Robert Kennedy's role as attorney general and the intimate professional relationship with his brother would exacerbate the problem in years to come.

*   *   *

Bobby Kennedy hadn't wanted to be named attorney general. But his brother and father had other ideas. In fact, it had been the day after the election that Jack first broached the idea that Bobby serve as attorney general. Bobby was immediately reluctant. "It was the first post he mentioned," Bobby recounted in an oral history for the Kennedy Presidential Library. He foresaw serious problems with taking on that job. "In the first place, I thought that nepotism was a problem. Secondly, I had been chasing bad men for three years, and I didn't want to spend the rest of my life doing that. I thought there was a certain amount of things to be done with the Department of Justice, but I thought I could get those things accomplished without being in the Department of Justice." Among Bobby's priorities for the new attorney general would be "organized crime and . . . finishing doing the prosecution part of the Teamsters that hadn't been done, where the cases hadn't been adequately handled, and . . . obviously civil rights."

After the election Bobby went on a short vacation and upon his return became involved in helping his brother select Cabinet secretaries and White House staff. Jack soon broached the subject of the attorney general's spot, but Bobby continued to balk. He was interested instead in a position at either State or Defense. "We talked about me going over to the Defense Department," Bobby said later. "He thought about asking Gates [current secretary of defense Thomas S. Gates, Jr.] to stay on with the understanding that he would get out in a year. I would go in as undersecretary of defense, and then become secretary of defense after a year." But the political operatives, including Kenny, opposed this idea, worrying that giving Gates more visibility would just make him a stronger potential Republican candidate for governor of Pennsylvania in 1962. Bobby went as far as to talk to others who had served as the undersecretary of defense to get a sense of the job. But once Kennedy chose Robert S. McNamara as defense secretary, the idea of Bobby serving as undersecretary became impossible. As a condition of his taking the spot and leaving the presidency of the Ford Motor Company, McNamara had insisted that he be able to choose his own underlings. Jack Kennedy agreed.

Some had broached the idea of Bobby's going to the White House
as a staff member, but that idea he rejected. "I didn't want to work in
the White House. I was opposed to it . . . it was just the fact that I had
been working with my brother for a long time, and I thought maybe I'd
like to go off by myself. I thought maybe I would travel or, I don't know,
read, teach or write or something. Well, maybe establish my own life."
But, as had been true in the 1952 campaign, Jack knew what Kenny and
so many others had learned—that, as Kenny had said, "if you don't
come it won't get done."

During a postelection visit to Washington, Bobby and Kenny's Harvard teammate Nick Rodis would hear Kenny and Bobby's arguments
firsthand over dinner at the Shoreham Hotel. Rodis was fascinated to
hear Kenny and Bobby talk about the new administration and what
Bobby wanted to do. They had come a long way from the locker room
at Dillon House, where Kenny and Bobby regularly stole other people's
towel allotment from the lockers. Rodis listened intently. Deep down
he sensed Bobby really wanted to be either secretary of defense or
state. "Bobby didn't think he could be secretary, but there were lots of
other positions that were possible in those departments," he would say
later.

"Bobby, it won't work," Kenny told him. "You can't have a position
under someone else. You're the president's brother, his best friend. I
think you should look at Justice."

As Kenny O'Donnell remembered it, "The Cabinet member who put
up the strongest fight about being pulled into the boat was Bobby Kennedy. The Bobby problem began to worry all of us for selfish reasons.
Since 1952, when Bobby came to Boston to straighten out Jack's disorganized senatorial campaign, Bobby had been our only reliable inter-
mediary in our dealings with his brother. We were all Bobby Kennedy
men. When we wanted to let Jack know about a problem too sensitive
for one of us to mention to him, Bobby could tell him about it and
bring back the answer. When Jack was in one of his inaccessible moods,
Bobby could always reach him and make him listen to reason. Now
Jack was Mr. President, and we were about to begin working with him
in the White House. Without Bobby?" Impossible.

"What if he does happen to be my brother?" the president-elect argued down in Palm Beach on vacation that December with Jackie, Caroline, and the newly born John Jr. "I want the best men I can get, and they don't come any better than Bobby," the president-elect told his confidant Dave Powers.

Joe Kennedy and Kenny O'Donnell both told Bobby that because he would be involved in all the major White House decisions anyway, to take an undersecretary position would make the job far more difficult for whoever served above him. "My father," Bobby said, "was very strongly in favor of me going as attorney general. He wouldn't hear of anything else. He said, in the first place, you can't go in anything other than a Cabinet position. . . . He felt that the president should, Jack should, have somebody that was close to him, and had been close for a long period of time when he went into his job. I was against it; we had some rather strong arguments out here, all the family; a couple of my sisters, Jack and Teddy and I, and my father.

"And then, finally, I thought about it a good deal and I went and called [Jack] up and said I wanted see him. I called him up the day before I was supposed to be announced and told him I'd finally decided, and I'd thought about it, and I decided I wasn't going to do it, and that I'd gone through it all and I considered it all, and my mind was definitely made up that I wasn't going to do it."

Jack listened, and when Bobby finished, he said that before he made his final decision he wanted Bobby to come over and have breakfast with him the next morning at his house in Georgetown. Bobby agreed.

It was a long way from that day in New York in 1957 when John Seigenthaler had first met Bobby Kennedy and disliked him so. After Bobby had sent his rackets committee investigators down to Tennessee, the two men began to develop a mutual respect and eventually a bond of friendship. John Seigenthaler would help Bobby write his book *The Enemy Within*. While working for Jack's national campaign he had found himself in the middle of a crisis over the jailing of the civil rights leader Martin Luther King, Jr. The judge would not offer him bail.

A young JFK campaigning for the Senate, with Rose Kennedy at lower right, 1952. *Courtesy of John F. Kennedy Library and Museum.*

Kenny O'Donnell, assistant to campaign director Bobby Kennedy, maps election strategy during JFK's 1952 senatorial race. *Courtesy of John F. Kennedy Library and Museum.*

Dinner at the Kennedys', circa 1957. *Courtesy of John F. Kennedy Library and Museum.*

McClellan (Rackets) Committee staff photo, 1957. Pierre Salinger, Carmine Bellino, and Bobby Kennedy are in the first row, third, fourth, and fifth from right. *Courtesy of AP/Wide World Photos.*

Bobby conferring with an unidentified staffer, circa 1957. *Courtesy of John F. Kennedy Library and Museum.*

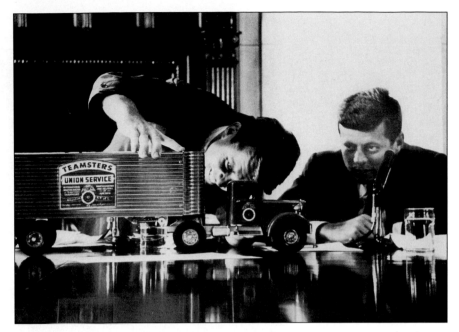

Bobby and Jack Kennedy during Teamsters testimony. *Courtesy of John F. Kennedy Library and Museum.*

The Kennedy brothers relaxing at Hickory Hill, the family estate, 1957. *Courtesy of John F. Kennedy Library and Museum.*

Bobby with Ethel after he was named Father of the Year, 1959. *Courtesy of John F. Kennedy Library and Museum.*

Bobby with Bill Walton in West Virginia during the 1960 presidential campaign. *Courtesy of John F. Kenndedy Library and Museum.*

Kenny boarding the *Caroline* just days after the election. *Courtesy of John F. Kennedy Library and Museum.*

Kenny "the Cobra" O'Donnell at his desk outside the Oval Office. *Courtesy of the White House.*

A Harvard-Columbia football game, October 19, 1963. In the fourth row from
the top are, *left to right*, Kenny O'Donnell, Dave Powers, Edmund Muskie,
Jack Kennedy, and Larry O'Brien. *Courtesy of Harvard University.*

Jack and Jackie, Washington, D.C., 1961. *Courtesy of United Press International.*

Kenny and Pierre Salinger with the president in Venezuela, 1961. *Courtesy of John F. Kennedy Library and Museum.*

The "Three Brothers" in the Rose Garden. *Reprinted by permission of* The New York Times.

Kenny and Jack enjoy a light moment with John Jr. *Courtesy of John F. Kennedy Library and Museum.*

Jack, Pierre Salinger, and Kenny at Fort Bragg, North Carolina, on October 12, 1961. *Courtesy of John F. Kennedy Library and Museum.*

Angela Novello guards the door to the office of Attorney General Bobby Kennedy *(back to camera)*. *Reprinted by permission of* The New York Times.

The attorney general meeting with New York District Attorney Robert Morgenthau *(second from left)* and his staff, circa 1962. *Courtesy of O'Donnell family.*

The president's last trip abroad, Dublin, Ireland, 1963. Kenny is standing in the second car. *Courtesy of John F. Kennedy Library and Museum.*

Kenny and Dave Powers *(center)* in Limerick, Ireland. *Courtesy of John F. Kennedy Library and Museum.*

At Love Field in Dallas, November 22, 1963. *Courtesy of John F. Kennedy Library and Museum.*

Aboard Air Force One. Kenny is at far right. *Courtesy of John F. Kennedy Library and Museum.*

According to Seigenthaler and historian David Garrow, Jack Kennedy, at the urging of Sargent Shriver, had called Dr. King's wife Coretta to express his concern. The call made national news. It was also the cause of an explosion between Kenny and Bobby.

Kenny had been with Jack when he had made the phone call to Mrs. King. He had not had a chance to tell Bobby about it. Once the news broke, Bobby was upset that he had not been told or consulted. Calling Kenny on the phone, the two men argued furiously. Finally Bobby said, "Look, we are all dealing with people all over this country and we're getting calls from people in the South who are raising hell—and it would have been so easy to deal with if we had just known in advance the call was going to be made." Kenny stood his ground. "Bobby, Jack wanted to do it and that was it!"

Bobby had to leave Washington for New York that day. As he was preparing to go, he asked John Scigenthaler to find the phone number of the Georgia judge who had denied King bail; he wanted to see if he could change the judge's mind. Seigenthaler tracked down the judge's number and gave it to Bobby. As he drove him to the airport for his flight to New York, he argued strenuously against Bobby's calling the judge. As he climbed out of the car at the airport, he was relieved to see that Bobby had finally agreed. Headed toward his flight, he said, "Okay, okay, you're right. I won't call."

Seigenthaler went back to the Esso Building headquarters. Later in the afternoon, Roger Tubby, the press secretary who worked for Pierre Salinger, entered his office upset. "John, that crazy judge in Georgia said Bobby called him up and chewed him up and he is really mad!"

Seigenthaler laughed, shaking his head. "Well, issue a denial. He didn't make the call."

Tubby, relieved, left and promptly issued a denial to the waiting press corps. A little while later, the phone rang at Seigenthaler's desk. It was Bobby. "What's going on?" he asked quietly, sounding tired.

"Nothing really," Seigenthaler said. "That crazy judge in Georgia said you called him up and chewed him out. So I had Tubby issue a denial. It's okay."

There was a moment of silence on the other end of the phone. "Well," Bobby said, "better withdraw it quick. I called him."

Seigenthaler was stunned. Hanging up the phone, he rushed off to find Roger Tubby and Pierre Salinger to get them to withdraw the denial. As Seigenthaler understood it, "the more Bobby thought about what the judge was doing to Martin Luther King the more angry he got. Every man had a right to bond, and Dr. King is being held on a misdemeanor charge; this denial of bond is nonsense. So he called the judge and said, 'Look, as a lawyer, I am calling you and telling you I think your denial of bail is unconscionable.' "

Kenny more than anyone understood Bobby's need to make that call. He and Shriver had persuaded Jack to call Mrs. King. As Kenny knew, Bobby would take a political risk to do the right thing. Which is why Kenny thought he would make such a good attorney general.

John Seigenthaler accompanied Bobby to his brother's home on N Street that morning. Bobby entered the house determined to put to rest the question of his being the attorney general, thus giving Jack enough time to find someone else.

It didn't work out that way. "We talked about forty minutes," Bobby would say later, during which Jack told him "he thought it would be helpful to have somebody in government—that all these people that he had been selecting were people that he didn't know particularly well, and . . . he thought that he would want . . . to make a difference, to have somebody that he could talk to over some of these problems, and so he thought it was important that I become attorney general."

Bobby was still hesitant, but Jack was not willing to wait; they had all thought and talked enough. "Let's go out and announce it," he told his brother.

"So, I think it was that day it was announced or maybe noon; that was at breakfast, and I think I said I'd come back," Bobby remembered. "And then I came back, and he told me to brush my hair, and I brushed my hair, and we went outside and announced it."

"The Kennedy wisecracks flew fast and furious that morning," Kenny said. "Jack said only half jokingly, 'I'll stick my head out the front door, and look up the street and down the street, and if nobody's around, I'll whisper it's Bobby.' " If Bobby Kennedy was impossible to say no to, as Kenny would be the first to admit, then Jack Kennedy was even more difficult to rebuff. One brother could not turn down the other.

16

THE WHITE HOUSE

*I do have a liking for the word "politics." It's the way
a president gets things done.*

—JACK KENNEDY

On Inauguration Day 1961, poet Robert Frost gave John Kennedy a valuable piece of advice: He told the president to "be more Boston than Harvard." Kenny O'Donnell, his Ivy League education notwithstanding, embodied that entreaty. As the Kennedy brothers knew well, Harvard Yard could win impressive reviews and even provide some tools necessary for leadership, but Kenny's education in the mean streets of American political life could help win the White House. Bobby had recognized this talent early in his association with Kenny. By the time they arrived at the White House in 1961, Bobby himself was more Boston than Harvard, having accomplished what he had in politics and government alongside men who shared a background with his original college friends Nick Rodis, Paul Lazzaro, Wally Flynn, and Chuck Roche. Says Sander Vanocur, "I think Kenny O'Donnell and Bobby Kennedy went to Harvard and they both spent the rest of their lives doing their best to live it down."

Bobby and Kenny did make sure that all the crew from Harvard was invited to the inaugural events. At Kenny's behest, his sister Justine called brothers Cleo and Warren, still in Massachusetts, and helped track down everyone, sending them tickets, booking them hotel rooms, and getting them invited to all the events surrounding the ceremonies. Wally Flynn recalls that "when they sent out the invitations for Jack's inauguration, we all got a little letter from Bobby telling where to check in and so forth. It was wonderful."

Paul Lazzaro, now treasurer of the Massachusetts town of Wakefield, was one of the Harvard football players who received one of Bobby's letters, complete with a reference to a practical joke now some fifteen years old. While Bobby was living at Harvard's Lowell House, he had stopped by the Varsity Club one afternoon and found Lazzaro with Rodis and Cleo in Rodis's room. Lazzaro was massaging something into Rodis's scalp. Bobby watched in amazement. "What's up?" he asked. Rodis was going bald, he was told, and this was the Greek way to make the hair grow back. "Nick, you don't look like you are losing hair," Bobby said in surprise.

Soon Paul Lazzaro got up and, running his fingers through Bobby's deep locks, said, with serious concern, "Bobby, you know, you're really losing some hair along your hairline." Bobby dismissed them with a wave of his hand. But Rodis and Lazzaro weren't done yet. They told Kenny, who in turn made sure that everyone who encountered Bobby remarked on his receding hairline and thinning pate. The final blow came one day when Bob walked into the Varsity Club game room and the room went silent. Bobby looked uneasy. Kenny walked over and ran his hand through Bobby's hair. "My God, you *have* really lost a lot of hair since the beginning of the week." Everyone agreed, horrified. With this, Rodis and Lazzaro were able to convince Bobby to go with them to the Boston's Lahey Clinic to get some hair tonic from the doctors for premature baldness. The bill for five dollars is still in the records. The doctors were not amused by young Kennedy and his friends, promptly sending the bill to the ambassador, who found even less to laugh about. Bobby had a long memory, as his pre-inaugural note to Lazzaro made clear.

December 28, 1960

Dear Paul,

With your bald head—don't take off your hat to anyone.

I am sending you and Leo invitations to the Inauguration. Anything you and Leo sell while you are down here Kenny and I get a split! If they elect you as Treasurer in Wakefield then that whole community must be corrupt.

Best regards,
Bobby

At Bobby's invitation, Kenny had the Harvard gang attend Hickory Hill for a party after the inauguration, where the guests included such luminaries as Jack Paar, Harry Belafonte, and Kim Novak. The veteran football players were especially attracted to Novak. After much teasing from other members of the team, Paul Lazzaro managed to get up the nerve to introduce himself to Novak. "The wise guys, all of us were all standing there, we had surrounded Kim Novak," Nick Rodis recalls. He got up the nerve to introduce himself to Novak and get a picture taken of himself kissing her. "Kim Novak asked who I was and what I did. Kenny introduced me as the ambassador to some country, that I never heard of, telling her that Mr. Ambassador was a very close friend of the president. Well, boy, was she impressed. She spent the entire rest of the time calling me Mr. Ambassador. Bobby overhead the whole thing while he was talking to somebody else, and barely got through his conversation before he burst into laughter."

When Bobby was working for the rackets committee, he had used his connections in the State Department to send Nick Rodis to Greece to give basketball clinics. At the time Rodis was coaching football at the University of Connecticut, and the trip was an opportunity to visit his parents' homeland that he could not otherwise have afforded. When he returned he went to see Kenny and Bobby at the Old Senate Office Building to thank them, catching them in between hearings on Jimmy Hoffa and the Teamsters. Sitting in the conference room of his office, Bobby shook his head, running his hand through his hair as he talked. "Nick, you've got to get out of coaching. Your family has never had any money and you're never going to make any money coaching. I have great connections. I want you to go see four or five of my friends. Just go talk to them."

Nick shook his head. "No, Bobby, thanks a lot, but I don't want to. I want to be in football. I don't think I would be comfortable."

Bobby looked at Kenny, who shrugged. "Well, keep it in mind, Nick."

Now that Jack had won the White House, Bobby and Kenny intended to bring Rodis and as many of their other Harvard men to Washington as possible to expand the Kennedy team. Kenny offered Rodis a place in the Commerce Department. When he protested that he didn't even know anything about commerce, Kenny told him, "You're going, Nick." And soon the right job opened up and Rodis was in the Commerce Department working for President John F. Kennedy.

After John Kennedy had taken the oath of office and told his fellow Americans not to ask what their country could do for them but what they could do for their country, Bobby Kennedy had to endure what promised to be a difficult confirmation hearing for attorney general. He was young and relatively inexperienced, and he had a lot to prove. Bobby had done his homework and had brought in help. John Reilly, who would become chief of the U.S. attorneys, compiled a list of all earlier attorneys general who might have had less experience going into the job than Robert Kennedy. "We went through all the former attorneys general to find anyone, I mean anyone, with less experience than Robert Kennedy. We couldn't find one! I mean not one. Bobby was making all kinds of jokes about it, he was very funny, but it was kind of embarrassing really. I think he knew this would be the case and it was one of the reasons he fought so hard against becoming attorney general." While Reilly did not find an attorney general with less experience, he did uncover Warren Harding's attorney general, Harry Daugherty, who had forty years' experience and had gone to jail in the Teapot Dome scandal; experience was not necessarily a mark of competence or honesty. "We planted the question of experience with one of the senators who was friendly to us, because we wanted the question asked and answered. Bobby answered with the information about the Teapot Dome scandal. Bob loved it and so did everyone else." After Bobby's confirmation, Reilly won his own permanent spot; he worked for the new U.S. attorney, who was quickly becoming one of Robert Kennedy's closest confidants, Byron White.

*   *   *

Reporter Rowland Evans had first met Bobby during the rackets committee hearings and by 1960 had gotten to know Bobby well. His wife Katherine and Ethel had become close friends. On inaugural morning, in Ethel's dining room, he was conducting an on-the-record breakfast interview with Bobby, when Red Fay, one of Jack's PT 109 crew, came down the stairs. "I said to Bob, 'Who the hell is that?' He turned and looked. 'Oh, Red Fay.' " The interview was frustrating for Evans; Bobby was responding evasively, with a one- or two-word answer, telling Evans he wasn't certain of some new administration plans. Fay joined them for breakfast and listened to the conversation. "Suddenly," Evans remembers, "Fay interrupted and said, 'Bobby, what do you mean you aren't sure? Don't you remember Jack said it last night?' Then Fay would tell me the whole story—it was great! Bobby was just chuckling and shaking his head. Finally, Bobby said to Fay, 'Hey, don't you know who this guy is? He is a big time columnist for the *Boston Herald* and a political reporter! Shut your mouth up!' Bobby was as close to the president as could be, but nevertheless he was very tough to get stuff out of unless he wanted you to. It could be frustrating. Kenny was very similar."

Evans and Kenny O'Donnell had also grown close during the 1958 campaign and beyond. "If Kenny liked you he would talk to you, and he liked me, so I was lucky. He never would tell you a whole lot of inside stuff, but he would give you the feel for the story and what was going on. He would also steer you away from a false lead, so you wouldn't waste your time. He would sit up there in the bus with us— we all traveled by bus. He was the first one off the bus and the last one on; he was like that in the White House as well. He was always alert, watchful, protective of the president and Bobby. If Kenny was there, from a reporter's standpoint, you knew the president meant business."

Once Kenny O'Donnell reached the White House, Evans saw him in action with the same fierce single-mindedness he had employed on the campaign trail. Once over lunch, Kenny told Evans about an encounter he'd just had with the vice president. "Lyndon was in my office today. Stopped by. He asked me how one of his nominations was doing, and I said, 'Well, Mr. Vice President, we haven't done anything about it. In fact—' " With that Kenny reached down into a desk drawer, pulling it out about two inches, so Johnson could see inside. "That's where it is right now, in that drawer, Mr. Vice President, and that is where it is going to stay!" With that Kenny slammed the drawer shut. Stunned, Johnson walked away. It turned out that Jack Kennedy and Kenny had been pressing Johnson to lobby for a specific piece of legislation and Johnson had resisted. According to Evans, this was Kenny's way of saying, " 'Fuck you, Mr. Vice President. You will get your goddamn nomination when I am good and ready to give it to you! Do your job first!' Kenny had great power that way, and it was real power. He didn't glory in it, he didn't lord it over anyone, he used it when it was necessary to use it to achieve the aims of John F. Kennedy."

Kenny's desk was right outside the Oval Office. As special assistant and appointments secretary, he was the gatekeeper to the president. He was as relentless and tough in his new job as he had ever been on the campaign. He was widely known as Kennedy's political chief of staff, with Ted Sorensen the coordinator of the president's legislative programs and the master at turning Jack's wishes into eloquent prose. Soon Kenny won the nickname "the Cobra." "Kenny used his position to advantage," recalls Sander Vanocur, then a correspondent for NBC. "If you wanted to get around Kenny to see Kennedy, you might do it once through Evelyn Lincoln, but better not try it twice because if you did you were done with Kenny O'Donnell."

"There were three words that epitomized Kenny O'Donnell in Jack Kennedy's White House," says White House aide Letitia Baldrige. "Those words were 'Cut the crap!' " That attitude made him valuable to President John Kennedy, who knew he could rely on Kenny to handle what needed to be handled, preserve the president's time, and protect the president's back. "Kenny was devoted to the president and to Bob," Ron Linton agrees. "Everyone knew he spoke for them. He was always fair, direct, no bullshit. That's why Jack and Bobby liked him, wanted him, and trusted him."

The nature of Kenny's position would inevitably create conflicts. Jack and Bobby wanted Kenny in that position because they understood how the presidency could foster an environment where people are less comfortable telling the president what he needed to hear than what he should hear. "It's a very difficult thing," says John Seigenthaler—who would become Robert Kennedy's Kenny O'Donnell at the Justice Department—"when four or five people are telling Bob or Jack only what they thought Bob or Jack wanted to hear. Kenny would never do that. Kenny would speak out against four or five people in a room; even if he was the only one disagreeing with them, he would speak his mind. If he felt they were wrong and we were wrong or that the other side needed to be aired and wasn't being aired, he would say so."

"Kenny was always direct, always spoke his mind," remembers Paul Lazzaro. "The White House was no different. I think in some ways he thought it was even more important to speak out there, because so much more was at stake."

Bobby Kennedy himself agreed. "Kenny would strip away the veil and tell it as he saw it, no matter what." It was something that Jack and Bobby Kennedy would come to rely on even more in the years ahead.

Jack Kennedy's strategy to put Lyndon Johnson on the ticket had worked. Now they faced the question of a new majority leader. Jack told Kenny that he was looking forward to working with Senator Mike Mansfield, a Kennedy Democrat from Montana. Mansfield was especially drawn to Jack Kennedy because they had both served in the House and Senate together along with Prescott Bush, father of the future President George Bush; Barry Goldwater; Stuart Symington; Henry Jackson; and Albert Gore, father of the future vice president. When Johnson got the vice presidency, Jack Kennedy sent him to see Mike Mansfield to urge him to become the new majority leader—just as he had told Kenny he would during their bathroom confrontation during the convention. Johnson went to see Mansfield, pouring on the heavy Johnson charm, but the Montana senator was adamant. He didn't want the job. He was naturally reserved and didn't like to strong-arm people, an activity the position required. Failing to get the answer he sought, Johnson sent Dick Russell to see Mansfield, who still resisted. John Kennedy himself had to intervene and Mansfield acquiesced.

Kennedy had gotten what he wanted—a vice president who helped him carry the South and a majority leader who would be more friendly to the Kennedy legislative program than Johnson would have been, after having lost the nomination and been passed over for the number two spot. Kenny O'Donnell saw how crafty a strategic thinker Kennedy was. The choice of Mansfield had a personal benefit for him; he and Mike Mansfield were to become close friends. "Kenny became my conduit to the president," Mansfield says. "We exchanged notes and kept each other fully informed in all respects. He kept his word to me always and he never, ever, tried to block access to Jack Kennedy or use his position to work out his own agenda. Kenny was the point man on all areas of the president's concern, not just legislatively, all areas. In my view the president relied completely on Kenny and he was the key to every decision."

The Kennedy staff had in essence grown up with each other. Many had been together long before they ever entered the White House, and although there were tensions, most were familiar with each other and that helped. "I must admit," says Meyer "Mike" Feldman, who worked with the so-called Sorensen group in the White House, "I wondered, Ted Sorensen wondered, and several others wondered if Kenny's first responsibility was going to be to Bobby or to the president." Kenny had been known as "Bobby Kennedy's guy" as he himself freely admitted; many saw him as simply an extension of the attorney general's reach. "Was his responsibility going to be to John or Robert Kennedy? And when he spoke was he speaking for John or Robert? We on the staff were John Kennedy people and Kenny O'Donnell was a Bobby Kennedy person, which wasn't the same thing at all, and frankly we were not sure of him fitting in or if we could trust him."

Bobby and Kenny were not the same person, however. An early episode involving Hy Raskin, a lawyer and a savvy politician who had been invaluable during the 1960 campaign, symbolizes the difference in attitude and temperament between Kenny and Bobby, which made them largely independent players in the New Frontier. Raskin had not wanted a position in the White House; instead, he wanted to open his own Washington law firm. To help him open his business with a bang, Kenny had arranged with Jack to announce that Hy Raskin had just turned down a key post in the administration. When the president-elect made the statement from the door to the house on N Street, he exchanged a quick amused glance with Kenny, as the assembled press corps tore through their briefing sheets trying to find out who in the hell Hy Raskin was and what post he was up for. "The president thought the whole thing was funny as hell," Kenny told Reilly. "Hy had never asked me or the president for anything in his life. If that's all he wanted the president said, 'Hell, that's fine; that's an easy request to fill!' and so we did it. It was great."

Bobby was not amused. "Bobby thought it was stupid and kind of unethical to give people an impression like that when it really wasn't true. It really ticked him off. He didn't think you should do things like that and he thought it was stupid to play with the press like that." Kenny disagreed; in his view, it was a political favor, one that was simple and easy to grant. "Kenny and Bobby could really argue and disagree with each other," Reilly says. "A lot of people were afraid of both of them and they knew it, but they were never afraid of each other, and they would really take each other on sometimes. It was funny to watch the two of them go at it with each other. They were tough as hell on each other. Nobody would have dared speak to either one of them the way they spoke to each other. In many real ways, Bobby helped keep Kenny down-to-earth sometimes. Kenny, the 'Cobra,' was tough, very tough, sometimes too tough on people. Bob helped to kind of remind him of the human element of decisions. Bob could be tough too, but underneath he knew there was a human element to things, and I think underneath he had a very gentle streak to him that Kenny didn't necessarily possess." Kenny was a real politician and Bobby had never thought of himself that way, especially now as attorney general.

Nick Rodis agrees with John Reilly's assessment of the two men's differences. "They had different views and different jobs, and they were always friends, but from the days at the Varsity Club to Bobby's days with McCarthy, they had no problem going at each other. I think nobody else would have dared."

Wally Flynn also saw the two men from a broad perspective. "I think that is why Bobby liked Kenny and liked the football team, and why they got along so well, because Kenny was never going to kiss his ass and tell him only what he wanted to hear. Many people were afraid of Kenny, but Bobby had no problem telling him if he thought he was doing something stupid."

According to Paul Lazzaro, "Bobby understood that kind of friendship is not something you can buy in life, and so he treasured it."

One of John Reilly's jobs was to do background checks for candidates for the U.S. attorney appointments made by the attorney general. In a practice different and perhaps more workable than that in use today, Bobby ordered Reilly to have a background check done on someone who actually got the job. Otherwise, he didn't want the check done, because if the FBI questioned a prospective appointee's employees and personal acquaintances, it could be needlessly embarrassing for both the administration and the candidate. For many U.S. attorneys, the most difficult adjustment was the realization that once they began to work in the United States Attorney's Office, they were no longer political. 'They were really startled," Reilly recalls. "It hit them hard. But, Bobby would have them in to a meeting and he would really lay it out for them, really direct and sternly."

"When I became attorney general I was forced to put politics aside in order to do my job and do it well," Bobby said. "To be a successful attorney general politics can have nothing to do with your decisions." Bobby's fierce commitment to that principle would soon lead to major conflicts with both his brother, the president, and Kenny—starting with a case involving the brother of one of Jack Kennedy's early and most fervent supporters, Congressman Eugene Keogh from Brooklyn, New York.

Keogh had been a key figure in Jack Kennedy's primary victory in New York, and many people, including Kenny O'Donnell and Jack Kennedy himself, credited him with swinging the New York delegation to Kennedy. Keogh's brother Vincent was a state judge in New York and had been accused of taking bribes in order to deliver lenient sentences to those brought before the court. The Justice Department "get Hoffa squad" investigating Jimmy Hoffa and his ties to Tony "Ducks"

Corrallo had "backed into the Vincent Keogh case" recalls Bill Hundley, a Justice Department career lawyer Bobby asked to take over the case.

Hundley had first met the new attorney general in 1951 during Bobby's own tenure with Justice. "I remember when he left" to work for his brother's campaign, Hundley says. "We all told him that he was crazy because we could see the big Republican sweep coming. Of course neither we nor the Republicans had counted on the tenacity of Robert Kennedy." The two men had also known each other when Bobby was minority counsel to the McCarthy Committee. "Roy Cohn was chief counsel of the committee and none of us could stand Roy Cohn and most of all Bob Kennedy. He was pretty unhappy and frustrated at the time. I remember he was working on something with regard to China, and I remember thinking he wasn't going to last there very long." During the McClellan hearings, "Bob Kennedy, Kenny O'Donnell, Paul Tierney, Walter Sheridan, Carmine Bellino, and Pierre Salinger were the core of that committee." Hundley and Kennedy would clash over the progress of some of the cases involving the Teamsters union; Bobby wanted Justice to be more proactive in going after the Jimmy Hoffas, the Dave Becks, and their friends in the underworld. "We ended up so angry with each other," recalled Hundley, "that we literally ended up on our feet standing, chairs pushed back, screaming at each other."

Bobby was furious. "It makes me sick to my stomach, Bill, when you tell me you can't bring this case!"

Hundley shot back, "Bob, look I can't be responsible for your gastric juices." The two men nearly came to blows, separated only by Kenny who pushed them both into their chairs and told them to "knock that shit off."

Now, Hundley says, "Bob was right, of course, but there was nothing I could do at that time. Bob was tough, really tough. Kenny was at all of those meetings and he was just as tough as Bob, but in a quieter way. They made an incredible team. The team came almost intact to the Justice Department when Bob became attorney general.

"When Bobby Kennedy became attorney general one of his first acts was to fire me," Hundley says, laughing. Bobby told the longtime Justice lawyer that he wanted to put his own person in Hundley's job. Instead, he would stay on as Bobby's special assistant. His new status allowed him to take command of the Keogh case. It would be to Bill Hundley that Bob Kennedy would turn when confronted with his most tricky, politicized prosecutions.

Jack Miller, Bobby's choice to head the department's Criminal Division, also found himself involved in the Keogh case—and caught between Bobby and Kenny. An acquaintance of Bobby's during the Jimmy Hoffa investigations, Miller had barely known Robert Kennedy. "We weren't social or even political friends, especially political," says Miller, who was a registered Republican.

In early 1961, Miller came home from his law office to find his wife demanding to know what he had done wrong: "The attorney general of the United States called and he wants to speak to you."

"Then," says Miller, "even I got a little worried." Rushing to the phone he quickly called the number that Bobby had left and soon was speaking to Kennedy's private secretary Angie Novello, who passed him on to Bobby, who told him abruptly, "I want you to be head of the Criminal Division in the Justice Department." When Miller protested that he was a Republican precinct chairman and worked for a law firm that represented the notoriously conservative *Chicago Tribune*, Bobby told him he didn't give a damn. "When can you start?" he asked.

"How about next week?"

"It was clear that Gene Keogh had been very important in the election and probably swung the whole state for Kennedy. I don't think Gene ever expected Bob Kennedy to prosecute," recalls Bill Hundley. Jack Miller knew that the evidence was clear: The brother had taken a bribe, broken the law, and should be prosecuted. "I know," Hundley says, "that Gene Keogh didn't go directly to Bob Kennedy, but he did go to Kenny in hopes that Kenny could get Bob to back off." Kenny never directly asked Bobby to decide not to prosecute, but he made the political implications clear to both Kennedy and Miller. "It was a very difficult situation," says Hundley. "You were either damned if you did or damned if you didn't."

Jack Miller recalled seeing Kenny during this period once at Hickory

Hill during one of Ethel's parties. "I can't believe that you can't let it go!" Kenny told him.

"Look, Kenny," said Miller, hoping not to get punched in the nose, "he broke the law—that's all there is to it." Walking away, Kenny gave him the dirtiest look he had ever received in his life. Joe Dolan remembers a Hickory Hill party during the height of the Keogh investigation, where four or five people from Justice and the White House were arguing with Bob. "Are you sure?" they were asking. "Do you really have enough?"

"Kenny and I would have a lot of conversations," said John Seigenthaler. "The Keogh case was a prime example—we commiserated about that one a lot. Kenny would call me and say, 'Can you tell me what's going to happen? Gene called me.'" Seigenthaler would tell him, "As soon as I know I will tell you."

One evening during the height of the investigation, right before the decision would be made whether or not to indict, John Seigenthaler accompanied Bobby and Ethel to a White House reception. As they walked up the steps that led into the hallway near the reception room, they saw a group of assistant attorneys from the Justice Department standing off to the side, obviously waiting to see the attorney general about the Keogh case. Catching up to Ethel, Bobby, and Seigenthaler near the reception room, one of them said, with more than a little sarcasm, "Well, I hope we are this meticulous when it comes to Jimmy Hoffa!" Seigenthaler flared and said something sharp in return. Before the other assistant could reply, Bobby put up his hand. "I hope so, too," he said, very deliberately. The point was lost on no one.

Finally, Hundley told them the evidence against Vincent Keogh was incontrovertible. They had to indict. "It was really difficult for him," Hundley says. "I am sure he was under tremendous pressures and I think he felt really bad, but he had a job to do. He knew the political implication—the guy's brother was a friend—but what could he do?"

When Hundley had finished his presentation Bob made only one statement. "Okay, if you feel we have a case, then we've got to bring this case, but you damn well better win it!"

"It was typical of him," Hundley declares. "Once he knew we had a case, that we weren't just fishing, he made up his mind to prosecute, do the job, and do it right. He gave me all the support in the world."

Seigenthaler called Kenny at the White House to tell him the news. "Who's gonna tell Gene? I'm certainly not going to do it."

Ultimately Seigenthaler made the call, breaking the news to the congressman as gently as he could. Bobby would be willing to talk to him, he told Keogh, but he hadn't wanted to intrude on what he knew was a painful family matter he had helped to cause. To his surprise, he heard weeping on the other end of the phone.

"John, I know Bobby wouldn't do this if he didn't have to," Keogh finally said. "I'm terribly hurt. I love my brother very much. But, I would like to call Bobby myself. I know this is as painful for him as me."

Seigenthaler couldn't believe his ears. "Congressman, he wants to talk to you if you want to talk to him. But he has told me specifically that he would like to do you the courtesy of his calling you."

"John, please don't be silly. Give me his number."

Seigenthaler put Keogh on hold and on his other phone furiously dialed the attorney general at home to warn him that Keogh was about to call. Then he gave the congressman Bobby's private number at Hickory Hill.

They didn't talk about the case, the attorney general told Seigenthaler the next day. "It was more about how sad it was to watch his brother and his family go through this. He couldn't stop crying. I felt terrible," Bobby said. "I mean, he just wept, and I know I am destroying this family, but he broke the law and nobody can be above the law. There was nothing more I could do. He just wept and all I could do was listen."

"The Keogh case showed the delicacy of Robert Kennedy's position and I think in a way showed clearly the difference between Kenny's role and Bobby's role," John Reilly says. "Bobby understood very well that because he was the president's brother he was privy to a lot of decisions and information that otherwise he wouldn't know anything about. But because he was the president's brother there were going to be inevitable gray areas." Robert Kennedy used the Keogh case to demonstrate clearly that he was not a man to dwell happily within those gray areas. "I think sometimes during the Keogh case and others, we drove Kenny and the president crazy," Joe Dolan says. "I think Kenny especially saw Bobby and many of us at Justice as a bunch of do-gooders who had no political sense whatsoever."

"Working for Bobby," says Seigenthaler, "I tried to be as straightforward as Kenny, because that was something to measure against. I found both Kennedy brothers had more respect for people who engaged them in arguments and stood up to them." Once the attorney general and Kenny had an argument over somebody Kenny thought should be fired over at the Justice Department. After much arguing, Bobby finally agreed and told Seigenthaler to fire him. "No, I am not going to do it," his assistant told the attorney general. "You and Kenny are wrong. If you want it done, do it yourself." Bobby was furious. John argued right back. "I don't think he deserves it. Either get somebody else to do it or do it yourself. It would be better, by the way, if you did it." Both men were angry and hurt. The next day Bobby called Seigenthaler into his office and told him "he had decided to give the fella another chance. He did and it turned out all right."

Seigenthaler's model in this issue had been Kenny. "He had the guts to say, 'Look I don't think so' for both the president and Bob. I felt it was my job to be able to do that for Bob. I watched Kenny and nothing bothered him — if he thought someone was wrong he would say so."

"The president's assistants all fascinated me," remarked Letitia "Tish" Baldrige, who had come to the White House as the First Lady's lieutenant. "They were such a motley group, that's what I called them, because they had represented everything and anything. There was no 'type.' They were not slick politicians. They were a mixture of everything. As much as they were different, they had one common bond and that was John F. Kennedy. They were all devoted to him." Baldrige knew at least one reason why he would inspire devotion. "He would listen to you, which is a rare thing among politicians. God, what a wonderful thing that is for your ego to be listened to by the president of the United States!"

As much as Baldrige respected his political ability, she and Kenny were mostly at odds. Baldrige had known Jackie since they were girls in Washington. Her parents were friends of Janet and Hugh Auchincloss, Jackie's mother and stepfather. Jackie had been three years behind Baldrige at their boarding school, Farmington, and then followed her to Paris and the Sorbonne. Baldrige's experience as Clare Booth Luce's assistant in Paris made her an ideal candidate to be Jackie's amanuensis and advocate in the White House. When she first met Kenny, he gave her his cool stare and said, "If you think I'm going to trust you, you can forget it."

Baldrige, the daughter of a onetime Republican congressman, knew politics and gave it right back to Kenny. "I saw the twinkle in his eye when I was finished giving him 'what for.' I knew then we would fight constantly and get along famously. I would tease him and say, 'Ken, if the devil runs for president as a Democrat, are you going to stay with your party?' He would look at me, trying to intimidate me, and say, 'Absolutely. Can't stand switch hitters!' Which was of course a reference to my Republican lineage." In due course, Baldrige would earn Ken's respect. "We had quite a good time," she says now. "We were unmerciful with each other, but the bottom line is that everyone in the White House really worked together because we all loved John F. Kennedy."

The parties Jackie hosted were a source of constant battle between Baldrige and the president's special assistant. "Kenny couldn't figure out what good all the social stuff was. All these parties of Jackie's were taking up the President's valuable time," Baldrige says Kenny thought. He would constantly try to book the president out of the social events that Baldrige and the First Lady had planned, which meant Jackie would have to approach the president later in the evening and get him to relent, or else restore it to his schedule herself, only to have Kenny remove it once more. After several of these round-robins, an irked Kenny went to see Baldrige to tell her these events were foolishness. Baldrige rose from her desk to face him. "Kenny, this is useful to him. Jackie wants it, she knows it's good public relations, and it will have an impact. She knows what she's doing!" Kenny, unmoved, went to plead his case directly to the president. Caught between his wife and his closest aide, the president let Jackie have her way. "In time," Baldrige says, "Kenny began to see what Jackie already knew—that the public loved it. The public loved seeing Jack and Jackie together. They were in essence king and queen of the country and the public adored it. Kenny began to see that these social events could be used for political purposes, and then we had no more trouble with the schedule."

Soon the debate revolved around the invitation list. Once Kenny sent over a set of names Jackie was to include as guests. When Baldrige called to demand who these people were, Kenny replied tersely, "These people are very important to the president. That's how he got elected and will be reelected. That *is* the idea, you know." Baldrige sent a memo to Jackie listing the names submitted by the various Cabinet members, together with Kenny's list of no fewer than twenty-three names. Jackie wrote a terse note back: "Forget it. We don't need these politicos with no manners; tell Kenny forget it!"

Rather than calling Kenny, Baldrige sent a memo, thinking it was safer. As she expected, Kenny came storming over to her office. "Why aren't these people on the guest list? What does she mean, forget it!"

"Kenny, there isn't enough room," Baldrige began delicately.

"Room my ass," Kenny snapped. "Does Jackie realize that without these people the president wouldn't have been elected, and you people wouldn't be here to have your damn silly parties? Do you realize that you are going to need these people during the next campaign?"

Putting up her hands, Baldrige acknowledged him. "All right, all right Kenny, I know—my father was in Congress—but you have to compromise as well. Jackie will give you a certain number, but you can't have the whole thing!" Kenny reluctantly agreed, culling his list to seven. From then on, per the president's orders, Jackie and Tish Baldrige knew that Kenny would get at least some of his politicos invited.

The night of the first formal event that Kenny's invitees attended, Baldrige spied Kenny standing unobserved against the wall in the State Dining Room, still wearing his business suit, watching the entire scene. Tish wandered over and stood next to him. "Geez," Kenny said, his lips barely moving. "I'm surprised I got any of my people here tonight. See, look at him, Tish, he's wearing shoes—he's not so bad." Nodding toward another man he said, "Look at him, he's got a tie and a shirt on. Don't be so critical—they know when to put clothes on!" All Tish Baldrige could do was laugh.

Ethel and Bobby, along with Kenny and Helen, rarely even attended White House affairs. "I never saw a group that was less interested in getting invited to the White House than Kenny and Helen or Bobby and Ethel," Baldrige remembers. "They could come whenever they wanted, so they had none of the political insecurities about it. When they did come, Ethel and Helen were always comfortable, made others feel welcome, and were themselves. It was refreshing." On the other hand, congressmen, senators, Joint Chiefs of Staff, Cabinet members, and staff were all vying to be invited. The battle to be included had reached such a fever that at one point a prominent senator called Baldrige and said, "I must be invited to one of the Kennedys' parties; otherwise I will be divorced. My wife says that I am a nothing because I haven't been invited to one of Jackie's parties!" The Kennedys, not wanting to be responsible for ruining the senator's marriage, obliged.

"My lasting image of him is during a visit by a group of retarded children," Baldrige says of her memories of Kenny. "They were in the Rose Garden and it was during the height of one of the presidential crises. The president wasn't going to be able to see the children, we were told. To my astonishment I walked out into the garden and saw him standing there talking with the children. He stayed for almost an hour visiting with them. I turned and saw the Cobra leaning against the White House wall, ever watchful, catlike—ready for action. As I approached him, he gave me that small, flirting smile of his. 'He's something, isn't he?' he said, nodding toward the president."

"It's been a terrible day," Kenny went on to say. "With all the stuff and the problems he has on his mind, he gives up the only time he is going to have today and has been out here for almost an hour with these kids. But then that's him, isn't it?"

Baldrige turned back from looking at the president, astonished at seeing Kenny show his gentler side. "You're right, Kenny. He is really a very special, wonderful man." She caught Kenny's black eyes giving her that sideways glance. "How are your friends? The unemployed dilettantes? Haven't seen them lately."

"Fine," Baldrige replied, giving it right back. Now, this was the Kenny she was used to. "How are your political hoods? Looking for shoes?"

In his role as the president's troubleshooter, one of Kenny's responsibilities was to handle FBI reports that would determine whether or not somebody should be hired. White House aide Mike Feldman recalls that Kenny "often took the blame. Some guy would get mad because he was rejected and they would get mad at President Kennedy. Kenny would stop them. 'No, it was my decision. If you are going to be mad at anyone, be mad at me.' He took the blame for things he didn't have to take the blame for, and as much as everyone was unsure of him at first we really grew to trust him. We saw how tough he was. He wasn't phony tough; he didn't pick on people who didn't deserve it. He took on people who had to be taken on because it was his role to protect the president. There was no ego problem there. He was protecting the president, it was that straightforward and simple."

Though Bobby and Kenny maintained the warmth of their friendship once they were in the executive branch, they were all business about business. Jimmy Kenary remembers sitting with Kenny "at his desk in the White House, chatting and laughing, like old times, when the president came out—there was some visiting dignitary coming or something. I started to leave and Kenny said, 'No, sit there, this will take a couple of minutes.' Kenny became all business. He was intimidating almost. It was an amazing transformation."

Bill Geoghegan, who had come to Washington to be assistant attorney general, recalled many times, especially at the height of the civil rights crises in the South, when he would be in the attorney general's office while Bobby was on the phone to Kenny. Bobby never worried about anyone overhearing anything confidential in his conversations with Kenny. As Geoghegan recalls, "Bob didn't ask me to leave or anything, because who the hell could figure out what they were saying to each other? Most of the time it made no sense, just harsh tones—'mm, uhm, yup, fine, no, no, yes, okay.' Occasionally it might get really chatty and I would hear, 'yup, yup, mm, uh, yup, gotcha and yeah, okay, that's okay, and fine.' That was pretty much how it sounded when Bobby and Kenny were in the middle of discussion at the height of any crisis."

Mike Feldman was seated at his desk one day, in the Sorensen enclave within the White House office, when Kenny called about a political contributor the president didn't want to see. They were planning to subpoena a prominent labor official whose support was important to John Kennedy's future plans. When the union leader called on Kennedy, presumably to talk about Bobby's investigation, Feldman had agreed to meet with him. On the day of the encounter, Feldman's phone rang. "Look," Bobby Kennedy said, "we have got to get his testimony. We think there is something wrong in the way that union is operating. You ought to know that before you sit down with him."

"Okay," Feldman replied. The labor official arrived, announced he didn't want to testify, and while he didn't ask for any favors outright, he made a clear point of raising the fact of his past and future support of Senator John Kennedy. After he left, Feldman called Bobby. "You know what this fellow wants done, don't you?"

"Yeah," Bobby said. "I have an idea."

"Well, Bobby, what do I tell him?" Feldman asked.

"You just tell him that we have to do our duty, no matter the consequences."

That had been Feldman's first real conversation with Bobby, which now, in 1961, gave him an idea of how the new attorney general would respond to the company executive's implicit request. "I really want to talk to the president myself," the man told Feldman. "No offense, but I am entitled in view of what I have contributed to the Democratic National Committee."

Feldman called Kenny, who grudgingly agreed to get the executive in to see the president. Kennedy greeted the man warmly, showed him and Feldman to seats, and sat for twenty minutes while the man recounted his antitrust woes. He felt persecuted by the Justice Department, he said.

The president sat in his chair, looking at the man thoughtfully, his chin resting in his hand. "There is one major thing wrong with this administration," he finally said. "I have to admit it—and it is simply something that I can't control!"

Startled at the admission, the executive leaned forward. "What is it, Mr. President?" he asked anxiously.

John Kennedy looked at him with a straight face, with "not the slightest touch of humor or sarcasm," as Feldman would say later. "To be candid, we don't have an attorney general we can fix!"

Not only could John Kennedy not fix the attorney general, but sometimes it was the attorney general's own decisions that frustrated John Kennedy the most. Bill Geoghegan remembers well one incident—the only time he ever took a direct call from the president. Geoghegan had been sent by Bobby to meet with Senator Allen Ellender from Louisiana, chairman of the Senate committee that was handling a farm appropriations bill and tangling with the administration over potential revisions. The committee and the administration were fighting over the potential revisions. Bill Geoghegan's reason for meeting with Ellender had nothing to do with the farm bill. Rather, it involved the U.S. attorney that Senator Ellender wanted appointed in Louisiana. Ellender had been pushing hard for a candidate named Louis McClure. The FBI background on him had checked out but had indicated he had relatives associated with organized crime.

When Geoghegan and John Reilly said that the Justice Department could do better, Bobby agreed—on condition that Geoghegan tell Ellender firsthand. Geoghegan wasn't delighted with that prospect; he had been in this exact situation just months before, when at Bobby's request he had had to tell the powerful Senate Appropriations Committee chairman, Oklahoman Bob Kerr, that Justice had found *his* candidate for U.S. attorney unqualified and ask him for another name to nominate. Kerr had thrown Geoghegan and Reilly out of his office, bellowing, "I have been here long before Bob Kennedy and you came, and I will be here long after you are all long gone!" Senator Kerr had gotten on the phone to Kenny, who came up with a solution. He sent Seigenthaler and Geoghegan out to Oklahoma to conduct a week-long independent investigation. Kerr ultimately got his U.S. attorney candidate appointed a federal judge instead, which was enough to satisfy the senator.

Ellender also threw Geoghegan out of his office and called Kenny O'Donnell, demanding to see the president. Kenny quickly agreed. An irate Senator Ellender arrived in the Oval Office to tell both Kennedy and Kenny that the "damn farm bill is not going to move until I get my U.S. attorney." As Kenny later reported to Bobby, Ellender had been so furious he couldn't even remember Bill Geoghegan's name, but at the top of his lungs kept referring to him as "one of those boys, Bobby's boys from the Department of Justice!" John Kennedy's considerable charm was no match for Ellender's fury; after making his ultimatum the crusty senator from Louisiana stormed out of the White House.

At about 6:30 the phone rang at Bill Geoghegan's desk at Justice. A secretary's voice came on the line and said that Mr. O'Donnell was waiting

Minutes later he heard the voice of Kenny O'Donnell — there was no greeting, no chitchat. "The president wants to talk to you, Bill."

"Oh sure, Ken, sure!" said Geoghegan with good humor.

"I understand you were up seeing Ellender this afternoon!" As Geoghegan started to stammer a response, the Cobra cut him off. "Do you know what the fuck your conversation is going to do to our farm bill!? Do you have any sense at all? Well, now you have really screwed up and you are in for it. The president wants to talk to you, and you better handle it!"

"Oh, cut the bullshit, Kenny!" said Geoghegan defensively. "I was only doing my job!"

"Really?" said Kenny with a sarcasm that reached through the phone and tapped you on the shoulder.

Then Geoghegan heard only silence—broken by the accent, that famous Boston accent. "Bill," said President John Kennedy, "what the hell is this all about?" Clearly this was no joke, and John F. Kennedy, the president of the United States, did not sound in the least bit amused. He didn't yell, but his tone almost made Bill rise from his chair. "I understand that you are not going to appoint that—what the hell is his name, Kenny?" Geoghegan could hear Kenny hiss the name—"Louis whatever the hell his name is to be U.S. attorney. And who in the hell was stupid enough, I mean who was fucking stupid enough, to tell you to go up and tell Senator Ellender about this? Who?"

Your brother whom you appointed attorney general, Geoghegan wanted to say. "Mr. President," he began again, nervously, "I cleared it all with the attorney general of the United States. He sent me up and agreed with our decision not to appoint this man." Silence. "Sir," he added quickly and nervously.

"Oh, shit!" the president muttered, slamming the phone in Bill's ear.

The only thing that had given Geoghegan courage in the face of the president's anger was the knowledge that he had Bobby behind him. Like it or not, John Kennedy had an attorney general interested first and foremost in justice.

"I don't know anybody Bobby Kennedy ever fired or deprived of a mouthful of food in his whole life," Kenny O'Donnell would declare years later. "Now, his brother wasn't like that at all. If you couldn't do the job, he'd just say, 'See you later, fellow. I got my own problems.' Bobby was very, very compassionate. We used to con him, the president and I. One day, a fellow wanted a job on one of the commissions. Bobby, I know, didn't care much for him. Bobby thought he was lazy. Actually, he wasn't lazy, he was a politician! I said to the guy, 'You go over and tell Bobby you've got five kids and you need the money. Give him a little sob story.' Fifteen minutes later the phone rang. 'We got to take care of this guy,' said Bobby. 'Will you talk to the president and see if you can't put him on this commission? I understand there's an opening. He's got five kids and geez, his wife is sick.' 'Sure,' I said. You never heard such claptrap in your life, but it worked. That was Bobby."

"I remember once sitting in the president's office with Kenny," Mike Feldman says. "Kenny was leaning against the wall, arms folded. Suddenly Bobby, the attorney general, walked in. The president was at his desk and looked up. 'Well, how does the second most important person in the world feel today?' Bobby and Kenny burst out laughing. Jack, Bobby, and Kenny seemed to have their own language, their own understanding, and the bond was so evident. It made any earlier concerns about trusting Kenny seem absurd. Sitting there watching the three of them laugh and joke, then turn to such serious matters of state, I realized they were like three brothers, they had this beautiful relationship between the three of them, like a band of brothers."

After resting up after the election, Jerry Bruno had worked with Dave Powers on the Inaugural Committee, and then Kenny had sent him to the President's Committee on Equal Employment. By 1962 he was beginning to miss the campaign trail, which is why he welcomed Kenny's phone call. "Teddy is going to run for senator in Massachusetts. I want you to go up and help him," Kenny told him. Bruno headed up to Boston and met up with Kennedy brother-in-law Steve Smith, the low-keyed genius behind so much of the family's success. Kenny's orders had been clear: They were to stay under cover and help Teddy get nominated for his brother's Senate seat, being careful not to draw any attention to the White House.

According to Bobby, "Some of the people at the White House sort of mumbled about the fact that Teddy shouldn't run or it would hurt the president, but as far as the president and I were concerned, I was pleased that he was running. I think the president was pleased he was running." Kenny's concern was practical: If Teddy was going to run, he had damn well better win, and the Kennedy organization had better make sure of that. Once Teddy won the nomination, Kenny sent Bruno to help advance the president's congressional campaigning trips during the 1962 midterm elections, in such stops as Cincinnati; Springfield, Illinois; St. Louis; and San Francisco.

The beginning of the trip went well, but Bruno noticed that Kenny was tense and more uncommunicative than usual, often spending time talking quietly with the president. Kennedy's visit to Abraham Lincoln's tomb in Springfield, the first stop, disturbed him. The president was on his way out of the tomb when the Secret Service pulled him aside to take a phone call. Bruno saw him take the call and look concerned. From there they went to the fairgrounds, where the president gave a speech before a large and positive crowd; as they went to leave, again the Secret Service called him aside. Another phone call. Bruno knew something was up. Yet despite the distraction Kennedy was in top form, laughing, joking. Bruno went ahead to St. Louis, where Kenny called him. "The president has a cold," he said, rapid-fire. "We are going back to Washington."

A cold! Bruno had just seen the president; he didn't have a damn cold. "Kenny," Jerry began.

Kenny cut him off. "You go on to St. Louis and prepare like we're gonna go. If anybody says he's not going to be there, tell them they are wrong and set it up as if he's going to be there. Make sure you tell them the president will be in St. Louis and is looking forward to the visit."

Mystified, Bruno went about his work setting up a big rally at a shopping center. The city spared no expense, building a huge wooden platform. Returning to his room, he waited for Kenny's call. The phone rang, "Tell them we are not going to go, there has been a schedule change — tell them what you need to tell them, apologize, make them happy, pretend you are as shocked as they are. Go on to San Francisco tonight, but make sure you check in with Pat Brown," the governor of California. "Be very positive and upbeat, make all the plans, and don't tell anyone that he's not coming."

When Bruno began to protest, Kenny again interrupted him. "You gotta listen to me! You gotta be very, very, very accurate on this, do you hear me? You gotta be positive, and you know without question the president is going to be in San Francisco."

Governor Pat Brown was planning to host a fund-raiser for his reelection campaign against Richard Nixon and hoped the president could come. Normally, Bruno would immediately tell such petitioners not to expect anything. The president hated doing those things, and Kenny rarely allowed events like this on the schedule. This time, since Bruno knew and nobody else did that John Kennedy was never going to make it to San Francisco, he saw no harm in telling Brown yes. Pat Brown was delighted. Ten minutes, he said, was all he needed of the president's time. "I promise, ten minutes and he will be out of there." More out of there than you know, thought Bruno. The mayor of San Francisco wanted five minutes for President Kennedy to speak to a labor group that was giving him trouble. Is there any way he might have time? "You can have him for five minutes," Bruno told him. In all, Bruno must have acceded to a hundred requests for that trip to San Francisco. He left everyone happy. Then Kenny called and told Bruno to watch the president's speech, 4:00 California time. Then he would understand.

In October 1962 Bobby Kennedy asked Bill Geoghegan if he wanted to fly back to Cincinnati on Air Force One with the president on a campaign trip. Geoghegan was flattered at getting a chance to visit home in style, and he was grateful to Bobby for thinking of him. Such acts made him even more loyal to the attorney general.

On Air Force One, the president made his way through the plane, stopping and chatting with various people. Geoghegan had spoken briefly to Kenny, but he seemed preoccupied. The president sat down next to him. "So, you're one of Bobby's boys," he said, reminding him playfully of poor Senator Ellender and the farm bill. Geoghegan was impressed that Kennedy remembered him. He sat and listened as the president dictated a speech to his secretary while smoking one of his cigars. He kept dropping his ashes on Geoghegan's pants. Some of those ashes fell on him still red hot, but who was Bill Geoghegan to say, "Excuse me, Mr. President, could you get an ashtray?"

Once they arrived, Geoghegan rode in the motorcade with Kenny and Larry O'Brien. They were friendly, but tense. Geoghegan assumed it was always this way when the president was on the road. He left the presidential entourage in Cincinnati, thinking how hale and hearty the president seemed. Air Force One flew on to Chicago. The next morning as he shaved while listening to the radio, a news report announced that the president of the United States was canceling his trip because he had a severe cold. "A heavy cold?" Geoghegan asked himself. He had sat next to the president the whole way from Washington, cigar ashes and all. No, something was up. Geoghegan changed plans quickly and headed back to Washington, back to the Justice Department.

It was evident as they gathered in Bobby's office the next morning that the attorney general had been up all night. He looked haggard and he was wearing the same suit he had on the day before. Bobby said little and seemed distanced. When the meeting broke up, Geoghegan lagged behind. "What's up?" he asked Bobby as casually and quietly as he could. Bobby shook his head, the etched lines around his eyes deep. "Sorry," he said softly, "can't talk about it. No offense. You'll know soon enough."

At 5:30 that evening, Bobby called his "boys" together in his cavernous office. The president was scheduled to speak to the nation at 6:00. Bobby described with quiet concern what was going on. The Soviet Union had sent missiles to Cuba, aimed directly at the United States. President Kennedy would insist that they be removed. He was, he said, "deeply concerned, very deeply concerned, about the outcome" of the crisis. Through all the crises they had endured together, Bill Geoghegan had never seen Bobby like this before. Later he would decide it was Bobby's manner more than his words that unnerved him, though his pronouncement was chilling. He closed the meeting by saying quietly, "Look, we don't know how this is going to end up. I just wanted you all to hear it from me directly. I wanted to give you time to call your wives and families. This well may end up in a nuclear exchange."

When he ran for president in 1968, Robert Kennedy would tell interviewer David Frost that he most valued his work during the Cuban Missile Crisis, "where the question was whether or not the world was going to be blown up or not. It is at that moment that I felt I made the most important contribution. In the final analysis," Bobby continued, "in choosing a president it comes down to judgment. . . . Of the fourteen people who were involved—who were very, very significant, bright, able, dedicated people, who all had the greatest affection for the United States [and] I suppose they were the brightest kind of group you could get together under those circumstances—if six of them had been president of the United States . . . the world would have been blown up. Now you miscalculate in a major way it is the last miscalculation you will make. . . . President Kennedy spent more time giving the Soviet Union time to calculate their position than to get the missiles out of Cuba. There is no question you could have brought it to a head at a much earlier time. And, there were those involved in counseling president Kennedy, who wanted to do it immediately—the idea of giving the other person time to understand what the consequences of his actions are is so important. To have some judgment about what he is going to do and will not do."

After the president spoke that night in October 1962, Geoghegan drove home thinking about his mother and father in Cincinnati and his mother-in-law and father-in-law and other relatives spread across the country. He was relieved that he and his family were in Washington, D.C. — at least Washington would be hit first. Then suddenly he realized, in a moment between a light turning from red to green — Washington, D.C., Jesus, that's us, that's my family. He stopped and bought five gallons of bottled water.

Those five gallons would sit in his basement for years, five gallons that reminded him of how close the nation had come to nuclear disaster. After Soviet premier Nikita Krushchev had removed his missiles from Cuba and the hottest of Cold War crises had abated, Geoghegan, like many others, would realize that Robert Kennedy's judgment had helped to make the difference between opening or ignoring those five gallons of water.

During John Kennedy's trip to South America after the Cuban Missile Crisis, "Kenny was very uptight," Jerry Bruno says, "because Nixon had gone to South America as vice president and had a tough time. They tried to overturn his car." He also got pelted with rocks and garbage in Caracas. To advance the trip, Bruno headed to Colombia first. It was during the height of the blockade Kennedy had imposed upon Cuba, and Jerry found tremendous support of Castro on the country's college campuses. Kenny and the Secret Service were both particularly concerned about Bogotá, Colombia. Right before Bruno left, Kenny had said to him, in those low, direct tones, "We gotta be careful about any activities at the university, and [these activities] should give us some indication of whether or not there was going to be trouble." It was evident to Bruno that the Cobra knew more than he was letting on.

Jackie Kennedy was scheduled to accompany the president on this trip, and Kenny had several times made a point of expressing to Bruno his concern for her safety. Nothing could be left to chance. Jerry and the Secret Service met with the Colombian military, which was not thrilled to hear that Mrs. Kennedy was coming as well. The military leaders kept insisting that if they were going to be responsible for protecting the American president, then the president would have to use their car. Bruno resisted, but finally, in frustration, said, "Okay, let's go look at the car." They all jumped into a military jeep and drove to a nearby military base. There they entered a huge garage, and as the door slowly closed behind him Bruno felt a bit uneasy. As his eyes adjusted, he saw what the Colombian military called the "car" they wanted Jack Kennedy to ride in. It was less a car than a tank, its armor punctuated with tiny peep holes. Bruno, shocked, demurred. Jack Kennedy loved the enthusiasm and energy he got from crowds. He would ride in an open car.

"You gotta be out of your mind," Bruno told the military brass. "Do you think the president of the United States is going to ride in that tank?" The generals were stunned at Bruno's reaction and kept insisting that their car was the only vehicle that Kennedy and his wife could ride in. A phone call to Kenny in the White House solved the problem. Jack and Jackie would have extra protection, but they would ride in a motorcade as they always did, in an open American car.

When Air Force One landed in Bogotá, as was the custom, Kenny was the first one down the steps. He immediately sought out Bruno, as if this were another ordinary campaign stop. "Any problems?"

"No," Bruno told him. "I don't think so." Kenny looked dubious. Bruno pointed up toward the hills. "Unless the peasants come down and overtake the nice dictators, we should be okay." Kenny allowed himself a small smile.

Jack was a huge success and the crowds loved Jackie and her command of Spanish. No peasants came down from the hills, and the dictators stayed nice.

In Venezuela, Kenny O'Donnell's personal and political lives converged in a singular way. He was sitting in a conference room with Kennedy and the president of Venezuela when he was called out for a phone call. The Americans in the room watched him leave. They all knew that Helen was expecting a baby. Was this that call?

When Kenny returned, he resumed his seat against the wall, his arms folded, his visage blank. John Kennedy couldn't wait. "Well?" he demanded, interrupting the president of Venezuela.

"Helen had the baby," Kenny said.

"Boy or girl?" demanded John Kennedy.

Kenny looked surprised at the question. "I don't know," he said finally. "I never asked."

The president couldn't believe it. Getting hold of a phone, he called the hospital himself and got put through directly to Helen. After chatting with an exhausted yet delighted Helen O'Donnell, the president hung up the phone and turned to his special assistant. "It's a girl," he told Kenny, with a look from those blue eyes that said more than words could have. Her name would be Helen Kathleen.

"Fortunately, John Kennedy was nice enough to call," Helen would say years later, laughing. "I think he was more excited than either Kenny or I. Kenny didn't even ask."

"It was pretty scary," Bruno says of the South American trip, which was fraught with personal and political peril. "I remember we were flying back on Air Force One, and Kenny was walking from the front of the plane to the back, his jacket was off, his sleeves rolled up slightly, which for Bobby was usual attire and for Kenny was unheard of. He had his coat off, which he never took off. His mind was clearly elsewhere."

To his astonishment, Bruno saw Kenny had a gun. It was alongside his belt, tucked in a holster, and was deliberately visible, Bruno realized, even under his suit jacket. "It was the first time I realized that he carried it. I knew now how he got the nicknames 'the bodyguard' and 'the Cobra.'" Bruno's face must have revealed his surprise, for as soon as Kenny caught his expression, he quickly found his suit coat and slipped it on. "I think he always kept his coat on and was careful to conceal it when he had to. He had it, though, the whole time we were in South America. Bruno would eventually realize that Kenny often carried the gun. He never questioned Kenny about it. Kenny did not invite such questions.

*   *   *

The Irish trip was perhaps one of the most memorable of all the trips that Kenny took with Jack Kennedy. Yet when the president first mentioned his intention to visit Ireland, during his European trip, nobody including Kenny took him very seriously. "One day when I was discussing with the president our plans and dates for the journey to Germany, Italy, and England, the president said, 'I've decided I want to go to Ireland, too.' "

"Mr. President, may I say something?" Kenny asked. "There's no reason for you to go to Ireland. It would be a waste of time. It wouldn't do you much good politically. You've got all the Irish votes in this country you'll ever get. If you go to Ireland, people will say it's just a pleasure trip."

"That's exactly what I want—a pleasure trip to Ireland!" the president told him.

Kenny left the meeting, not paying too much attention to the president's request. There were too many important items on the agenda during the European trip for him to worry about Ireland. After talking with national security adviser McGeorge Bundy, who agreed with Kenny's assessment that the trip to Ireland would be a waste of time, Kenny went in and informed the president.

"Kenny," the president told him, "I am the president of the United States, not you. When I say I want to go to Ireland, it means that I'm going to Ireland. Make the arrangements!" Kenny knew better than to question Jack Kennedy twice.

The trip exhibited the power of the presidency and the aura of Jack Kennedy. It would be the trip to Ireland that Kenny would remember most when he would reminisce about his time working for Jack Kennedy. Kennedy's last words to the Irish people at Shannon Airport, his vow that he would "come back to Shannon in the springtime," would come to symbolize the tragedy and the loss inherent in his murder.

The trip was not without its more humorous moments for Kenny, Jack, and Dave Powers, even if they didn't seem quite that funny at the time. As was necessary, Jack Kennedy spent much of the trip at official dinners and functions, including an enormous amount of time in the company of the president of Ireland, Eamon De Valera. A hero of Irish independence, he was now partially blind and deaf, which did not make for easy conversations. Kenny and Dave used the opportunity to escape from the president and visit various Irish pubs and generally have a grand time. One evening, the president was returning from a state dinner when he decided to stop in and see Kenny and Dave at one of their new haunts. Both were well into their cups by the time the president caught up to them. The president collapsed exhausted into a chair and listened to a relaxed and unusually talkative Kenny spin stories about the people they had met during their crawl through the pubs. As he listened he grew more and more annoyed. Pub hopping through a town in Ireland was something he wasn't allowed to enjoy. His neck and face were turning red. Dave Powers tried to catch Kenny's eye, but Kenny continued with his tale, clearly enjoying watching the president's discomfort.

Finally, Kenny finished his story. "That's just terrific, Kenny," the president said, glaring at him. "It's just terrific that the people of Ireland are so nice. I wonder what the hell happens to them when they get on the goddamn boat and come to America!" With that Kennedy rose from his chair and stalked out of the room.

"We almost fell on the floor laughing," Kenny told John years later. "That was the great thing about John Kennedy—even when he was president, he was still himself. He never changed or let any of the trappings go to his head."

The president's planned trip to Italy had been postponed twice when Pope John XXIII died suddenly. One day Kenny called Bruno and told him to pack his bags; the trip was back on. The advance man told Kenny he was surprised, because the College of Cardinals had yet to elect a new pope. "Don't worry—in three days the name of the new pope will be announced," Kenny said. He hung up the phone. He was right.

After an audience with the new pope, Paul VI, and an adulatory response from the Roman people—coordinated by Jerry Bruno—the president was to go next to Naples. Bruno was not handling Naples and headed to Capri for a short vacation. He had barely unpacked when

Pierre Salinger, Kennedy's press secretary, called to interrupt him. No advance work had been done in Naples. Someone had screwed up. "The president wants this trip to end with the biggest turnout of the whole European tour. He wants you to get your ass back here now!" So much for Bruno's vacation.

Arriving in Naples, Bruno decided to approach the place just as he would a campaign stop in Wisconsin. Calling the mayor of Naples, he introduced himself and said, "Sir, the president of the United States, John F. Kennedy, needs your personal help. We want your cooperation in turning out a crowd—and everything depends on you!" The mayor, properly flattered, began inviting everyone, including a local band. But Bruno also called every mayor within fifty miles; all were told to bring a band. He told the mayors that they should place themselves and their bands at each street corner and that the president would stop and shake hands with each of them personally. Fortunately for Jerry Bruno, the crowds were so tremendous that every mayor and his band got lost in the crush, so that the president couldn't keep Bruno's promise to stop and shake their hands. "Thank God!" he recalls. "Jesus, I would have been in real trouble if John Kennedy had to stop and shake hands. That would have been my last trip!"

The president was amused. He was also grateful for the size of the crowds. Kenny invited Bruno onto Air Force One during the return trip. He got to sit up with the president; as the visit to Palm Beach had been earlier, such company was their way of saying thanks. "Bruno," said Jack, "how the hell did you turn that crowd out?"

"Mr. President, they're all my relatives!" Bruno declared. The president laughed; he liked the sass in his advance man's answer.

17

MR. ATTORNEY GENERAL

I do the very best I know how, the very best I can,
and I mean to keep doing it so until the end.

— ABRAHAM LINCOLN

The attorney general's vast and stately office had never seen anything quite like Robert Kennedy before: children running through, their drawings hung on the mahogany walls; the attorney general, a man of thirty-six, his hair uncombed, sleeves rolled up, tie pulled down, suit coat thrown on the floor. This was the setting for Robert F. Kennedy's Justice Department. It even included a dog.

Bobby was inevitably accompanied to the Justice Department by his huge Newfoundland, Brumus. "Bob would bring him to the office every day. The administrative guys at GSA [the General Services Administration] used to go crazy," says Angie Novello. "One day one of them called me and said, 'Please tell the attorney general that we don't allow dogs in federal buildings. It's against the law!' The obvious point being, after all, he was supposed to enforce the law." After hearing that message, Novello got up from her desk and walked into Bobby's office. It was a sizzling Washington summer day, and Brumus was lying there, looking up at her with huge, sad brown eyes, as if he knew what she was about to say. Bobby looked up from his desk. "What's up?"

Novello took a deep breath and told him what the fellow from GSA had told her. Bobby looked at her for a moment and then looked at Brumus. As if on cue, Brumus looked up and exchanged a sad, fateful glance with Bobby. "Well, Ethel and the kids have gone to the Cape for the summer and Brumus is home alone. It's just Brumus and me. I can't leave Brumus home alone all day. He'll be lonely."

He looked up at Novello, his blue eyes intense and serious. She looked from Bobby to Brumus; both had the same "how could you do this to me" expression. "Oh, what the heck," Novello recalls she said. "It makes perfect sense to me."

What the hell were they thinking by putting Bobby Kennedy in there as attorney general, Joe Dolan asked himself. Byron White, whom Bobby had chosen as deputy attorney general, called his friend and fellow political operative in Denver. "Take your pick, Joe," White had told him. "You can have one of three spots. You can be U.S. attorney and have a fight with Senator Carroll," the Colorado senator who would have to assent to his nomination, "but if you're willing we are willing. You can be my assistant, or you can be Bob's assistant." Dolan had told Byron he would think about it and get back to him.

The more he thought about Bobby Kennedy as attorney general, the more concerned Dolan became. "It's ironic, looking back now. He turned out to be the best attorney general in history, but when I finally decided to go to Washington as Byron's deputy, I was doing so because I really believed that I was going to help protect the country from Robert Kennedy. I mean, he had never questioned a witness under oath, he had only been in a grand jury room once, and had never even handled a case as a practicing lawyer. So I called Byron and told him I would come on board as his deputy. As much as I wanted to be U.S. attorney, I just thought I have got to protect this country from this guy. It's so funny now. I mean, what was I thinking?"

Robert Kennedy himself was not unaware of the profound reservations about his appointment that came from Kennedy people like Joe Dolan as well as critics of the new administration. He took their concerns with a measure of wit and the determination to do a good job. Traditionally, the attorney general appears before the U.S. Supreme Court each year. For the entire first year of his tenure, Bobby had been pressing Solicitor General Archibald Cox about arguing a case. It was finally decided that

Bob would argue one of the congressional reapportionment cases before the Court involving the one-man one-vote principle, a civil rights measure that had begun to cause political controversy, especially in the still largely segregated South. Joe Dolan sent his wife, Martie, to watch Bobby argue what would be his first case ever. "Bobby figured that the government wasn't paying you to go watch him give speeches."

Following his argument, Bobby headed down to the basement of the Supreme Court building to meet his car, and ran into Martie. "Bobby," she said, "you were just wonderful. You know, Joe is a lawyer, my father is a lawyer, and my uncle is a lawyer, but this is the very first time I sat through a whole case!"

"Really!" said Bobby. "Me too!" With a brief kiss on the cheek he hopped into his car and sped back to the Justice Department.

Often Bobby would make impromptu visits to various staff offices within the Justice Department, introducing himself to career attorneys and staff members, many of whom had never even met an attorney general, much less have one talk to them about their job and experiences. Shortly after settling into the post, Robert Kennedy decided that he wanted to spend as much time as possible visiting with other United States attorneys across the country. No previous attorney general had ever taken such an extraordinary step. John Reilly organized the trips and traveled with him.

"We would arrive in some town and walk into the lobby of the federal courthouse where Bobby was visiting that day," Reilly remembers. "There would be people hanging over the rafters and over the balconies, screaming and yelling. Oftentimes the crowd would surge forward and just try to touch him." Bobby Kennedy found the attention amazing. It was a foreshadowing of what he was to face during his own campaigns in later years. "Bobby understood it was not a personal response to him; it was the work that he was doing and the president was doing that made the crowds come out." Paul Lazzaro, from Harvard, who had remained behind as treasurer of Wakefield, Massachusetts, put it another way. "That was the real beauty of the man; he never had some grand vision of himself. He knew who he was. He didn't need that and understood what it was all about. He knew it was about the work that was being accomplished.

After coordinating Bobby's highly successful trip to Chicago, Reilly returned to receive a phone call from Kenny O'Donnell. "Were you with the attorney general in Chicago?" Kenny growled into the phone.

"Yeah," Reilly replied, instantly wary.

"Did you call Mayor Daley?"

"Daley? No. No, we did not."

"Why the hell not?" the Cobra demanded.

Damn, Reilly thought, why are you calling me? After all, the attorney general is your friend. Instead he said, "Bob is there as attorney general and he doesn't feel that it is appropriate for him to do something that might be perceived as political, such as calling Mayor Daley."

This remark was met with silence. "Look, Jesus fucking Christ, Daley helped elect John Kennedy president of the United States. You tell the attorney general that he wouldn't fucking be attorney general if it weren't for Mayor Daley, so he damn well better pick up the phone and show him some goddamn respect!" John tried to respond but Kenny cut him off. "He is not just the attorney general, he is the president's brother, and he has got to make these calls. You're traveling with him, you're running things—you make sure it's done! Got it?"

Deciding whether or not to urge Bobby to follow Kenny's injunction, Reilly had to ask himself whom he was more scared of, his boss or Kenny O'Donnell. Getting up the nerve, he broached the subject with Bobby. "No," he said with simple defiance. "I just don't feel comfortable and I won't do it. I am the attorney general and I am going to get a lot of scrutiny as you know, and it's best if I keep myself removed from politics. Call Kenny and tell him no."

By the time the next trip came up, John Reilly had come up with a solution he thought would keep both Kenny and Bobby happy—and keep the politicos happy without getting caught. The key to success lay in the bathtub. Kenny referred to the bathroom as the "usual Kennedy place." Like his brother, Bobby had learned to relax by retreating into a steaming hot bath whenever possible, especially at the end of the day.

He could work undisturbed and then change clothes before what was usually a full evening of dinner and meetings. His memos would often be sent out water stained, and the assorted books and documents usually took a hit or two from the overfilled bathtub as well. Just as Bobby was emerging relaxed from his bath, Reilly would come in and tell him that one or another local politician was on the line. "Oh," Bobby would reply thoughtfully. He hadn't heard the phone ring, but after all he was in the bathtub. He would grab a towel, wrap it around his waist, and come out to take the call. John was able to keep up this practice for months without Bobby's catching on. The attorney general's conversations were usually short and comfortable courtesy calls—good political public relations.

During a visit to Louisville, Kentucky, Bobby was in his "usual Kennedy place" when Reilly called out that former congressman Burns was on the phone. This time Bobby was sure he hadn't heard the phone. Sitting on the edge of the bed, still soaking wet, he grabbed the phone from Reilly and said, "Hey, Congressman, how are you? What's up?"

Reilly felt his stomach sink. Bobby's blue eyes were staring right at him and Reilly was sure he had figured it out. Turning to walk toward the window, he thought, Well, it was fun while it lasted. "I didn't call you! You called me!" he heard Bobby saying. Reilly stared hard out the window, wondering if he should just jump. Finally, after a good several minutes of the former congressman's puzzled protests, Bobby got off the phone and stood up. Sweeping his still wet hair away from his brow, while still holding the towel with his other hand, he said, "You've been doing this for months! I told you no!"

"Look, Bobby, I'm scared of both of you. I couldn't say no to Kenny because he's Kenny, and I can't say no to you because you are you, and so I didn't know what to do."

Bobby looked at him amazed. He shook his head. "Okay, John, I guess Kenny is going to get his way one way or another, so we might as well both go along." He turned and headed back to the bathroom. "It's okay, it's tough to be caught between the two of us." Reilly heard Bobby laugh from the bathroom. "You know, you're probably right to be more scared of Kenny than me. He's meaner!"

From then on, if Bobby thought that it was appropriate and the people involved had nothing pending before the Justice Department, he would make a political call. He was thus able to remove Reilly from standing between a rock and a hard place. "That was the thing with Kenny. Sometimes he had no idea how tough it was to pull off his orders. He didn't care. His orders just got followed. He didn't care how you did the job—just do it. Ironically, Bobby was the same way, and I guess that was one of the reasons they worked so well together. But, it could be tough to be the staff guy caught in the crossfire between the two of them. They were both strong-willed people who were used to getting their way."

On one early trip Reilly realized that Bobby never carried any money. His assistant found himself dipping into his own pocket to pay waiters, maids, airport guys, bellmen, and even street people who would recognize the attorney general and approach him for money. During any encounter involving money, Bobby would simply look toward Reilly, who would find himself reaching for his wallet. Reilly felt he had no choice but to cover for Bobby. "After all, it was bad enough that people called him 'ruthless.' You didn't want them calling him 'cheap' too." Reilly would regularly run through so much money that his wife began to get annoyed. Knowing he had to do something about it and unwilling to confront Bobby, he decided to stop by Kenny and Helen's house after work one day.

The O'Donnell house had become a regular haunt for members of the administration. Helen had found what would be the first of two homes that the family would occupy in Bethesda, an easy commute from Washington. The schools were close and convenient, which made sense for the growing family, now numbering four children. In addition to Kenny the oldest, and the twins Kathy and Kevin, Mark Francis had been born in 1958. By December 1961 a fifth and final child would be born, Helen Kathleen. "No matter what time you went by, there were always people there," Reilly remembers. "Always administration people, always talking business." Kenny might have left the White House for the day, but he took his responsibilities and friendships home with him.

Helen was enjoying her new life. Her husband was home more often and their household was more settled. She had also established a group of friends to help her through any difficult times. She didn't mind being alone so much, since so many of her friends were also widowed by campaigns, politics, and government. They had much in common. Additionally, although Kenny's government salary was not enormous, perhaps twenty thousand dollars a year, it was more than enough for them to live comfortably.

In many ways the O'Donnell household in Maryland was a match in numbers and activity with the Robert Kennedy place across the Potomac in McLean. Hickory Hill was the site not only of a large animal menagerie and children's games, but regular dinners and parties that often included Kenny and Helen, Walter and Nancy Sheridan, the John Seigenthalers, and many others from the administration. Often the O'Donnell kids would spend their weekends at Hickory Hill, and Kenny and Kevin became friends with young Joe Kennedy. Nick Rodis remembers the vital chaos of those Hickory Hill weekends. "Once we were at Bobby's for some party, and we were in the living room and there were all these people and kids and dogs everywhere. Bobby was talking to me and looking around at all the dogs. Finally he said to me, 'You know, I don't know who these dogs belong to. They aren't ours. Do you know whose they are?' I said, 'Bobby, it's your house. I don't know half the people here, and I don't think you do either!' "

Kenny and Bobby would send gifts to each other's children for Christmas that would require the recipient's parents to stay up the night before Christmas to put the complicated toy together. Kenny and Bobby kept up their informal competition with no clear winner, until finally one year Bobby sent the O'Donnells a full-size train and track set that children could sit in and ride. Kenny and Helen were up almost until dawn putting it together. Finally, an exhausted and frustrated Kenny retaliated by calling Ethel and Bobby and waking them up out of bed to yell at Bobby and admit defeat.

It was to Kenny that John Reilly turned with his minor but persistent problem with money and the attorney general. Over drinks one night at Kenny's house, he said, "I'm going broke. I can't afford this. The guy never carries any money. We take a taxi cab and he never has any money and I have to pay for everything. He never offers to pay you later. What the hell do I do?"

Kenny's face clouded over and dark eyes stared directly at Reilly, who suddenly felt guilty for criticizing his host's longtime friend. "John, it's not a character defect and don't put it that way, because I don't like it and I'll deck you. He isn't cheap or a bad guy. It's just that in his entire life he hasn't had to think about or worry about money. You would be the same way if your entire life money was never an issue. He doesn't even know what things cost. He doesn't have to worry about that. That's why he can afford to do what he does. He doesn't have to be doing this. He could be off in the Caribbean, for Christ's sake. He just doesn't realize what the problem is. So you keep track of how much you spend, and then you go to Angie Novello and let her know and she will cut you a check from his personal account. Angie takes care of everything."

Reilly took Kenny's advice, kept his receipts and regularly went to Novello. He was impressed with how well Kenny understood Bobby and accepted him.

"When Bob told you something," Reilly says, "you just went and did it. You didn't ask, you just did the job. Whether in the Justice Department, at a speech, or on the street, when people approached the attorney general with questions or requests, the job of responding went to whoever was standing closest to Bobby. Jurisdiction didn't matter."

After a luncheon event in New York, Bobby saw a book and music store and went inside. Reilly browsed the shelves, keeping one eye on the attorney general. Bobby was not the browsing type. He walked straight to the album section, picked up something he wanted, and headed for the cashier. When Reilly asked him what he'd gotten, Bobby held up a recording of Shakespeare's *Henry V*. "When are you going to get time to listen to it?" Reilly asked.

"I can listen to it in my bathroom in the morning when I'm shaving. I didn't really get to read it in school. I really didn't concentrate on it and I've always wanted to. I didn't understand it then, but I want to learn it now." As John reached for his wallet, Bobby told him, "I have this little record player Ethel got for me, so I can listen to albums like this, since I don't have time to sit down and read. It's perfect," he said. "I'm learning something and not wasting time. It works great!"

Robert Kennedy lived life as if he knew time was short. "I can't tell you how many times we would do these breakneck runs through an airport at the last minute," Reilly remembers. Once after they had made a successful dash up the jetway to a plane's closing door, Reilly asked him, "Bob, next time why don't we get to the airport a little earlier so we don't have to do this kind of stuff?"

"He looked at me like I was from Mars. 'Why?' Bobby demanded. 'What am I going to do at the airport? I can't get any work done there. My God, that would be a waste of time — just to sit around an airport and not accomplish something!' "

During another grueling week, when the two of them were headed back to the Justice Department, after Bobby had testified before a Senate committee, Bobby sat in the front seat going through some papers, with Reilly directly behind him. To break the silence he finally piped up, "What are you doing this weekend, Bob? I'm taking Saturday off to take my kids to a ball game."

With his eyes still on his papers, Bobby replied sarcastically, "I'm working." Then he turned around and looked at Reilly. "I'd love to spend it with my kids, but I have to work. Big deal, Reilly, you're father of the year, who cares?" With that he returned to his stack of papers.

Reilly felt guilty. "I could meet you in the office early and then take my kids in the afternoon." Bob didn't even turn around; he just burst out laughing. On Saturday, both men arrived early at the Justice Department, departing around noon to spend the afternoon with their children, after getting in a good five or six hours' worth of work.

Angie Novello would often witness how Bobby would have his children join him for hamburgers at the office, supplied by the chef of the Justice Department dining room. "The attorney general's office had the most enormous fireplace. In the winter it would be lit every day and it was cozy and nice. Once a week the children would come in and they would have lunch around a huge round table in the office. Bobby would take the raw patties the chef had brought up and grill them in the open fireplace. He would make them lunch, put aside all his work for an hour or so, visit with his children, have lunch with them, and then pack them up and Ethel would take them home."

"We used to bring all the dogs," said Bobby's late son Michael Kennedy, "and the horses."

Occasionally, lunch would in fact include a visit by the horses, which the children would ride in the open outdoor space in the center of the building. "It was a sight to behold," Angie Novello says. Eventually these lunches and horseback rides grew to include underprivileged children from various homes and schools in the area. "He just had a warm heart. Bob just loved his kids and really all kids. There are really no words to describe it. When it came to children, and especially his own, he was really passionate about them. When his children would come to the office with him it made a reevaluation into who Bob Kennedy was. I mean, you think you love your children, but then you would watch Bob Kennedy with his own children and you can't imagine having such a special bond between a father and his children. There are really no words. His children were like part of his soul.

"Brumus used to come in with Bob and he was huge, just huge, and he would plop down right in the doorway, in the double doors leading to Bob's office," Novello remembers. "All the ambassadors and important people would have to step over Brumus to see Bob." On one occasion Brumus almost caused an international incident. The dog was prone in his usual place, blocking the entrance of an ambassador, who hadn't had an opportunity to meet with the president and was coming to see Bob. He was upset and the meeting was important. As the ambassador stood waiting, Novello not so gently kicked Brumus with her foot. "Brumus, move," she said.

Bobby heard her. Without looking up, he said, "Angie, don't do that. He's very sensitive."

"Well, he was such a big lug of a dog! Sensitive! Anyway," Novello recalls, "the unfortunate ambassador and his staff were forced to leap over Brumus."

*   *   *

By the end of a long day, Bobby's desk would be lost under a blizzard of documents and notes. Every night he carried home a briefcase of homework. If he and Ethel weren't entertaining, the two of them would have dinner and visit with his kids as best he could; before going to bed he would put in a couple more hours' worth of work. Even when they had official guests, Bobby would often disappear with his briefcase. "Without question, Bobby was a workaholic," his prep school friend Sam Adams says. "He just was. He used every minute and believed in giving it his all."

"Someone had sent Bob a photograph of this horrible-looking boat," Angie Novello remembers. "It was a sleek, metal-looking, shiny boat, like a motorboat with a sail on it." For days it sat on Bobby's desk, floating among the layers of papers that covered his desk that only she could easily excavate. "He was always impressed when I came in and was able to lay my hands on whatever he was looking for immediately," she says. She got tired of moving the photo around. Finally, frustrated, she put a note on it: "What do you want me to do with this?" At the end of the day, after Bobby went home, she found the picture with a note from Bobby: "Order two for the Cape and one for the pool."

Bobby would get up at the crack of dawn for a vigorous horse ride in the Virginia countryside, usually with one or more of his children. Then he would return to the house for a big breakfast with Ethel and the children and sometimes a staff member or reporter. He would arrive at the office, hair windblown from the drive in his convertible. "He would always come in the door looking so fresh faced and healthy," Angie Novello remembers. "He always looked so refreshed after he had spent time with Ethel and the kids. I think it rejuvenated him. He would come in, take off his suit coat, and toss it at the rack. It would miss, land on the floor, and there it would stay. He would throw his briefcase on the couch. Sometimes it would fall on the floor and spill open. It never bothered him. He was so focused and so intense about the work that he had to do that nothing bothered him. He was immediately focused once he walked in that door." Once when Bob had dropped his coat on the floor one too many times for Novello's taste, she finally mentioned it to him. "Bob," she said as she picked up his coat, "you really shouldn't do that. You should pick your things up."

Bob looked up from his desk. "Why? It's okay. Somebody will pick them up." Novello was not amused.

His days might last until late in the evening. When he was in Washington he would spend a full day at the Justice Department, sometimes staying until nine or ten in the evening, or during difficult times often until early hours of the morning. If he had to attend an evening event, he would often return to the office afterward. At times of crisis, he would often spend the day at the White House and then return to a full day's work at the Justice Department. When he was on the road, his schedule was even more intense. "Bobby could always keep at least eight balls in motion at the same time," says David Hackett, whom Bobby had known since Milton, and who now worked in the Juvenile Justice Division. "What amazed me the most is that if you asked him about any one of those balls he would know every detail about it. He was intense and so in motion that it made you work twice as hard just to keep up."

The president wanted to name the mayor of Gary, Indiana, George Chacharis, as ambassador to Greece. Kenny was leaning on John Seigenthaler to have the Justice Department hurry with its background check; Chacharis's supporters were pressuring the president and wanted to have Congressman Ray Madden come in with Mayor Chacharis to see Bob Kennedy, which, during the 1960s, was not an unusual request. It was going to be a difficult meeting. Chacharis was not going to be ambassador to Greece. In fact, Robert Kennedy's Justice Department was about to indict him because evidence showed that Chacharis and his pals had regularly accepted money from companies and businesses that were looking for city contracts and licenses. Kenny wasn't surprised, but he still wanted Bob to hear them out.

As Congressman Madden pleaded to Bobby Kennedy the case of George Chacharis, "he listened," Seigenthaler says. "He expressed sympathy but remained unmoved in his decision to indict."

"Bob," the mayor said, sitting in a chair in front of the attorney general's desk, hands outstretched, "you know I spent some of that money on your brother's campaign."

Seigenthaler winced. He looked over at Bobby, who did not flinch. He went on to let Chacharis have his say. Then, shaking his head, his voice clear and firm but not loud, he finally said, "I have no choice. You stole the money. I have no way not to indict you. I'm sorry. You left me no choice."

The final words hung in the air for a moment before they took full effect. Then Chacharis blanched. He put his head down on Bobby's desk and began to cry. Congressman Madden began screaming at Bob.

Bobby remained impassive, his pain and discomfort evident only to Seigenthaler. Finally, Madden spat out, "Look, Bobby, the Eisenhower administration started this! Why can't you let it go?"

Bobby looked at him hard. "That's right, Congressman, the Eisenhower administration started this and I am going to finish it. I have to finish it."

The Dean Landis case caused Bobby and Kenny a great deal of turmoil. Landis was a good friend of the Kennedy family and very close to the ambassador. Dean of the Harvard Law School, he had served with the ambassador when he was chairman of the Securities and Exchange Commission and was a fixture within the Kennedy family, frequently visiting their house, working for the ambassador, and occasionally helping out John Kennedy as well. Now he worked in the Justice Department, writing speeches for Bobby. "He was a wonderful old guy," Seigenthaler says. "He loved scotch, and every night I would take him a Pinch bottle of scotch back to the little room he worked in. He would write well into the night. It was wonderful, fluid prose."

Dean Landis hadn't paid his income taxes for six or seven years. "To Kenny," Seigenthaler says, "the Landis case was just a question of compassion. Bobby understood that, but he also believed that the law was the law. No matter who was involved."

John Seigenthaler had returned to the Tennessee newspaper world by the time the Justice Department indicted Landis. On a return visit to

Washington, he met Bobby outside his office. "How are you doing?" he asked. Before Bobby could reply, Seigenthaler added, "I'm upset that you indicted our old friend Dean Landis."

Bob tossed down the papers he was holding and looked Seigenthaler straight in the eye. "*You're* upset! *You're* upset! Tell me you're upset! Come in," he said gruffly, trying to marshal his temper. He slammed the door behind them. "What would you have me do? This man is dean of the Harvard Law School, my father's good friend, close to my family. He has violated the law—and you want me to give him a break? Tell me what would that do to the law? How would that affect the law for the rest of America? What would that mean to the average guy on the street who doesn't have friends in government?"

"Bobby, I'm sorry I said it. I just had a human reaction. I am sorry you indicted my friend Dean Landis. I didn't mean anything more than that."

"*You're* sorry!" he repeated, his voice softer now.

"He wanted me to understand why," Seigenthaler says, "but he also wanted me to know how much pain he felt." It was moments like these when he wished he hadn't allowed his brother to persuade him to take the job.

Kenny continued to be the key link between the president and the rest of the government. When Bobby was around he always dealt with Kenny himself. Sometimes though, he wasn't available and others in the Justice Department got the bulldog treatment. When Bobby and Ethel were on an official trip to Europe and Byron White was laid up in the hospital, Archibald Cox was acting attorney general, which made Joe Dolan acting deputy attorney general. A major airline hijacking had occurred. Dolan's first thought was to talk to Kenny. "Kenny, who's handling the hijacking situation over there? Bob isn't in town."

"The president," Kenny shot back. "Is that all right?"

Both the president and Bobby would often use Kenny for cover, not only to deliver messages that people might not want to hear, but to communicate with Bobby without letting anyone know he was calling. If Bobby was out of the office and the president wanted to be sure a message got through, he would call and talk to Seigenthaler, except that Seigenthaler wouldn't know it was the president until he was on the line. The first time it happened, a secretary announced that Mr. O'Donnell was on the line. As he reached for the phone, Seigenthaler saw Bob's private line was lit up. It was fairly typical for Kenny to call on Bob's private line. Picking up the phone, punching the private line button, Seigenthaler, expecting Kenny, jumped right in. "What's up?"

After a brief moment of silence, he heard, "How are you?"

John didn't catch the voice right away, "Kenny?" he asked.

"No," said the voice, "this is me." Seigenthaler recognized the unmistakable accent.

"Hello, sir," he said, not wanting to identify out loud who he was talking to.

"Tell Bobby I want to talk to him right away."

"Yes, sir," Seigenthaler said. "I'll take care of it."

"It was a regular thing," Seigenthaler recalls. "He wanted to get a message through and he didn't want to wait, so he would use Kenny as a cover. You would pick up the phone expecting to chat with Kenny and it would be the president. The first couple of times it happened it was unnerving, but then you got used to it."

Paul Lazzaro, who became head of the General Services Administration, asked Kenny once, "What do you do when people ask you for favors?"

Kenny's advice was straightforward. "If they have the nerve to ask, you have the nerve to say 'no.' "

"These guys were phenomenal," said Nick Rodis, whom Bobby had found a post at the State Department. "They had nine million things to do at the White House and over at Justice in running the country and yet they took the time to take care of all of their friends and make sure everyone got a job and was taken care of. Amazing. Bobby never forgot a birthday, even later as senator and when he was running for president."

"I would go in to see Bobby, and he would have these major civil rights crises going on," Wally Flynn says. "There would be ambassadors, senators, lined up outside his office. Then Angie would whistle, I would sneak in the back door, and he and I would stand in that goddam office throwing the football and talking sports while all these big shots waited."

Burke Marshall, head of the Civil Rights Division, was Bobby Kennedy's point man on how to handle the Freedom Riders (who were traveling through the South challenging the segregation laws) when they arrived in Alabama. The situation in Alabama had deteriorated badly. John Seigenthaler was in the hospital, having been knocked unconscious and attacked while trying to save one of the Freedom Riders from a mob. Before Marshall headed to Alabama to see the situation firsthand, he asked Bobby if he had any advice. Bobby, weary from the Justice Department vigil over civil rights, quipped, "Well, if you get your head laid open like John did, nobody would criticize me for at least thirty days."

Marshall's team was headed down to Alabama to help organize the eight hundred or so federal marshals, the paramilitary group Bobby had assembled to protect Dr. Martin Luther King, get the Freedom Riders safely out of Alabama, and preclude the need to call in federal troops. Robert Kennedy later explained his decision to send in marshals this way: "The reason that we sent the marshals in — it was to avoid the idea of sending troops. Now, we thought that marshals would be much more accepted in the South, and that you could get away from the idea of military occupation — and we had to do something." It was a decision fraught with dangers. The force of federal marshals had been developed during the Eisenhower time and under Robert Kennedy had become a crucial element in enforcing court-ordered integration.

Louis Oberdorfer was called out of a tax meeting by a call from Bobby Kennedy and summoned to the attorney general's office. Bobby wanted Oberdorfer to step in and take charge of the marshals. Oberdorfer told Bob he would go, but told him that he thought it was impolitic to send him down. Oberdorfer explained that he was Jewish and he had family in Alabama. "I would be glad to go, but I think you should be very careful how this is seen, Bob." Given the strong anti-Semitic feeling in the South, Oberdorfer didn't think it was wise politically to have a white Jewish lawyer defending blacks' rights there. In the end, the attorney general asked Byron White to take over, and Byron literally was forced to drag himself from his sickbed and go down and run the operation in Alabama.

Bobby recalled the dramatic situation at the church that Sunday night: "I remember [King], he wanted to get out [of the church] . . . and I said that we were doing the best we could, and he'd be as dead as Kelsey's nuts if it hadn't been for the marshals and the efforts we had made."

As the marshals took up positions between Dr. King's followers gathered at the church and the growing angry mob outside, Bobby remarked on the danger faced by all involved: "Sunday night, I talked to Dr. King several times and I talked to Governor Patterson. Martin Luther King was concerned about whether he was going to live. And I was concerned about whether the place was going to be burned down. Dr. King kept getting reports that the crowds were moving in and that they were going to burn the church down and shoot the Negroes as they run out of the church." In fact, the mob did burn a car right in front of the church. As the situation grew worse, Bobby tried to calm Dr. King. "I said [to him] that our people were down there, and as long as we were in a church, he might say a prayer for us. [Dr. King] didn't think that was very humorous. He rather berated me for what was happening to him at the time. And I said to him that I didn't think he'd be alive [if not for the marshals] and that they would keep the church from burning down."

The Kennedy team flew to Alabama in a private jet owned by Najeeb Halaby, a Kennedy family friend who had been named head of the Federal Aviation Administration. On the plane were the Justice Department team, several secretaries, and stacks of law books. Because most of them had been corporate lawyers in private practice before coming to work for Bobby Kennedy, they had never faced this kind of situation. As corporate lawyers, they were unprepared to be on the front lines of the civil rights struggle. "We learned the law on the plane," Oberdorfer remembers. "I dictated a memorandum to my secretary about the presidential power to take this action literally on the plane on the way down."

The team landed at Maxwell Air Force Base in Alabama, where some eight hundred federal marshals had been assembled. They had been assembled from the ranks of the Border Patrol agents, prison guards, and IRS agents. Many of the prison guards had been flown in from a federal prison in Ohio, and according to Oberdorfer were "a rough-looking bunch. They looked at us in our suits and ties, as if to say, Where the heck are you guys from?" The group included special agents from the Internal Revenue Service, and it would also be the only time that Bob was able to use them. Several of them complained to Oberdorfer and were angry at being thrust into such a volatile situation. Later Treasury Secretary Douglas Dillon complained to the president, and the marshals were left out of future Justice Department operations.

The federal effort was pretty much a paramilitary operation, complete with a base radio and walkie-talkies. Bobby, in touch with White by telephone, instructed him to send two of the marshals down to the church where Martin Luther King was to speak that night, to watch over the church and keep them apprised of the situation. Taking a look at the motley group of eight hundred men, White pulled out two of the Border Patrol guards, dressed them in civilian clothes, and sent them to the church. His instructions were clear. "One of you sits in the car. The other one stands by the church and keeps a channel to the base open, no matter what happens!" Byron stayed on the base with the walkie-talkie, in touch with the two marshals at the church the entire time. The remaining marshals were dispatched in post office trucks.

Lou Oberdorfer had procured the post office trucks through the postal service in Atlanta. Bobby teased him that he was trying to make his reputation by getting postal trucks the way General Gaynley had commandeered taxi cabs in World War I in Paris to take the soldiers out to the front. It was a reference that only Bobby understood, leaving his guys to figure out what he was talking about later. "His mind," Dolan says, "was always ten steps ahead of you."

The marshals were gathered inside a large garage where the postal trucks were lined up. White, Oberdorfer, Dolan, and the others stood outside and watched as the postal trucks began to drive to the church where Dr. King and many of the Freedom Riders had gathered. There was only one problem, Dolan saw, as the trucks drove by: They were empty. "It was a real ad hoc operation. The marshals were standing at attention and nobody had told them to get into the postal trucks. It would have been funny, if it weren't so damn serious." Fortunately, White and Dolan had some wartime experience, which kicked in as they took command. As Bobby's men watched the last of the marshals head out in the postal trucks, White broke the uneasy silence. He said he hoped he could rely on the marshals—white men who by background and temperament were not necessarily going to be sympathetic to a black civil rights leader.

King was giving a speech at the church that evening in preparation for a march the following day. The segregationists, threatened by King's presence, were prepared to take the law into their own hands. The marshals were brought in to protect King from being lynched.

Back at the garage, the Justice Department team monitored by radio the developments at the tense standoff at the church.

"The marshals have arrived. They have arrived in the Post Office trucks."

"The marshals have been deployed on the perimeter of the church."

"Roger," White said. Bobby Kennedy was listening on an open line from his office in Washington. He had previously been on the telephone with Dr. King, reassuring him that the marshals would protect him from any disturbance.

"Police say there is a mob forming at the foot of the Dexter Avenue hill."

"How many in the mob?" White asked the marshal on the other end of the radio transmission.

"I don't know."

"Find out!" the attorney general commanded.

Intelligence went back and forth about the size of the mob.

"The mob is coming up the hill!"

Oberdorfer began to worry about how the marshals, many of them "ridge-running revenuers from the hills of north Georgia, east Tennessee, and Alabama," would react to the crowd climbing the hill toward them.

"The mob is approaching the line of marshals."

"Roger."

"The mob is stirring around and getting very angry."

There was a pause, the noise coming clearly over the radio.

"The marshals have gone into action! Over!"

There was a long pause. Then, breaking the silence, Robert Kennedy asked, "On which side have the marshals gone into action?"

In late September 1962, Bobby sent Joe Dolan and Justice Department tax division head Lou Oberdorfer to Millington Naval Air Station near Oxford, Mississippi, to work with the team escorting James R. Meredith to register as the first black student at the University of Mississippi. John Doar, Bobby's tough-minded right-hand man on voter registration and civil rights, had been able to spirit Meredith into his dorm on campus. Negotiations with Governor Ross Barnett had broken down; he would not enforce the court order requiring integration at the state university. Bobby, feeling betrayed by the governor, had no recourse except to call in federal marshals, to be followed by federal troops. On Sunday night, Bobby called from the White House to tell Dolan to use the army to keep back the crowd of segregationists and safeguard Meredith's registration.

By the next morning, after Dolan picked up Deputy Attorney General Nick Katzenbach from the airport, they found that segregationists had already gathered outside the Lyceum, a building on campus, the federal headquarters for the operation. As the two men headed inside to meet the rest of Bobby's team, they were greeted with shouts of "bloodsuckers," racial epithets, and the occasional hurled bottle. "We could see that things were going to build up and that it was going to be something bad," Dolan says. "It was clear that we were not going to get Meredith registered that day."

The situation remained tense over the next several minutes. Over the open phone line, Bobby and the White House team could hear sporadic gunfire coming from the campus. As the federal marshals held out against the growing mob surrounding the Lyceum, the president tried in vain to get the army moving, but it seemed unable to respond to this kind of crisis. At one point, Ed Guthman, press secretary for Bobby, was on the phone line with Bobby. As the mob howled in the background, gunfire cut through the southern night air, and bottles broke against the walls, the attorney general asked quietly, "How's it going?"

"It feels a little like the Alamo," Guthman told him.

After a brief pause, Bobby Kennedy, his gallows humor evident, said, "Well, you know what happened to those guys, don't you?"

According to Dolan, "They were shooting into the hallway, putting holes in the windows while Guthman was talking to him. Bob could hear the bullets in the background. But there was nothing we could do but hope the marshals could hold out until the army got there. Bob knew that; he knew there was nothing he could do. That was Bob Kennedy's humor. When things were tough he always knew the right thing to say. It got us through."

Meredith and all of "Bobby's boys" survived the harrowing night in Mississippi, but for Bobby it was one of the most painful experiences. The real fear of the situation in Mississippi was that it would come to a point where United States troops were facing off with Mississippi troops. Bobby envisioned the Civil War all over again. Recalled Bobby, "Basically what I was trying to avoid was having to send troops and create a federal presence in Mississippi. In my judgment what [Barnett] was trying to accomplish was the avoidance of the integration of the University of Mississippi, number one, and if he couldn't do that, to be forced to do it by our heavy hand, and his preference was with troops. He was trying to satisfy and please me, and still try to talk me out of sending, or having James Meredith come, to the University of Mississippi."

Bobby believed he had miscalculated by trusting Governor Barnett and had thus cost people their lives. "I think he was wrong to second-guess himself," Dolan says now. "His choices were limited. You couldn't believe the governor or his men, but you had to take the chance, I mean he was the governor, you wanted to believe he would do his job under the Constitution. The governor was a liar and it would have been political suicide for him to cooperate and in the end, the governor chose politics over the Constitution. Bob didn't have a great many choices; he had to do his job as attorney general and enforce the law."

Eventually, Bobby invited even J. Edgar Hoover to the Tuesday and Thursday Justice Department staff luncheons. The longtime director of the Federal Bureau of Investigation, who had urged Bobby to take the post of attorney general, had since come to loathe him, especially since Hoover felt Bobby was determined to limit his access to the president. In addition, Hoover also resented Bobby's insistence on forcing the Federal Bureau of Investigation to focus on issues that Hoover found personally distasteful, such as civil rights enforcement and organized crime.

Hoover's resentment eventually extended to Kenny O'Donnell. Hoover, trying to bypass Bobby Kennedy's authority, would send FBI reports directly to Kenny, labeling them for the "President's Eyes Only," to get around Bobby's insistence that Hoover go through him and maintain the order of command, which no previous attorney general had been able to maintain with him.

Kenny would send Hoover's reports back to Bobby without even showing them to the president. Kenny knew Bobby would decide what the president should see or not. Frustrated with Hoover's constant attempts to go around Bobby, one day Kenny called him directly. "Mr. Hoover? Don't you work for the attorney general of the United States?"

"Yes," Hoover replied, his fury already evident.

"I suggest from now on you go through your boss, the attorney general, Robert Kennedy. Then he can talk to the president as he sees fit."

J. Edgar Hoover behaved only as long as John Kennedy was alive. And he would obtain the ultimate revenge by becoming the one to deliver the news to Bobby that his brother, the president, was dead.

"Hoover stopped coming over to the Justice Department the day after the assassination," Dolan says. "Hoover said to Bob, 'You know now we deal directly with the White House. We don't deal with the brother anymore — cut him out!' " The next day Hoover had the direct phone linking him to the attorney general's office removed. Hoover had always resented that phone. Now with the brother gone and Hoover's friend

Lyndon Johnson in place, a man who did not like Bob Kennedy, Hoover no longer felt any obligations or pretense. A couple of days later, Dolan was talking to Bobby on the phone and told him the story. Bobby said sadly, "Those people don't work for us anymore."

Kenny O'Donnell remembered that shortly after the Bay of Pigs disaster in April 1961, where Castro had captured many of the motley invasion force, the president came into his office one morning looking tired. "I was thinking about those poor guys in the prison down in Cuba. I'm willing to make a deal to get them out of there," he said.

Making the deal fell to Bobby. In December 1962, when Castro agreed to release the prisoners for $28 million in tractors, bulldozers, and medicine, Bobby called on his lawyer friend John Nolan to monitor the deal, which had been negotiated by Jim Donovan, a former OSS officer who had also negotiated the exchange of Colonel Rudolph Abel with the Soviet Union. Donovan had spent much of his time traveling between Cuba and New York, allowing only the Cuban Missile Crisis to interrupt his negotiations. "Bob Kennedy perplexed Jim Donovan, but Donovan did not perplex Bob Kennedy," Nolan says. "Bob decided that he would rather deal with Donovan through an intermediary. Bob Kennedy was relatively fast and very concise in his speech and thought. Jim Donovan was philosophical; he would discourse. If you asked him a question, he would rub his chin, sit back, put his feet up and sigh, and give you this long-winded answer that often didn't answer the question. That kind of thing drove Bob crazy." Nolan's job was to see how real the deal was that Donovan said he had hammered out with Castro. As it turned out, Donovan had lots of pledges for baby food and other goods, but it would take a lot of effort to deliver on the promise to Castro and bring the prisoners home before Christmas. At the last minute Castro would demand another $1.9 million, and Bobby was forced to scramble, calling on Boston's Cardinal Cushing and General Lucius D. Clay—famous for masterminding the Berlin airlift—for help in raising money.

Bobby turned to his law school friend Barrett Prettyman, now in private law practice, to find a way to transport the goods to Castro. "A whole group of us was asked to just give up everything and go to the

Justice Department and virtually live there while we tried to run this operation. We all did it without a second thought. If Bobby asked, you just came."

The attorney general was able to get help from the private sector. "Bobby assured these companies that they wouldn't be prosecuted for sending this stuff overseas. He also arranged to give them a tax break in order to get them to cooperate." As soon as the companies realized they were getting a tax break they began moving out of their warehouses a lot of junk, which was mixed in with the valuable goods requested by Castro. Day and night, Nolan, Prettyman, and the rest of Bobby's ad hoc team worked on procuring everything on Castro's shopping list. Prettyman was able to get a company to donate the use of an old ship that looked like something out of the *African Queen*. Everything was going smoothly and there were only a few days before everything was to be shipped when Castro got wind of a rumor that he was being sent a lot of junk.

The Cuban leader was furious and knew he risked great embarrassment; he had arranged for the international media to be on hand when the ship landed in Havana and was unloaded. He sent a group of agents to Florida to inspect the ship and make sure the United States wasn't pulling anything on him. By the time Prettyman and the others had gotten word of their arrival, it was too late for the Cuban agents to do anything; most of the material both good and bad had already been packed.

Prettyman was pleased he'd managed to evade the prying of Castro's agents and told Bobby so. Bobby was not happy. "I guess you'll have to fly down to Cuba and explain to Castro why he is getting all this stuff, that I told him he wasn't going to get," he said calmly. "You will have to tell him that you screwed up and hope he understands." The next thing Prettyman knew, he was on a plane to Cuba with no passport and no clothes except the ones he was wearing, and no diplomatic explanation ready to give the Cuban leader.

John Nolan and Bill Donovan were already on the island negotiating with Castro for the release of the prisoners. They were more than a little surprised to see Prettyman arrive. They introduced him to Castro. "We started chatting. I was trying to figure out when was the best time to tell him about the ship and exactly what to say to him about it. I kept putting it off. I felt like a little kid." Finally, a thought popped into his head. "By the way, where is Hemingway's place?" he asked.

Castro looked surprised. "Would you like to see it?"

"Sure," said Prettyman, thinking that Bobby Kennedy would fire him for not telling Castro immediately.

"I would be honored to show you," said Castro.

Hoping at worst to stall the inevitable and at best to build up some goodwill, Prettyman followed Castro and his retinue into an armed jeep and roared up the hill with him to the Hemingway compound. As they drove along, with Castro pointing out sites, Prettyman pondered whether Castro would kill him and throw him into the hills when he found out he was getting a fair share of cast-off American junk. Soon the jeeps had come to a stop at the great writer's longtime retreat. After a short search for the key, they entered, with Prettyman following Castro inside. It turned out that they were the first people to enter it since Hemingway's death in Idaho two years before. "He had his bottle of booze there and he had his weight written on the wall in the bathroom. Everything was just exactly as it had been when he left it and nobody had touched the place since he died."

Hemingway's old manservant, Castro, Prettyman, and several military men headed into the kitchen, where Hemingway used to watch the fights on his small television and then smoke cigars and drink. Castro pulled out some glasses and cigars. Soon they were all standing around smoking cigars and drinking Hemingway's booze. Still Barrett said nothing about the shipment. Castro began telling wonderful stories about Hemingway that Barrett had never heard, and he certainly wasn't going to interrupt.

Finally they all climbed back into the jeeps, and after a stop at a housing project for the poor, where Castro was mobbed, they finally made it back to the wharf. The old ship had already arrived and was being unloaded, the baby food and medicine stacked sky high on the pier. Castro was ecstatic and the press was attentive to his every move. It was now or never, Prettyman thought. He slipped quietly over to

Castro, pulled him aside, and explained as best he could that the ship-ment was not all it seemed. Castro just stared at him. He looked puz-zled, and then he began to laugh. Prettyman himself was relieved; at least he had followed Bobby's orders.

Castro shook his head and walked away, throwing a glance back at Prettyman and smiling. He had gotten his medicine and his media at-tention. He had won.

"The next morning I was on the first plane out with all the prisoners. We got to the end of the runway and they had the engines all revved up and ready to go. However, we ended up sitting there for quite a while, because the Soviet MiGs were taking off and landing." There was not a human sound on the plane. The plane had just begun to move when through the window Prettyman saw several military cars come careening toward the plane, pulling in front of it as if to block it.

Oh God, Prettyman thought, he finally figured out what I was trying to tell him.

It turned out that Castro had ordered some Cuban families and sick children to leave as well. After the plane was finally loaded they took off. The plane headed down the runway and as it left the ground chaos erupted, the freed prisoners yelling, screaming, and crying. They grabbed and kissed Prettyman, thanking him, John Kennedy, and Bobby Kennedy. Prettyman was as relieved as they were, but for different rea-sons.

When he returned to Washington, Prettyman met with Bobby who was curious to hear about Castro. When his guilt took over, Prettyman confessed to Bobby his aborted attempt to confess to Castro. Bobby just stared at him in disbelief for a moment and then laughed. "Who are you more afraid of, Castro or me?"

In addition to his other duties, Bobby managed to find time to work with kids, both in his official capacity—by starting programs for juveniles and meeting with gang members in New York—and on his own. If he had any free time during the day, he'd call Barrett Prettyman, who had joined his staff in 1963, and say he wanted to visit a school. "I would call the school and then we would rush out to some local school in

Washington. He would talk to the kids, going from classroom to class-room." If the school knew he was coming they would often have the students lined up in the auditorium, and he would address them there; but always he managed to escape and look around the school and talk to the kids individually. Often he would get a visiting sports figure or movie star to join him.

At school after school, Bobby was taken aback by the bad conditions, the violence, and the fact that many kids had nowhere to play. Wash-ington, D.C., said it lacked money to fix up the schools, the pools, and the playground. Bobby called Prettyman in his office one day. "Find out what the worst area of the city is and find someplace to build a playground. Let's get the private sector involved and fix it up." The worst area that Prettyman could find was at 7th and P streets, a former play-ground that had begun being used as a city dump for abandoned cars. Bobby called the chief of police and told him to move his abandoned cars elsewhere. Next he contacted O. Roy Chalk, a wealthy black entre-preneur in Washington, enlisting his help to raise private sector funds for the playground. The air force donated an old plane for the play-ground. Others donated a tugboat.

Prettyman visited one school with Bobby that, unlike most schools in Washington, had a swimming pool. The swimming pool was closed. Bobby wanted to know why. He was told by school officials that the pool had been a big success, attracting not only kids who would linger there after school but also their parents. The local crime rate dropped. But the pool broke down and no one had the money to fix it. Bobby just stared at them. They were all standing beside an empty swimming pool in the sweltering Washington heat. "That doesn't make any sense. How much does it cost to fix it?"

"Thirty thousand dollars, Mr. Attorney General."

"We'll raise it and get the pool fixed." Turning to Prettyman, he began, "Barrett—"

"I know. Raise thirty thousand dollars and fix the pool."

Bobby nodded. "Get it started, tell me who to call, and we'll get it done."

Bobby raised the thirty thousand, all from the private sector, called the school, and had the pool fixed. It had seemed to him a simple solution. "If you help kids early," he said, "then you don't have to save them when it's too late."

Sitting in his hotel room in upstate New York one night, Bobby was reading a speech he was going to give on civil rights. "This is too serious," he told John Reilly and Fred Dutton, from the White House staff, another friend of Kenny's. "John, call that comedian Milton Berle. I just saw him last week and he was great. He likes my brother and I know he wouldn't mind."

"Sure," said Reilly, with meritless confidence. He and Dutton looked at each other, leaving Bobby to make some more calls. It was a Sunday, and they had no idea how to reach Milton Berle. Maybe Angie Novello would know how to track him down; but after repeated calls they couldn't even track down Angie Novello. Time was getting tight. They tried calling cold out to L.A., but that didn't work either; Milton Berle was not listed in the phone book. "We didn't know what to do," Reilly says. "We couldn't ask Bobby. He wouldn't know how to find anyone without Angie, and we couldn't reach Angie!"

In desperation, Dutton and Reilly decided to make up their own jokes. They actually thought their one-liners were quite funny and proudly walked in and handed the paper to Bobby, pretending they had got them from Milton Berle. As he was getting dressed, Bobby read them over. He looked up at Dutton and Reilly, surprised. "God, is he slipping! I just saw him at the house last week and he was great, but these are awful. I mean they are really bad. I can't use any of them. He's really losing his touch." Bobby shook his head. "Isn't that too bad."

"We couldn't say a word," Reilly remembers, "because he would have known we lied to him and then we'd be dead, so we just skulked out of the room."

18

❦

DALLAS

We are sheep without a shepherd when the snow shuts out the sky.
Oh! Why did you leave us, Owen? Why did you die?

—IRISH BALLAD

Kenny had opposed American combat involvement in Vietnam almost from the beginning. His reservations were not specific, but for him this narrow strip of Southeast Asia didn't seem the kind of place where the United States needed to make a stand. Burned by the quality of intelligence he'd received from official sources during the disastrous Bay of Pigs invasion of Cuba by Cuban exiles that the United States had backed in 1961, President Kennedy sent Mike Mansfield to Indochina for an independent report. At the end of his trip, Mansfield met up with the president in Palm Beach, joining him on a boat ride on Lake Worth. Mansfield handed the president his report. The president reached over and casually took it out of Mansfield's hand and went to find a secluded place to read it.

Mansfield watched as the president finished reading the report. His blue eyes were stern. He looked displeased. Kennedy got up and came to sit down across from the senator. Holding the report aloft, he said, "This isn't what my advisers are telling me!"

Senator Mansfield felt uncomfortable. "Mr. President," he said, "you asked me to go and review the situation in Vietnam. This report is the result of your invitation and honestly reflects my finding and my viewpoint on Vietnam. We should not get involved there. It would be a mistake."

The president was angry; his face was flushed and his neck got very red. "Well," said the president, finally, having mastered his anger. "I find all of this hard to believe!"

Mansfield shook his head. "It is an honest assessment of the situation and where it is headed."

The two men spent a couple of hours together and then parted. "The president was angry," said the senator. "Not too bad. I had seen worse. I think he was surprised by the information in the report. It clearly didn't reflect what he was being told by the military."

Over time, Mansfield reports, "Jack Kennedy was switching more and more against Vietnam." Kennedy had in essence inherited the simmering conflict from Dwight Eisenhower. Eisenhower had sent what were called "advisers" to assist the South Vietnamese in their battle against the Communist North. Kennedy had increased their numbers.

Both Kennedy and Mansfield had previously encountered Ngo Dinh Diem, now president of Vietnam. Mansfield remembered best a luncheon for Diem that he and Kennedy had attended as senators, hosted by Supreme Court Justice William O. Douglas. Diem's brother was a Catholic bishop. Diem himself had spent a couple of years at a Maryknoll retreat house in New Jersey. Both senators were duly impressed with Diem and were very supportive of his attempts to become president of South Vietnam. By 1963, however, President Kennedy was growing disenchanted with Diem because of his inability to control his brother's growing corruption, as well as Diem's increasing crackdown on dissent. As much as Kenny O'Donnell and others were convinced that the United States government should not become involved in supporting the Diem military, they nevertheless remained convinced that Diem was the best solution to Vietnam's problems.

"Diem was assassinated in Vietnam; both brothers were killed. I know this occurred without the approval or knowledge of John Kennedy," Mike Mansfield says. "He didn't even know of the plot until after the fact. John Kennedy may have questioned him. He did not however—did not," Mansfield repeated with conviction—"withdraw his support for him as a leader; neither did I, nor have I ever since. I still think Diem was the best man for South Vietnam. His brother Nhu and his wife began to take more and more control of the government. John Kennedy began to see that it was that segment of the family that was causing the biggest problems and making it difficult for Diem to remain credible. Personally, I think that Diem was honest, dedicated, and his heart was in the right place. It was unfortunate that he was killed, because following his death things went from bad to worse. I nevertheless always felt that in the end it always had to be their fight, not ours."

Kenny would usher Mansfield into the Oval Office three months later and linger in the background as the senator and the president talked. "I think you were right in what you had to say about Vietnam," Kennedy told the majority leader. "I'm going to pay more attention to the contents of your report. I agree with you that we shouldn't get involved any further in Vietnam. I was wrong. I am going to withdraw approximately a thousand troops. I can't do it at the moment, but I can do it after the next election. Once the next election is over I am going to implement further withdrawals until we are completely out of Vietnam. I wanted you to hear it directly from me."

Mansfield looked up and caught Kenny's eye. He was smiling faintly.

Just three weeks later on November 20, 1963, John and Jacqueline Kennedy, Kenny O'Donnell, and the entire presidential entourage left for Dallas. As Kenny prepared for the trip he told Helen, "The president has so much planned for after the election. I can't wait to win and get started."

"You're going to Texas," Kenny told Jerry Bruno. Texas governor John Connolly was feuding with Senator Ralph Yarborough, and Bruno had strict instructions from Kenny not to get caught in the middle as he advanced the president's trip. Arriving at the airport, he was greeted by both Yarborough and Connolly people and knew what a delicate job he had ahead of him. Connolly tried to hand him a schedule for the president's visit. Bruno shook his head; he was accustomed to being in this position. Rare indeed were opportunities like the one in San Francisco, where he got to tell everyone yes. "Look, Governor," Jerry said, as gently as possible, "this schedule is why Kenny sent me down here. They are going to look at your proposed schedule when I go back and Kenny will see what things they agree to do and what things they won't. It's up to Kenny, really."

Connolly sat back in amazement. "Oh no, sir. No, no, no, that's not the way things work in Texas!" he bellowed. Standing up, he went for the phone and said in a voice loud enough for everyone to hear, "Operator, get me the White House." Once the White House came on the line, Connolly announced, "This is Governor John Connolly of Texas — get me Kenny O'Donnell!" Glaring at Bruno, Connolly waited for Kenny to come on the line. As soon as Kenny picked up the phone, Connolly began outlining his outrage over Bruno's behavior and the schedule, finishing with "That's not how things are done in Texas!" Bruno said little; he knew what Kenny's response would be. The governor would just have to hear it for himself.

Kenny cut Connolly off halfway through his tirade. "Look, Governor," Kenny growled. "Go over the schedule with Bruno and he will bring it back to Washington and we will give you our answer later!" With that Kenny hung up the phone. Angrily replacing the receiver, Connolly returned to the table visibly upset. He was not accustomed to that kind of treatment.

The next day Bruno traveled through Texas to reconnoiter potential campaign stops. Kennedy might go to San Antonio and then a Houston testimonial dinner for Congressman Carl Albert, after which he might drop by another event and spend the night at the Rice Hotel. For the next day he could give a speech in Fort Worth and address the students at Texas Christian University, then go to Dallas by car and talk to a business group at the Hilton Hotel and that evening head to Austin for a fund-raiser, spending the night at the LBJ ranch.

After spending the day going through the schedule with Connolly's people, Bruno thought San Antonio was fine and Houston seemed all right, but Fort Worth presented some problems. Bruno spoke to the school trustees where the president was to speak and asked them about presenting an honorary degree to the president, which was customary. The school officials explained that under no circumstances could they present such a degree to a Catholic. Bruno was stunned. This was really going to go over big with Kenny, he thought. Bruno told the officials, "Governor Connolly says President Kennedy was going to get an honorary degree and that is the only reason that the president is coming here." The trustees were adamant, Bruno was told. It was against school policy.

Bruno was livid. Returning to see Governor Connolly, he told him what the trustees had said. Connolly professed horror and said he would intervene. Bruno then headed on to Dallas and the Hilton Hotel to check out the ballroom for the president's business speech, only to discover that the ballroom was already booked by a bottlers' convention. The hotel had explained to the bottlers that they needed the ballroom for the president of the United States. They had been unimpressed. Bruno was flabbergasted. Standing in the lobby of the Hilton Hotel, he searched out a bank of phones. He was going to have to call Connolly. This whole trip was turning out to be a pain in the ass.

Getting Connolly on the phone, Bruno explained the situation. Connolly came up with the Trade Mart, a local exhibition and meeting hall. "Fine," Bruno said. From there Bruno met with Connolly's representative at the Dallas Citizens Council, Bob Strauss, along with one of Lyndon Johnson's advance men. Connolly called saying he had been unable to persuade Texas Christian University to give Kennedy an honorary degree. He was a Catholic; it didn't matter that he was also president of the United States. Governor Connolly had a suggestion: Skip the university and have the president address the Fort Worth Chamber of Commerce. From there he could go directly to a luncheon in Dallas, either at the Trade Mart or the city fairgrounds.

The new plan called for the president to spend the night at a hotel in Fort Worth, speak at a Chamber of Commerce breakfast, and then fly all of thirty miles to Dallas rather than drive, so that he might hit Dallas at midday and do a motorcade through the city. It sounded like a good plan. Jerry Bruno thought finally he had come up with a trip schedule that would keep the Texans happy, but most of all keep Kenny O'Donnell happy.

The Trade Mart was what remained the most pressing concern for Bruno. The ground floor area where the luncheon was to be held was an enormous open space. The second floor contained shops and five catwalks that connected a variety of shops. Walking through the main cavern of a room, his eye wandered to the catwalks above it, crossing overhead like the steel extensions of tree branches. There had been demonstrators in Dallas, Bruno knew. Lady Bird Johnson had had trouble with protesters on a recent visit. Stevenson had been spat upon. Texas was feverish in its varied political views. Extremists had been flying the flag upside down, and far-right leaders had been running ads declaring that John Kennedy ought to be tried for treason. "I was scared that somebody was going to get up on the catwalk and try to embarrass the president," Bruno recalls. Bruno and the Secret Service men accompanying him agreed that the place would not work. Finding a spot to sit, Bruno borrowed paper and a pencil and then drew a diagram of the room for Kenny.

Upon his return to Washington, Bruno met with Jerry Bain of the Secret Service, outlining the schedule for him and discussing his concerns over the Trade Mart. Then they went to Kenny. He was typically quick in his assessment of the information. San Antonio was fine; Houston was fine; the Texas Christian University controversy appalled him; Kenny thought the Bruno decision to go with Fort Worth and Dallas worked better. Bruno made his case for the Texas fairgrounds and against the Trade Mart, showing Kenny his diagram. "Well, Connolly won't agree with that. He's already called." Bain pressed the case further. The catwalks were too dangerous; it was too risky, given the uneasy Texas atmosphere. Kenny finally agreed, saying he would take care of it with Connolly. But ultimately they were unable to get Connolly to budge; the luncheon was scheduled for the Trade Mart.

Kenny and Bruno worked out a motorcade route to the Trade Mart. The Secret Service raised some objections. Kenny decided the final route he had chosen to the Trade Mart made sense. It was a minor detail in a major trip. His decision would haunt Kenny for the remainder of his life.

At 12.30 P.M. central time on November 22, 1963, President John F. Kennedy and his wife Jacqueline sat in the open rear seat of the presidential limousine as the motorcade turned left into Dallas's Dealey

Plaza, about to go under the underpass and on to the Trade Mart. Kenny and Dave were in the car directly behind the president and Jackie. Jerry Bruno was at the Democratic National Committee office in Washington. "I was on the phone with my Secret Service guy—mundane stuff, really—and suddenly the guys starts screaming into the phone." His screams were so loud that Bruno could hear the words ringing in his ears days, months afterward. "There have been shots! There have been shots!"

Bruno, stunned, understood but could not quite comprehend. The Secret Service man was in the motorcade directly behind Kenny. His voice resounded with hysteria and disbelief. "Shit! Shit! There have been shots, there have been shots. Dear God, they have shot him, they have shot. Dear God, they are shooting, they are shooting, he's hit!"

"Suddenly the line goes dead and I don't hear nothing until the ticker tape tells me Jack Kennedy is dead," Jerry Bruno remembers.

"When we were riding through Dallas on our way from the Love Field to the Trade Mart luncheon, the sun was shining brightly and warmly. The crowd at the airport had been warm, enthusiastic, and friendly. The crowds lining the streets were equally warm and friendly. In the backup car, next to Dave Powers, I turned to Dave and said, 'There is certainly nothing wrong with this crowd.' The misgivings of the Secret Service, my own concerns, and the *Dallas News* black-bordered anti-Kennedy tirade in mind, I was relieved. It would seem all the concern was unnecessary.

"Sitting on the two jump seats of the Secret Service backup car, only about ten feet behind the president and Jackie, we could see their faces clearly when they turned to nod and wave to screaming people pushing into the street beside them. The president seemed thrilled and fascinated by the crowd's noisy excitement. I knew he had expected nothing like this wild welcome.

"When we were making the sharp left turn around Dealey Plaza in front of the School Book Depository building, I asked Dave what time it was. Ahead of us in the back seat of the Lincoln, the president was sitting on the right side of the car with his arm outstretched, waving to the crowd in front of the Depository. Mrs. Kennedy, in her pink suit with her matching pink pillbox hat perched on the back of her head, was beside him on his left with red roses presented to her at the airport on the seat between them. Governor Connolly was on the pull-out seat in front of the president and Mrs. Connolly was on the pull-out seat in front of Jackie."

"It's twelve-thirty," Dave said, looking at his watch.

"Fine," said Kenny. "It's only five minutes from here, so we're only running five minutes behind schedule."

"I had just finished speaking when we heard shots, two close together and then a third one. There must have been an interval of at least five seconds before the third and last shots, because, after the second shot, Dave said to me, 'Kenny, I think the president's been shot!' I made a quick sign of the cross and said, 'What makes you think that?' 'Look at him,' said Dave. 'He was over on the right, with his arm stretched out. Now he's slumped over toward Jackie, holding his throat.'

"While we both stared at the president, a third shot took the side of his head off. We saw pieces of bone and brain tissue and bits of reddish hair flying through the air. The impact lifted him and shook him limply, as if he were a rag doll, and then he dropped out of our sight, sprawled across the backseat of the car.

"I said to Dave, 'He's dead.' "

Jerry Bruno ran into the office of Dick Maguire, treasurer of the Democratic National Committee, Arthur Garrity's law partner, and a charter member of Kenny's Irish Mafia. Justine, Kenny's younger sister and his secretary, jumped from her seat at the sight of him. She no longer remembers his exact words; it happened as if in a dream. She thought he said, "There have been shots, shots in Dallas in the motorcade — they are shooting at the motorcade." As if in a trance she rose from her desk and started out the door, when someone else stopped her, his face alabaster. "Did you hear, shots in Dallas, shots — an agent has been killed, an agent has been killed."

Justine turned to face Jerry Bruno. "It wasn't an agent, it was Kenneth," she said. She left the building and ran up to St. Matthew's Cathedral, through the heavy doors and into the cool sanctuary to pray in the dusty midday light. Praying, she knew it was her brother who had been hit. It was his job to protect the president. Surely he would have stepped in front of the bullet. She fought her tears back. She would have to be brave now, for Helen would be alone with those five children. At least the president was all right. He and Bobby would take care of Helen and the kids.

As she sleepwalked back out onto the street, toward the committee headquarters, she was startled to see her coworkers walking toward her, their faces blank, tears streaming down their cheeks. No words were exchanged as they turned her around and headed back to St. Matthew's.

As they entered the cathedral and knelt, a priest came to the altar and, weeping, began a Mass for the soul of President John F. Kennedy. That was when she realized, Dear God, it wasn't Kenneth, it was the president. Her relief about Kenny was swiftly replaced with horror. He would never be able to live with himself. He would believe he had failed his president, failed his president's wife, failed his country, and failed his best friend, Bobby.

Air Force One took off from Love Field carrying the body of President Kennedy. "As soon as we took off, Johnson asked me to come up and see him," recalled Kenny. "I talked to him for a few minutes and he used the famous line he used on every single staff member, 'I need you more than he ever needed you.' He came back, and he was changing his shirt with me and he said, 'You can't leave me. You're the only one that I really get along with there. You know that I don't know one soul north of the Mason-Dixon Line, and I don't know any of those big city fellows. I need you. My staff doesn't know anything, they don't know anything. They don't know anyone outside of Texas.'

"I'm noncommittal at the moment. I went up and talked to him about ten minutes, but I wanted to stay with Jackie. So I went back and sat with Jackie."

Helen O'Donnell was having lunch with some of her other politically widowed women friends at Paul Young's restaurant in Washington, on Connecticut Avenue, exchanging stories about their children along with a little political gossip. Helen was talking when she saw the waiter, his face ashen, rush up to her, breathless. "It's terrible news, terrible — the president has been shot and I think your husband has been shot too. I think he's dead."

She wanted to vomit. She couldn't. She couldn't make a sound. She just tried to breathe. She thought of her children and what she would say to them. Even moments later, when the news of the president's death came over the radio and her fear for her husband abated even as her grief grew, she knew her life and Kenny's would never be the same. Helen O'Donnell would always say that Kenny wished that bullet had hit him instead of his president.

For Helen, November 22, 1963, would mark the beginning of the unraveling of her life. There were times in the dark days ahead when she knew that the assassin's bullets had found another mark. They had ripped a hole in her husband's heart.

She would watch him as he shrank from going to the White House, where he had practically lived for the previous thousand days. At home she would hear him pace for hours, often in the darkness. She urged him to talk to her, and if he couldn't talk to her then to put his words on tape, to articulate his grief. He was horrified. It wasn't his way. "For history," she had said. To him that notion was cold and sickening. In time she would blame herself: If she had been able to get him to talk, if she had been able to reach him . . .

Only Bobby would understand. Bobby would make Kenny move on. As Bobby had written her in 1947 after the sad and abrupt death of his sister, "It's hard to know God's plan." At least they still had Bobby. He would hold them all together.

19

BEGINNING AGAIN, 1964

The future does not belong to those who are content with today.

— BOBBY KENNEDY

Bobby's first official act after his brother's assassination was to dedicate the newly completed playground at 7th and P streets. "It was the saddest day you can imagine," say Barrett Prettyman. "There were thousands of kids around, and all these officials and press, and Bobby was doing the best he could, but he was so remote it was hard."

Afterward, Bobby began walking toward the car. He had brought Brumus with him. As he approached the car, he turned and faced Prettyman. "I'm going to walk back to the Justice Department. I want to be alone." With that he turned and began to move away, Brumus loping along beside him.

"Bobby," Prettyman called after him, reluctantly. "Look, we have to have someone go with you to guard you, whether you like it or not."

"No. I don't want to be guarded. Leave me alone." He turned down the street. "I don't want to see any cops near me," he growled without turning around.

Panicked, Prettyman ran to find some plainclothes officers. By the time he did, Bobby and Brumus were well on their way down the street.

"It was the saddest sight," Prettyman remembers. "He had no coat or hat on, it was cold, Brumus was walking along beside him, kids trailing along, and we had all these plainclothes cops walking way behind, so he wouldn't spot them. I just watched him and my heart ached. There was nothing I could do or say. There were no words for the pain."

After John F. Kennedy was killed, Kenny and Bobby would walk to-gether for hours. They would meet at the Justice Department and walk over to the monuments, then go up to Arlington Cemetery. He was dead. All they had planned had died with a gunshot. A man they both disliked and distrusted now sat where John Kennedy should have sat. They walked in the cold gray of the Washington winter afternoons, just before dusk, hands stuffed in their pockets, wearing neither coat nor hat. They said little on these walks. Kenny would say later, "There were times when we would talk for a while, that I think we both made each other feel worse. There were times we couldn't even talk." They were accompanied only by the sound of their footfalls as they climbed to Jack Kennedy's grave site.

"I let him down," Kenny would say to Helen, "I failed. I let him down." Helen tried to probe his grief over Jack's death but he withdrew from her. Helen and Ethel tried to cope with their husbands' pain and their own, even as they worked to continue raising their active families, shield-ing them as much as possible. For a while they were left to do so alone. They did not complain. They never cried publicly or let their anger show on the public stage. For now they soldiered on alone.

"Kenny and Bobby were walking around as if in a fog," says Nick Rodis. "You couldn't reach them. We were all fogbound, but those two were lost to us." Both men gained as much strength from Jacqueline Kennedy as from anybody. In the aftermath of the assassination, she had moved from the White House to a house in Georgetown owned by former New York governor Averell Harriman, and then later to a house she bought herself. "Bobby and I went over every afternoon to see Jackie," Kenny would say later. He and Bobby would sit in her living room and tell stories about Jack—remembering being an Irish way of dealing with pain. They thought they were there to console her, but in the end, it was she who helped them. She enjoyed the political war stories, which showed her a side of her husband that she had not often witnessed. He had married her because she asked the opposite of what politics required; she was grace, beauty, and gentleness. She was also, Kenny said, "wickedly funny," which was always an asset when it came to being a Kennedy.

"On a regular basis Kenny would get three or four of us from Capitol Hill, who had worked with Jack Kennedy, together at Jackie's house," then Congressman Dan Rostenkowski recalls. "We would sit around Jackie's living room with Bobby, eat sandwiches, have some drinks, and tell war stories. Jackie would laugh so hard her side would hurt sometimes. I think that Bobby really appreciated everyone reaching out. One particular time I was looking over at Jackie and suddenly realized, 'My God, she's a kid!' She was just thirty-four years old. It dawned on me just how much Jack had protected Jackie from his political life and kept her apart from it. I think it was as amazing for her to see a glimpse of what his political life was like as it was for us to see through her this glimpse of Jack Kennedy's personal side." It was as if both aspects of John Kennedy had finally been introduced to each other and discovered they liked each other very much.

"It was Kenny that we most worried about," Bobby would say later. Others agreed. "Kenny drank too much after the president died. I was really worried," says Dan Rostenkowski. "He seemed haunted somehow. I couldn't reach him. Finally, I said, 'Kenny, look, you gotta slow down on that stuff and take care of yourself.' "

The Cobra just looked at him coldly. "Go to hell and mind your own business." Rosenkowski didn't mention it again.

Jackie noticed Kenny's drinking also. She talked to Bobby; Bobby talked to Kenny. They talked to him together. It worked. He seemed to step forward back into human company again.

Kenny had to decide whether or not to return to the White House. On the plane ride back from Dallas, Lyndon Johnson had asked him to return to his job, but Kenny could not give him an answer. He agonized over his next move. "I can't stay with this guy," he told Nick Rodis. "I just can't do it." Kenny would have the same conversation with Helen and also with Justine. As she and her brother talked late one evening, Kenny paced the den as he made a confession. "Sometimes I have conversations with Mother and Dad," he told Justine. Alice had lived long enough to see her son work in the White House and her daughter go to work for the Democratic National Committee. She had died of a heart attack while in Washington, while baby-sitting for Kenny and Helen. Bobby had arranged for one of the president's planes to fly Alice's body, Helen, Kenny, and his family up to Worcester for the funeral. Bobby had gone himself, embarrassed by the press coverage of his attendance.

"I can imagine," Kenny said softly to his sister, "what Mom and Dad would say. Mom would say, keep the job—who would have imagined you would work in the White House for the president of the United States? Dad would say, get the hell out of there! You don't like the guy, he doesn't like you, he needs to get his own people there. I just don't know."

Kenny finally returned to the White House early one morning just before Christmas to clean out his desk. Walking into the White House, he felt almost physical pain. He tried the lock to his office door. The keys didn't fit. Puzzled, he tried again. When he found a guard, he was told the locks had been changed. He would have to get new keys. The transition of power had begun. In John Kennedy's White House, nobody would have even changed the locks without checking with Kenny. But this was Lyndon Johnson's White House.

Kenny had come to say goodbye, but the president asked him again to stay, at least through the 1964 election campaign. Kenny told the president that before he made his final decision he had to talk to two people, Bobby and Jackie.

Kenny and Helen flew to Palm Beach to spend Christmas with Jackie and the kids. It was one of the saddest Christmases anyone could remember. At dinner with Jackie, Kenny and Bobby got into a discussion about their obligations and what to do next. "We got into this great discussion about obligations to the Democratic party," Kenny recalled, "which I thought we had obligations to beyond Johnson or anybody else. I think it was the first time that Bobby realized that I intended to stay through the election. He wasn't happy."

Kenny would follow Alice's advice, but in the end, by the end of 1964, he would be gone. He was more Cleo than he would like to admit.

"I knew they would get one of us, but I always thought it would be me," Bobby once said.

"Bobby wasn't really around for long periods of time after the assassination and when he was, he wasn't much with it," Kenny would say. The pain in his face was so visible, said one friend, that it almost hurt to look at him. "I think what disturbed Bobby more than anything else was that he found some of those fast friends that he had made weren't fast friends at all," Kenny would declare. "They had really talked to him and been friendly to him simply because he was the president's brother. It upset him very much. I am more callous than that. I realized people cared because of the power and the prestige and when it's gone, those same guys who used to jump on the phone when you called would never return your call. Bobby didn't understand that; he really believed that some of those people were genuine. I think that was as big a shock for him as anything."

Bobby didn't return to the Justice Department until February or March. When he did return he would often stare out the window of his office for great periods of time, lost in thought.

"When Bobby was first coming back, the children's pictures had been up for such a long time that I took them down to put up fresh ones. I hadn't had time to put up the new ones yet. Bob came in and saw the empty walls. He turned to me and said, 'Angie! Where are the pictures?' I immediately began to put them back up. I think at that time his children were what kept him going."

"He was very distraught," said Kenny, "as he should have been. This wasn't the president, this was his brother. Nothing really interested him very much anymore at this time, politically or otherwise. I don't think he really had even had a thought about his own career." He was feeling, he told Kenny, that he just had to get out. "I just want to get out of Washington," Bobby told Kenny.

But there was brewing, among those who refused to let the flame die, a push to draft Bobby Kennedy as Lyndon Johnson's vice president on the 1964 ticket. "President Johnson didn't like it," Kenny would say later. "He had moved in his own political fashion to stop Bobby. He had a fear of Bobby that was beyond belief. Bobby Kennedy had no part in it whatsoever. It was just strictly a one-way operation, but now the press had begun to conjure up whether there would be a confrontation between Robert Kennedy and President Johnson."

It made great copy as the presidential campaign began to get under way in early 1964. The talk began to heat up just as the New Hampshire primary approached. "Bobby was just coming around to talking politics and sense. Then the New Hampshire thing boils up," Kenny said. "Bobby and I had our first political discussion over this and as I recall he told me he had no part in it. He understood there were friends of his that were involved in it, Kennedy people, Jack Kennedy people. Like all the rest of us, they didn't want to give up the White House." Bobby, said Kenny, was the heir apparent to them and they didn't know or care about Lyndon Johnson. They had been opposed to Johnson for ten years, and their resentment became almost an emotional transfer from Jack to Bobby. Johnson stood in the way; the fact that he was president became a minor point.

Kenny had managed a fairly solid relationship with Johnson. "I think President Johnson trusted me," he would say later. "He didn't think I was a liar. He may not have liked my attitude on some occasions. But I think without any question that if I had been willing I would have been appointments secretary. He came out one day and said, 'I don't want anybody [else] ever to sit at this desk as long as I'm president of the United States.' And he meant it. He had great confidence in my judgment politically, and we talked every single day. He chased me all over the place."

Now, however, sitting at the same desk where he was when Jack Kennedy was president, Bobby Kennedy's best friend was the most suspect person in town. "The situation obviously created a very suspicious relationship between the president and myself. He couldn't believe that the [Bobby Kennedy promoters] Bill Dunfeys, Bernie Boutins, and the John Kings weren't getting their instructions from me."

At one point Bobby did call Kenny and ask him what he thought about his running for vice president. "I told him I thought it was asinine — find whoever is doing it and tell them they ought to stop. And then we had a discussion about him making a statement and I said, 'Well, if you're not involved in it, then you should not make a statement.' 'Why?' Bobby asked. 'Because I think that magnifies it. I think you ought to tell the president of the United States you're not involved in it.' " Johnson did want Bobby to make such a statement, and he made that clear to Kenny. Kenny disagreed. "Look, Mr. President, why should he deny something that he isn't involved in?" Johnson was forced to let the issue go — temporarily. "President Johnson needed me more than I needed him at that point," so Kenny got his way.

But the president wasn't sure he needed Bobby. On the way to the funeral of Philadelphia mayor Bill Green in December of 1963, Johnson made his position clear to Kenny. "If I need Bobby Kennedy, I'll be the first guy to ask him. We'll wait around and look at the situation. If I can't win the election without a Kennedy on the ticket, I am going to take Bobby Kennedy. I'm not that proud. But I don't want to go down in history being elected by a Kennedy if I can help it. I would like to be President Johnson."

"Bobby had to think of his own future, and the thought of running for the United States Senate first entered his head at that moment, I'm sure," Kenny would recount. "Running for the Senate was suggested by friends in New York, more than by himself and by newspapers, who had made the vice presidential thing a *cause célèbre* now for a period of four months and were looking for something else to write about." For his part, Bobby really looked askance at the whole idea of being vice president. "He downgraded it because many of the people around him downgraded it," Kenny said. "It was something that he and I argued about. I said to him, 'Look, Bobby, the vice president is the second most powerful job in the world. Your brother ran in 1956; he tried to kill people to be elected vice president of the United States. When have we reached the moment of arrogance in our life that we say it's not important? I don't mind you not wanting the job, and I don't think you should take it either. I think you should run for Senate. But let's not downgrade the position either.' " Bobby had never envisioned himself as a political candidate. In years past he had evaded Kenny's pleas to become a candidate in Massachusetts. "He was leaning toward New York, but politically he was just not mentally there yet."

Of Kenny's role after the departure of the attorney general, Bobby would say, "I don't know what he is trying to prove—he spends more time at the Democratic National Committee than at the White House. He just can't stand being at the White House." Yet the new president was relying heavily on Kenny's savvy and connections as he made the transition into assembling his own staff. "He may not like me," Kenny told Bobby of his relationship with Johnson, "but I'm the only one of the Kennedy people he can trust." Theodore Sorensen and Arthur Schlesinger had resigned. The Irish Mafia remained intact: Kenny and Larry O'Brien were at the White House, with Dick Maguire at the Democratic National Committee. Some Johnson people made it clear they were wondering why O'Donnell and O'Brien didn't leave. "Our relationship with Johnson was pretty good, considering," Kenny said. He remained tense and uncomfortable at the White House. Johnson, sensing his discomfort, offered Kenny the executive directorship of the Democratic National Committee and said he could keep his job at the White House, plus the DNC.

Yet he remained wary of Kenny's continuing connection to Bobby. At about six o'clock in the evening, he would invite Kenny into the Oval Office, close the door, and have a few drinks. It was then that Johnson would begin to grill Kenny about Bobby's intentions and how Kenny would handle a direct conflict between the two of them. "I told him over and over again," said Kenny, "that if Bobby Kennedy decided to run for vice president of the United States in a direct confrontation with the president of the United States, then I would resign from the White House and go to work for Bobby Kennedy that next minute. Because my loyalty would be to Bobby Kennedy. I would recommend against Bobby doing it, but Bobby was my friend. Period." Johnson would ask again and again. Kenny's answers would always be the same.

The more Bobby discussed it with Kenny and Jackie, the more sure he was that he had to make an independent place for himself on the political landscape. By May 1964, he had really made up his mind to run for Senate from New York. The final decision was reached at a meeting at Hickory Hill attended by Fred Dutton, Steve Smith, Teddy Kennedy, Larry O'Brien, Kenny, and Ethel. "Teddy was the strongest that he ought to run for Senate," Kenny said. "Teddy had three or four discussions on the vice presidential matter and convinced Bobby that he really ought to get out and run for Senate. If there was one person who was responsible for helping Bobby move towards the Senate and the next phase of his life, besides Jackie, it would have to be Teddy."

Bobby knew he could have the New York Senate nomination if he wanted it. Although some behind-the-scenes maneuvering was required, the political pros would hand him the nomination for the asking. He would be the strongest candidate they could field against Republican incumbent Kenneth Keating. The members of the Kennedy team all agreed that Bobby should not seek the vice presidency but that the buzz about his potential run could benefit his political visibility. "It finally came down to this: Bobby would refuse to withdraw his name from the nomination," Kenny said. "So there went a moment of silence for about two weeks while Lyndon kept dropping bons mots all over town about who was going to be vice president, from Eugene McCarthy to Sarge Shriver." The whole purpose of Johnson's campaign, explained Kenny, "was to get rid of Bobby, smoke him out in some way and get him to announce for Senate, get him the hell out of the ball game." Bobby remained dutifully silent. Kenny balanced between his responsibilities to his current boss and his fealty to the Kennedys.

"There was not much give on either side," Kenny would say. A birthday party for Jackie at the F Street Club demonstrated the difficulties and strains Kenny felt in the relationship between the Kennedys and President Johnson. Both Kenny and Johnson, having just come from the White House, were all dressed in business suits. "We got there and everyone else was in white tails and it was a very important social event" featuring such Kennedy administration luminaries as Douglas Dillon, Robert S. McNamara, and McGeorge Bundy. Kenny was greeted warmly by the Kennedy crowd, especially by Bobby and Jackie. With many of them still in shock over the death of John Kennedy, events like this were especially important for maintaining the bonds that had brought them together. "Nobody, I mean nobody, spoke to Johnson," Kenny said. "He was sitting there in a rather baggy old suit like he always wore anyway. If you ever saw a fish out of water it was he. Everybody was surrounding Jackie and Bobby; they could hardly move. Finally the poor man came up to me and said, 'Kenny, would you mind coming back with me to the White House and have a drink?' "

Kenny gave Johnson his barely noticeable smile. "No, I would love to."

The two men left the party, climbed into the car, and headed back to the White House. "Geez," the president said to Kenny, "they just don't accept me. I am president of the United States and they just don't accept me!"

By July 1964, just as the Republicans were going to nominate the vocal conservative Barry Goldwater, who would almost certainly lead the party to defeat in November, Johnson knew he didn't need Bobby Kennedy anymore. The showdown came quickly. On July 29, Johnson asked Bobby to come to the White House. When Bobby arrived, he stopped outside the Oval Office to talk for a moment with Kenny. Much had changed in their level of comfort around the White House; their conversation was brief and whispered. "I had warned Bobby before he went in there," Kenny would say later. There was no question, Kenny told Bobby, that Johnson was going to tape the conversation, "so judge yourself accordingly." Bobby nodded. He understood.

After Bobby went in to see the president, Kenny left the White House and headed for the Sans Souci restaurant. Larry O'Brien was already there, waiting for him. Kenny's decision to leave the president and Larry's eventual decision to stay with him would in time mark the end of their friendship. Right now, they each took a drink while they waited for Bobby to join them. Finally, Bobby appeared. He was, said Kenny, in a very good humor. Shaking his head he slid into the booth, ordered a drink, and started to tell them what had happened. Bobby said that Johnson made clear he had thought a great deal about the vice presidency. He told Bobby "he wanted a vice president who could help the country, help the party, and be of assistance to him . . . and he concluded [his remarks] by saying that that person wasn't me." Bobby, admittedly relieved, said he would be glad to help the ticket in the fall.

A waiter brought a phone to the table, saying that the president of the United States was looking for Mr. O'Donnell. Kenny picked it up, "I just talked to your friend," the president began, "and I told him he's out and we got to write a statement."

Before Kenny could stop him, Johnson began telling his version of events. Based on what Bobby had already told him, it sounded to Kenny as if Johnson and Bobby had been in different rooms. "He talked about Bobby licking his lips," implying that he was highly nervous. "I just knew it was nonsense. I had told Bobby about the tape machine, that he was going to record every word he said, and I am quite sure Bobby's version was the honest one. Without a doubt."

Before the president could dig himself in deeper, Kenny cut him off. "Mr. President, for your information, I am sitting here now with the attorney general of the United States." Never would he call him "Bobby" to President Johnson. "So I don't want to be talking out of both sides of my mouth at the same time now."

There was silence. Perhaps Johnson thought he should have realized that Bobby and Kenny would be together. "Oh, fine," the president said, being as gracious as possible. "Would you come over here? I want to work with you on that statement."

Kenny left Bobby and Larry at the restaurant and headed back to the White House. Johnson was waiting. Calling him into his office, he again told him his version of the conversation, which according to Kenny was the exact opposite of what Bobby had just told him. Then they wrote out the statement. "It was that great historical statement where we knocked the whole Cabinet out. He was trying to think of some way to knock Bobby out by putting everybody from the dog catchers to Dean Rusk in the statement. In fact, they called poor Dean Rusk and these guys all over the country and said, 'Sorry you are not the candidate.' Dean Rusk, among many, said, 'I never knew I was under consideration.' It was a comedy, a comedy, and that's how I treated it, frankly." It was not the way John Kennedy would have handled anything. The transition of power was complete.

Bobby went back to the Justice Department where his "boys" were waiting, eager for news of his White House encounter. "I am sorry to have taken so many good fellows over the side with me." Bobby was joking about Johnson having to eliminate the entire Cabinet in order to disguise the fact that he was getting rid of Bobby. Robert F. Kennedy was now on his own. The man who had never wanted to be in politics, who always preferred the background, was finally, irrevocably, forced front and center.

First, however, he would take care of his friends. Nick Rodis saw no reason to stay in government; Bobby wanted to help him get a more lucrative job at IBM but Rodis demurred, opting instead to take a job coaching at Brandeis University. During their meeting in Bobby's Justice Department office, Rodis did make one promise. "Bobby," he said before he left, "I'll come back here when you are president." Bobby just looked at him.

While Bobby was privately committed to a Senate race in New York, publicly he kept himself theoretically available until it was clear Hubert Humphrey was going to be Johnson's choice for the number two spot. By giving everyone the impression that he was still interested in the vice presidency, Bobby was ensuring Johnson's choice of Humphrey, whose voting record was acceptable to the Kennedy forces. It was only the very real fear and threat of Robert Kennedy's candidacy that ensured Hubert Humphrey's selection. According to Kenny, "It was one of the greatest services that Robert Kennedy ever did for the United States of America and meanwhile the press is knocking his brains out. He wouldn't have taken the vice presidency if they gave it to him on a silver platter, but he was doing what we had asked him to do. I didn't just speak for me," Kenny said, "I spoke for Walter Reuther, George Meany, and for all these guys. They were Hubert Humphrey guys and they all felt that Bobby was the only threat that they had over Lyndon. They felt Lyndon would take anyone over Bobby, and if he had to go to a second choice, he would take Humphrey. Bobby was the only way to force that to happen. Bobby played the game perfectly and got murdered for it then and afterward."

He announced his candidacy for the Senate just before the Democratic National Convention in Atlantic City, where he was scheduled to introduce a film about his brother. Even though Bobby had made his political intentions known, Johnson still harbored a deep fear that he would stampede the convention, and he would be forced onto the ticket. Johnson was taking no chances. His aide Bill Moyers had asked Bruno to head to Atlantic City and set up the convention for him. Bruno had checked with Kenny about the ethics of working for the new president and Kenny had encouraged him to do it. "When they got word that Jackie was going to appear, Marv Watson, who was chief of staff for Johnson, said to me, 'I want to know everything that the Kennedys are going to do. I want you to watch them very carefully and let me know immediately. We are not going to let Bobby and Jackie Kennedy steal this convention.'" Bruno was amazed that he was asked to conduct surveillance on the very man he had been loyal to for so long.

"The film tribute was supposed to be at the beginning of the convention," Bruno says, "but Johnson was so fearful of a stampede of the delegates for Bob Kennedy that he rescheduled it to prevent that." Jackie and Bobby were supposed to host a tea for the delegates. They had expected five thousand people, and Jerry said he thinks they got fifteen thousand instead. The crowd was so enormous that the glass doors leading to the reception room shattered from the pressure of people surging forward, hoping to either shake hands with or at least glimpse the former first lady and the late president's brother. It was an unnerving experience for both of them.

Jerry Bruno did stick close to Bobby Kennedy before he spoke to the delegates, but not because Marv Watson had told him to. He went to Bobby's hotel because he wanted to keep an eye on his old friend when he was under such stress. Bobby was worried about getting through his introduction in one piece, and he was concerned about the delegates' reaction. From Kenny, Bruno, and others, he knew how Johnson had manipulated the timing of his speech and this tribute. It made him uncomfortable, for it only further dramatized the difference in his relationship with Lyndon Johnson compared to what he had with John Kennedy. With his brother, he had been the ultimate insider. Now he was the outsider, the person the man in the White House disliked and feared the most. It had all happened too fast for him to fully grasp. Now they were in Atlantic City with all those forces under one roof, with him standing where his brother should have stood. It was a lot for one man to handle.

"Let's go," Bobby said. He and Bruno left the hotel and walked toward the convention. Bobby needed the air. They entered a greenroom behind the main platform. Bobby joked that Lyndon had probably stuck them in this room and wouldn't let them out until the convention was over.

"He was really tense, nervous. He didn't know how the delegates were going to react to what he had to say," Bruno remembers. "He wanted them to be more focused on John Kennedy than on him. He didn't want anything to take away from the tribute, and I think he was uncomfortable being center stage. He hadn't grown accustomed to it yet." They climbed the steps to the platform and he was introduced. The crowd erupted into cheers and deafening applause. This was the moment the Johnson camp had feared. "They wouldn't stop," said Bruno. "They just kept going and going, on and on and on. There was nothing anyone could do to stop them. Bobby tried; he finally had to give up. The moment and the sentiment just carried it on and on. He was barely able to contain his tears. In the end he couldn't."

His speech left the delegates weeping. After finishing it, he walked off the platform, behind the podium, where Bruno sat on the steps. "He came down and sat right next to me and we watched the film on his brother together," Bruno says. "It was almost physically painful for him," Bruno says. "The steps were so close to the screen that in order to see it, Bobby had to tilt his head back. He would watch for a while, then drop his head down again. When he lowered his head, I couldn't see his face anymore." After the film ended, he patted Bruno on the shoulder. "It's over. Let's go." With that, almost unnoticed, Robert Kennedy walked out. It was the end of the past and the beginning of his future.

20

THE SENATOR FROM NEW YORK

I realize as individuals we can't just look back,
that we must look forward.

— BOBBY KENNEDY

By the spring of 1964, Bobby's and Kenny's trips to the grave site, and their long walks and talks, had brought neither one much solace. Kenny spent most of his time at the DNC, avoiding the White House, with its memories and ghosts of what might have been. Bobby dropped two shirt sizes and seemed lost, without a compass. In June 1964, Edward was injured and nearly killed in an airplane crash in western Massachusetts. Stung by yet another Kennedy tragedy, Bobby remarked to Jackie, "Somebody up there doesn't like us." Bobby briefly considered leaving public life altogether. After all, politics was not his first choice; he never saw himself as a politician. In search of direction, he traveled with Ethel and some of his children to West Germany and Poland. The huge crowds and outpouring of emotion convinced him to finish his brother's journey. Recalls oldest son Joe, now a congressman, "The trip was amazing. The guy went through more car roofs than you could believe. People just wanted touch him, see him, and be touched by him." Upon his return to Washington, Bobby began to explore his options again. The trip had been exhilarating, lifting his spirits. LBJ's decision on July 27 to keep Bobby out of the vice presidential spot made the New York Senate seat the clear choice. Bobby announced on August 25, 1964, his intention to seek the New York Senate seat. On September 3, 1964, Bobby resigned as attorney general of the United States. He and Ethel met with LBJ in a cordial, if slightly uncomfortable, meeting at the White House. Bobby was gone, his brother was dead, and Kenny would soon follow Bob's lead. "[Bobby's] ambition was not for himself," said journalist Jack Newfield, "but to complete his brother's journey."

Bobby Kennedy was not a natural candidate. He was more accustomed to being campaign manager than the man in front of the voters and the media. He hated that some saw him trading on the Kennedy name as a candidate. Congress was not necessarily his first choice for political office either. According to Kenny, "Bobby was more interested in being governor than senator, but he was not constitutionally eligible to be governor of New York." To run for governor of New York he would have had to have lived in the state for the preceding five years as a registered voter, which he had not. "He either ran for the Senate or retired from politics," Kenny said.

Kenny used his position at the Democratic National Committee to send most of the old Kennedy crowd up to New York to work on Bobby's campaign. Almost as important was the money Kenny and Dick Maguire raised for him. "He ran his own campaign — well, really Steve and he ran the campaign in New York," Kenny said. The two political pragmatists Steve Smith and Kenny O'Donnell knew that Bobby would need a strong showing from Johnson at the top of the ticket to win his own race against a strong Republican incumbent, Kenneth Keating. New York City mayor Robert Wagner was a great help, but according to Kenny, "strangely enough Bobby Kennedy was in trouble with the very groups who should have been his greatest support and who should have been with him all the way," The New York liberals distrusted and resented Bobby's entrance into the New York political arena. Following the lead of *The New York Times*, the liberals were suspicious of Kennedy, citing his work for McCarthy and his campaign against Jimmy Hoffa, conveniently forgetting his lengthy record of accomplishments. Smith and O'Donnell already knew, and others would find out: Bobby was not Jack, and this was going to have to be a very different campaign from the ones the Kennedys had run before. Jack had always made it look so easy. As Bobby had learned again and again since Milton, some things didn't come easy to him.

*   *   *

Bobby's Justice Department assistant, John Nolan, and Ed Guthman, his departmental press spokesman, would spend the second half of 1964 helping out in New York and saw firsthand the transition Bobby had to make from political operative and administrator to public figure. During a day-long press interview that occurred as Bobby campaigned through lower Manhattan, they could see that Bobby was clearly uncomfortable with his new role. Jack Kennedy would have laughed, finessed the questions, made it all look easy. As a woman reporter from the *New York Post* tried to ask him questions as he drove from one campaign appearance to another and then another, Bobby was elsewhere. "Bob was sitting in the front. She was sitting in the back between Guthman and me," Nolan remembers. "Her questions were detailed. They went on a long time. He was not doing well with the answers. He would either say one or two words or sometimes not answer her at all. Ed and I were looking at each other, thinking, This is not good." Finally, she asked a particularly fuzzy question. Bob let it hang in the air for a moment. Finally, he turned completely around and looked right through her with a kind of half smile. "I'm sorry," he said, gently scolding, "I just don't do well with questions like that, and to be honest I simply don't like your questions."

"It was awful," Nolan says. "There was a really long, long pause with nobody saying a word. You could hear the sounds of the tires hitting the pavement." Bobby had turned around and was staring out the side window, lost in thought. The reporter "was so flustered that she never recovered." She continued to ask questions and he would answer with a simple yes or no, or more often than not say nothing. As John Nolan was learning, Bobby Kennedy couldn't fake it. "If you didn't get the beat, you didn't get to dance with Robert Kennedy."

"People would come up to Bob Kennedy to shake hands and ask him a question and Bob would often answer with a yes or a no," Nolan says. "The person would stand there kind of lost. People thought he was being rude, but he wasn't. He just wasn't a hail-fellow-well-met type of guy. He was not a back slapper. He couldn't do it."

Kenny was not a conversationalist either, Nolan points out. One day during their Justice Department tenure when the weather turned bad, Nolan had gone to Bobby to see if they should shut the government down. "We were getting calls from agencies asking if we were going to shut the government down because of the weather. Bobby told me to call Kenny, who said, 'Turn 'em loose and send 'em home.' Bob Kennedy could be very much the same way. He never used three words where one would do." Campaigning politicians often had to do the opposite.

The campaign had its painful moments independent of Bobby's demeanor. Kennedy was immediately accused of being a carpetbagger, a stranger come to New York just to run for office. In an attempt to blunt the charges, Bobby took John F. Kennedy, Jr., to visit the Kennedy childhood home in Westchester County, just north of New York City. There was only one problem; the advance people had gotten the wrong house. "It was awful," says Joe Dolan, whom Bobby had told to continue working at the Justice Department, against Dolan's protests that he wanted to join the senatorial campaign. "John had brought this huge stuffed seal with him, and so here were these photos of the two walking around Westchester County, Bob, John, and this stuffed seal by themselves, with all these photographers around, and they can't find the house!" The next day the phone rang in Dolan's home around 2:30 A.M. "Bobby said you can come," Ed Guthman told him. "First thing in the morning!" Dolan headed to the airport at dawn and called his boss, the acting attorney general Nicholas Katzenbach, telling him where he was going.

Johnson was going to beat Goldwater nationwide by twenty million votes, in Kenny's estimation, which made it difficult to get his people to cooperate with the Kennedy campaign in New York. Because of the personal animosity Johnson held for Bobby, the thought of Bobby as an independent senator was almost more frightening. "The two campaigns fought the entire time," he would say later. "If we didn't have our own fellows there, they would have given Bobby the shaft to his eyeball." During the last week of the campaign, Bobby was to campaign in Brooklyn and wanted Johnson to join him. The race was extremely difficult for Bobby because he wasn't a natural politician. He was much better attuned to being a campaign manager than a candidate. He was uncomfortable campaigning with President Johnson. It fell to Kenny to obtain Johnson's cooperation. The president was campaigning in Denver when he called Kenny in Washington at the DNC. "Kenny," said the president, "I don't mind your doing everything for Bobby Kennedy. I know you're working for Bobby and you should be. But I don't have to spend a whole day campaigning for him. You've got me all over the city of New York!"

"Mr. President," Kenny told him, "to be frank with you, I don't think he needs you." There was silence on the other end. "Did you read the latest *Daily News* poll?" Kenny asked. He knew well how to work Johnson. "He's going to win easy. If I were him, and I suggested to him just a few minutes ago, he's much better off alone because you're going to win anyway easy, but he needs a little more exposure. When you are there you will get all the adulation of the crowd and he's just there with you. I told him he's a hell of a lot better to go by himself."

"You did?" asked the president, surprised.

"Yup," Kenny replied. Soon Johnson was deciding that maybe he should go; after all, he didn't want to leave Bobby to campaign alone with all those crowds. "If there was going to be any crowd there he was going to go," Kenny said later.

Jerry Bruno had planned to do the New York advance work for Johnson, but he felt the Johnson people deliberately kept him away, fearing he would use the opportunity to make Bobby look good at the president's expense. With Kenny's intervention, he did get to handle one appearance with Bobby and Johnson. "There was one stop and it was in Manhattan. They had this motorcade together; I had really worked it in advance and the crowds were terrific. I rode in the motorcade with Ethel and Bobby. The crowds were huge and so enthusiastic that Johnson ate it all up."

"Jerry!" Ethel exclaimed to Bruno. "I don't know how we can ever thank you for the work that you're doing! You've done a wonderful job!"

"Ethel, he's working for Lyndon!" Bobby told her, waving to the crowd.

"Oh," Ethel said. They all began laughing.

*   *   *

After the election, President Johnson called Kenny into the Oval Office. He wanted, he said, to discuss who would be the next attorney general. Kenny was puzzled. Nick Katzenbach had been acting attorney general and had done a great job; Kenny had assumed, as had many others, that he would get the spot. "That's your decision, Mr. President," Kenny told him.

"No," President Johnson said. "No, I want you to make it. I want you to give me a list of five names that you recommend for attorney general of the United States, and then I will pick one of those five names."

Kenny said nothing. He never gave Johnson the five names, because as he explained later, "He would have just figured that I just got them from Bobby thirteen minutes before. Those five guys would be the first five guys who wouldn't get the job."

Bobby thought the story was very funny when Kenny related it to him. In the end, Katzenbach received the nod as attorney general. Down the road, it would be Katzenbach who would find himself in a strange position, several times at odds with his onetime boss and mentor, Senator Robert Kennedy. Katzenbach and Bobby clashed especially over Hoover's release of documents citing Kennedy's approval of wiretapping Martin Luther King, Jr.

Kenny himself was leaving the White House. He had decided to return to Boston and pursue his ambition, long put on hold, of running for public office. Since he had explored running for Congress in Worcester back in the early 1950s, he had held his own electoral aspirations in reserve. With John Kennedy's death, Kenny sensed this was the time to take the risk. He had never considered going to work for Bobby in the Senate. They would remain friends; he would still be one of Bobby's closest advisers. But now they would pursue different goals. Even if they were not partners they would be allies. "There was no question," Nick Rodis says, "that if Bobby needed Kenny, he was there; that was just it."

"When Bobby went into the Senate," Kenny said later, "he was determined to be a good senator. He wasn't thinking of the White House at all then. But soon events would overtake him. Vietnam was on the horizon."

Bobby, being a freshman, moved into one of the smaller Senate offices, which was soon jammed with furniture, staff, kids, dogs, and visitors. The office was located on the first floor of the building and became a natural stopping place for all sorts of visitors from all over the world. Although President Johnson had large Democratic majorities that allowed him to put through the social legislation that would make up what he called the Great Society, Bobby saw trouble on the horizon as the military buildup in Vietnam began in earnest. "I think that by the end of '65 Bobby had begun to make some judgments that Johnson might not last," says Kenny. At that time nobody agreed with him, but he would be proven correct.

One of the first pieces of legislation that Bobby Kennedy addressed as senator was the Appalachian bill that would provide extensive assistance to those suffering the ravages of poverty and it was part of the Great Society program. Bobby Kennedy had seen severe poverty in New York, among other places, during the 1964 campaign, and he wanted to amend the legislation so that certain southern counties in New York could benefit as well.

It was a cold, late January afternoon, when Senator Robert F. Kennedy rose to speak for his amendment. "Bob was waiting for his moment of recognition, when they called the bill up and you asked to be recognized," recalls Ron Linton, who was then working for the Senate Public Works Committee. "He was nervous, I could tell, because he was quiet and his hands shook slightly." He sat in his seat and kept rereading his prepared statement over and over again. "This was his first time speaking on the floor as senator. Nobody from his office was there, and he was quiet, intent on his statement." Just before he began to speak, he turned to Linton. "Where is Javits?" he whispered. "I want to do this with him." Bobby wanted the state's senior senator, Republican Jacob Javits, present to provide moral and political support.

"Senator," Linton told him, "respectfully, what do you care where Javits is? The minute you offer your amendment he will burst through those doors over there. Don't worry—he'll be here."

Bobby looked over toward the doors that Linton had pointed toward. At the very moment the Senate president recognized the senator from

New York, the doors opened and Javits came charging onto the floor. Bobby offered his amendment, and immediately Javits sought recognition to endorse it and make his own speech. As he was preparing to leave the chamber, relieved, he turned to Linton. "How did you know he was going to come in here from that way?"

"Because that is the Republican cloak room through those doors," Linton said to him. He had long known his way around the Senate. "The minute they saw you stand up they were on the phone to his office. They had been watching you through there from the moment you stepped on the floor, watching every move you made." Bobby chuckled as he headed back to his office. "Bobby may not have realized it," Linton says now, "but the minute he arrived in the United States Senate, he eclipsed every other senator there and was automatically in contention for the presidency." The only one who didn't seem to realize that was Bobby.

Bobby got as much attention outside the Capitol as he did within, both in New York State and nationwide. "He used to get tremendous crowds upstate; he just loved the people," Jerry Bruno remembers. "We would start at one end of the state and work our way across. We would go into these really little villages, and people would be just amazed to meet Bobby Kennedy." He was deeply interested in the issues that involved the often neglected northern part of the state. Often these terribly depressed communities vied against each other for both federal and state aid. Bobby helped to form a north county council that allowed them to work together to get aid and then share the money in the most effective manner. He wanted thirteen more downstate counties to share in the Appalachian aid.

Bobby toured the tenant farms of the economically ravaged Allegheny County. Bruno set up an encounter where Bobby was to meet a sheep farmer. As they walked into the woman's shack, the press in tow, Bruno watched Bobby react to the dirt floor, the potbellied stove, the cot, and the lone table and chairs. The farmer explained to Bobby that she lived on poverty assistance along with the little she got raising sheep. As she was talking, Bobby's eyes came to rest on the wall where a single

Kenny and Jackie Kennedy remained friends after Jack's death. *Courtesy of John F. Kennedy Library and Museum.*

Teddy and Bobby at the Senate, 1964. *Courtesy of John F. Kennedy Library and Museum.*

The O'Donnell family, 1966. The author is holding hands with her father. *Courtesy of John F. Kennedy Library and Museum.*

Left to right: Michael, Bobby, and David Kennedy, circa 1964. *Courtesy of John F. Kennedy Library and Museum.*

Jo and Dave Powers, Kenny and Helen, and Bobby during Kenny's gubernatorial race. *Courtesy of John F. Kennedy Library and Museum.*

Kenny campaigning for governor of Massachusetts, 1966. *Courtesy of John F. Kennedy Library and Museum.*

Kenny at a breakfast meeting with President Johnson, Senate President Carl Hayden, and Senate Majority Leader Mike Mansfield. *Courtesy of O'Donnell family.*

Kenny with LBJ, greeting officials from the Republic of China. *Courtesy of John F. Kennedy Library and Museum.*

Bobby and Kenny, 1966. *Courtesy of John F. Kennedy Library and Museum.*

Bobby surrounded by exuberant fans during his 1968 presidential campaign. *Courtesy of Helene Borinsky/John F. Kennedy Library and Museum.*

Bobby relaxes with his dog, Freckles, on his campaign plane, in 1968. *Courtesy of Helene Borinsky/John F. Kennedy Library and Museum.*

"My brother rode a white horse once." Erie County Fair, New York State, 1967. Jerry Bruno is on the right. *Courtesy of Jerry Bruno.*

photograph was hanging—a picture of a handsome young man in uniform. "Who's this?" Bobby asked.

The woman pulled herself to her full height. "This is my son. He's a soldier in Vietnam."

Bobby looked at her, concerned. "When your son returns from Vietnam, what is he going to be doing?"

"Well, I guess he'll help me take care of the sheep."

"Is that all he has planned for the future?" Bobby asked her. "To come back here, live here, and take care of the sheep?"

The shadow of poverty fell back across the woman's face. "Yes, sir," she said. "What other future is there for people like us?"

After they left the shack and headed back toward their car, Bobby walked with his head down, hands stuffed in his pockets. As they climbed into the car, he let out a torrent of frustration. "I can't believe this woman's son is going to come home from Vietnam, if he comes home, and live like that and take care of the sheep after sacrificing so much for this country. That's all we have to offer?"

Bruno didn't know what to say. Bobby stared out the window, tapping his hand on the dashboard just the way his brother used to when he got nervous or upset. He was now talking as much to himself as anyone, "I just can't believe this administration! I can't believe he doesn't realize what is happening to the poverty programs because of Vietnam! Doesn't he see that he could help these people out of poverty by putting the money from that war into these people's lives? And there is not a damn thing I can do to stop it!" Maybe he was thinking of how things would have been so different if his brother had lived, Bruno thought, how much more power he had to make changes when he was attorney general, brother of the president. "If anything stirred Robert Kennedy it was the programs that Johnson had gotten passed and then was gutting," Bruno says, "not taking them off the books—leaving them on the books—but funneling the money toward the war in Vietnam. To Bobby, that woman represented the real horror of what was wrong with this country and wrong with that war. Bobby thought we really owed an obligation to people like that woman and especially to her son. If anything drove him crazy, really ate at him and motivated him to run for president, it was his frustration that he saw all this happening and was helpless to change it."

Bobby had long been preoccupied with the living conditions of tenant farmers and migrant workers, not just in California but in New York State as well, and told Bruno that he wanted to witness the camps for himself. Bruno had resisted. "He was determined to see these camps and nobody could talk him out of it. So I reluctantly set it up. They were dangerous places and I wasn't keen on bringing him in there." Bobby and Senator Javits, with the press corps trailing, went to see one of the worst of the camps, right outside Rochester, where migrant workers picked onions, cherries, and apples and were housed in abandoned buses. Bruno had wisely not told the owner of the local farm that the senators were coming. Bobby and Javits climbed out of the car and headed toward the gate where the farmer was standing. The farmer stood menacingly at the gate, his shotgun pointed at Bobby. Waving the gun at him, the farmer said angrily, "Senator, I'm just telling you I don't want you to come on my farm. Don't try it!"

Bobby Kennedy looked straight at the man. "If you aren't doing anything wrong, you shouldn't have anything to fear." Senator Javits stepped forward, urging the farmer to put the gun down. The standoff lasted for what seemed to Bruno an excruciating several minutes. After some time the farmer finally relented, the presence of the news media making it difficult for him to turn Bobby down. The two senators finally got in and walked toward the buses. Bobby climbed aboard one. On the first bus there may have been ten or fifteen children crawling around on filthy mattresses. Some had the bloated stomachs that signaled malnutrition. There was no running water and no toilet facilities. As they toured the buses, Bobby talked to the workers and stopped to hug the children whenever he could. "The scene was horrible," Bruno says. "It was so awful it was hard to put into words."

Before they left, the two senators announced to the press that they were going to introduce legislation to regulate and prohibit camps like these. "This is why you go into politics," Bobby said when they got back in the car, "because you can use your position to help people in trouble." Neither Senator Javits nor Bruno replied. Bruno caught a side glance at Bobby. He was sitting straight in the seat, his face a portrait of sadness. Catching Bruno watching him, he turned away, but not before Bruno caught the tears welling up in the corners of his eyes. They drove in silence the rest of the way.

Ethel had remained home during a ski trip the Kennedys made to upstate New York, because she was a month away from delivering a baby. On January 11, 1965, Ethel woke up in the middle of the night, realized she was in labor, and called the police, who rushed her to Georgetown Hospital, where she gave birth to Matthew Maxwell Taylor Kennedy at around 4 A.M. After receiving a call from Joe Dolan, Bobby flew down to Washington, encountering several flight delays, and arrived late the following afternoon to find the press camped out around the hospital. He didn't want to have to face them and explain why he had only just arrived. According to Dolan, "He was mad at himself for not being there when Max was born, and he didn't need the press in his face as well." Because the front entrance of the hospital was closed for construction, the press were surrounding the side door. Dolan decided to spirit Bobby in through the front. The two men hurried past the startled construction workers. When they encountered some other press people, Dolan quickly ducked into a hallway that took them through the pantry and the kitchen. Bobby made it safely upstairs, spent over an hour with Ethel and Max, and emerged from the side entrance, where he was nearly overrun by the press. The headlines, which were front page the next day, read, BOBBY KENNEDY BARELY MAKES IT IN CLOSE RACE WITH THE STORK! Looking at the papers the next day in his Senate office, Bobby remarked to Dolan, "I guess that's what you call 'spin'!"

From the very beginning, for Edward Kennedy, the senator from Massachusetts, Bobby's coming to the Senate created challenges. Dave Burke, who was Ted's administrative assistant, remembers his boss's reaction to his brother's arrival. Burke had not yet seen Bobby at full throttle. "I'm telling you," Teddy explained to him, "he's going to drive us crazy. He'll have us doing this and doing that—we really have got to get cracking because he really is going to be all over me if we don't have everything on the ball and we aren't really accomplishing things!" At first Burke thought Ted was overreacting, until Bobby took his Senate seat. "It was like a hurricane arriving. He worked all the time and he drove his staff at a hundred miles an hour. Bobby to me was like an electric charge. He came into the Senate, hitting the ground running. He was always on the run. You knew then he was headed toward the White House—where else could he go? He wasn't going to play the usual Senate games—meaning you go along, do what you're told, and keep your mouth shut until your turn comes. That was not Bobby's style. He'd always been in Teddy's life, but now he was affecting my life, and I began to see why Teddy was so wired about his coming."

For Teddy the Senate was a career he was building for the long term. He saw himself as a Senate man. For Bobby, the Senate seemed to be more a stopping place en route to the White House. "Therefore in a strange way they were not competing with one another," Burke says. "Teddy would pull Bobby aside and say, 'You know, Bobby, you don't just barge in here and do that. Why don't you go talk to Senator X or pay more attention to Senator Y before you make that speech or offer that amendment. You don't want to offer that amendment without at least talking to the guy. You don't want him to hear about it on the evening news.' Teddy wasn't trying to criticize Bobby, but he was trying to show him that this is my house, my place, I have been here a while now, and I know how it works. I need you to respect my place."

In the chamber or at a hearing, the Kennedys always drew a crowd. "Whenever the two brothers appeared together, the whole Senate would come to a complete halt," Burke says. "Bobby would get furious because Teddy would always ask these really, really tough questions that he knew Bobby wouldn't be able to answer."

Trixie Burke, Dave Burke's wife, recalled another kind of interaction. "Teddy was making a speech on the Senate floor, and Bobby walked by and leaned down and said, 'Dave tell you to say that? He must have— you wouldn't even know what it meant!' Teddy got flustered and lost his place. He didn't think it was so funny at the time."

Experiences such as the ones he had in upstate New York brought home to Bobby how difficult it was as a senator to effect change. One of 535 legislators, he could no longer see a problem and simply take direct action to resolve it. For him the transition to freshman senator was particularly difficult, and in some way reiterated how much had been lost in November 1963.

Kenny knew that Bobby was an "action guy," as Joe Dolan put it, and the pace of the Senate frustrated him. "Bobby wasn't interested in making a speech for the speech's sake like a lot of guys are in the United States Senate," Kenny said. "He had worked for the so-called McCarthy Committee in '54. He had a lot of experience in the Senate. . . . I suppose particularly when you're an attorney and there's these guys making speeches for the TV cameras, it gets a little frustrating.

"Bobby Kennedy could have been a United States senator in 1960 like breaking sticks!" Kenny continued. "All he had to do was say, 'I'll take the seat.' But he didn't think that was where the action was. Bobby Kennedy was the kind of guy who wanted to do things. He didn't have the patience to sit around and deliberate and sort of tell a few fibs here and there about where you're really going. He thought things were too important for that. He and I talked when he took the attorney general's job. We walked around Washington for hours. I was urging him to take his brother's senate seat in Massachusetts, but he said no, he just didn't want to be a United States senator. Then his brother dies and there he is, because of circumstances in 1964, sitting in the Senate with Lyndon Johnson as president until 1972—seeing eight years of rustling around with these problems. I'm sure it was frustrating—nothing was being done, the situation was getting worse, and for him it was a very frustrating experience.

"This stuff about whether you're a Senate man or not a Senate man is just a lot of junk. You're a Senate man if you hang around and do what you're told for about ten years. Maybe then they'll let you be a Senate man. Until you get a committee that's worthwhile, it isn't really worth much. For Bobby to spend his days as a freshman senator when he's been attorney general of the United States, sitting on the National Security Council and certainly the closest man to the president of the

United States, that's pretty tough stuff. I am amazed he had the patience to do what he did."

Once in the Senate hearing room, Bobby was forced to wait his turn while two other senators droned on about some minor point of order. Bobby tried to be recognized or to interrupt, but was ignored or scolded. He sat in his chair, his face getting tighter and tighter, gripping the papers in his hand. He had a plane to catch. In total frustration, he growled, "Oh forget it," and threw his papers in the air, letting them cascade to the floor as he turned and stormed out of the hearing room. "The senators were stunned. They just sat there in complete silence," says Dave Burke. "They couldn't believe it. They had never seen anyone like Bobby before."

"That kind of senatorial stuff wasn't important to Bobby," according to Trixie Burke. "Bobby was used to taking executive action. Teddy was a legislator and Bobby was an executive—that was the real difference."

Bobby decided the way to handle the Senate was simple; he would try to work around it. So he identified the issues that meant the most to him—not just Vietnam, but the conditions of migrant workers and the poor, the Bedford Stuyvesant Project in New York—and then addressed them publicly, forcing the Senate to take up his public agenda.

In 1966, labor leader Walter Reuther approached Bobby's aide Peter Edelman, urging him to persuade the senator to attend a Senate hearing in California on the conditions of migrant workers, whom Cesar Chavez was trying to organize into a union. Reuther and his lieutenants believed a hearing featuring Senator Robert Kennedy could help Chavez win the national recognition he needed. Kennedy was reluctant to fly across the country, but he was persuaded.

Edelman knew that once Bobby began his questioning he would agree it was a good thing that he had, as he put it to Edelman, "dragged my tail all across the country." When they arrived at the hearing, already in progress, Bobby slipped into his seat just as a local sheriff was telling how he handled striking migrant workers. "We're arresting these farm workers while they are picketing, for their own safety."

Edelman watched from the side of the room as Bobby's face transformed. "Excuse me, Sheriff, what did you say? You are arresting these people why? Again please?" Bobby's experience from the McClellan Committee hearings was kicking in once again.

The sheriff shifted uncomfortably in his seat. "Well, Senator, we're arresting these people because we're afraid something is going to happen to them out there." Bobby asked the same question three times in three different ways, getting the same response from the sheriff each time. Edelman watched as the lawman dug himself deeper and deeper.

Just as they were about to break for lunch, Bobby leaned forward, staring straight through the sheriff. "Sheriff, while we are out at lunch, I suggest you read the Constitution of the United States before we come back for the afternoon session."

Cesar Chavez and the farm workers had the champion they needed. "He was a different kind of senator," said Edelman, "he saw the justice of Chavez's cause and he was very taken with individual leadership. He realized he could use his position to give voice to the voiceless. It wasn't always popular, but he was willing to take the risk and to make the difference. Isn't that what political power should be about?"

21

PUBLIC MEN

*At stake is not simply the leadership of our party or even our
country. It is our right to moral leadership of this planet.*

— BOBBY KENNEDY

For the O'Donnell household, the move from Washington to Boston in
1965 was a difficult turning point. The three older children, Kenny,
Kevin, and Kathy, had to leave high schools and friends behind. The
transition was easier for the two younger siblings, Mark and Helen. It
was perhaps hardest on Kenny's wife. Helen O'Donnell dreaded moving
back to Massachusetts. Helen loved the Washington whirl and her
friends like Ethel were all there. She had no friends in Boston and didn't
enjoy the prospect of being to close to her family. She had tried to talk
him out of it and begged him to work for Bobby in the Senate, but she
could not move him. Kenny had put aside his own ambition for public
office to work for John Kennedy, but now that was all gone. He was
free to make his own choices, just as Bobby was.

He and Jack had once discussed their futures after the White House,
as they stood on the Truman Balcony of the White House at the end
of a long and grueling day in November 1962, smoking cigars in the
cold air. John Kennedy began by outlining the upcoming campaign.
They needed to win by a landslide, a mandate that they hadn't had the
first time, so that they could accomplish all that Jack intended in his
second term. After the president outlined his plan for the next administration, Kenny asked him what he would do after his second term was

over. John Kennedy smiled; he had already decided on that. Jackie and the children had had enough of politics and campaigns. He would return to Cambridge and teach at Harvard University. "It's what I have always wanted to do. You're coming with me, aren't you?"

Kenny thought for a moment, Harvard—teach at Harvard after the White House? He had never thought of returning to Harvard and was stunned that the president wanted to go back and teach. After a moment Kenny found himself saying, "Yup."

John Kennedy nodded. "Good, I had planned on it."

His own fate had been bound up in the Kennedy brothers. It was only now that his experience in politics and government with Jack and Bobby had given him the platform to take the greatest risk of his life.

His first campaign event was an appreciation dinner, held on January 22, 1966, at the Sheraton-Boston Hotel. Kennedy speechwriter Dick Goodwin had written an eloquent speech for the event. Despite a snowstorm, two thousand people overflowed the Sheraton ballroom. Mike Mansfield and Ted Kennedy came, along with many other luminaries. Kenny was nervous giving his speech and spoke so fast nobody understood a word he said. Like Bobby in New York eighteen months before, he was not a natural candidate. *The Boston Globe* described the event this way: "It was all a Kennedy affair—the people, the style, the smoothness of the operation. There were many of the familiar faces of the 1000 days of the Kennedy administration in Washington."

One of those familiar faces belonged to Bobby Kennedy. Bobby had been eager to help Kenny, but it had been up to Kenny to ask. With the campaign kickoff looming, Helen urged Kenny to summon Bobby to Boston. Kenny wouldn't. "He wouldn't admit that he needed Bobby's help," one friend says. "I guess he didn't want to ask." Helen had no trouble asking. Tracking down Bobby in New York, she told him flat out, "Get your ass up here. He needs your help."

"I am very pleased to be here," Bobby announced as he began his speech. "I am pleased to come to a place where they understand my accent!"

It's really marvelous what Edward Kennedy has done with the Democratic party in Massachusetts. You know, not everyone could unite it like he has. I keep reading all these stories about the older Kennedy brothers never came back and paid any attention to the Democratic party, but that he did. I thought they emanated from his office—those stories!

They talk about me being ruthless—I've read in the paper about the fact that he wants an open convention and he wants a free choice by representatives of the Democratic party of all candidates in the State of Massachusetts—I see that. His idea of an open convention is to get all the delegates and have a free debate, have a free discussion of the candidates and then let him make the choice!

I understand that Kenny O'Donnell was not going to run for office unless at least two or three voters spoke to him and asked him to run. But I am delighted to be here and join with you in honoring him, and in paying tribute to him. Not only have I come today because he has been a life-long friend of mine and because we have been through many battles and struggles together prior to the time that we ended up in Washington in the fall of 1961. I come here chiefly, because of the great contribution that he made during a difficult time of history in the United States.

I can say quite honestly and openly that there wasn't a major decision that was made by President Kennedy during the period of 1961 to November 22, 1963, that Kenny O'Donnell didn't share in. There wasn't a problem brought up—and I am really not even restricting it to major decisions—there wasn't a question that arose in the White House that the president of the United States passed on that Kenny O'Donnell didn't know about or really wasn't involved in.

Any matter that needed counsel or advice from someone with determination, courage and good sense, Kenny was turned to. I don't care whether it was in the field of civil rights, the problems we had in Mississippi, or whether we should send legislation to Congress. Kenny O'Donnell was called in and his advice and counsel was asked. During the Cuban Missile Crisis he was one of the two or three major advisers to President Kennedy. During Berlin, the crisis of 1961, 1962 Kenny O'Donnell's advice was sought by the president of the United States . . . his advice more often than not was good advice. He seemed to always come down on the right side of these matters.

I come here not because of the long friendship that I have enjoyed with Kenny — it goes back to 1944 and 1945 — but I come here because I feel that he is a distinguished public servant — because he has given of himself. He has the courage and the tenacity of purpose and because he had dedicated himself to his country, to this state and to the people of the United States — which is an inspiration to all of those of us who served with him. I am honored and pleased to call him my friend.

"There was no better statement of their friendship than Bobby's speech that evening," Justine O'Donnell says.

Robert Kennedy did not endorse him that night because Kenny hadn't asked him to, because he hadn't announced his decision to run for governor. Paul Kirk, son of a locally famous jurist, ran the O'Donnell-for-governor campaign, often traveling with Kenny to various events around the state. Kirk later himself became chairman of the DNC. They would joke about how everywhere they went people knew who their fathers were — Judge Kirk and Coach O'Donnell — but nobody knew who they were. Kenny had a lot of work to make himself a well-known and viable statewide candidate. Justine ran the main headquarters on Tremont Street; Kenny's crackerjack secretary Marge Evans stayed with Kenny at the Arlington Street office.

By the middle of the campaign, running against Republican John Volpe, Kenny had hit his stride and felt more comfortable giving speeches and meeting voters. However, the man who had always been in the background and made the wheels turn was ill suited to be a political candidate. He was not comfortable in the venue and, as his sister Justine would realize, it showed. "I was after him to come in and meet the volunteers in the Tremont Street headquarters. Finally, he came in. Walking in the office, he spotted the daughter of one his close friends, made a beeline straight for her, talked to her about her father for several minutes, and then turned and went into the private office to talk with his brothers about the day's events. I went in after him and told him he had to come out and meet each volunteer and shake their hands. He shook his head. 'Look, Justine,' Kenny said, 'I just can't do that phony stuff. I don't know how.' "

"Learn," Justine ordered. "You should have thought of that before. Now get out there." He nodded. He went out and did the best he could.

Kenny's older brother, Cleo, and younger brother, Warren, dropped everything and got involved in the campaign. They were both gregarious, charming, witty, and funny. They would tease Kenny often that if he just stood there and talked politics and government, the two of them could stand in front of him to do the hand-shaking and the voter-wooing. As Justine put it, "Cleo and Warren had all the charm and warmth. If they could have gone out and campaigned as Kenneth, he might have won!"

Money was the real problem. There was just never enough of it. They didn't have the Kennedy money or the Kennedy name that could help them build a war chest. Making the situation worse was Kenny's abhorrence of asking people for money. It was something that had taken root in him as a young man in Worcester. He hated money, hated worrying about money, and refused to seek it out. In running a major statewide campaign, that was a problem.

Helen hadn't adjusted well at all to being front and center in public life. Out of her element in Boston, with her friends left back in Washington, she felt alone and terrified. She had always enjoyed the Washington ambiance, the Washington life—being a big shot, as she and Kenny had joked. But never did she ever think that she and Kenny would be out front in public the way they were now. That was the sort of role to be played by Jack and Jackie or Bobby and Ethel. She hated speaking in front of crowds, feared the press, and hated that he was doing this to her. She found refuge more and more in alcohol, holing up in the huge brick colonial they had bought in Jamaica Plain, missing scheduled events, showing up late or not at all.

The first time she failed to show up at an event that featured her,

Kenny was shocked. Helen had always been at his side—she was the tough one, he had joked. Helen had been scheduled to speak at a women's garden party. The press, curious about the reclusive Mrs. O'Donnell, would show up in significant numbers. Two hours before the event, she called Justine. She wasn't coming. She couldn't. Justine could not persuade her. It was too late to cancel, and Justine couldn't find Kenneth, who was on the road; she had no choice but to go herself. Racing to Filene's, Justine bought a dress, had her hair done, and barely made it to the event in time to speak briefly and painfully before the garden party crowd.

Kenny was furious. In the end, he would never forgive her for letting him down, and she would never forgive herself for letting him down again. She had not been able to help after Jack died, he secretly felt. Now she had abandoned him again. Neither he nor she nor anyone else acknowledged the true culprit, the disease of alcoholism, which would creep in like a thief to steal their love and destroy their marriage. The downward spiral of the bottle had begun. In the end it would consume them both.

Paul Kirk said, "Kenny was at once a private man who, by 1966, I believe, wished to continue to be a public personality. Running for governor in 1966 was the right thing for him to do, and if he had only had a better staff he might have succeeded and found the public challenges he needed to satisfy his public and professional day-to-day activities." He needed something, as Kirk put it, to "fill the void."

Kenneth O'Donnell lost the Massachusetts governor's race by a scant two votes a precinct.

Shortly after Bob's election to the Senate, Barrett Prettyman got a call from Ed Guthman. Guthman asked Barrett, "Could you come to New York after Bob has seen Tom Watson of IBM to get his thoughts?" "Sure," said Barrett, sitting in his law offices at Hogan & Hartsen in Washington, D.C. On Sunday night, Barrett boarded the train north, got a small room at the Statler, and first thing on Monday got in touch with the Federal Housing Administration, which had told him about eight pieces of property in New York City already owned by the city adjacent to federal housing projects. Bobby was hoping to use the property to build a playground for inner-city kids. The FHA supplied him with a car, a driver, and a guide, and until 4 P.M. that afternoon they toured the worst parts of New York City. Only for Bobby Kennedy would he put himself through this, thought Prettyman as they left the last place. At four he called Ed Guthman at the Carlyle, where Bob had an apartment, to tell him of the day's events. "Why don't you come over?" suggested Guthman. New York traffic being what it was, it took three quarters of an hour to make it there.

When Prettyman got to Bob's apartment, Guthman let him in. Bob was meeting with the head of the public school system. Prettyman was exhausted, hot, and in need of a shower. Guthman directed him toward a bathroom, where he showered and put on the new cuff links that he'd bought at Gimbels for ninety-nine cents (he had forgotten his own). Emerging from the bathroom, showered and refreshed, he got his first lay of the land, so to speak. There were three phones in the apartment with four or five buttons on each. They rang about every five minutes, and a girl in the living room would answer and take messages. The apartment had a big hallway, a living room, two big bedrooms, and two baths. Barrett didn't notice any kitchen. Having seen Ethel and Bob's kitchen at UVA, he was sure they must have help. At least he hoped they did. The beds were covered with unsigned thank-you letters, congratulatory telegrams, and magazines with stories about the Kennedys. On the table were pictures of John Kennedy, Bob's kids, and the whole Kennedy clan.

Finally, the guest left, and Barrett found Bob in the living room. After greeting him warmly, Bob said, "I've got to go to the doctor." So Bob, Prettyman, and Guthman all grabbed their coats and headed out the door, leaving the girl to manage the phones herself. When they walked out of the hotel, there was a car waiting, driven by a New York detective assigned to Bob. Bob rode in front as usual, Guthman and Prettyman in the back. They headed to another hotel and straight into the doctor's office, going through an anteroom full of waiting patients. Guthman and Prettyman followed the wave of Bob's hand as they walked into the examining room. It was typical Bob Kennedy, never wasting a minute;

they could talk while the doctor worked. Entering the room, the doctor greeted them. Bob took off his trousers and pulled himself onto the table. He grunted in obvious pain and almost jumped off the table when the doctor felt his calf muscle. In the meantime, Bob was relentlessly giving the doctor a hard time, telling him how terrible he felt, that the only leg that felt good was the one the doctor hadn't touched; the other one was as bad as the first day he had walked in. As Prettyman watched, the doctor nervously seemed to enjoy the ribbing, although at other times he seemed unsure. Finally, the doctor told Bob he was going to have to begin to take better care of himself. He would have to get a shot, treatment for two days, and then another shot.

Bob looked unhappy. "Are you going to hurt me now?"

"Yes," said the doctor.

"Well," said Bob, feigning an intimidating expression, "can't you think of something else to do?"

"No," said the humorless physician.

With the examination over, the three men headed down in the elevator, and Bob began telling Guthman and Prettyman that a night or two before, one of his sons had fallen all the way down the stairs. Ethel, who was pregnant at the time, had been resting but heard the commotion and rushed to find the boy unconscious at the foot of the stairs. Terrified, she called a neighbor who was a doctor; he came in and said he thought the boy had a broken neck. Ethel was terrified. Fortunately, she kept it together and stayed with her son as he was rushed to the hospital, where the neighbor's diagnosis was found to be incorrect. The boy was fine and went to school the next day. All in all, said Bobby, it showed that the stuff Ethel dealt with was far tougher than anything he had to handle. It had been scary. As they left the hotel, there were the usual gapers—young girls standing with their mouths open; old ladies who practically hugged each other at the sight of him; men who looked, turned back, and looked again, admiring him but not wanting it to show. Barrett watched to see if Bob had gotten used to it yet. He decided he had not. To deflect the situation Bob joked that he shook hands with them only as part of his job, and Guthman said the only people he ever got to shake hands with were the rabbis. The trio climbed back into the detective's car and Bob asked the driver to stop at Jackie's (he called her Mrs. Kennedy). When the driver pulled up in front of Jackie's building, Bob said he would go up and meet the others back at the Carlyle. Guthman and Prettyman decided to walk from there, discussing the 1964 convention and the recent election along the way.

Returning to Bob's apartment at the Carlyle, Guthman and Prettyman began working through the unsigned telegrams and signed notes of congratulations. They were from everywhere: governors, mayors, diplomats, friends, and entertainers. Notes from Kenneth Royal, Josephine Baker, Kirk Douglas, and George Lodge—from everywhere. Eventually, the persistently ringing phone interrupted too many times for them to do anything coherent. Needing a break, they left a message at Jackie's that they would be in the Carlyle bar. Guthman and Prettyman were joined in the bar by a fellow named Ernie, a young politico Robert Wagner had assigned to Bob. Eventually Bob arrived in the bar. He slid into the booth and ordered a drink, and then discussion of the recent campaign began. Mrs. Jacob Javits was sitting at a nearby table with Ogden Reid. Mrs. Javits called over to Bob, who went over to her table and talked to her for about ten minutes, leaving his drink untouched except for perhaps a sip. Returning to the booth, he immediately announced that he was hungry and wanted to go. As they left the hotel bar to go to a restaurant for dinner, Bob borrowed twenty cents from Prettyman for a newspaper. Picking up the paper, he spied a huge headline saying that Jackie Kennedy thought she might have saved her husband if she had turned toward him after the first shot. Bob got upset, his hands trembling slightly; that haunted look returned momentarily to his blue eyes as he shook his head and said softly, to nobody in particular, "Damn, why didn't I take that out of her testimony? I didn't even see it. Why didn't I see that? Now she has to read it in the paper." As they headed toward the exit and the car, Bob's mind was racing back to Jackie, the testimony, what else he'd forgotten, his brother, what he could have done . . .

En route, Bob began to ask Prettyman about the reason for his visit— the playground. "Well, on the playground," Bob said from the front seat, as the New York detective dodged, honked, and worked his way through New York traffic, "are we going to do it?"

"Yes," said Prettyman from the backseat, leaning forward to talk to Bob, who was still facing front. Prettyman went on to tell Bob there were two sites he thought would work as playgrounds, either one in Harlem or one on the East River.

"How much would it cost?"

"Well," said Prettyman, unsure — he hadn't had time to figure out the costs — "the D.C. playground cost two hundred and fifty thousand dollars, plus donated equipment and services."

Bob whistled. "We'll never get that here. Tom Watson says the businessmen despise me. And we need to raise another ten million dollars for the Kennedy Library — we have gotten thirteen million to date."

Prettyman thought for a moment. The playground had worked in D.C., so "let me think about it and see if I can do something."

"Fine," said Bob.

They arrived at the restaurant, La Caravelle, and took their seats, Bob and Ernie facing Guthman and Prettyman. They ordered a round of drinks. The headwaiter was extremely polite, overly so, hovering around Bob, who seemed oblivious. They discussed the campaign again: how much Bob had learned since, in this case, he had been the candidate. It had been a different kind of experience for him. At some point during the dinner a "lighthearted" discussion of unity in the New York State Democratic party began, and quickly the conversation became tense. "I would have gone to Wagner and Harriman in advance and talked to them, and found out from them what they could all agree on, and then gone to the meeting with an agenda to discuss only those items, and agreed, and come out of it with harmony!"

Ernie replied, "Yes, but I couldn't go see them."

Bob looked at him intently. "Why the heck couldn't you? That's ridiculous!"

Ernie began to shift uncomfortably. "You don't understand local politics and what these guys are like."

Bob's blue eyes looked right through Ernie. "Don't tell me I don't understand!" said Bob, clearly annoyed. "I didn't go through all these campaigns for nothing. I know what they're like. I have a little political experience." Prettyman and Guthman winced, as Bob continued, "Look, all I am saying is, I think you did a lousy job. Now that's what I think. You screwed it up. You asked my opinion and now you have it. Don't ask if you don't want to know what I think." Ernie sat uncomfortably for a moment while Bob sipped his previously untouched drink. He rarely did more than sip his drinks—Prettyman decided half the time he ordered them just to take a couple of sips to relax him and have something to do with his hands. Bob could never seem to sit still for long.

Prettyman tried to fill the silence by discussing the financial committee to advise on a proposed Washington-to-Boston high-speed train run. Listening to the difficulties Prettyman was having, Bob suggested that he go see Harriman in Washington on Friday. If it could be done, he would help; if he couldn't help, he wouldn't waste your time. The conversation then shifted back to the New York State Legislature, and whether Bob was going to keep his hands off the legislature. Bob was annoyed. "Look, Ernie, would it be smart or stupid for me to meddle with the legislature?"

Ernie looked down at the table, not sure how to reply. Bob Kennedy was not the kind of politician he was used to dealing with. "Stupid," said Ernie tentatively.

Bob stared at him for a moment. "Do you think I'm stupid?"

Ernie shook his head vehemently, playing with his drink. "No, I think you're smart."

Bob looked at him, blue eyes snapping. "Then why do you have to come to me with that kind of question? Why can't you tell them yourself, emphatically, that I am not going to meddle with the legislature? That is why you are here, isn't it?"

Ernie shifted in his seat, exposed and uneasy. "Well, I—"

Bob cut him off. "What I resent," said Bob, not yelling, his voice quiet and deadly direct, "is that you're calling me stupid. That's the implication."

Ernie shook his head, color draining from his face. Clearly this was not going the way he intended. "No," said Ernie, "I am not. But these guys want me to talk to you—"

Bob cut him off again. He was tense. Hands fiddling with the glass, blue eyes staring right through Ernie, Bob said, "Do you think I give a darn what they want? What have I got to do with the legislature? The trouble with you guys, Ernie, is that you've been backbiting and conniving and suspicious for so long among yourselves, and trying to guess what the other guy's motives are, that you don't know any better—you can't believe someone is just playing it straight. God," said Bob, his frustration in full view now, incensed that someone, anyone, would question his honesty, "my son David knows better than that! My father used to say, 'Even my son Teddy knows better than that,' and Teddy was four at the time. My father was still saying it twenty years later, until Teddy came to him and said, 'Look, Dad, you've got to stop that. I'm twenty-four now, and it looks bad.'" The humor deflected the conflict. Everyone laughed including Ernie, who was embarrassed but relieved that Bob had let him off the hook.

Discussion turned to the so-called "well-oiled Kennedy machine," and Guthman told a related story about one of Bob's sailing trips in Maine: A salty old seaman had come aboard and, after having watched the Kennedys in action, remarked, "If they are running the boat the way they are running the country, we are all in trouble!" Everyone laughed, and then the white wine Bob had ordered with dinner arrived. The waiter poured a small amount in a glass for Bob to taste, but Bob, thinking such gestures foolish, paid no attention to him. The waiter stood there confused, until finally Ernie nodded to him. The waiter shrugged, still confused, and filled all the glasses. Bob was never in need of theatrics or pretense; it was the political point he had been trying to make to Ernie. Bob devoured his dinner and then, as they were talking, began eating off Prettyman's plate, asking if he was going to eat his roll or this or that, not waiting for an answer as he helped himself. Having known Bob since law school, Prettyman was hardly fazed.

After dinner when Bob rose from the table, Prettyman noticed what he had seen all through dinner: that all eyes were on Bob. People had tried hard to pretend they were paying attention to their partners, but the entire time they had been focused on Bob. As they left, the head-waiter shook hands with Bob and followed them out into the street.

The men stood in the street talking for some time. The detective talked about Mrs. Kennedy, how it took a detail of twelve agents to guard her. She still got a minimum of four or five death threats per week, which was fewer than Bob received, but Bob, the senator, refused protection, feeling it was foolish. Look at how much protection his brother had had. It had all been for nothing.

Bob began telling about how Jackie had suggested that he give a luncheon for local politicos, since they were still so suspicious of Bob. They had tried to arrange dinner at "21," but found that even a hamburger without drinks cost eight dollars a plate, and Bob said he couldn't give anyone a hamburger—it would be an insult. "We called Toots Shoor, who said we shouldn't pay over eight dollars with drinks, so we dropped the idea and decided to write letters instead. Jackie said she would be happy to give them cocktails, and we agreed that if she did that, we could feed them newspapers." Everyone laughed.

Suddenly a woman appeared at Bob's side. She had a bet with her husband that it was really Robert Kennedy. Was it really him? Bob looked surprised. "It was really him," he said, slightly embarrassed. He shook hands with them both. That was when Prettyman noticed that while they had been standing there talking, a crowd had begun to gather. The woman and her husband seemed to open the floodgates, and suddenly everyone was pressing forward, shaking Bob's hand. People waved or yelled from their cars; some stopped in the middle of the street. The lone detective was nervous and began pressing Bob toward the car. Finally he succeeded in getting Bob away from the crowd and into the vehicle.

When they returned to the Carlyle, Bob stopped Ernie to make one last point. "You just don't understand us"—his voice was direct but softer this time—"do you? You don't understand what Ed Guthman and Barrett Prettyman and all of us—what we are doing, what we want. You don't think there are things that should be done, and we think we can do them." Ernie stared. He was trying to understand, but he had never before met a politician who actually believed politics was about accomplishing what you set out to do.

Frustrated, Bob said good night to him and, with Guthman and Prettyman, got into the elevator and headed upstairs. Bob looked sad and discouraged in the elevator, so Prettyman tried to break the silence:

"Ernie seems like a pretty good man." Bob nodded. It was 10:30 and the long day, the long campaign, had begun to take their toll. He looked tired but still had several hours of work—phone calls, letters, reading— to do tonight. "Yes, he is, but of course he is the best of the whole lot. But he still doesn't understand, none of them do. To them it's a game. To me it's people's lives." Bob shook his head.

They entered the apartment. Prettyman got his briefcase and bade Bob good night, leaving Guthman and Bob to continue working their way through the masses of paper and telegrams. Heading back to his hotel, Prettyman decided that Bob was getting used to it now, the recognition, the way the crowd tore at his clothes and his hair during the campaign. But as he sat in the cab weaving its way through New York traffic, he decided Bob was really going to make a difference, turn politics in this county on its ear. Yes, he was going to be fine, and he was going to be around for a while.

Bobby Kennedy spent much of the fall of 1966 campaigning for Democratic candidates around the country and in the process began to realize the extent of his own popularity. "The crowds were tremendous, just tremendous. It was like a presidential campaign. It gave him the feeling of what it would be like," Jerry Bruno says.

In California, Bobby debated Ronald Reagan, who was running for governor against the Democratic incumbent, Pat Brown. As Bobby left the event, he turned to Bruno and nodded his head toward Reagan. "Reagan is a really sharp cookie and everyone is underestimating him," he said. "He's somebody to watch. I think he could go all the way." At the last stop, in Washington State, where they campaigned for Tom Foley for Congress, Ethel had made a huge sign that she held up for the cameras: JERRY BRUNO IN '66, HIS BROTHER IN '68! "She was teasing me but also sort of hinting about what she thought Bob should do in 1968. If he didn't know where things were going, she had a sense very early that he was going to have to be himself," recalled Jerry Bruno.

Bobby's twenty-seven-state tour was a different experience for him; there were crowds at the airport, along the motorcade route, and everywhere he appeared. At one point he remarked to Bruno, with a mixture of sadness and amazement, "I think they are really here for me, not just him." Moving out of his dead brother's shadow, Robert Kennedy was coming into his own.

President Johnson and Bobby were scheduled to campaign together across upstate New York. Neither man was looking forward to the experience. After Bruno had set it up, he picked Bobby up and they headed to the Syracuse Airport to meet up with Air Force One. "Do I have to do this?" Bobby kept asking, even though he knew the answer. As the plane rolled to a halt, Bobby insisted that Bruno join him for the jumps with Johnson from one upstate city to another. Sitting side by side with him on Air Force One, Bruno watched Bobby "holding on to the arm rest, then tapping his teeth, looking out the window, his whole body tense, uptight. Every time I would get up to go to the men's room or anything, Bob would grab me hard by the arm and say, 'Where are you going? Sit here!' forcing me back into the seat next him. I sat sort of as a buffer between him and Johnson. Johnson and Bobby didn't really talk. Johnson tried a few times, but Bobby didn't really respond. He would answer with one- or two-word answers. Bobby didn't make any effort to talk to him. It was a very, very cool ride on Air Force One. Very cool. The problem," Bruno sums up, "was that if Bob Kennedy didn't like someone, he couldn't fake it. He just wasn't capable."

As they disembarked from the plane in Newburg and climbed into Bobby's car, Bobby visibly relaxed. They started to leave the airport when Bruno had an idea. "How about some ice cream?" Bob loved ice cream, especially Howard Johnson's chocolate. Wherever they were, whether in New York or across the country, Bruno would always make sure he located the local Howard Johnson's. He would make sure that in Bobby's hotel room there was a half gallon of ice cream waiting for him. After the White House doctor Janet Travell had once told him his cholesterol was too high and that he had to cut out steak, butter, sour cream, and ice cream, especially ice cream, Angie Novello caught him devouring a bowl of chocolate. He smiled and said, "Well, I stopped for the day she told me!"

Now as they drove, Bobby stared out the window, lost in thought. Finally he said, "That was the first time I have been on Air Force One since my brother died. The last time I was on it was to take his body off." Bruno didn't reply. There was little he could say. It had never occurred to him, or to President Johnson.

"When he went into the Senate he was like a flower in speed up that would blossom more and more every day," Barrett Prettyman declares. "He learned about life as he went along. He was always growing. The important thing about Bobby is not just that he experienced things, but that he said we have got to do better. He experienced things and then he did something with those experiences. It wasn't just speeches. He saw something that was fundamentally wrong and didn't make sense, it was unacceptable; and so he would fix it, change it, improve it. The Senate pace sort of made him crazy. He never yelled or screamed. He would give you the eye and say something to you very softly, so nobody else heard, but very directly; you got the point. He very seldom shouted or said flowery things in speeches. Bobby was at his best when he was at his quietest."

He also recognized the political power inherent in his own personality. "He was very genuine," said Prettyman, "but he understood his impact with people. Once Bobby and I were going through the Atlanta airport coming up on a bank of telephones, and there was this young girl, nineteen or twenty, talking to her friend on the telephone. She turned and spied Bobby. He was walking along, brushing his hair back in that absentminded way, jacket on, but tie pulled down, his hair too long, and suddenly the girl starts screaming into the phone, 'Jane, Jane, you won't believe it! Bobby Kennedy is walking by—no, really, Bobby Kennedy is walking right by me! No, I swear Jane, I swear he is walking by, he's coming along here and he's almost here! God, he's gorgeous!' She had her hand over her mouth, as if he were a rock star or something. Bobby took the phone from her and put it to his ear and said, 'Jane, it's me. Just wanted to chat with you. How are you anyway? Okay. Yes, it's really me. Have a good day!' The girl was just standing there. She couldn't even speak. He gave her the phone and we walked along and Bobby and I just started to laugh. How many senators do you know have that kind of impact?"

On March 3, 1966, Prettyman met with the senator on some dealings around a New York playground project Bobby was supporting. As the meeting broke up, Prettyman told Bobby, "If you ever need me to do any advance work, go on trips, carry out special assignments, et cetera, you only need to let me know and I'll try to arrange my schedule. I will of course pay my own way."

Bobby nodded and grinned. "How would you like to go to Alabama?"

Startled, Prettyman agreed and ten days later met Bobby and Ethel at their new New York City apartment at the United Nations Plaza and flew with them to the University of Alabama, where Bobby would give a speech that had already been highly publicized. The plane trip was awful. They had to switch to a smaller plane to make it to the university, and the weather was terrible, tossing the plane through the air like a piece of paper. Ethel clung to Bobby's hand. Prettyman could only think how difficult this had to be for her. She had lost both parents and her brother and sister-in-law in plane crashes, and yet here she was. The pilot kept announcing that he didn't know where they were, but he was sure they would come out of this soon. Finally landing, the group headed to the campus. Ethel, Prettyman, and the others all sat in the front row of the auditorium, which was packed to the rafters with students.

Just as the senator was being introduced, a state trooper began to approach Prettyman. Leaning down, the trooper whispered, "I'm sorry. Mr. Prettyman, would you follow me." Ethel looked up at them, surprised.

Prettyman excused himself and followed the trooper through a side door into the hallway, where several state troopers and campus police were standing in a semicircle.

The trooper's face was deadly serious. "We just had word that the son of a professor is on his way over here with a gun to kill Senator Kennedy."

A sick feeling welled up in Prettyman's stomach. "Do you have people here who can recognize him?" Prettyman heard himself asking.

"Yes," the trooper told him. "But would Senator Kennedy consider not making his speech?"

Prettyman knew the answer, but he went out into the auditorium and handed a note up to Bobby, who sat waiting for the introductory speeches to conclude. He read it, crumpled it in his hand, and waved Prettyman off. Bobby had long ago decided that he wasn't going to live his life in fear and intimidation.

Prettyman spent the rest of the event on edge, watching the audience, the doorways, every stray movement in the audience. The young man's mother and father arrived, distraught, standing by the front doors in hopes of recognizing their son. The audience gave Bobby a thunderous ovation, after which he shook hands and stopped to talk to the students who had waited hours to hear him. They were grabbing, touching, screaming, pulling at him.

It turned out later the young man had been caught and stopped in the parking lot. It never made the papers. Bobby never asked about it or mentioned it. Only occasionally would he remark, as he had at the time of his sister Kathleen's death, "It's hard to plan ahead too far. You just never know."

Bobby was so busy that often he was oblivious to much of what was going on at Hickory Hill. His children were always his priority but being head of a large and chaotic family meant he didn't always have a command of what was going on in his own household. "Bobby had to go to New York one Monday morning," Joe Dolan remembers, "so I was picking him up at Hickory Hill to take him to the airport. It was November, a brisk, really cold day with the wind blowing. Bob came out of the house to get in the car; Ethel walked him out, as she usually did, to kiss him goodbye. Bob opened the back door and tossed his briefcase into the back. 'I'm going to go to New York, but I'll be back tonight, probably late.' 'Fine,' Ethel said. Before she could say anything else, Bobby's eyes drifted toward the workmen down by the pool house. 'Ethel, what are those workmen doing down by the pool?' Ethel looked around, wide-eyed. 'Oh, Bob, what are you talking about?' she asked innocently, easing him into the car. I could tell she was trying to avoid the question, so I just said the first thing that popped into my mind. 'They're building a movie theater, Bob!' Ethel gave me the dirtiest look you can imagine, and then she kind of pushed Bob into the front seat and slammed the car door and said sweetly, 'Oh, he's kidding, Bob!'

"Well, it turned out they *were* building a movie theater—expanding the pool house. You could go in the pool house and there would be forty pairs of shorts, bathing suits and sneakers—Bob and Ethel would just tell you to grab one that fit. The movie theater was supposed to be a surprise for Bob," Dolan says. "I almost blew it, but I didn't know. Afterward, every once in a while Bob would call me up, since we lived so close, and invite us to watch a movie with him. We rarely went. We sort of felt that was his time with his family."

For a September 1965 sailing trip, Bobby borrowed a beautifully restored schooner, the SS *Nehris*, built in 1917, which would be rechristened by the end of the Kennedy voyage, the SS *Nervous*. For a sail from Sag Harbor, Long Island, to Hyannisport, Barrett Prettyman accompanied Bobby, Ethel, and ten children ranging in age from five to fourteen. Six of the children were Kennedys, and four were friends, including one of Kenny O'Donnell's kids. The captain stared in disbelief; this was his crew.

Once the boat was under way, Bobby and the captain immediately had a disagreement over the sails: Bob wanted the sails up, but the captain never put them up until they were out of the harbor. The boat was aswarm with children, the entire section belowdecks strewn with clothes, duffel bags, and food all over the galley. "The Kennedy children live freely and without restraint," Prettyman says. "Every child obeys. The girls still curtsy when they meet people. They all play hard and dangerously, yet the competition seems to be within themselves rather than between each other. I never heard one say or do anything against another one during the two-day trip. They sing, they tell jokes, and they read a great deal, from comic strips to minor adventure stories." The captain was clearly unaccustomed to dealing with kids; he was constantly telling the kids not to touch things, and they ignored him.

Bobby told the captain that he wanted to get the dinghy ready so they could water-ski. The captain was horrified. There were sharks, he said, visibly upset, and besides the dinghy didn't have much gas; if it ran out, it would be difficult to turn the schooner around to retrieve the smaller vessel. Bob shrugged off the protests. They had come to have fun; they couldn't just lie around the deck. And the dinghy had a gas gauge — how risky could it be? Despite the captain's concerns, Ethel and Bob were soon water-skiing with the dinghy, driven by twelve-year-old Joe.

When the gauge got low, Bobby, Ethel, and their son returned to the ship. Over lunch, Barrett Prettyman finally had a chance to talk with Bob. He talked about Jack's desk, how Jackie wanted it for the Kennedy Library, and how Lyndon Johnson's press secretary Bill Moyers had in effect turned him down, saying that Mrs. Johnson might want the president to use it. When he finished, he stared out at the whitecaps. Prettyman told him that if Jackie really wanted the desk, she ought to call Moyers herself. Turning down Bobby was one thing, but turning down Jackie herself was far more risky. Bobby agreed. Then one of the kids asked if they could swim. Bob said, "Sure."

The captain went white. "No," he insisted, "it's too dangerous." Bob bit his lip and waited until the captain disappeared belowdecks. Then Bob ordered the front sail up. All the children lined up at the front of the boat and as the boat sped along, each child would jump off into the water, surface, reach out, and grab the ladder that was put over the side as the boat sailed swiftly by them. In time, even the adults had joined in, all with the exception of five-year-old Kerry, who was too young. Bobby doused her with buckets of water so that she could get wet too. The captain came back up on deck, saw the water and the wet kids and adults and knew it was hopeless to protest. Within half an hour they saw the dark fin of a shark swim by.

As dark settled in they dropped anchor at the Newport Yacht Club and met up with their host, the state's senator, Claiborne Pell. At the club there was the usual excitement at the sight of the Kennedy clan, and the shy grins and the confusion that greeted Bobby Kennedy's arrival in most places. Although others may have thought of him as a big deal, to Prettyman neither he nor Ethel nor any of the children seemed to feel that way. Jackie arrived; she was staying at her mother's home, Hammersmith Farm, and Bobby had arranged in advance for her to join them. She brought along with her Jack Kennedy's friend, the artist Bill Walton. The evening included lots of storytelling, including tales of politics and Jack Kennedy.

The next morning Prettyman woke at 8:30. While he was dressing he looked out the window and saw the entire Kennedy crew, with Bob and Ethel in the lead, dressed and headed for Mass. Bob suddenly turned and ran into the house, and soon he was charging through Prettyman's door. Prettyman had expectantly taken five dollars out of his pocket; Bobby grabbed it and disappeared. He had breakfast with fourteen-year-old Kathleen, who had stayed behind to take part in a horse show and would meet up with the family in Hyannisport. She was excited. She had won the cup twice before; if she could win it one more time she could retire the cup. About 12:30 the whole family piled into the Pells' car and headed back for the boat.

Soon the SS *Nervous* was under way. Almost immediately they sensed that today's sail was different. They were the only boat out and the wind was fierce, with the water growing ever more choppy. They had been out for a while when they heard a siren. Looking back they could see they were being followed by a Coast Guard cutter with lights flashing. Bobby and Ethel exchanged nervous glances; Bobby joked that they were probably going to be arrested for being silly enough to be out in this weather. The Coast Guard boat came dangerously close. From the boat's bullhorn, Prettyman heard the captain say, "Senator Kennedy, your daughter, Kathleen, has been injured by a horse and has head and internal injuries. But the doctors say she is all right. Do not be concerned. Pull in your mainsail and we will try to come close to reach you and take you to her."

After a moment of shock, both parents went into action. Ethel told Bobby that she had to go to Kathleen and that Bobby should stay with the children on the boat. Bobby watched the water and the wind whipping the two boats around and shook his head. "You stay," he told her. Then he steered the boat, staring directly ahead, blue eyes intense, thinking the thing out. "We can't lower the mainsail," he said, turning to face the captain and his crew of family. "We would lose rather than gain control, and it wouldn't do any good anyway. The cutter still would be smashed if it tried to move alongside in these waves." The only alternative was for him to go over the side and swim to the cutter.

He gave the wheel to the captain and walked over to the side of the boat facing the Coast Guard cutter. He moved as if he were going to jump, and Ethel screamed at him, urging him to wear a life preserver. They argued, their voices loud against the wind. Finally Bobby gave in, putting on the life preserver to ease Ethel's mind more than anything else. He leaped over the side and disappeared into the waves. The Coast Guard men on one boat, and the friends and children on the other, searched the water for sight of him. At last he appeared on top of the waves, fighting not to be pushed under again. The cutter maneuvered close, Bob was somehow able to grab the ladder, and they pulled him on board. Bobby would later admit that the preserver had nearly strangled him under the water, making swimming nearly impossible. Once he was on board, the cutter took off at high speed, chopping violently into the top of the waves. The force of one wave caused Bobby's chair to break. When he leaned down to examine it, the next wave came crashing through the window, sending splinters and glass shards all around Bob and the driver, who was savagely cut. Bobby helped him to a seat and took the wheel temporarily until someone else took over. Had he not been bending down, he might have been maimed or even killed. Finally, they arrived at Woods Hole, and the police rushed Bobby to the hospital and his daughter Kathleen's side.

Four and a half hours later, the SS *Nervous* arrived in Woods Hole and Ethel joined her husband and daughter. Kathleen's condition had been critical, more serious than the Coast Guard had intimated. When Prettyman joined them he was struck by how calm and upbeat they were. Joe, who had been lowering one of the sails when the boat was tossed by a wave, had been struck full force across the back and also had to be checked. Prettyman was amazed at the boy's bravery; he didn't moan or complain as he lay on the deck being comforted by Ethel, even though Prettyman worried that the boy had broken his back. Ethel moved with admirable nerve, comforting first one scared child and then the next. In the middle of it all, the chaos and confusion, he heard Kerry singing, "Roses are red, violets are blue, your nose is as big as a B-52!"

Bobby was torn between staying with his kids and attending a five-thousand-dollar-a-person fund-raiser featuring Sammy Davis, Jr., on Long Island. They left the children and headed back to the Kennedy compound. Eunice came over for a while; Marlene Dietrich called from England, having heard about Kathleen on the news. Arthur Schlesinger called; so did Rowland Evans. Bobby wanted to stay with his family, but he felt obligated. They flew to Long Island. Prettyman went along, and they discussed Larry O'Brien's appointment by Johnson to be postmaster general and the escalating war in Vietnam. After the fund-raiser, Bobby, Prettyman, Sammy Davis, and three members of Davis's band headed toward a friend's house for a drink. The car was low on gas and Sammy thought they should stop, but Bobby said, "No, don't stop at a station. They'll think we are a bunch of Freedom Riders coming to picket." The car erupted into laughter. After finishing their drinks, Bobby prepared to drive off to the airport to return to Hyannisport. As they parted, Prettyman thanked Bobby for the sail. Bobby interrupted him, telling him that he was glad Prettyman had come and stayed over. "Next time, plan to stay a couple of days, because I have this new small sailboat and we could sail over to Martha's Vineyard, have lunch, and sail back!"

Prettyman stopped him before he was finished. "I think it might be a few days before I'm ready to sail again. Let's do it again—but don't call me, I'll call you!"

Bobby chuckled, thanked Sammy Davis, and disappeared from sight down the road. Davis said reflectively what Prettyman had long known: "That cat sure is some man."

The poor had found their champion in Bobby Kennedy, and Bobby had found a way to make being a United States senator mean something more than entanglement in legislative protocol. In April 1967, he and Peter Edelman flew down to Mississippi for hearings on possible extensions of the federal poverty program. On this trip Edelman would meet his future wife, Marian Wright, with whom he would propound anti-poverty programs, children's issues, and civil rights long after Bobby's death. He would also witness an image of Robert Kennedy that would haunt him — and help him understand why Bobby had no choice but to run for the presidency of the United States in 1968.

Marian Wright had set up a trip that would take Bobby, Edelman, and CBS newsman Daniel Schorr through the Mississippi Delta and allow him to see the effects of poverty and hunger firsthand. At their first stop, Bobby encountered children with swollen bellies; when he went in and opened the refrigerator, there was nothing in there. The children were covered with running sores on their arms and legs. As they moved on to the next house, Bobby told Edelman that this was as bad as anything he had ever seen in a third-world country.

They went into the next house, as the CBS crew stayed outside to film something else. Edelman and Wright waited in the doorway as Bobby went in. For some reason, there was a small child all alone in the house, sitting Indian-style before a bowl of rice. Edelman assumed the child was a boy, but he was so dirty and forlorn it was almost impossible to tell the child's sex. Bobby walked up to the child and reached down, trying to lift him, but the child's legs buckled. He could not stand. Bobby sat down on the filthy floor directly across from him, speaking gently, trying to get a response. The child's eyes were dull from hunger and his belly was swollen, his skin oozing sores. With one finger he stirred the rice in the bowl before him.

Edelman and Wright said nothing; they didn't want to interrupt Bobby, who was acting as if he were alone. They didn't want him to think they were following him everywhere. Still, they did not leave. They couldn't. Bobby touched the child's hand to his face, brushing the child's dirty hair back from his eyes. No response. Edelman watched as pain creased Bobby's face. In one motion he scooped up the child and held the small form against his chest, kissing him. The boy laid his head on Bobby's shoulder.

22

"RUN, BOBBY, RUN"

A life without criticism is not worth living.

— PLATO

Kenny O'Donnell had been opposed to the war in Vietnam since 1961. His wariness about American involvement in Southeast Asia escalated even as the war did. In early 1965, President Johnson pushed the Gulf of Tonkin resolution through the Senate with only Senators Wayne Morse and J. William Fulbright dissenting. This sense of the Congress resolution gave the president the right to send in American combat troops to repel Communist provocation and aggression. Kenny's objections grew even stronger. And slowly but surely, Senator Robert Kennedy would share his opposition.

During the Kennedy adminstration, "I think Bobby fell under the spell of Maxwell Taylor," the Chairman of the Joint Chiefs of Staff, after whom he named one of his children. "I think at first Taylor convinced Bobby that the price wasn't as high as we're paying today—that this was sort of an exercise and you're almost playing at something." Back in 1962, Taylor, according to Kenny, could make the case for American intervention in Vietnam this way: "We don't have any combat units in and our casualty rate is limited totally to volunteers. We don't have any draftees. It was that whole counter-insurgency thing. But by 1963 and '64, Bobby was beginning to wonder. He still had a mental commitment to it, because of his brother." He was still grief-stricken over Jack's death, and by coming out so early and so strongly against the war, he was afraid he would be repudiating his brother.

"I was involved in the Tonkin Gulf, if in fact what did occur happened. There was no reason at the time to say it didn't occur. I disagreed with Senator William Fulbright, believed he was probably wrong in that one. I don't think the military tell that many lies. I think they take you down a lot of garden paths, but I don't believe they would outright lie to the president of the United States. Lyndon Johnson in good faith accepted it because I was in on the meeting at the time," recalled Kenny.

It was to Kenny that Bobby first expressed much of his concern over Vietnam. "He and I used to argue quite a bit. I had come under the influence of Mike Mansfield and [columnist] Walter Lippmann, very early, so I was clear in my views and Bobby was not quite ready to be that clear yet. He was working his way there. Bobby doesn't like to argue things that he hasn't really made up his mind about. I don't think it was until 1966 that he began to see that the war was absolutely futile. Bobby was just too honest to have pulled off of it and just said it's wrong because he had an involvement" in formulating the Kennedy administration policy. "Most politicians would have said, 'The hell with it. I am saving myself. I am saying I don't even know what occurred when I was attorney general. I don't have anything to do with that stuff.' Bobby was too honest to do anything like that, so he was always in that ambivalent position, where he'd like to say — and what he ultimately did say — was 'I was wrong too, but I am prepared to change my mind.' Which was the honest approach to it — it was the only way Bobby could be, really. Bobby and I used to battle back and forth. When we finally reached some agreement on the military aspect of it, we would fight about and argue about the political implication of it here in the United States of America. It was how we worked through things."

Since their debates at the Varsity Club, Bobby and Kenny had argued their way into decisions on important issues. Their friendship was as much based on disagreements as concurrence. Nick Rodis says, "Bobby didn't need or want people around him who were always going to agree with him. That's why he and Kenny were so close, because they fight and work through these things. It's how you make good decisions."

"In February of 1966 Bobby gave his first major speech on Vietnam," Peter Edelman remembers. The speech had been heavily planned and worked through by every adviser, but especially with Dick Goodwin and Arthur Schlesinger. Goodwin did the major crafting of the speech. "It was the Sharing and Responsibility speech," said Edelman, in which Bobby proposed involving the National Liberation Front in a negotiated settlement on Vietnam. Bobby's proposal was greeted with a barrage of criticism. The *Chicago Tribune* led the charge with an editorial calling Bobby "Ho Chi Kennedy." Johnson was furious and immediately trotted out Maxwell Taylor, Hubert Humphrey, and Robert McNamara to attack him. Bobby was really upset, Edelman recalled. "Johnson was deliberately hauling out Robert Kennedy's friends to beat him up in a public manner that would inflict the most personal pain on Kennedy. It was very hurtful and painful for him both politically and personally for several days. We were very, very isolated in Robert Kennedy's office after that speech. It rained down on us from every sector — his old friends, every sector of the government, every newspaper, and the public itself."

Johnson had his people calling the editorial pages of every newspaper, telling them Robert Kennedy was unrealistic and immature. "I think Bobby was not prepared for the depth of the assault," Edelman said. It would take Bobby another year before he said publicly what he had been pondering privately since 1964 — that America had to get out of Vietnam. "In 1967 Bobby went and gave a speech on the Senate floor about who gives us the right to rain terror down on others," says Edelman. "It was largely extemporaneous and I think his passion got away from him and he was out ahead of his game plan a little bit. But by that time he was not calibrating so carefully, because his opposition had become so fervent. He was seeing what I think Kenny saw earlier — that these so-called friends were hanging him out to dry. When he faces that, he then becomes free to act, to be himself."

"Bobby Kennedy was a complex guy," Kenny declared. "He had extreme loyalties, and he would never talk about people. He resented it among others. He comes across to people who don't know him as cold, ruthless Bobby Kennedy. He was one of the least petty fellows about other people and the most forgiving human being that I've seen in my life. That used to be a bone of contention between him and me. I'm pretty hard on a guy. When I thought a guy made a mistake, I was pretty tough about it. I really didn't want to give them another chance. Bobby would give them another chance every time. He could think of more reasons why Bob McNamara did something or Mac Bundy or Max Taylor, or anybody that was his friend. Even when these guys were killing him, it was hard for him to see it. You know, we would go out for a few drinks. I would tell Bobby, you know, Max Taylor is giving you bum advice. He's killing you. Bobby would say, 'Oh, we all make mistakes — you make mistakes too, misjudgments. You aren't perfect.' 'Fine,' I would say, 'but I'm not telling you I am.' If you have a weakness though, it's a pretty nice weakness to have. . . . He just had this outrageous loyalty to people. He could still make the tough decisions, but often he would take the hit for somebody else's bum advice. I would have thrown 'em over the side. Bobby couldn't; he took all the responsibility."

As 1967 progressed, American opinion on the war in Vietnam would move from wary support of U.S. policy to a stronger desire to have the whole conflict over. The situation in Vietnam continued to deteriorate; the poverty programs continued to falter, and Lyndon Johnson was finding it more and more difficult to fight the war abroad and at home. The president found himself fighting a rearguard action against national antiwar opinion — just as a presidential election loomed. As it did for so many other Americans, the war would force both Kenny and Bobby to make decisions they hadn't expected to make. "By the New Hampshire primary really, this thing had gotten deep into the American craw," Kenny would say. "Bobby had no choice but to go, no matter the risk. That was my view.

"By 1965 he had begun to really focus in on what he thought were the two great things disturbing the United States. One was poverty and the other was the war in Vietnam. Johnson started to fade terribly in

'65. By 1966 Bobby believed somebody really had to do something about it and that the president was doing a rather poor job, in his judgment. He began campaigning in '66 around the country. The polls began to show he was more popular than Johnson. That started him thinking now that he might possibly be a candidate in '68—or more to the point that he possibly had an obligation to be a candidate in '68. . . . Coming up late in the year of '67 we talked rather regularly.

"The thing that disturbed him most of all was the misinterpretation of what his motives were. He resented that people thought that he just wanted to get the White House back, that the Kennedys wanted the presidency back. This really upset him personally very much. I think when it came to making the final decision to go that became the one real drag in his thinking. I think if his name had been something else, Bobby Kennedy would have announced for president in 1967 and taken Johnson on without any question whatsoever. Yet he couldn't. Bobby felt that number one, it would be misinterpreted—that it not only would be wrong from his own viewpoint but that he probably would be defeated because of the fashion in which he entered into this thing. It would be viewed as some sort of personal vendetta." Bobby had to think all these issues through—starting with a meeting in Pierre Salinger's hotel suite at the Regency in New York in 1967.

Salinger called Kenny to join the war council to discuss Bobby's political options. Kenny had been working as a consultant. Now he was hesitant. "I wasn't enthusiastic about some of the people who were going to be there, because to be frank . . . a lot of the ones who were going to be there love to talk to the newspapermen. My association was too close to the president in a political sense. I thought that it would be politically hazardous for me to be there." Together he and Salinger culled the list of prospective attendees. Kenny made clear his belief that Robert Kennedy should not attend the meeting. He believed that Bobby's presidential ambitions would not be able to survive such a meeting, should his presence leak out. "I talked Bobby out of going to the meeting. I told him there were people that were going to be at that meeting that are going to talk to the newspapers even if you threatened to shoot them."

Some of the newer Kennedy staffers had, in Kenny's view, more enthusiasm than political acumen. "They are very bright, high-minded young fellows, but they really don't know the ball game. They really were pushing Bobby in a direction where he was reluctant to go." Their reasons, in Kenny's view, "were very immature. They didn't realize the type of potential opposition that they really were dealing with. Ted Sorensen was disinterested, almost, to some degree." Fred Dutton was more practical than most. "Fred is a pol, he is a realist, he knew the difficulties involved. Pierre loves to get in the middle of things. He was more enthusiastic for Bobby involving himself than Bobby was. Dick Goodwin was all rather highly excited about it. I think Dick Goodwin was probably more interested in beating Lyndon Johnson than in getting Robert Kennedy elected. I don't think he meant that, but that's what I got out of it. Teddy Kennedy was the most reluctant, and the most practical. I think he saw the peril in it very clearly. Obviously Steve Smith just sat and listened." Kenny believed that, like him, Smith was reluctant to run for the White House just for the sake of running. There was too much risk involved. They knew the difficulties and they understood, more than most, the risk.

Kenny didn't want to attend the meeting himself, telling Bobby nothing was ever accomplished at such sessions. "Still," he said, "I didn't want him to get mad at me so I went. The meeting was the most inconclusive bunch of crap thrown around. No one knew what they were talking about really, or where they were going, or what the real problems were. Nothing came out of it. Nothing. If I had said I think Robert Kennedy ought to run, I think it would have had an awful lot of influence. But I didn't. I wasn't prepared to say that. At the moment," reflected Kenny, "I wasn't sure he ought to run. I wasn't sure of the direction that he was going in or he was thinking about. And I certainly was very unsure of the direction of some of those urging him to run. Whether their interest was for him or for themselves confused me. In the end, I made one point and I repeated it over and over again: If the issue were Vietnam and really the character of the United States of America, hell, I thought Robert Kennedy had an obligation to go! But if the issue was just sort of 'we've got to get our guy back in the White House,' which it very clearly was almost certainly for some people around him, I thought it would be a terrible error. I thought the only issue was Vietnam and the character of the United States."

As he pondered his candidacy, Bobby had to be especially careful in how he addressed Vietnam. He knew his words would be scoured by politicians, the press, and American citizens themselves. Teddy could be far more free in his criticisms, a difference David Burke ascribed to their divergent personal experiences with Vietnam. "Bobby had been so close to executive power and the heir apparent to President Kennedy that his actions on Vietnam always provoked mixed reviews. Teddy could express outrage. Teddy could focus on the civilian casualties, refugees, and children, using the political argument he was comfortable with, which was, How do you expect to win the minds of the people, if you are rolling over them like a steamroller, if tons of weaponry and bombs are shattering their lives and you're creating refugee camps and hospitals that are nothing but breeding grounds for the Vietcong? Teddy could say things like that. If Bobby said the same thing, all hell would break loose.

"When Bobby was going to be on *Meet the Press*, he would sit in a chair in his living room with myself and two other people on a couch with a coffee table in between. Then we would fire questions at him. The questions would be miserable, horrible questions, terrible questions, to give him the worst possible barrage." Bobby and Burke knew that nearly all the interrogation would concern Vietnam and the possibility of a presidential run. Burke accompanied Bobby to the *Meet the Press* studio, with a tiny American flag stuck in the pocket of his jacket. During the broadcast, Burke says, "Bobby would look at me and I would pull out my American flag and wave it and put it back in my pocket. Then Bobby's answer would be patriotic, right down the middle. The problem was Bobby would say always what he believed, of course, but we wanted him to say it a little more carefully. He wasn't a careful politician, he would get emotional and angry, and it would show in his answers. We wanted to keep him from tearing the cover off."

✳   ✳   ✳

Deciding whether or not to run was weighing heavily on Bobby's mind. "He would play headgames with himself," Joe Dolan remembers. "He didn't want to disappoint people. If he was going to run, he would need to do all these political events and favors. Still he hated doing them, so it was a constant battle." Once Bobby was scheduled to go to former governor Averell Harriman's upstate New York home to speak at a dinner for a pro-Johnson congressional candidate who didn't have a chance of winning. As Dolan and aide Phil Ryan drove him across the George Washington Bridge on their way to the dinner, Bobby announced he felt sick. "You can let me off here," he told them. "Don't worry about it. I'll walk and get a cab."

The car pulled over, and Bobby got out, walking back across the bridge. "Phil couldn't believe it!" Dolan says. "I kind of knew what was on his mind, but I wasn't going to say anything. So we go on up to the event, and the crowd is waiting, all excited, screaming, yelling, signs and all. The car door opens and out steps Phil! You could hear a pin drop." The next day, Dolan saw in the newspaper social column a small item that said at the Met opening the previous night were Mrs. John F. Kennedy accompanied by Senator Robert F. Kennedy. He looked just fine in the photograph. Dolan chuckled to himself.

Bobby called Dolan into his Senate office and told him he was thinking of running for president. What did Dolan think? The senator's aide wanted to say that this was what he'd always been waiting for, what this Senate operation was all about. Instead, he began ostentatiously to turn in his seat, looking all around the office, then looking underneath the chair he sat in. Bob watched, puzzled. "What are you doing?" he asked finally.

Dolan straightened up in the chair. "Looking for *Candid Camera*," he deadpanned.

"Cut it out! What do you really think!"

Dolan began by relating the conversation he had just had with a supporter in San Francisco, who had made an eloquent plea for Bobby to run. "Look Bob, win or lose, the Democratic party would never be the same. You might be able to stop that damn war."

Bob listened, thoughtful. "Would that be so bad?"

Dolan went home, talked to his wife, and the next day told Bobby that he needed ten days off. "I need to go rest. It's just a matter of time now."

"Fine," Bobby said.

To Kenny the meetings to discuss Bobby's candidacy highlighted the difference in style between the two brothers. "In the first place," he said, "despite what the press said, we did not meet with President Kennedy as a group at any time to discuss particular issues. There are those there that he pretended to talk to but when he got down to the political decisions, he would meet with some people separately, but he would never put Bob Kennedy, Ken O'Donnell, and Ted Sorensen into a group. He would take us one by one, or he usually would take Bobby and me together, then talk to Sorensen alone. He and Sorensen had their own relationship. He might talk to Arthur Schlesinger, but he wouldn't group us, because we have such divergent and strong person-alities and approaches that what comes out of those meetings is nothing. We end up being mad at each other most of the time, because one of us usually thinks we're smarter than the other fellow is. That's why I didn't want Bobby to have these meetings. . . . I told him I thought it was an inconclusive bunch of crap and that he ought to be very, very wary that he make his own decision and go in his own direction, and not be pushed by these high-minded people, who, in a high-minded fashion might have their own motivations that don't have anything to do with the real interests of Bobby Kennedy." Bobby listened. Within twenty-four hours of the first meeting at the Regency Hotel, as Kenny had predicted, he received a call in the office on Arlington Street in Boston. The call was from *The New York Times*. The story was out.

Frank Burns was a wily California politician. An ally and confidant of California House Speaker Jesse Unruh, he had become very close to Kenny O'Donnell starting with the 1960 campaign. Burns first got to know Bobby in 1967, during a San Francisco fund-raising trip. He be-came involved in Bobby's presidential deliberations when Jesse Unruh brought him in. "I had just come off an operation for what they thought was lung cancer. It turned out not to be, but still the recovery period was long, so my wife and I had taken the last cruise on the *Queen Mary* as part of my convalescence. It was my birthday, December seventh, when it began for me. Jess had me run down on the ship, and asked me to come back early and meet him in New York for a meeting with Bob Kennedy. We met with Bobby. It was clear to me the man was seriously considering a run."

It was decided at that meeting that Unruh and Burns would do a poll in California testing the level of support for Bobby in a primary against Senator Eugene McCarthy, who was already a candidate, and Lyndon Johnson. The deadline for filing for the June primary was approaching; Bobby would soon have to make a decision on whether or not to run, since California would be central to his effort to win the nomination.

On January 19, 1968, Kenny attended a fund-raising dinner in New York for the state committee, where Bobby was the featured speaker. Afterward they had drinks and Bobby asked Kenny, "Would you come to Washington?"

Kenny was on his way back to Boston; he had a speaking engagement scheduled for the next day. "Why?" he asked Bobby.

"Jesse is coming in from California," Bobby explained. The results of the poll were in and Unruh and Burns were taking the red eye to Washington to discuss them. "He's your pal and I'd like to have you sit in on the meeting if you would. It will be at my house."

"Fine," said Kenny, resignedly.

The meeting began at 11:00 with lunch on the back patio of Hickory Hill. In addition to Bobby, Kenny, Unruh, and Burns, also attending were Ted Sorensen, Fred Dutton, Burke Marshall, Steve Smith, and Ethel. "It was interesting," Burns recalled. "Jess and I were making all the arguments for Bob running, which was obviously why we were invited. Sorensen was making the argument against Bob's running, and Jess was challenging him. We had the California poll results that clearly showed if he announced in this state, in a three-way race he would win. But Sorensen was reluctant and being difficult." The meeting inevitably led to a showdown.

"I never came out and said he ought to run," Kenny recalled. "When we got to it, I said, 'Well, I'm going to be cold and practical about it.

If you're in this to get back in the White House, I don't think I'll be for you. If you feel as strongly as I think you do about this situation in Vietnam, then naturally I'll be for whatever you want.'" Kenny turned to Jess. "Jess, you're a practical politician. Now, you know what a convention is. You know what you're talking about. What odds do you think there would be that Robert Kennedy could be nominated by the Democratic party? I think," said Kenny, "the odds are three to one against!"

Jess shook his head, "No, five to one. But I still think he ought to run." Then Jess made what Kenny would later call a "very eloquent little speech about how the character of the party has been destroyed by Lyndon Johnson." According to Unruh, the party and the country were both sick. Someone had to pick up the pieces even if he lost the White House, so that the party could retain its integrity.

"Sorensen made a statement, which I frankly thought was well taken," Kenny recalled. "He said, 'Jess, let's all be practical. You're interested in yourself. You want to be chairman of the slate which, with Robert Kennedy's name, would probably win in California and make you a big hero. Then you will run for governor.'"

"Jess was furious," Burns said. "He really cut Sorensen off at the ankles and said, 'Ted, after all those high-flown phrases about making a difference, and putting the country first! I have never been under the impression that any of us were virgins in this business, and if you think that Bob Kennedy doesn't think about Bob Kennedy when he makes a decision, then he's not the Bob Kennedy I know! And, if you think Jess Unruh doesn't think about Jess Unruh, then you're looking at the wrong Jess Unruh!' Sorensen started to get really mad. I think Kenny thought Ted was making a good point, but he sort of just let Jess and Ted go at it."

Jess went on to declare that since Sorensen was working for General Motors, relied on his access to the White House, and had a strong relationship with Johnson, then Sorensen was thinking about Sorensen. "Ted was really angry at that point," said Burns. "Fortunately, Ethel stepped in and kind of ended it." Cutting off the argument, Ethel, in characteristic fashion, brought the discussion to the bottom line. She had been around Bobby long enough to know his priorities. "Well, it's all big talk!" she said. "But let me ask you two, just what will you do if Bob Kennedy announces for president of the United States?"

There was silence for a moment. Burns says, "I think Ethel's question kind of brought everyone back and sort of put everyone on the spot: What will you do if he takes this huge risk?"

Jess spoke first. "I'll tell you what I'll do. I'll resign as speaker of the California House, because I think it would be a conflict of interest for me, and I'll round up all those legislators and set up a slate and we'll carry California for him. I will devote full time from this minute on. That's how much I think of him, and that's how far I'm prepared to go!"

Ethel turned to Kenny. They had been friends for a long time, since 1946. They had been through great achievement and great pain together. "Kenny, what will you do?"

Kenny returned her gaze. "I'll be in Washington the day after he announces. I will give him my full time and all the people I can lay my hands on. If he wants to run, then win, lose, or draw, we're with him."

As the meeting broke up, the Kennedy children weighed in as well, unfurling a huge banner from the top windows of the house saying, RUN BOBBY RUN!

Lyndon Johnson was still very much in the political game. Unruh and Burns were invited to the White House on the following Sunday afternoon to meet with him. Jesse Unruh's defection to Bobby was something Johnson knew he could not afford. "Lyndon was really doing a masterful performance," Burns says.

"Jess," Johnson bellowed, "you're a state legislator, and you should be a senator from California!" There was not much immediate prospect of that, but to keep Unruh out of Bobby's hands, Johnson was prepared to pull out all the stops to get him elected senator. "The Tet Offensive had just started," Burns says. "We were in the mansion itself and Johnson was at his most charming. He could really put it on. But there was this disturbing undercurrent. Johnson kept getting up to take phone calls about the war. At one point he came charging back into the room and announced to us that it was going to be all right! Jess and I kind of exchanged glances, like what is he talking about? Johnson went on to say that they had just located the headquarters of some Vietcong general, whose name I didn't even know, and that the raid was going forward over such and such a hill. They were sending in B-29s or maybe it was B-17s, but they were sending them in to demolish General Such and Such's headquarters. We were going to win that battle and take that hill! Jess looked just amazed. The color drained out of his face and he was very quiet for the rest of the meeting.

"After we left the White House, Jess said, 'Let's walk.' So we walked over to the Lincoln Memorial and finally back to the hotel. Jess was quiet. He hardly spoke at all. His head was down and he looked like he was miles away. We got to the hotel and had a drink. Jess finally spoke. 'He is never going to be able to get out of that war. The president is so immersed in the war that he is down to the level of a company commander. He will never be able to end that war without complete victory, which is impossible. The slaughter will just go on and on. Come on,' Jess said."

The two men went to Jess's hotel room, where he called Bobby Kennedy. "It was the moment of real truth," Burns says. "That was when Jess decided Lyndon had to go and Bob had to run. Johnson had offered to make Jess a United States senator, but Jess turned him down flat. He knew there was only one hope now."

"Teddy was absolutely against Bobby's running in '68," Kenny said. "Teddy hated the 'you must run' crowd. He feared that Bobby was going to be literally forced to run for the presidency because if he didn't, then Bobby wasn't a good man, he wasn't a moral man, he lacked courage, he wasn't decent. They would get so emotional and go on and on, as if Bobby was the only one who could stop the madness. Teddy resented the pressure it put on Bobby, thought the times were dangerous. He felt that Bobby could still have an effect on the course of the war and wait and run in 1972. I think, sadly, Teddy was right."

Dick Goodwin in particular wanted Bobby to run. At an event at Hickory Hill for the schoolchildren of Washington, D.C., Goodwin came up to Bobby and announced, "I wanted to know this very day, as to whether you are going to run for president. Gene McCarthy has already announced and is in New Hamphshire and I want a decision right now!" Bobby looked stunned, taking a step back, and looked around, trying to find a place where they could talk in private.

"So Dick Goodwin, Bobby, Teddy, and myself end up in the pool house, in the ladies' room of all places," Burke recalls. "It was the only place for privacy because this big event was going on. People were hovering. For some reason, whenever we had a serious discussion we would always end up in the bathroom. We had to get away from people and really be able to talk." At various points during the conversation, someone would try to pull on the door, or call to see who was inside the bathroom and taking so long. The men didn't answer and spoke in sutble tones. Goodwin told Bobby that if he wasn't going to run, "in the trunk of my car is the typewriter, and I will leave here today and drive directly to New Hampshire to work for Gene McCarthy."

Burke says, "I think Bobby wanted to punch him right in the face. Teddy was trying to keep Bobby from losing his temper and trying to smooth over the waters. The look in Bobby's eyes made you want to reach for a winter coat. Bobby didn't like being pressured and the more Dick pressured him for an answer, the more sullen he became. In the course of it, it became quite clear Bobby wasn't going to run, or at least at that point hadn't made up his mind. Then Dick started getting nasty, saying, 'You aren't running! You don't have the guts to run, do you?' That was it for Bobby. 'No,' said Bobby, 'I am telling you today that I am not running. No, I am not running!' " Goodwin was livid. He stormed out of the bathroom and toward his car. Teddy gave Burke a look that sent him scurrying after the speechwriter to calm him down. He slipped out of the bathroom and heard the door lock behind him.

"Dick, give him time," Burke entreated. "Nobody likes to be pressured like that. He is getting it from all corners. He needs time to breathe." Goodwin didn't want to hear it. He headed for New Hampshire, his brilliant prose quickly evident in McCarthy's speeches. The Minnesota senator's strong showing in New Hampshire encouraged Johnson not to seek another term. Right now, as Bobby struggled to make a decision, Teddy and others resented the pressure on Bobby. He would risk more than they would.

On March 16, 1968, "the morning of Bobby's announcement that he was going to run, Teddy and I were upstairs with him going over his final statement," Burke recalls. "He was picking out what tie to wear. 'Do you like this, Dave? Do you like that one, Dave?' He couldn't decide. Ethel was flurrying all around, and everything I liked she hated. He wasn't really worried about what he was going to wear. He was worried if he was doing the right thing. So finally Teddy said to me softly, almost sort of mouthed, 'Let's get out of here.' We walked downstairs and went out into the backyard at Hickory Hill. Teddy was really upset. He said, 'I'm really afraid for him. I have a terrible feeling about this whole thing. I'm sure I'm wrong, and yet—' Teddy just couldn't shake this feeling. It was one of the saddest conversations I have ever had."

23

THE FINAL PLAY

You know, my brother rode a white horse once....

—BOBBY KENNEDY

Bobby Kennedy's campaign for the presidency began messy with promise. The California poll had shown that in a three-way race among
Johnson, Kennedy, and McCarthy, Johnson and Kennedy were at a dead
even 36 percent—not bad for an unannounced challenger of an incumbent. It was the general election results that were probably most convincing. In a straight contest between Robert Kennedy and the likely
Republican nominee, Richard Nixon, Bobby in the words of Frank
Burns, "cleaned Nixon's clock."

On March 17, the day after Robert Kennedy announced he would
seek the Democratic nomination for the presidency, he flew to New
York to appear in the St. Patrick's Day parade and then went on to
Boston to appear at the parade there with Teddy. Lester Hyman, who
had run for attorney general when Kenny ran for governor, would meet
them there. Kenny had been his political mentor, and they had grown
quite close. Over lunches, Kenny would joke with him about his man-
gled hand, which had been operated on for Dupuytren's contracture.
"This fucking claw will cost me the election!"

"We used to kid him about that," Hyman says. "He had a wonderful
sense of humor and was very low-key. A lot of people really feared and
resented Ken, but he was always nice to me. I was a kid so he took me
under his wing and taught me politics." As an assistant to Governor

Endicott Peabody, Hyman would represent Massachusetts in White House meetings with the Cobra, Kenny O'Donnell. Once Kenny motioned him into the Oval Office to meet John F. Kennedy. It would be the first time he'd ever seen Kennedy as president.

The president looked up from his desk and took off his glasses. "Lester," Jack Kennedy said, "You get outta here! You are the kiss of death!" Lester was stunned and broke out into a sweat. He looked over at Kenny for help.

"Don't faint, Lester," Kenny ordered, his demeanor serious.

Finally Hyman found his voice. "Mr. President, sir, what did I do?"

The president leaned forward, hands on the desk. "What did you do?" he asked, seemingly shocked that the young man didn't know. "You worked for Eddie McLoughlin for Congress and he lost. I told you to work for Leverett Saltonstall for Congress, you did—he lost! I told you to work for Johnny Powers for mayor, and you did—he lost!" Jack enumerated eleven candidates Lester Hyman had been associated with, all of whom had failed at the polls. "I'm up for reelection next year. Lester, you get out of here!" With that his face broke into a wide grin. Kenny joined in.

On St. Patrick's Day morning, when Hyman arrived at Ted's apartment at Charles River Square, Ted's driver, Jack Crimmins; Dave Burke, Ted's aide from Washington; and his cousin Bob Fitzgerald were already there. Ted greeted him warmly. The two men were the same age. Ted was clearly nervous. Now that Bobby had made the decision and would kick things off in Massachusetts, Ted wanted everything to go well. But since it was Sunday, could they even find a place to get signs made heralding Bobby's presence in the South Boston parade? "I know," said Ted, as they sat in the living room planning the event, "let's take the paper lining out of the drawers in the bedrooms." Soon they had several dozen WELCOME BOBBY signs made—and clothes strewn all over Teddy's bedroom.

When they set out to pick Bobby up at the airport, the car's ignition died. The men all sat in silence. Teddy stared at his driver Jack Crimmins in disbelief as he tried again and again to start the engine. He put his head down between his legs, holding his handmade sign, and groaned, "The fucking Kennedy machine rides again!"

For Senator George McGovern from South Dakota, if there was one compelling reason for Bobby Kennedy to run for president, it was Vietnam. McGovern had been a critic of the war since early 1965. He had supported Johnson in 1964 partly because "I felt like he was really going to end the war and get out. That's how he was talking and a lot of us on the Hill believed him." The first indication that something was amiss came very early. "Hubert Humphrey was by then vice president and he was my neighbor in Washington. I got wind from Hubert that they were going to move the other way and escalate the war. I was concerned." In an audience with the president, McGovern made his case to end the war. Johnson seemed very understanding and attentive to everything he said but made no firm commitments. McGovern left, convinced he had gotten Johnson to listen. Later when he had told Bobby about his meeting, Bobby had just smiled. As McGovern and others would find out later from Hubert Humphrey, after the South Dakota senator left the White House that day, President Johnson turned to press secretary Bill Moyers and said, "You know what really bothers me about McGovern and the rest of them? I think they are right. I think this damn war is a sink hole." Having said that, President Johnson steadily began to increase the war effort, eventually becoming so involved that he could brag to McGovern, Kennedy, and others that "a shithouse doesn't get bombed unless I know about it!"

Even before the presidential campaign got under way, McGovern had witnessed Bobby become the object of a furious public outcry after he announced that Americans should not hesitate to give blood to the victims of American bombing in the North—that Communist victims should be helped just on humanitarian grounds. In the same week Teddy had denounced the regime in the South as "corrupt and rotten through and through." Teddy, with Dave Burke's help, had backed it all up with documentation and research. While Bobby was being crucified for his statement, Teddy was being applauded for his. Standing on the Senate floor beside Senator McGovern, Bobby shook his head, saying ruefully, "Teddy is a much smarter politician than I am politically. I come out for giving blood to Hanoi and Teddy comes out for getting rid of the crooked bums! And it's South Vietnam we are allied with. Teddy is on the side of cleaning up the crooked bums and I emerge as a bleeding heart liberal!"

"Teddy was more like Jack than Bobby," McGovern says. "Teddy was a pragmatic politician and Bobby would react from his heart, and it often got him into trouble. Bobby was more inclined to address things directly. Bobby was not a natural politician." Perhaps because he had never expected to be one or really wanted to be.

While Senator McCarthy was campaigning against Johnson in New Hampshire, McGovern held a meeting in his office, including Congressman Frank Thompson of New Jersey, Montana senator Lee Metcalf, and former Interior Secretary Stuart Udall, to pressure Bobby Kennedy to run—but to do nothing until after the New Hampshire primary. "We told Bobby that if he came to New Hampshire at this point, it would almost look as if he were in a spoiler role—that you would get a division of the New Hampshire vote, with part going to McCarthy and part going to Bob, neither one of whom would get enough to defeat Johnson, and Johnson wouldn't get the message. We begged Bob to stay out and let Gene have his day in the sun and then after the primary in New Hampshire he could make his announcement and go in." Bobby had been frustrated, but had agreed. "We had this practice of getting together once a month. Bob and I and several senators who were opposed to the war. Whether or not Bob should run and, if he did, when he should go had been a regular topic. Now that he had decided we wanted him to wait. He was frustrated and angry, but agreed that it was only fair to Gene. It was an unselfish thing for him to do. Even if nobody understood it, because it wasn't his nature to explain himself."

"We had one meeting," Kenny said of the Kennedy for president 1968 campaign. "It was the first and only formal staff meeting we ever had." No titles were handed out, except to Teddy and Steve Smith, who were the campaign managers. "Teddy and Steve were interchangeable, which was acceptable to everybody," said Kenny. "There was no conflict with either of them. They're relatives, brothers really, and we'd all worked with them both." Kenny was the only one with a clear assignment, which was to organize the political machinery and the labor vote. "I was left alone, because frankly I am not that nice a fellow to get along with in the first place. I had a pretty sizable staff of my own fellows and I always did and always will run my own show."

As the campaign raced forward, Kenny watched as Bobby slowly progressed into an effective national candidate. He was impressed but not surprised. His Senate race had been a helter-skelter effort, and he was running in a state where he did not have a personal organization; moreover, he had been a first-time candidate without a natural knack for the political simplifications the stump requires. "Bobby never really got on track in New York," Kenny would recount later. He didn't have real control of the political organization in the state. "Now with the presidential campaign, you are in a situation where you are running for president of the United States. Bobby had seen enough of it so he understood it, but that's the first time I saw Bobby Kennedy withdraw and look at Bobby Kennedy and do what his brother Jack did so magnificently—talk about himself in the third person. He was analyzing his performance on television, how he comes across, and he said to me, 'I don't come across well on set affairs. I do very well with question and answers. I don't think the set format is my milieu. I don't think that's my strongest suit.' "

Kenny saw the transformation happening in Ohio. "We set up a meeting in Columbus that Bobby flew into and was about three hours late for. I must have called him nineteen times. I said, 'Bobby, I know you are getting great crowds and I don't know how many times I have tried to impress this on you—it doesn't impress one single delegate. You are begging them to vote for you. They don't care how many crowds you get. They want to know whether you can win the election and what kind of guy you are. As of right now, they don't like you! Don't be late to this meeting, because they think they're "King for a Day." Now, for God's sake, arrive on time!' " The meeting involved some 145 delegates and was crucial to the nomination, in Kenny's view. "A little drinking was going on among the delegates. I got up and gave a speech to use up some time . . . I finish, the phone rings. It's Bobby, proud as a peacock; he's with the mayor and he's five minutes early. He'll be right over. Well, we sat there and we sat there and I have to shut the bar down three times, because I figured by the time he gets here the delegates will all be drunk. I must have made seven speeches. I told every Kennedy story I could think of. I don't even remember which stories I had told. . . . I am looking at my watch—where the hell is he? Turns out he had gone through the black section of Columbus en route and the crowds had been ten times what were expected. He couldn't get through. It was wall-to-wall people.

"By the time he arrived the delegates were so mad they were almost sullen. Then he got up and made the best damn speech I have ever heard in my life to those delegates. They went wild. They are a hard-bitten, tough crowd of guys, and they were so taken aback by him. . . . Here is this nice-looking young fellow who gets up and says, 'Look, if I were you fellows I'd be doing just what you're doing, be uncommitted. I would stay uncommitted if I were you! Bob Kennedy may go out to California and get murdered! I don't want your vote. If I can't get elected president of the United States, I don't want you to vote for me, and if I can't win California, I can't be elected president of the United States. All I am here for is just to ask if you would please wait and give me a chance to talk to each one of you individually and tell you what I am going to do if I am president. . . . I am a regular Democrat and an organization guy, regardless of what you have been reading in the newspapers.'

"They loved it," Kenny said. "They just loved it. He went into a room and took fifteen minutes or longer with each individual delegate. They couldn't believe it. He heard them out. Bobby did a really beautiful political job. He'd come so far I couldn't believe my eyes. He was his brother! He was as loose as a goose. He knew just what they wanted to hear and he acted like he loved being there. Bobby had always been impatient, he couldn't get out fast enough to go somewhere else. He just handled himself beautifully. He was his brother. It was fantastic.

The women just went ga-ga over him. They were unanimous—all the old pros were just taken aback by how much they liked him. This was not the Bob Kennedy they had read about. This was not the ruthless, arrogant young fellow. All they kept saying was, 'He's just like Jack! He's just like Jack!' I knew he could go all the way then. Once he had California in his pocket, he would have Daley and all the pros were going to love him. I was never worried about the general election."

Kenny would be vital to this second Kennedy presidential candidacy, just as he had been to the first. "Kenny was like an extension of Bobby and Jack," Jerry Bruno says. "He thought like they did. They had total confidence in him. Kenny knew what they wanted, he knew what they were thinking, he could almost read their minds. He especially knew Bob Kennedy. He knew exactly what Bob Kennedy wanted and when he wanted it done. There was this—I don't know how to explain it in words, it was almost eerie, scary really—this feeling of direction when Kenny said, 'Here's the way it is or the way Bobby wants it done.' There was never a question that Bobby had said it. It was strange—sometimes Kenny would say Bobby wants this or that and then later Bobby would say, Did you do this or that, and I would say, 'Yeah, Kenny told me.' Bob would say, 'Really? Good, I only just thought of it. I meant to mention it to him.' It's hard to explain. It was something that the three of them shared—then the two of them, and then there was just one."

Lester Hyman took to the campaign trail with Teddy Kennedy. The pace was hectic and grueling. They were all over the country from Michigan to Maine, trying to line up party leaders who hadn't already signed on with Hubert Humphrey. On one of his occasional weekends home, he was greeted warmly by his six-year-old son, David, who was in public school in Newton. Lifting the boy up in his arms, he was startled to see a black eye. Putting the child down, he asked, "David, what happened?"

"I got into kind of a fight at school," the boy said shyly.

Hyman was surprised. "David," he said sternly, "you know better than to fight. What was it all about?"

The boy looked up embarrassed and a little guilty. "Daddy, it was about the presidential election. All the kids at school are for Senator McCarthy and I'm for Bobby and I told them so and they beat me up!"

The next week his itinerary coincided with Bobby's and he pulled the candidate aside to tell him the story. "Bobby, do you ever have problems like this with your children?"

"Yes, yes, yes," Bobby said quickly. His face was drawn with exhaustion, his hands cut and swollen from the crowd who would reach for him at campaign appearances. With that Bobby walked away. Hyman was furious. He thought to himself, what an insensitive son of a bitch. Then he explained the incident away to the candidate's exhaustion and put it out of his mind.

At week's end, Hyman arrived back in Boston to find his son ecstatic. Holding up a letter in his hand, his face bursting with pride, his son said, "Daddy, look, Bobby wrote me!"

Hyman thought he hadn't heard right. Taking the piece of paper from his son's hand, he read the letter, recognizing immediately Bobby's famous chicken scrawl.

Dear David,

  Your daddy told me how much courage it took to stand up for me against all odds. I shall never forget you.

                              Your friend,
                              Bobby

Two weeks later, Hyman saw Bobby again on the campaign trail in Indiana. "Bobby!" he called out sharply, to get Bobby's attention. Bobby turned and looked at him, his blue eyes quizzical. "Why didn't you say something to me?" Hyman demanded. "I was so angry at you and you do this beautiful thing for my son. Why didn't you tell me?" Bobby looked at Hyman, puzzled and annoyed. "Jesus, Lester," he said. "You're not the one with the problem—your son is! Don't be such a baby. It was for your son, not you! It wasn't about you!"

Lester Hyman felt his face flushing red. He couldn't respond. "Look," Bobby said, perhaps aware of his staffer's embarrassment, "I'm coming up to Boston for a speech next week. I'm staying at the Statler. I'll give you my room number. You put your son in my room. I don't want you there. Just put your son in there and I will spend some time with him and teach him how to handle these difficult things. Okay?"

"Fine," Hyman said, embarrassed, watching Bobby walk away. "Thank you," Hyman said after him, although Bobby was probably too far away to have heard him. He would make sure to thank him next week. As he turned to join the others, Lester thought to himself, Bobby is really something—we'll have to think of something nice to give him when he's in Boston next week—right after the California primary. It was June 2, 1968.

Even as he wanted to show his appeal in major states like California and New York, Bobby also wanted to show his strength in South Dakota and other conservative states. His loss to Eugene McCarthy in Oregon made a victory here even more imperative. Bobby was doing shuttle campaigning between South Dakota and California.

George McGovern had remained friendly with both Bobby and Hubert Humphrey. He had told both men that he would publicly support Bobby, but whenever Hubert was in South Dakota he would introduce him as well. Rising to introduce Bobby during one of Bobby's appearances at the Corn Palace right before the primary, he found himself saying, "I think the people of South Dakota know and appreciate the love and affection I have for the late President John Kennedy, but I honestly believe that if Robert Kennedy is elected president, that he will be an even greater president than John Kennedy!" After he had said it, McGovern gave the microphone to Bobby, unsure of how he would receive his introduction. As he rose to go to the podium, Bobby squeezed McGovern's hand hard. He was not a verbal man. Later, Ethel called to thank him.

"Bobby felt at home out there in South Dakota," said George McGovern. "I was surprised. He really felt at home with the people, the farmers, the ranchers, and the Indians. The last day he was there, he was physically exhausted, out of his head, just wiped out physically. I had never seen anyone so physically exhausted and yet still on their feet. Bobby insisted on pressing ahead, keeping a full schedule. We took him to the Corn Palace and he was so tired that he was no longer effective. Face drawn, eyes dull from exhaustion, lines marking his face."

McGovern introduced Bobby to the overflow crowd, quoting the song from the musical *Man of La Mancha*, about the need to pursue an impossible dream. Bobby's speech at the Corn Palace didn't work. The crowd was restive; he was too tired to speak clearly; his voice was somewhat hoarse; and the audience responded indifferently with only smatterings of applause, and murmured conversations spread through the six thousand rally-goers who jammed it to the rafters. Finally, realizing he was losing them, Bobby asked for questions from the audience, which responded well. Later that evening as they sat in the comfort and warmth of the Lawler Hotel café, McGovern thought Bobby looked pensive, tired, and very quiet. Finally, after a particularly long pause, Bobby looked across at his friend, his blue eyes haunted. "I know there are times," Bobby began, almost out of nowhere, "when I am not as capable or as forceful as Jack was. There are times like today, when I realize I just don't perform very well. Jack was the one, I just am not Jack, I can't do what he did. I am not Jack." Silence hung around the table. Nobody knew what to say. "George," Bobby continued, his voice low, "going back to what you said earlier today, do you really think the dream is impossible?"

McGovern was taken aback. He had meant the reference only as a throwaway line. Now, looking at Bobby's face, he regretted his use of the phrase, but he had to be honest. "Bobby, I think it's going to be awfully tough. I think you are up against a president who is going to back Hubert all the way, especially against you. The party machinery has already been tapped into by the White House. It really is going to be awfully tough to get the nomination. But, nevertheless, I'm still glad you are trying."

Bobby made no reply, staring out the window into the evening. A few moments later, they slid out of the booth, and Bobby said almost nothing as they walked over to the hotel. The next morning McGovern went to see Bobby off at the airport. He was still subdued. He had his springer spaniel Freckles by his side—a replacement for the late Brumus, and a smaller, easier animal to travel long distances with. Bobby thanked McGovern for his help and walked some distance over the tarmac to his chartered plane. McGovern watched him walk away into the early morning mist, his head down, suit coat swung over his shoulder. Freckles walking beside him, his head turning constantly up to his master. Bobby turned and gave McGovern his first smile of the day. "Bye, George," he said, waving, his words carried off by the wail of the engines. Then he and his dog climbed into the small plane that would take them on to California.

"As I watched him stand there and say goodbye, I felt something, something I couldn't explain and still can't," George McGovern remembers. "It was a brief glimpse, only a glimpse, only for a moment. For that brief moment, I saw into Bobby Kennedy's soul better than I ever had before. I saw what a deeply human, compassionate person Bobby really was. He was just so sad and wistful. It was like his guard was down and he was letting me in just the tiniest bit. Something held me there, held that image of him in mind. He's so small, so alone. He looked so human, so vulnerable. I never saw him again."

By 1968 Robert Kennedy was a different man than the one Jerry Bruno had met eight years before. His admiration for his first boss's younger brother had only grown. "Bob Kennedy would lead an audience. Most politicians wait to see how the audience or the people are moving, but Bob Kennedy would challenge the audience, tell them things they didn't want to hear. He had some really rough times on the college campuses he visited — he would get booed and they would give him a real rough time — but he didn't care. The more hostile the crowd the more he loved it.

"One time we were in this town and Bob was going to speak to a group at a synagogue. There must have been five thousand people there, jammed into the place. The sheriff got news of a bomb threat. He found me at our hotel and took me aside in the lobby and he told me about it."

Bruno found Bobby in his room making phone calls. "Are all those people still in there? Has anyone told them?"

Bruno was caught off guard. He didn't know; he hadn't asked. His thoughts were for Bobby, not the gathered audience. "I don't know," he told Bob. "I'll go find out."

"No," the sheriff told him, "we didn't want to panic them."

When Bruno told Bobby what the sheriff had said, the candidate rolled down the sleeves of his shirt, fixed his tie, and grabbed his jacket. "If people are still there, then I'm going to go."

The sheriff was furious. "He can't go," he insisted, ordering his deputies to block Bobby's car from leaving the hotel. "We won't allow him to go." Bruno caught Bobby as he came off the elevator and told him what the sheriff had said. The sheriff stood in the hotel doorway.

Bobby kept walking forward, hands stuffed in his coat pockets. "I'm going to go. That's fine if they want to block my car. I'll walk the three blocks. They can't stop me and neither can you. So come on." The two men walked past the sheriff and the phalanx of police cars blocking Bob's motorcade and walked to the meeting.

"We walked in," said Bruno, "and it was wall-to-wall people. He got up to the microphone and told them there was a bomb threat and they shouldn't be scared. The audience became deathly quiet. Bob said to them, 'If you want to leave you should leave in an orderly fashion and not panic. Be careful of the children.' But Bob added, 'Anyone who wants to stay, I will stay with you.' "

The room was quiet. Bruno studied the faces. He looked over at Bobby, standing at the microphone, his face lined with concern but with not the slightest indication of fear. The audience all resumed their seats. Those standing in the aisles stood their ground. "Not one person left the room," Bruno remembers. "Not one."

Jerry Bruno had accompanied Bobby to a county fair in Buffalo, New York, in 1967. The organizers kept pressing Senator Kennedy to wear this hat, kiss this baby, pick up this animal. He hated stuff like that. They kept pressing. They wanted him to ride this beautiful white horse. Finally Bruno said to Bobby, "We are never going to get out of here. Just ride the horse." Bobby's blue eyes twinkled mischievously. He agreed.

Bobby climbed on the white horse, turned it around and, much to the horror of the organizers and the crowd, began chasing Jerry Bruno across the fair grounds. "He was chasing me with the horse! He was galloping around and chasing me all over the damn fair grounds. The people thought we were nuts! Finally, we got into the car to leave. Bob was real quiet, like he would get sometimes. Withdrawn, gone someplace else, staring out the window, tapping his teeth. I thought maybe he thought he had looked silly or done something wrong, so I said to him, 'Bob, they loved it! I mean, the crowd, the people, they were caught off guard at first, but they really loved it! They did!'"

Silence. No response. Bruno began to drive. Suddenly Bobby put his hand on Bruno's arm. Bruno pulled the car over and turned to face Bobby. Bobby grabbed his arm. "I don't know if I did the right thing getting on that white horse. My brother rode a white horse once." He let go of Bruno's arm, turned and looked out the window. They rode in silence the rest of the way.

George McGovern spoke to Bobby on primary night, June 5, 1968. The Kennedy campaign had already won in South Dakota. He had won the Native American precincts by 100 percent. "I called Teddy, who was in San Francisco, and told him the results of the election," McGovern says. Teddy told him to call Bobby at his Los Angeles hotel. "He'll want to hear it from you. He hasn't gone downstairs yet." Calling Bobby on the phone at his suite, McGovern gave him the good news. Bobby wrote the results down on a piece of paper as they talked. In fifteen minutes he would go downstairs to give his victory speech. Before they finished the conversation, George tried to tell Bobby he was wrong, he was sorry he had used that quote about an impossible dream. Bobby's hotel suite was bedlam, and the conversation had to be cut short before they got to finish it properly. They didn't even get to say goodbye.

Fifteen minutes later Bobby descended into the ballroom of the Ambassador Hotel. Bobby's handwritten notes from his conversation with George McGovern would later be retrieved from the podium.

Kenny had talked to the redoubtable Mayor Richard Daley of Chicago. If Bobby could win California, then Daley would come out for him and bring most of the regulars along. Everything hung on California. Kenny was in Washington that humid June evening, having dinner at Paul Young's with Congressman Dan Rostenkowski. After dinner they walked back to the Mayflower Hotel to watch the primary night returns. Kenny was expecting a call from Bobby about the next step after this last, vital race. After tonight, Kenny was confident Bobby had what he needed to win at the convention in Chicago.

"We were in Kenny's room," said Rostenkowski. "We all had drinks, we were sitting around some in chairs, some on the beds, all political people, tough political guys." Kenny was on the phone with Bobby. It was a typical conversation—grunts, yups, uhs and 'you got it.' Kenny hands the phone to me and I talk to Bobby. Bobby says to me to commit to support him for president. I knew they were talking to Daley and I told him Daley is my guy, I do what Daley tells me. Daley was the boss. You win California, you get Daley, we all come along. Bobby understood. He was real nice, he asked about my wife and joked around, we talked about what was next. I gave the phone back to Kenny. Kenny, for the first time that evening, looked pleased. They started joking, something about Harvard, I don't know, something about Nick Rodis or somebody like that.

"Kenny's face broke into a wide grin. Bobby must have said something. Kenny said back, 'Bobby, you did it, you son of a bitch!' At the end I hear Kenny say, 'Never doubted you, Bobby. See you tomorrow.' "

It was the last call Bobby took before he headed downstairs to claim his victory.

Kenny hung up. He was so pleased. "He's got it," he told the gathered friends. "He's going downstairs now to accept and I'll catch up with him tomorrow back here. Never doubted him."

Ron Linton woke up late on Wednesday morning, June 6. He didn't have time for coffee or the morning news. He tossed the newspaper, still furled in its rubber band, into the backseat of his car. He had gone to sleep early last night, just when it was clear that Bobby Kennedy would win the California primary.

Ron Linton had a meeting with Kenny O'Donnell at the Mayflower Hotel. Bobby Kennedy had been after him for some time to get involved in the campaign. Linton had been forced to turn him down. He had just opened his own firm and needed to get his work stabilized. He couldn't go. Bobby had called right before the start of California. "I need you now," he had said. It was more of an order than a question.

"Okay, Bobby, after you win California I'll come." Bobby had been happy about that.

Kenny O'Donnell had called the previous morning, the day of the primary, to tell Linton to meet him for breakfast to discuss the campaign's next step. On the drive over to the Mayflower Linton never put on the radio. His mind was racing, wondering where Kenny would send him and what was next. Parking near the hotel, he hurried to meet Kenny.

Kenny was not in the restaurant. The hotel was eerily quiet. Linton went up to Kenny's room, the same one he always stayed in when he was in Washington. He knocked. The door was slightly ajar. He walked in.

Kenny was sitting on the bed wearing a white shirt, his sleeves rolled up. His tie was draped around his neck. He clearly had not slept. His face was not white. It was as gray as death, Linton thought. When he looked up, those Cobra eyes that Linton had feared and grown to love didn't seem as black any more. Linton stood in the doorway. Other men were in the room—Dick Maguire, Dick O'Hare, some of Jack Kennedy's "Irish Mafia." The room was littered with glasses, with booze everywhere. A mirror had broken.

From the droning television, Ron Linton learned what Kenny could not tell him. Robert Kennedy was dead. Horror. Linton turned to Kenny, helpless. What could he say? "Kenny . . ." was all he could get out.

Kenny smiled, his slight smile. "It's okay," he said, his voice barely above a whisper. "Bobby was the emotional one in the family. I'm all right. I just winced a little bit."

Bobby was dead. What about the campaign? Linton found himself asking.

"Why bother?" Kenny told him. "What the hell does it matter?"

CONCLUSION:
"THE SILENCE WAS DEAFENING"

"Vietnam was like a ball coming down a hill. Nobody could stop it and everybody wanted to stop it. Bob was the only one who really could put a stop to it. He knew it, Teddy knew it, Kenny knew it, Ethel knew it, Jackie knew it, and we all knew it. And yet the price was what we feared," says Dave Burke. "We all agreed. Bobby was right about that— our country was committing really horrible, horrible crimes against a bunch of kids in diapers for Christ's sake, and they were killing us! So Bobby, Kenny, and Teddy knew that we had to be large enough and tough enough to stop it. But for Ethel, Teddy, Kenny, and the rest of the family, you were talking about asking someone you love to step into that breach and then have your worst fear realized. For Kenny, who believed so firmly that Bobby had to stop that war, there was no consolation.

"Bobby Kennedy had the ability to be a successful politician in life, while carrying within himself this heart, this compassion, and this caring," Burke says. "You look at pictures of Bobby Kennedy with a black child or with Cesar Chavez, and you know he cares, that he will take risks. You knew what Bobby's real feelings on Vietnam were; you saw him go through his own torment on the issue. You knew you were dealing with a really decent person. Whatever Bob Kennedy touched in life, it was only going to be good. You wouldn't want to live with him twenty-four hours a day while he was doing that. That's why God created Ethel, because nobody else could handle him except Ethel."

"That was the great sadness," Nick Rodis says. "When he died, it just stopped, all at once, all that energy, compassion, brilliance, emotion — it all stopped. When he died there was just silence. For Kenny, for us all, there was just silence."

"Politics was never the same," Jerry Bruno declares. "There wasn't anybody that I would be willing to take that kind of risk for. It was like all of our lives just stopped."

For some, life after Robert Kennedy would eventually began again. But for Kenny the silence would become deafening.

George Sullivan had been eleven years old when he first met Bobby and Kenny and the Harvard football team of 1946. In 1968, he was a sports writer for the *Boston Herald*. When he heard that Bobby had been assassinated, his first thoughts were of Kenny, Helen, and then Ethel. Kenny had called soon afterward about the funeral. "Get your ass to New York," he had said. "Everything will be paid for. Check in at the Plaza. We have a room for you." Like the rest of the team, Sullivan went when the captain called.

"It was like an Irish wake without the body," Sullivan remembers. "Kenny had a room at the Plaza, an open bar, and we had a huge party. Bobby would have loved it. Maybe he did. It was all so surreal."

Nick Rodis remembers every moment of the mourning with precise pain. "We went out to get into the cars to go to the cathedral" for the evening vigil preceding the funeral. "All these kids were standing on the steps of the Plaza waiting for those hansom cabs to take them to the prom. Teenagers on prom night. They were all so young, dressed up in gowns and tuxedos and so happy."

"Here we were," Wally Flynn recalls, "it was the saddest day of our lives, and the contrast between those happy kids and the Harvard team in mourning for one of our own — it was like a Fellini film, a bad movie. You just wanted it to be over. I couldn't even look at Kenny."

Kenny had made all the arrangements for the team. FBI men came in cars and took the team down Fifth Avenue to St. Patrick's. There weren't enough cars for all these big men, as had been true at Ethel and Bobby's wedding in Greenwich. They jammed into the cars with their wives on their laps. "When we went to St. Patrick's to do the honor guard around Bobby, Helen had to sit in my lap on the way," Sullivan recalls. "She kept saying she needed some air. I didn't know why, because the car window was open. I think it was that none of us could really comprehend what had happened to Bobby. The whole team was there. I kept looking toward the door expecting him to walk through. He never did."

Fifth Avenue was so crowded with mourners in the middle of the street that the cars had to drive up on the sidewalks. The whole team filed out to enter St. Patrick's Cathedral, Kenny in the lead, as if they were headed to the Harvard playing field once more. Only Bobby was missing.

They walked into the cathedral among the candles, television cameras, and harsh lights. The casket abruptly loomed in front of them. The men stood in formation around it. From the moment he had extended his hand to each of them at Dillon Field House and said, "Hi, I'm Bob Kennedy," he had been their leader and their friend.

Kenny remained impassive. His face was drawn tight, as if he was afraid of what would happen if he opened his mouth. A black woman made her way to the casket. Kneeling down opposite Kenny, holding on to the casket, she began sobbing, crying uncontrollably, giving voice to the pain Kenny would not express.

At that moment, Nick Rodis glanced at Kenny. As he looked down at the woman crying and leaning on Bobby's casket, tears streamed down Kenny's face. He made no sound. The tears spoke loud enough for all who knew him to hear.

When Robert Kennedy died in June 1968, for my father, life seemed almost unbearable. The loss of his two dear friends, Jack and Bobby, the wounding of his beloved brother Warren, and Warren's death several years later only added to his sense of loss. His younger brother's death seemed to be one more burden he was simply unable to shoulder. It was now just Kenny and Justine.

After Bobby's death in 1968, my mother suffered a nervous breakdown. The walls of pain came crashing in on her, and she seemed unable to stem the tide. My older brother Kenny was drafted into the service and shipped off to Vietnam. My brother refused to ask my father to intervene on his behalf. Kenny understood his son, so like himself, and let "the monster" as Bobby had nicknamed him be shipped off to fight the war — the same war that Kenny had encouraged Bobby to run for the presidency to stop, the war that had cost his beloved friend Bobby his life. The decision to let Kenny go to Vietnam, like the decision to urge Bobby to run, like the decision to turn left onto Dealey Plaza, would continue to haunt Kenny, who held himself responsible for things beyond his control. He was bound up in pain, anger, and sadness — a pain that he could not give voice to, that he could not explain to himself or anyone else. "Perhaps Bobby would have understood," he would say in the darkness, as he paced back and forth, listening to the strains of Frank Sinatra's "That's Life." He was trying to heal from wounds that he could not acknowledge existed. My mother would sit in the den, watching lists of soldiers killed in Vietnam roll across the screen. Her depression grew worse, her alcoholism deepened, and she became harder and harder for us to reach. Bobby might have been able to reach her, Kenny would remark, pouring himself another drink.

Kenny Jr. did return from Vietnam, stronger, wiser, and the son my father always wanted, making his parents proud. He took my parents up to his farm in Vermont, where he had moved after his return home. Daddy stood outside the farmhouse door, looking around the green fields dotted with Jersey cows, and inquired of "the monster," "How the fuck do you get any votes up here?" Vermont hadn't been on Jack and Bobby's lists in 1960 or 1968, I guess.

My dad ran for governor one more time in 1970, in what was perhaps one of his most self-destructive acts. He had no chance of winning, yet he ran anyway. The journey begun so long ago back at Dillon Field House with a handshake was over. The game was finished but the captain couldn't leave the field. He had to try one more "Hail, Mary" pass. He lost the race in 1970 in what his friend Paul Kirk terms "the Kid's last fight." By 1977, both my parents would be dead.

Memories of my father and mother, although tinged with sadness, are of two loving, fun people; two people who had shared their love and friendship with John and Jackie Kennedy, and especially their love of Bobby and Ethel. I am lucky to have had such wonderful and giving parents, and I urge the reader to, as Ethel said when this book began, "remember the good times, not the sad, for we had a whole lot of fun and I think we made a difference." I know she is correct; they made a difference in politics, in public life, as parents, and mostly as friends. It was a friendship they shared with each other and taught their children, allowing Michael Kennedy and me to collaborate on *A Common Good*. As Michael said to me, "After all, we are now working on the second generation here. I think that's good." *A Common Good* is a book about two extraordinary men and the world they tried to change. It is a book

about the lives they lived and the lives they touched. I hope the reader
has also been touched.

*Nothing worth doing is completed in our lifetime; therefore, we
must be saved by hope. Nothing true or beautiful or good makes
complete sense in any immediate context of history; therefore, we
must be saved by faith. Nothing we do, however virtuous, can be
accomplished alone; therefore, we are saved by love.*

—REINHOLD NIEBUHR

INDEX